Poland
a country study

Federal Research Division
Library of Congress
Edited by
Glenn E. Curtis
Research Completed
October 1992

On the cover: Arched entrance to the monastery of Jasna
Góra at Częstochowa

Third Edition, First Printing, 1994.

Library of Congress Cataloging-in-Publication Data

Poland : a country study / Federal Research Division, Library of Con-
gress ; edited by Glenn E. Curtis. — 3rd ed.
     p. cm. — (Area handbook series, ISSN 1057-5294)
(DA Pam ; 550-162)
    "Research completed October 1992."
    "Supersedes the 1984 edition of Poland : a country study, edit-
ed by Harold D. Nelson" : T.p. verso.
    Includes bibliographical references (pp. 307-327) and index.
    ISBN 0-8444-0827-1
    1. Poland. I. Curtis, Glenn E. (Glenn Eldon), 1946-
II. Library of Congress. Federal Research Division. III. Series.
IV. Series: DA Pam ; 550-162.
DK4040.P57 1994   93-46235
943.8—dc20   CIP

Headquarters, Department of the Army
DA Pam 550-162

Reprinted without alteration
on acid-free paper

Bernan Press
Lanham, Maryland
August 1994

Foreword

This volume is one in a continuing series of books prepared by the Federal Research Division of the Library of Congress under the Country Studies/Area Handbook Program sponsored by the Department of the Army. The last page of this book lists the other published studies.

Most books in the series deal with a particular foreign country, describing and analyzing its political, economic, social, and national security systems and institutions, and examining the interrelationships of those systems and the ways they are shaped by cultural factors. Each study is written by a multidisciplinary team of social scientists. The authors seek to provide a basic understanding of the observed society, striving for a dynamic rather than a static portrayal. Particular attention is devoted to the people who make up the society, their origins, dominant beliefs and values, their common interests and the issues on which they are divided, the nature and extent of their involvement with national institutions, and their attitudes toward each other and toward their social system and political order.

The books represent the analysis of the authors and should not be construed as an expression of an official United States government position, policy, or decision. The authors have sought to adhere to accepted standards of scholarly objectivity. Corrections, additions, and suggestions for changes from readers will be welcomed for use in future editions.

Louis R. Mortimer
Chief
Federal Research Division
Library of Congress
Washington, D.C. 20540

Acknowledgments

The authors are indebted to numerous individuals and organizations who provided materials, time, advice, and expertise on Polish affairs for this volume.

Thanks go to Ralph K. Benesch, who oversees the Country Studies/Area Handbook Program for the Department of the Army. The authors also appreciate the advice and guidance of Sandra W. Meditz, Federal Research Division coordinator of the handbook series. Special thanks also go to Marilyn L. Majeska, who managed the editing and production process, assisted by Andrea T. Merrill; to Teresa E. Kemp, who designed the book cover and the title page illustration for Chapter 2; to Marty Ittner, who designed the other chapter title page illustrations; to David P. Cabitto, who provided graphics support and, together with the firm of Greenhorne and O'Mara, prepared maps; and to Tim Merrill, who compiled geographic data. LTC Peter J. Podbielski, United States Army, provided invaluable personal insights into the current status of the Polish military; Marcin Wiesiołek of the Foreign Military Studies Office, Ft. Leavenworth, Kansas, and Michał Bichniewicz of the Center for International Studies and Defense Analyses in Warsaw updated the national security section; and Karl W. Soper assembled basic source materials for preparation of Chapter 5.

The Polish Information Agency (Polska Agencja Informacyjna) provided the editor with a wide selection of current photographs of economic and military activities. Ronald D. Bachman and Sam and Sarah Stulberg also contributed numerous timely photographs.

The contributions of the following individuals are gratefully acknowledged as well: Sharon Costello, who edited the chapters; Barbara Edgerton and Izella Watson, who did the word processing; Catherine Schwartzstein, who performed the final prepublication editorial review; Joan C. Cook, who compiled the index; and Linda Peterson of the Printing and Processing Section, Library of Congress, who prepared the camera-ready copy under the supervision of Peggy Pixley.

Contents

	Page
Foreword	iii
Acknowledgments	v
Preface	xiii
Chronology of Important Events	xv
Country Profile	xxi
Introduction	xxix
Chapter 1. Historical Setting	1

Neal Pease

EARLY HISTORY UNTIL 1385	3
The Origins of Poland	3
The Medieval Era	5
Integration into European Civilization	7
THE JAGIELLON ERA, 1385–1572	7
The Polish-Lithuanian Union	7
The "Golden Age" of the Sixteenth Century	10
THE NOBLE REPUBLIC, 1572–1795	15
The Elective Monarchy	15
The Deluge, 1648–67	15
Decay of the Commonwealth	16
The Three Partitions, 1764–95	17
PARTITIONED POLAND	22
The Napoleonic Period	22
The Impact of Nationalism and Romanticism	23
The Era of National Insurrections	25
The Time of "Organic Work"	26
Social and Political Transformation	27
INDEPENDENCE WON AND LOST, 1914–45	28
World War I	28
Interwar Poland	30
World War II	34
THE POLISH PEOPLE'S REPUBLIC	39
Consolidation of Communist Power	39
From Stalinism to the Polish October	41
The Gathering Crisis of People's Poland, 1956–80	43
The Birth of Solidarity	45

The Jaruzelski Interlude 47
The 1989 Elections and Their Aftermath 50

Chapter 2. The Society and Its Environment 53
Glenn E. Curtis

PHYSICAL SETTING 56
    Topography 57
    Drainage 60
    Climate 61
ENVIRONMENT AND POLLUTION 61
    Environmental Conditions and Crises 62
    Environmental Groups 63
    Government Environmental Policy 64
DEMOGRAPHY 65
    Languages 65
    Population Growth and Structure 66
    Population Density and Distribution 68
THE SOCIAL ORDER 68
    Ethnic Groups 71
    The Intelligentsia 75
    The Working Classes 77
    Social Relationships 82
    The Role of Women 83
HOUSING 86
    Communist Housing Policy 86
    Polish Housing in Practice 87
    Housing after 1989 88
RELIGION 89
    The Polish Catholic Church and the State 92
    The Polish Catholic Church and the People 97
    Other Churches 98
EDUCATION 100
    The Education Tradition 101
    Eras of Repression 101
    The Drive for Education Reform 103
    Structure of the Education System 104
HEALTH AND WELFARE 107
    Health Conditions 107
    The Health Care System 107
    Health Issues 109
    The Welfare System 111

Chapter 3. The Economy 115
Zbigniew M. Fallenbuchl
NATURAL RESOURCES 118
    Minerals and Fuels 118
    Agricultural Resources 120
    Labor Force 120
THE ECONOMY UNDER THE COMMUNIST
  SYSTEM 121
    System Structure 121
    Development Strategy 123
DEVELOPMENT OF THE CENTRALLY PLANNED
  ECONOMY 124
    Establishing the Planning Formula 124
    Retrenchment and Adjustment in the 1960s 126
    Reliance on Technology in the 1970s 127
    Reform Failure in the 1980s 128
AFTER THE FALL OF THE COMMUNIST SYSTEM 129
    Marketization and Stabilization 130
    Macroeconomic Indicators for 1990–91 133
    The External Balance of the Economy 137
    The Privatization Process 138
    Economic Policy Making in the 1990s 139
STRUCTURE OF THE ECONOMY 140
    Fuels and Energy 141
    Extractive and Manufacturing Industries 147
    Agriculture 151
    Fishing and Forestry 154
    Transportation and Communications 156
    Banking and Finance 159
FOREIGN TRADE 162
    The Foreign Trade Mechanism 163
    Postcommunist Policy Adjustments 164
    Foreign Investment 168
ECONOMIC PROSPECTS 169

Chapter 4. Government and Politics 171
Ronald D. Bachman

POLITICAL SETTING 174
    The Round Table Agreement 175
    The Mazowiecki Government 176
    Popular Election of a President 177
    The Bielecki Government 179
    The Parliamentary Elections of October 1991 180

The Olszewski Government 181
The Pawlak Interlude 183
The Suchocka Government 183
THE CONSTITUTION 184
The Constitution of 1952 184
Constitutional Revisions after April 1989 187
GOVERNMENT STRUCTURE 188
Presidency 189
Sejm 191
Senate 192
Supreme Control Chamber 192
Council of Ministers 193
Regional and Local Government 194
Judicial System 194
POLITICAL PARTIES 198
Solidarity 199
Center Alliance 200
Democratic Union 201
Liberal-Democratic Congress 202
Beer-Lovers' Party 202
Peasant Alliance 202
Christian National Union 203
Party of Christian Democrats 204
Confederation for an Independent Poland 204
PZPR and Successor Parties 205
Polish Peasant Party 206
POLITICS AND THE MEDIA 206
The Early Opposition Press 207
Liberalization in the 1980s 207
The End of Press Censorship 208
Book Publishing 209
Radio and Television 209
FOREIGN RELATIONS 210
Soviet Union and Russia 212
Other Former Soviet Republics 215
Southern Neighbors and the Visegrád Triangle 218
Germany 220
The United States 222
Other Western Countries 224
International Organizations 225

Chapter 5. National Security 229
            Glenn E. Curtis

DEVELOPMENT OF THE ARMED FORCES 232
From Medieval Times to World War I 232

The Interwar Years 234
World War II 236
The Communist Era 237
NATIONAL SECURITY POLICY 244
Threat Perception 244
Military Doctrine 247
Strategy and Tactics 250
Military Cooperation and Exchanges 251
DEFENSE ORGANIZATION 253
The Communist Tradition 253
Evolution and Restructuring 254
National Security Agencies 258
Armed Services 259
MILITARY MANPOWER 267
The Military and Society 268
Recruitment and Service Obligations 270
Military Training and Education 274
DEFENSE AND THE NATIONAL ECONOMY 278
Military Budget 278
Arms Procurement 279
LAW AND ORDER 284
Internal Security 284
Crime 287
Penal System 289
Under Communism 290

Appendix. Tables 293

Bibliography 307

Glossary 329

Index 335

Contributors 353

List of Figures

1 Administrative Division of Poland, 1992 xxviii
2 Piast Poland, 966 to 1370 8
3 Jagiellon Poland-Lithuania, Fifteenth Century 12
4 Polish-Lithuanian Commonwealth from the Union of
  Lublin, 1569, to 1667 14
5 The First Partition of Poland, 1772 18
6 The Second Partition of Poland, 1793 20
7 The Third Partition of Poland, 1795 21
8 Duchy of Warsaw, 1807–13, and Congress
  Poland, 1815 24

9 Independent Poland, 1921–39 32
10 Occupied Poland in World War II 38
11 Postwar Territorial Adjustments, 1945 40
12 Topography and Drainage 58
13 Population Density by District, 1992 70
14 Distribution of Heavy Industry and Mineral
    Resources, 1992 146
15 Transportation System, 1992 158
16 Enlisted Ranks and Insignia, 1992 272
17 Officer Ranks and Insignia, 1992 273
18 Warrant Officer Ranks and Insignia, 1992 276

Preface

At the end of the 1980s, Poland, like the other countries of Eastern Europe, underwent a rather sudden shift away from communist rule and into an uncertain new world of democracy and economic reform. The events spurred by the repudiation of Poland's last communist regime in 1989 demanded a new and updated version of *Poland: A Country Study.* Because the emergence of the opposition Solidarity movement in 1980 increased the flow of information from communist Poland, reliable coverage of the 1980s has been possible. Thus, this new treatment of Poland is based on a number of authoritative monographs and a host of scholarly articles. The most useful of those sources are cited in a bibliographic summary at the end of each chapter.

The authors of this edition have described changes in the past ten years against the historical, political, and social background of Poland. Particular emphasis falls on the transition period that began in 1989 with the rejection of the last communist government. This period, a historic watershed not yet concluded in 1993, promises to have permanent impact on all aspects of Polish life. The authors have attempted to present a compact, accessible, and unbiased treatment of five main topics: historical setting, society and its environment, the economy, government and politics, and national security.

Polish personal names are rendered with full diacritics. The spelling of geographical names conforms to that approved by the United States Board on Geographic Names, including the use of diacritics, with the exception of commonly used international spellings such as Warsaw (Warszawa) and Oder (Odra). On maps English-language generic designations such as river, plain, and mountain are used. In the text, organizations commonly known by their acronyms (such as PZPR, the Polish United Workers' Party) are introduced first by their full English and Polish names.

Measurements are given in metric units; a conversion table is provided in the Appendix. To amplify points in the text, tables in the Appendix provide information on various aspects of Polish society, economic performance indicators, Polish political parties, and military strength. A glossary and a bibliography are also included at the end of the book.

The body of the text reflects information available as of October 1992. Certain other portions of the text, however, have been updated. The Introduction discusses significant events that have occurred since the completion of research; the Chronology, Country Profile, and Glossary include updated information as available; and the Bibliography includes recently published sources thought to be particularly helpful to the reader.

Table A. Chronology of Important Events

Period	Description
MEDIEVAL PERIOD	
966	Prince Mieszko adopts Christianity; traditional date of origin of Polish state.
1025	Bolesław I (the Brave) recognized as first king of Poland.
1079	Bishop Stanisław of Kraków martyred.
1226	Teutonic Knights introduced into Polish regions.
1241	Asiatic Tatars invade Poland and Central Europe.
1320	Following a period of disunity, Władysław Łokietek (the Short) recognized in Europe as king of Poland.
1333–70	Kazimierz III (the Great), reigns as one of Poland's most noted rulers.
1364	University of Kraków founded.
1385	Union of Krewo begins Polish-Lithuanian Commonwealth under Jagiellon Dynasty.
1410	Forces of Poland-Lithuania defeat Teutonic Knights at Battle of Grunwald (Tannenberg).
SIXTEENTH CENTURY	
1500–1600	Traditional "Golden Age" of Poland-Lithuania; period when political stability, prosperity, and cultural achievement reach their peak.
1526	Defeat by Ottoman Turks at Battle of Mohács leads to collapse of Jagiellon rule over Bohemia and Hungary.
1543	Copernicus publishes treatise defining heliocentric universe.
1569	Union of Lublin strengthens Polish-Lithuanian Commonwealth.
1572	Jagiellon Dynasty ends, and era of truly elective monarchy begins.
SEVENTEENTH CENTURY	
1648–67	"Deluge" period includes internal rebellion and foreign invasion.
1683	King Jan Sobieski breaks siege of Vienna.

Table A.—Continued

Period	Description
EIGHTEENTH CENTURY	
ca. 1700–25	Poland becomes virtual puppet of Russia during reign of Tsar Peter the Great.
1764	Stanisław August Poniatowski elected as last king of Poland-Lithuania.
1768–72	Confederation of Bar rebels.
1772–73	Austria, Prussia, and Russia impose first partition of Poland.
1791	Constitution of May 3 restores hereditary monarchy and reforms political system.
1792–93	Confederation of Targowica invites foreign intervention; Prussia and Russia carry out second partition of Poland.
1794	Tadeusz Kościuszko leads rebellion against foreign rule.
1795	Austria, Prussia, and Russia impose third partition of Poland, ending Polish independence for more than a century.
NINETEENTH CENTURY	
1807–15	Semi-independent Duchy of Warsaw established by Napoleon; abolished by Russian occupation, 1813; repartitioned by Congress of Vienna after Napoleon's final defeat.
ca. 1820–55	Era of Romanticism in Polish culture produces such figures as Mickiewicz and Chopin.
1830–31	"November Revolt" against Russian rule in Congress Kingdom of Poland proves unsuccessful.
1846	Polish uprising fails in Austrian zone of partition.
1863–64	"January Insurrection" in Russian sector culminates in failure, ending phase of nineteenth-century insurrections against foreign domination.
ca. 1864–1900	Period of "Organic Work" marks important transition in Polish politics and society.
TWENTIETH CENTURY	
1914–18	World War I results in collapse of all partition powers and rise of independent Second Polish Republic at war's end.
ca. 1919–21	War with Soviet Russia; Poland avoids Soviet conquest and gains narrow victory.

Table A.—Continued

Period	Description
1926	Józef Piłsudski gains power by coup and establishes *sanacja* government that rules until 1939.
1939	World War II begins with September invasions of Poland by Nazi Germany and Soviet Union; Polish forces defeated. After defeat, Polish government-in-exile forms in London under General Sikorski.
1940–41	Soviet Union incarcerates 1.5 million Poles in labor camps and executes thousands of prisoners of war before ceding Polish lands to Germans.
1941–44	All Polish territory comes under Nazi occupation, taking savage toll of Polish lives; Poland becomes main killing ground of the Holocaust; Polish resistance movements active at home and abroad.
1943	Discovery of Katyń Massacre causes breach between Soviet Union and Polish government-in-exile.
1944	Warsaw uprising by resistance Polish Home Army receives no Soviet assistance, is crushed by Nazis.
1945	Red Army occupies Polish territories and establishes communist-dominated coalition government.
1947	Communists consolidate political monopoly after rigged elections.
1947–49	Sovietization occurs, including nationalization of industry and business, attacks on organized religion, and imprisonment of opposition leaders.
1948–56	Stalinist period brings most severe communist rule; adoption of Soviet-style constitution; attempted collectivization of agriculture.
1956	Worker riots in Poznań result in numerous deaths; in defiance of Soviet Union, Władysław Gomułka chosen as Polish Communist Party leader; he announces commitment to reform and liberalization of system.
1968	Popular disenchantment with Gomułka begins to crystallize opposition that will mature in next two decades.
1970	Government price increase policy brings strikes and demonstrations on Baltic coast; met by lethal force, hundreds die; Gomułka deposed.
1970–80	Edward Gierek heads communist party; his policies result in severe economic crisis and intensified opposition sentiment; strikes and riots result from price rises, 1976.

Table A. —Continued

Period		Description
1978		Cardinal Karol Wojtyła, elected pope, takes name John Paul II.
1980		Nationwide worker strikes culminate in occupation of Lenin Shipyard in Gdańsk; state authorities sign Gdańsk Accords, acceding to striker demands and autonomy or the Solidarity trade union.
1980–81		Solidarity, spearhead of political and social reform movement, exists legally; constant friction between Solidarity and government; Warsaw Pact threatens intervention.
1981		General Wojciech Jaruzelski becomes party head, declares martial law, and carries out military takeover in name of communist party; Solidarity banned, its leadership imprisoned, other union activists driven underground.
1983		Solidarity leader Lech Wałęsa receives Nobel Prize for Peace.
1984		Father Jerzy Popiełuszko murdered by Polish secret police.
1985–1988		Period of gradual liberalization corresponding to advent of Mikhail Gorbachev in Soviet Union; economic crisis and popular frustration deepen.
1988		Renewed labor strikes convince Jaruzelski to initiate talks with opposition.
1989		Round Table talks produce formula for power sharing between communists and Solidarity; partly free elections result in sweeping Solidarity victories; communist regime crumbles.
1989	August	First postcommunist prime minister, Tadeusz Mazowiecki, forms coalition government.
1990	January	"Shock therapy" economic reform program of Finance Minister Leszek Balcerowicz goes into effect; PZPR formally dissolved and renamed Social Democracy of Republic of Poland (SdRP).
	December	Wałęsa becomes first popularly elected postcommunist president.
1991	July	Warsaw Pact alliance dissolved.
	Summer	Comecon economic grouping dissolved.
	August	Coup fails to take over government of Soviet Union.

Table A.—Continued

Period		Description
	October	Parliamentary elections seat fragmented Sejm; Jan Olszewski chosen compromise prime minister.
	December	Soviet Union officially breaks up.
1992	February	Parliament passes strict antiabortion law after bitter social and political struggle.
	May	Sejm's rejection of Olszewski economic program leads to Olszewski's ouster; final accord signed on withdrawal of Russian troops from Poland.
	August	Hanna Suchocka chosen prime minister. Her coalition government then oversees period of economic growth and continued political fragmentation.
1993	October	Prime Minister Waldemar Pawlak forms new government dominated by SdPR.

Country Profile

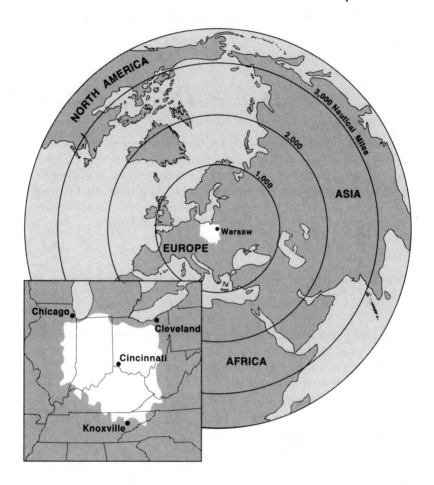

Country

Formal Name: Republic of Poland.

Short Form: Poland.

Capital: Warsaw.

Flag: Two equal-sized horizontal bands—upper white and lower red.

NOTE—The Country Profile contains updated information as available.

Geography

Size: 312,683 square kilometers, including inland waters.

Topography: Chiefly plains, most notably in vast central lowlands; significant highlands in southwest (Sudeten Mountains) and southeast (Tatra Mountains, northernmost part of Carpathian range). Only 3 percent above 500 meters, about 90 percent below 300 meters. Wide lake region above central lowland dotted with lakes occupying about 10 percent of surface area.

Climate: Dominant continental climate year round, but considerable winter snow and fog from maritime air currents. Summers less humid with occasional showers; rainy season in November. Longest growing season in southwest, shortest in northeast. Average annual precipitation 600 millimeters, higher in mountains. Summer precipitation averages twice that in winter.

Society

Population: According to 1981 official estimate, 36.1 million. According to 1991 official estimate, 38.3 million; projected 2000 population, 39.5 million.

Ethnic Groups and Languages: About 98 percent of population ethnic Poles; largest minority groups Ukrainians, Belarusians, and Germans; estimates of minority populations vary greatly. Polish, a West Slavic language, official and universally used; regional dialects do not impede communication.

Religion: About 96 percent of population Roman Catholic, according to 1991 survey; small numbers in various Protestant and Orthodox denominations and small Jewish population.

Education: About 98 percent of population over age fifteen literate. Eight grades of primary school compulsory; secondary program divided into college preparatory (26 percent in 1991) and vocational tracks. Institutions of higher learning include universities, polytechnical schools, and specialized academies such as medical and agricultural schools.

Health: Former communist system of free health care for all workers underwent reform in early 1990s. Privatization of medical practice, already common under communism, expanded but raised prices and did not make care consistently available. Obsolescence of equipment and shortage of medicines a continued problem; drive for consolidation closed many facilities; national health insurance plan slow in developing.

Economy

Salient Features: Wide-ranging measures taken beginning in 1990 to convert communist economy into market-oriented system, including commercialization of interest and exchange rates, abolition of price subsidies and wage indexation, and encouragement of foreign investment. Enterprise privatization, a central policy goal, met with uneven success; substantial portion of production capacity remained state-owned in 1993.

Mining: Major deposits of industrially useful minerals exploited, including coal, copper, lead, zinc, sulfur, and salt. Natural gas and petroleum reserves expanded, with new gas discoveries 1980s and early 1990s.

Energy: Coal, major energy source, generated 70 percent of electrical power, 80 percent of total energy, 1989. Imported and domestic petroleum and natural gas other major fuels. Imported fuel and power 21 percent of total import expenses in 1990. Nuclear program ended for financial, environmental reasons. Major reorganization planned for fuel-energy sector in early 1990s, including market pricing.

Manufacturing: Employed 25.2 percent of labor force in 1989. Principal branches food products, machinery and computer equipment, metals and metal products, textiles and clothing, transport equipment (including ships), and chemical products. In light and heavy industry, many plants outmoded and required wholesale modernization and Western investment. After 1990 consumer goods production up to bolster exports.

Agriculture: Never collectivized on large scale in communist era. In 1989 some 79 percent of agricultural production from private land, 17 percent from state farms. In 1989 agriculture employed 25.7 percent of labor force. Private farms, much more numerous, also mostly small and inefficient, suffering from poor availability of materials and infrastructure. Major reform and land redistribution contemplated. Main products: grains, potatoes, sugar beets, fodder, pigs, and cattle.

Foreign Trade: Principal exports coal, copper, coke, sulfur, ships, foods, and chemicals. Principal imports crude oil, iron ore, fertilizers, wheat, machinery, and electronic equipment. Maintained 60 percent of trade with members of Council for Mutual Economic Assistance (Comecon) in 1980s; major shift away from that group by 1990. Associate membership in European Community (EC)

1991 began reemphasis on opening Western markets; Comecon group export share declined to 9.8 percent 1991.

Currency: Zloty; exchange rate March 1993, US$1 equalled 15,900 zloty.

Fiscal Year: calendar year.

Transportation

Railroads: Standard gauge routes totaled 24,287 kilometers 1990, of total 26,644 kilometers in state network. Some 11,016 kilometers electrified. Locomotive fleet about 55 percent diesel, 41 percent electric, and 4 percent steam 1990. Substantial modernization planned for 1990s.

Roads and Road Transport: Of 363,116 kilometers of roads 1991, 159,000 kilometers hard surface and 257 kilometers motorway. Bus routes totaling 121,000 kilometers carried 2.6 million passengers 1989. Passenger cars 4.85 million, trucks 977,000 in 1989. Irregularities in petroleum import restrained road transport periodically in 1980s, early 1990s.

Pipelines: In 1987, operational domestic pipeline 6,846 kilometers, carrying crude oil, natural gas, and refined products. Druzhba Pipeline major source of crude oil from Russia.

Inland Waterways: About 4,000 kilometers navigable by regular transport services, 1989. Main systems Vistula (60 percent) and Oder rivers, connected by Kanał Bydgoski in north-central Poland. Total canal network 1,215 kilometers. Major inland ports Gliwice, Warsaw, and Wrocław. Inland waterways carried 3.8 million passengers, 9.8 million tons of freight in 1990. Some 69 passenger vessels, 1,380 barges in use 1989.

Ports and Shipping: Four large Baltic harbors: Gdynia, Gdańsk, Świnoujście, and Szczecin. In 1989 merchant fleet had 249 ships, total displacement 4 million deadweight tons, including 16 over 30,000 tons. Regular lines to London, Asian ports, Australia, and some African and Latin American countries.

Civil Aviation: State-owned Polish Airlines (LOT) operated nine internal, thirty-four international routes 1990, using Soviet- and United States-made aircraft. Fleet renovation began 1990. At Okęcie International Airport (Warsaw), largest airport, new terminal scheduled 1992. Eighty of 140 airports had hard-surface runways 1989.

Government and Politics

Government: Prescribed by 1952 constitution, its many amendments, and 1992 Little Constitution that defines executive powers. Legislative power centered in popularly elected bicameral National Assembly (upper, 100-member Senate; lower, 460-member Sejm). President, popularly elected to five-year term, acts as head of state, approves Sejm nominations for prime minister (head of government), and has decree power on many issues. Prime minister chooses Council of Ministers (cabinet), responsible to Sejm and president, to administer government.

Politics: Domination of communist Polish United Workers Party (Polska Zjednoczona Partia Robotnicza—PZPR) ended 1989. Umbrella opposition coalition Solidarity split several ways in 1990, joined by various new and revived groups in complex structure dominated by none. All governments 1989–93 based on at least seven parties in coalition, with constant threat of conflicting agendas causing collapse. Influential parties had religious (Party of Christian Democrats, Christian National Union), class-based (Polish Peasant Party, Peasant Alliance), or broadly political (Democratic Union, Liberal-Democratic Congress) agendas. Social Democracy of the Republic of Poland succeeded PZPR, maintained some power with democratized platform, and achieved plurality in 1993 election as dominant faction of Alliance of the Democratic Left coalition.

Administrative Divisions: Forty-nine districts and three municipalities (Warsaw, Kraków, Łódź) with special status. Counties basic form of local government, run by directly elected county councils. Both levels with substantial autonomy from central government.

Foreign Relations: After collapse of Soviet Union and its alliances, 1990–91, major shift toward relations with individual former Soviet states, especially Belarus, Lithuania, Russia, and Ukraine. Long-term national security goal integration into Western Europe, including European Community (EC) and North Atlantic Treaty Organization (NATO). Regional security sought in Visegrád alliance with Czech Republic, Hungary, and Slovakia. Improved relations with Germany, continued tension with Lithuania 1992.

National Security

Armed Forces: Polish Army (until 1990 Polish People's Army) divided into ground forces, navy, air and air defense forces, and territorial defense forces. Ground forces conscription for eighteen months, navy and air force two years. Mid-1992 total active-duty strength 296,500. Of 194,200 army personnel, 109,800 conscripts; of 83,000 air force personnel, 47,000 conscripts; of 19,300 navy personnel, 10,600 conscripts. Estimated 435,000 reservists. Territorial defense forces assigned as regional defense forces in case of invasion, reduced in size and role in early 1990s.

Major Military Units: Administered in four military districts, including Kraków district newly formed 1992. Major restructuring and streamlining undertaken 1990; in 1992 configuration, Pomeranian district had three mechanized divisions and a coastal defense unit, Silesian district four mechanized divisions, Warsaw district two mechanized divisions, and Kraków two mechanized divisions (projected). Navy operated three submarines, one destroyer, and one frigate. Air force operated 423 combat aircraft, 31 attack helicopters, in two air divisions. Substantial reliance on Soviet heavy equipment remaining from Warsaw Pact era; increasing domestic production of light equipment, early 1990s.

Military Budget: Major cuts 1989–92 during reassessment of doctrine and strategy. 1991 budget 16 trillion zloty. Equipment purchase reduced by high allotment for personnel maintenance in 1991 budget.

Internal Security Forces: Restructured and under civilian control after 1989. Office of State Protection, main state security agency after 1990, stripped of independent surveillance power but still object of public suspicion. Role of militia in riot control substantially reduced. Regular police upgraded, retrained, and reequipped. Border Guard streamlined, retrained for customs work and prevention of illegal entry.

Figure 1. Administrative Divisions of Poland, 1992

Introduction

A NEW ERA BEGAN for the nation of Poland in 1989, when the last communist regime ended unexpectedly and the Poles began to explore the potentials and pitfalls of true independence. That exploration process, which was accompanied by a firm commitment to democratic government, proved more chaotic and ambiguous than most Poles expected; it meant recovering long-dormant political and social traditions and reshaping them to meet Poland's needs as a capitalist member of post-Soviet Europe. It also meant inventing a political structure to accommodate the numerous interest groups that emerged from behind the communist monolith.

The cultural heritage of Poland, and the sense of nationhood that accompanies that heritage, evolved in a continuous process that began before the year A.D. 1000. Over the same period, the nation's history was a long series of dramatic shifts that included changes of dynasties, drastic realignment of frontiers, foreign invasion and occupation, and repeated partition by more powerful neighbors. Especially in the era that followed the collapse of Poland's 400-year federation with neighboring Lithuania at the end of the eighteenth century, the political and physical geography of Europe played a key role in Poland's fate. For the next two centuries, Poland was surrounded and often dominated by powerful expansionist Austrian, German, and Russian states. Poland's flat topography and central location invited invasion and made it strategically important during the many wars among European powers.

In the most recent phase of foreign domination, the post-World War II period between 1945 and 1989, Poland lay at the center of Soviet-dominated economic and military alliances, Comecon (see Glossary) and the Warsaw Pact (see Glossary), respectively. Socially, Poles suffered totalitarian repression of independent groups of all kinds, state-prescribed monolithic education doctrine, strict censorship, and repeated attempts to stifle their religious self-expression. Economically, Poland's subjugation resulted in a Soviet-style centralized planning system that produced early industrial growth but then stagnated in spite of repeated government restructuring programs. Comecon also isolated Poland's foreign trade from market competition throughout the communist era.

Politically, economic inertia and repression by communist regimes stimulated major incidents of nationwide social unrest that forced several changes of government between 1956 and 1981. Certain state controls were also relaxed during that period. The last and most enduring expression of social discontent was initiated by the Solidarity labor movement in 1980. Although officially illegal from 1981 to 1989, Solidarity was the symbolic spearhead of Poland's national revival and the foundation of the democratization movement that unexpectedly ousted communist rule in 1989.

In 1989 Poland was in the vanguard of political upheaval that swept communism from most of Eastern Europe and set the members of the Soviet-dominated Warsaw Pact on the course of drastic political and economic reform. In important ways, however, Poland had remained beyond the control of the communist political system that swallowed up Eastern Europe, even when that system was at its most formidable in the 1950s. As Poland's government bureaucracy, army, and internal security system assumed the classic forms of centralized totalitarianism, Polish society adjusted to official regimentation by establishing pragmatic alternative channels for economic and spiritual sustenance. The most visible and structured social institution of all, the Roman Catholic Church, actually increased in stature in the communist era. Most Poles responded to foreign domination by intensifying the unique linkage between their religion and their sense of secular nationality. Especially in the 1980s, the activism and stature of the church and labor groups prepared the ground for Poland to reassert the national independence that it had enjoyed only briefly in the previous 200 years.

The last communist government was voted out of office in mid-1989. In the reform period that followed, the groups that had mounted unified opposition to communist rule during the 1980s dispersed to pursue their own special interests in Poland's newly democratized political atmosphere. This dispersal lent a chaotic quality to the making of government policy on the country's most pressing problems: instituting rapid privatization of the key enterprises in Poland's formerly state-run economy; providing adequate social services during the severe dislocations of the privatization process; resuming economic growth while dealing with the desperately polluted environment inherited from communist industrial policy; and establishing a new set of foreign commercial and political connections to support Poland's new market economy and maximize national security. In 1992 experts agreed that, given Poland's strong sense of nationhood and dynamic entrepreneurial culture, the main obstacle to solving those problems was the acute fragmentation of its political system. In the second half of 1992, the new government of Prime Minister Hanna Suchocka began an energetic drive to refocus attention on issues of national concern and to regain the public trust that had eroded since the initial post-communist optimism of 1990.

At the stage when Poland emerged from Soviet dominance, it had a homogeneous ethnic culture. The near-unanimity of commitment to the Polish nation minimized the eruptions of nationalistic rivalry that plagued the postcommunist transitions of Czechoslovakia, Romania, the former components of the Soviet Union, and, most disastrously, Yugoslavia. In 1993 Poland was the only country in Eastern Europe whose borders were universally accepted, that faced no danger of disintegration, and that had no territorial claims on its neighbors. A monolithic ethnic structure was quite new to Poland, however: its cities had a long history as richly diverse cultural centers that tolerated religious and intellectual beliefs deemed heretical in other parts of Europe. Before 1939 the three largest ethnic minorities, the Ukrainians, Jews, and Germans, made up more than 25 percent of Poland's population.

World War II was the most recent and conclusive influence on Poland's ethnic structure. A large proportion of the prewar German and Ukrainian minorities were removed by forcible resettlement or the postwar redrawing of Poland's frontiers. Most of Poland's Jewish population (the largest in Europe in 1939) was exterminated in Nazi death camps; many of the surviving Jews emigrated after the war. Although the nation that emerged from those changes faced less ethnic unrest (the Ukrainians had been a particularly bothersome minority in the interwar years), many older Poles recalled that ethnic and cultural diversity had contributed much to the fabric of Polish life before 1939.

The Roman Catholic Church commanded the loyalty of Poles in such a way that communist dogma never penetrated much below the surface of Polish social or spiritual life. This status made the church the most powerful opponent of communist regimes in Poland throughout the postwar period. Most notably in the 1970s and 1980s, popular loyalty to the church forced communist governments to compromise in major church-state confrontations. Church support was vital to the initial success of the Solidarity movement in 1980 and to the movement's eventual accession to power in 1989.

In the political and social culture that emerged from totalitarianism in 1989, the church occupied an extremely influential and controversial position. After 1989, the church sought to preserve and extend the social leadership role it had played as an opposition force. Accordingly, it pushed legislation outlawing abortion, making religious education mandatory in public schools, and permitting active church participation in political elections. Politicians and the public were split between preserving the separation of church and state, which was a fundamental of the Western constitutional democracy to which Poland aspired, and preserving the thorough penetration of Polish secular life by religion-based ethics. Debate on the relation of church to state was especially heated in the prolonged framing of a new Polish constitution, a process that showed no sign of ending in early 1993.

Because the Soviet-modeled constitution of 1952 remained in force, with amendments, in 1992, all political factions considered a new constitution absolutely necessary as a foundation for Western-style commercial and human rights legislation. As in the other East European countries, governance in postwar Poland had been dominated by the national communist party, in this case the Polish United Workers' Party (Polska Zjednoczona Partia Robotnicza—PZPR). The party channeled policy decisions through a nominally democratic rubber-stamp political system that included a single-chamber parliament, the Sejm, and an executive Council of Ministers. After 1952 Poland had no president; the functions of chief of state were conducted by a Council of State elected by the Sejm. After 1989 those institutions proved inadequate for the return of democratic governance, however.

The Round Table Agreement of 1989, forged by the government of Wojciech Jaruzelski and by opposition forces led by Solidarity and the church, created a new presidency with formidable parliamentary curbs to limit the power of the communist Jaruzelski, who was expected to continue as head of state. The Senate was also restored as a second house of Poland's parliament, the National Assembly. Then the opposition unexpectedly won the national elections of 1989, and the total rebuilding of the Polish state began. Under those circumstances, the institution of the presidency was not powerful enough to push needed reforms through parliament. Lech Wałęsa, a strong personality committed to rapid reform, was chosen president by direct election in 1990. He faced twin frustrations: a government structure that constitutionally withheld most of Poland's executive powers from the president and a parliament fragmented among the numerous political parties that emerged when communist dominance ended. That fragmentation also blocked passage of a full constitution in the first three post-communist years. The Little Constitution, ratified in October 1992, was a pragmatic compromise that defined the roles of the president and parliament and quieted the power struggles that had flared in early 1992 between head of state Wałęsa and Prime Minister (head of government) Jan Olszewski. More important, previously irreconcilable factions of the Sejm finally compromised on a political system that would promote economic reform, which all sides recognized as Poland's top priority.

The Little Constitution helped reduce the confusion and near paralysis that had afflicted the central government since early 1990. The most controversial aspect of the document was the role assigned the president and the president's relationship to the Sejm, the lower house of parliament. Because the Little Constitution deleted the previous description of the Sejm as the supreme organ of state authority, many deputies feared that the president would now dominate the government. The new document empowered the president to submit a candidate for prime minister to the Sejm and to approve the prime minister's choices to fill cabinet positions. The president would also approve all important military and national security appointments and play a key role in selecting the most powerful ministers, those of defense, foreign affairs, and internal affairs. Thus, in contrast to the previous system, whose divided responsibility for naming a government had brought the gridlock of 1992, all roles were clearly delineated.

On August 1, 1992, a majority of 241 approved the Little Constitution in the Sejm. The issues resolved by the Little Constitution had been debated hotly and inconclusively many times before. Especially significant was the concept of the government's "special powers," which Wałęsa had advocated to avoid the legislative morass of Poland's multiparty parliament in building the legal framework for economic reform. Special powers meant that the government (cabinet) could now issue decrees with the force of law, provided the cabinet had the support of an absolute majority of the Sejm. The Sejm still decided, however, which policy areas were subject to such circumvention of the legislative process. According to the Little Constitution, areas protected from the force of decree were elections at all levels, constitutional amendments, the state budget, and civil and political liberties.

In early 1993, Prime Minister Hanna Suchocka requested expansion of the government's decree power to specifically include management of the economy, local government reform, public services, and adaptation of Polish laws to the standards of the European Community (EC)—areas considered vital to accelerate urgently pending economic decisions. According to her proposal, numerous safeguards would prevent the Council of Ministers from inappropriate action under the new law.

Because the Sejm retained substantial powers and met continuously, Wałęsa complained of the tyranny of the "Sejmocracy." Although the role of the presidency was better defined after mid-1992, the role of Wałęsa himself remained unclear. He continued strong advocacy of rapid capitalization of the economy, but in 1992 his traditional constituency, the workers in large factories, increasingly resisted painful transition steps such as wage controls and the closing of inefficient state-owned enterprises. Wałęsa failed to gain control of the national security policy-making apparatus in 1993, when the Sejm blocked legislation empowering the National Security Council that he had appointed.

In the first months of 1993, Wałęsa's position was destabilized by charges that his closest aide had collaborated with the communist secret police. This new phase in the campaign of Jarosław Kaczyński, Wałęsa's former chief of staff, to topple Wałęsa, aroused new questions about the deeds of present government officials in the communist era. It also endangered the unprecedented harmony that existed between Wałęsa and the Suchocka government in early 1993.

As an institution, the Sejm's performance in 1992 was mixed. Some sixty laws were passed, and numerous commissions met constantly. But most of the completed legislation covered rather narrow topics. Urgent and fundamental issues such as privatization, electoral law, the role of the prosecutor general, and financial and penal law, were tabled, and the Sejm often was preoccupied with trivial disputes. Passage of the Little Constitution was considered a remarkable achievement, but emotional issues such as separation of church and state made passage of a full constitution unlikely in the foreseeable future. Finally, the political qualifications of the average Sejm deputy were quite limited. Of the 460 members, sixteen were economists, twenty-two were lawyers, and few had significant political experience. This background had particular impact on the quality of legislation because in 1992 more bills were proposed by deputies than by the Council of Ministers.

The coalition government of Prime Minister Suchocka, who took office in the summer of 1992, brought together seven parties with diverse programs. By that time, Solidarity, the political linchpin of the anticommunist drive and the soil from which many of the ruling parties had sprung, had disappeared as a unifying force. The branches that emerged reflected two major lines of thought from the old Solidarity. The Suchocka coalition united most of the major parties on the right side of Poland's political spectrum. Within that grouping, the traditionalist right advocated continuing enough state intervention from the old communist system to protect social programs for the disadvantaged; at the same time, it backed strong state regulation in religious and moral issues such as abortion. The leader of this subcoalition was the strongly Catholic Christian National Union. The "liberal" group, led by Suchocka's Democratic

Union, advocated rapid introduction of a free-market system (with relatively little state protection from its inevitable social stresses), tighter monetary policy to stabilize the currency, and much less government intervention in personal freedom issues such as abortion and education. In the second half of 1992, the latter group was able to dominate economic issues by compromising on issues such as increasing church influence over policy on abortion, religious education, government control of broadcast programming, and the new constitution's position on separation of church and state.

In a national survey at the end of 1992, 80 percent of Poles expressed trust in Suchocka, a rating that had risen steadily through her first months in office. But, in a series of key parliamentary votes in early 1993, elements of her coalition defected, somewhat weakening her hold on power. Experts predicted that a confidence vote on the 1993 budget, due in midyear, would determine whether Suchocka stayed in power, but her position was not considered in immediate danger. Meanwhile, calls for a new presidential election multiplied as Wałęsa's political base eroded. Although his term would not be up until 1995, voices from both right and left suggested Suchocka and others as alternative candidates.

Suchocka was the first postcommunist Polish head of government with experience in foreign affairs. Under her government, Poland continued its strong efforts to solidify foreign relations with neighbors and, most urgently, with Western Europe. Poland's minister of foreign affairs, Krzystof Skubiszewski, remained in office through several changes of government and lent continuity to primary foreign policies such as fostering good relations with powerful neighbors Germany and the Soviet Union/Russia and moving Poland into the prosperous and secure sphere of Western Europe.

In 1990 Poland followed a two-track policy toward the Soviet Union. It maintained relations with central Soviet institutions while cultivating new relations with the Soviet republics. When the Soviet Union crumbled in 1991, Poland extended the latter policy by recognizing the newly independent post-Soviet states and seeking formal bilateral treaties with them. Thus, declarations of friendship and cooperation were signed with ''new'' neighbors Ukraine and Belarus in 1990 and 1991, respectively. In 1992 Polish trade and communications links increased with those countries in a fragmented, localized fashion. Poland also joined the Baltic Council, which theoretically linked it in a cooperative structure with the former Baltic republics of the Soviet Union.

Polish policy toward Russia had the short-term goal of expediting removal of the Russian troops that had been on Polish soil since

World War II. Thus early support for the independence of the non-Russian Soviet republics was stated carefully to avoid antagonizing Russia. In mid-1992 Russia accepted a troop withdrawal agreement that achieved complete combat troop removal in October 1992; all Russian troops were to leave by the end of 1993. Meanwhile, both nations saw the treaty of friendship and good-neighborly relations signed in May 1992 as beginning a new era of general bilateral cooperation.

The city of Kaliningrad was the capital of a small piece of Russian territory bordering northeast Poland and the Baltic Sea and isolated from the rest of Russia when Belarus, Lithuania, and Ukraine became independent in 1991. By 1992 the city had become a significant issue for Poland because of its continued role as a large Russian military base and its potential as a transportation and trading hub for the entire region. Although Poland and Russia held high-level talks on opening borders, regulating trade, and initiating joint transportation projects along their only common border, no other notable accords were reached in 1992.

In late 1992, Poland proposed new international standards for European border contacts, with the goal of easing multinational policies on issues such as the environment, regional development, communications, and transportation. By the end of 1993, two Euroregions had been established: the Nysa Euroregion at the junction of Poland, Germany, and the Czech Republic, and the Pomeranian Euroregion, including far northeast Germany and far northwest Poland (see fig. 1). The latter was viewed as a way of attracting support from the EC regional fund. Polish nationalist groups attacked proposals for such regions, however, as threats to the ethnic identity and the territorial integrity of the Polish state. In the fall of 1992, Poland signed a convention of the Council of Europe on cross-border cooperation. In early 1993, however, the Sejm rejected the government's proposal for Polish participation in a Carpathians Euroregion that also would include Ukraine, Hungary, and Slovakia.

In 1992 a new spate of European refugees moved northward and westward from war-torn territories of the former Yugoslavia and the countries of the former Soviet Union. Germany, the destination of choice for Muslim Slavs and other displaced groups, sought to return to Poland some of those who had entered Germany through Poland. Because Germany had acted without reaching agreement with Poland, and because Poland could not afford an influx of refugees, intense debates resulted over Poland's proper role and the economic and ethnic consequences of opening the borders.

After 1989 Poland entered two regional cooperation groupings of postcommunist East European states. The first was the Central European Initiative (CEI), which originally included Austria, Czechoslovakia, Hungary, Italy, and Yugoslavia. After the breakup of Yugoslavia in 1991, however, Poland distanced itself from the organization to avoid taking sides in the explosive Yugoslav political disputes that followed. In early 1993, however, Poland participated in many multinational working groups within the CEI and still considered the grouping potentially helpful in gaining entry into Western Europe.

A second grouping, the so-called Visegrád Triangle that included Hungary and the Czech and Slovak Federative Republic (see Glossary), was a promising economic and human-rights coalition aimed at moving its members faster into the institutions of Western Europe. The structure of that grouping was jeopardized, however, by the split of the Czech Republic and Slovakia at the start of 1993. In early 1993, Poland took a conciliatory role between the Czechs and Slovaks and between the Hungarians and Slovaks, whose relations had been strained for several years by ethnic and environmental disputes. In March 1993, after many postponements, the former triangle members (now known as the Visegrád Four or the Visegrád Group) established a free-trade zone that would eliminate customs duties among them by the year 2001. The agreement, whose timetable matched that already established between triangle and EC countries, signaled a shift in the triangle's attention from gaining EC membership to improving trade conditions within their group.

In 1993 Poles continued to feel anxiety about German reunification and the prospect of rapprochement between Poland's traditional threats, Germany and Russia. A strong opposing argument, however, held that fragmentation of the Soviet Union and the weakening of postcommunist Russia had significantly reduced the danger of domination from either East or West and that, on the contrary, Poland now had unique opportunities to establish advantageous relations with both sides. The latter assumptions formed the basis of Poland's policy toward Germany and Russia early in 1993.

In 1993 the national economy remained the most important issue to most Poles, but much of the country's economic policy remained unsettled. In 1990 the first postcommunist government had introduced the Balcerowicz Plan to introduce rapid market-oriented reforms in the national economy. (The first reform step, cessation of agricultural and food subsidies, occurred in mid-1989.) The general goals of the Balcerowicz Plan were macroeconomic stabilization, liberalization of prices from state control, deregulation of economic activity, privatization, and drastic industrial restructuring. In tandem with those steps would be ending wage indexation, taxation of excessive wage increases, and devaluation of Poland's unit of currency, the zloty (see Glossary). The plan initially eliminated shortages, curbed inflation, and prompted international financial institutions to pledge loans and encourage investment. But in 1990 and 1991, stabilization also drove unemployment far higher than expected while reducing real wages and productivity. The national budget deficit grew alarmingly because of Poland's negative trade balance and the inability of the state to collect taxes from large state enterprises. During the next two years, the contradictory short-term results of the Balcerowicz Plan fueled passionate economic debates.

In the first half of 1992, the government of Jan Olszewski attempted to soften the effects of the shock therapy. Olszewski's policy change was motivated by falling income, rising unemployment, higher prices, lower worker productivity, and a general feeling in Polish society that a market economy might not be worth the sacrifice needed to attain it. The worldwide recession that began in 1990 was a further disadvantage for economic recovery. Society's skepticism toward postcommunist reform was fueled by drastic budget cuts in education, health services, housing, and cultural activities. The idealistic egalitarianism of the old system, which many Poles cherished long after the end of communism, was sharply deflated by the rise of a small but visible wealthy class at a time when most Poles were struggling to maintain a minimal standard of living.

Olszewski's plan would have restored state spending for welfare, agricultural subsidies, and price supports, among other items. At the same time, it would have increased the national deficit, raised inflation, and destabilized the currency. This process in turn would jeopardize loan agreements with the International Monetary Fund (IMF—see Glossary) and other Western sources considered vital in the economic transition period. By the middle of 1992, those disadvantages had caused Olszewski to reverse the retrenchment experiment; his failure to carry through promised improvements contributed to rejection of his government.

Although the political chaos of early 1992 brought national economic policy making to a virtual halt, the Polish economy had begun a noticeable upturn by midyear. Price increases were the smallest since 1988, inflation showed signs of being under control, worker productivity increased about 12 percent, and the stabilization of unemployment at around 13 percent exceeded the most optimistic government predictions. The budget deficit, center of great controversy in the Olszewski government, was controlled enough in the first half of 1992 to fulfill IMF loan requirements.

The Suchocka government was able to stabilize somewhat the economic policy-making apparatus, which had been paralyzed by three changes in the positions of prime minister and finance minister between 1990 and 1992. In the first half of 1992, controversies in the crucial ministries of ownership transformation and foreign economic relations had further complicated economic planning.

Indicators at the end of 1992 confirmed some of the optimistic midyear figures: inflation for the year was 45 percent, unemployment 13.5 percent, and decline in production zero. In the last category, Poland's performance surpassed Bulgaria, the Czech and Slovak Federative Republic, Hungary, and Romania; Poland's inflation and unemployment figures were either better than or not far behind those of its former Comecon partners. Poland's end-of-1992 budget deficit, however, was about 50 percent higher than the midyear forecast. The size of the deficit ignited new acrimonious government conflict over budget cuts. In February 1993, after nearly three months of debate and Wałęsa's threat to dissolve parliament, the Sejm passed a stringent budget that promised additional short-term reductions in the living standards of many Poles.

In 1992 much of Poland's economic progress stemmed from growth in private sector productivity rather than from systematic government reform of the old system. Private firms were mostly small-scale and had minimal foreign-trade connections, but they generally adapted to recession conditions much better than state-owned enterprises. Thus between 1990 and 1992, employment in the private sector doubled, and by the end of 1992 well over half of Poland's workers held jobs in that sector. In foreign trade, the private sector provided 20 percent of sales, an increase of 3 percent over 1991. The magnitude of that statistic exerted great influence on the restructuring of industry and the development of capital markets in the early 1990s.

A second important factor in the upturn was 12.5 percent growth in hard-currency exports between 1991 and 1992. This trend included both Western and former Comecon trading partners, with the Czech and Slovak Federative Republic and Hungary (the partners in the Visegrád Triangle) registering the largest increases in the latter category. Poland's trade with EC countries rose much faster, however. EC trade reached a new high by the end of 1991, giving Poland the highest percentage of total exports (55.6 percent) to the EC among former Comecon countries. Experts considered this trend positive because it signaled the prosperity of firms able to survive in a Western market environment.

Germany retained its usual place as Poland's top overall trading partner. The combined countries of the former Soviet Union occupied second place overall, mainly because of large increases in sales of Polish agricultural and chemical products to those countries. Imports from most postcommunist European countries to Poland declined in 1992, however.

The permanence of the 1992 economic upturn was a matter of dispute at year's end because similar trends had proved illusory in 1990 and 1991. But falling inflation rates and a trade surplus now gave the government the opportunity to loosen restrictions on capital flow without again losing control of inflation. Also, the negative one-time effect of ending Poland's favorable trade status within Comecon had been absorbed fully by late 1992, and the unprecedented size of the private sector promised greater overall stability.

On the negative side, in the second half of 1992 strikes in major industries threatened to derail wage control policy and raise inflation while hampering productivity. But, by that time, the growing role of private enterprise and the service sector had blunted the traditional political impact of blue-collar labor actions. Although Suchocka's stringent economic policy continued to threaten workers in large enterprises through the end of 1992, labor failed to present a united front on the issue. Many strikes ended without inflationary pay raises, and by early 1993 worker discontent seemed to pose a diminished threat to government stability.

At the end of 1992, the financial structure of large state enterprises remained a severe obstacle to economic reform because those firms still supplied a major part of Poland's output and employment. Through mid-1992 the banking system had continued forgiving large debts incurred by such enterprises, a practice that automatically restricted credit available to finance new private enterprises. Many state enterprises had avoided bankruptcy (preserving their inefficient practices as part of the Polish economy) by making loans to each other, threreby creating a network of indebtedness outside the accountability of the national bank system. In mid-1992 the total state firm debt was an estimated US$24 billion, with 45 percent of state firms contributing to that figure.

In late 1992, the Suchocka government proposed a "pact on state firms" that would attack both the inefficient structure and the worker unrest in Poland's state firms. The basis of the proposal was a government grant of greater unemployment security and liberalized wage policy in return for active worker support of a range of privatization plans for their enterprises. The pact also would install Poland's first organized debt relief plan to allow both debtor and creditor organizations to regain financial health. The pact received considerable criticism. Many Poles feared that such a compromise would give trade unions too much power over government economic policy. And debt relief depended upon generous infusion of foreign capital into the national banking system, hence contributing to further indebtedness to the West. Under the 1990 agreement with the Paris Club (see Glossary) of seventeen Western creditors, Poland's total indebtedness was US$30 billion, with provisions for additional relief. At the end of 1992, the Polish government reached an agreement with the IMF for a loan of US$600 million that was expected to initiate a new series of negotiations with other Western lenders. But all agreements depended on Poland's demonstrating fiscal restraint by controlling its national budget deficit. That goal meant further cuts in pensions and welfare support and continued wage controls, policies that would affect most Poles in 1993.

The rate of privatization remained the single most important aspect of Polish economic policy. Between 1989 and the end of 1992, the most frequent form of privatization was liquidation, an interim solution that shifted ownership within the firm but retained state ownership. It predominated because outside private investment funds remained very scarce. Of at least 1,200 firms in liquidation in late 1992, more than half had declared bankruptcy.

The sale of shares to a joint-stock company was the predominant method of privatizing large state companies in the early 1990s. That process, which began with interim partnership with the State Treasury, went very slowly after that stage. Shares in state-owned firms were offered increasingly rarely on the Warsaw Stock Exchange, and only seven of 348 existing State Treasury partnerships were sold between January and August 1992. Overall, only twenty-five large or medium-sized companies had been sold to foreign owners on this plan.

The Ministry of Ownership Transformation, established to determine the type of disposal or restructuring required by Polish firms, faced political forces that prevented a comprehensive approach to transition. In late 1992, parliament was still sharply divided over issues such as foreign ownership and distribution of property rights, making liquidation the only generally accepted privatization formula. Long-term plans called for the Ministry of Ownership Transformation to begin a mass privatization program in 1994 that would move 400 state companies at one time into private ownership. Equity in the companies would be transferred into twenty national investment funds, shares of which would be available to all adult Poles according to a complex distribution scheme.

The predominance of debtor firms in Poland's major heavy industries made their restructuring a high priority in 1993. Among mines and steel mills, only a handful of firms showed a profit in 1992, and twenty of twenty-eight firms in the armaments industry were in the red. At the end of 1992, the power industry had amassed US$1 billion of credits from large enterprises, mainly shipyards, mines, and steel mills. The power industry had no leverage to collect its debts because energy supply could not be curtailed without hampering industrial output.

In late 1992, Polish mines were regrouped and their financial status examined, and plans were set for drastic shrinkage of the metallurgical industry, which was also a relic of communist inefficiency. Shipbuilding firms, expecting an upturn in their flagging international business in 1993, were spared major overhaul, but the armaments industry faced a depleted market and the prospect of retooling for some type of peacetime production. Such conversion promised a longterm "disarmament dividend," but it also required substantial short-term investment that had not materialized by early 1993. The insecurity of the post-Soviet arms market led to a series of illegal or quasi-legal arms sales by major Polish manufacturers.

Replacing or securing Russian fuel supplies was a major goal of industrial planners, who were dismayed by the disorganized state of the Russian fuel industry. Although two-thirds of Poland's natural gas came from Russia in 1993, two years after the end of Comecon the two countries still had not solidified terms of delivery or the standing of previous debts. Two factors made oil and natural gas vital to the Polish economy. Coal was recognized as a primary cause of Poland's environmental and health problems, especially because most coal-burning power plants lacked pollution controls. And Poland had ceased construction of its two nuclear power plants in 1990. Polish prospects for supplementing foreign fuel supplies were boosted in 1992 by discovery of large offshore Baltic oil deposits, however. Early estimates projected their output as 500,000 tons per year, compared with the 11.4 million tons of crude oil imported by Poland in 1990. Poland also sought agreements that would ensure regular fuel supplies from Russia and Ukraine, where political uncertainty had made export policy unreliable after the end of Comecon.

As Poles adjusted to the open exchange of ideas in the postcommunist era, certain issues of social policy became quite divisive. Central to this process was the Roman Catholic Church, to which about 98 percent of Poles professed allegiance in early 1993, and which had gained enormous prestige in the communist era. After ultimately winning the struggle to protect Polish spiritual life from the effects of communist dogma, the church immediately took a powerful role in determining social policy in the transition period. In doing so, the church successfully reapplied the linkage of religious and secular ethics that had become traditional in the communist era. Between 1989 and 1993, the promotion of "Christian values" became a routine element in the agendas of political and social groups, and by 1993 the meetings of nearly all political parties began with Holy Mass.

Significant numbers of Roman Catholic Poles, however, defended the idea of a "neutral state" that would set secular policy independent of ideological or religious tenets. Between 1990 and 1993, tension grew as the church sought to influence key items of legislation: religious instruction in public schools, abortion rights, government control of the broadcast media, and a new constitutional formulation of the relationship of church and state. Although mandatory religious instruction was reintroduced into public schools in 1991, public resentment toward the change escalated noticeably in 1992.

A majority of Poles also disagreed with their church's position that abortion was a crime and that the liberal communist-era abortion laws must be reversed completely. Although abortions in Poland already had decreased drastically in the early 1990s, parliamentary debates over illegalizing abortion were quite bitter in late 1992 and early 1993. Abortion rights advocates mounted a substantial drive for a national referendum on the issue, in the expectation that Polish public opinion would support their position. But Prime Minister Suchocka used her now substantial influence to block a referendum, calling it a bad precedent that might erode the government's recently acquired legitimacy.

In January 1993, the Sejm passed a bill outlawing abortion under most conditions. The Senate, where radicals considered the Sejm bill too lenient, forged with the Sejm a compromise provision that made abortion officially illegal except under life-threatening conditions. That version was passed into law in February 1993. At the same time, many Roman Catholic Poles who disapproved of dogmatic social positions and feared establishment of a theocratic state demanded internal liberalization, and some church authorities were alarmed by their institution's sharp drop in public trust in the postcommunist years. Open public criticism was a new phenomenon for the church, which in the communist period enjoyed strong public support when threatened by state authorities. In 1993, however, the conventional hierarchy of the Polish

Episcopate still possessed unprecedented political power and resisted strongly any policy-making democratization that would threaten its influence. Although the episcopate moderated its official positions on some social questions, individual priests used their pulpits to advocate radical change.

In 1992 Poland continued to feel the environmental and health consequences of previous communist policies. A 1993 report characterized 13 million Poles as living in regions of environmental danger, and disorders associated with environmental pollution—especially respiratory and circulatory problems—continued far above the European average. The report also noted bad living conditions, poor eating habits, smoking, excessive alcohol consumption, drug abuse, and poor personal hygiene as factors contributing to poor national health. National health care coverage remained in an uneven, poorly funded transitional stage between the full state-sponsored program of the old regime and a privatized system of yet unknown structure.

By 1993 Poland had environmental programs for protection of the atmosphere and forests and for water management. Funding, however, was a major problem. A high percentage of fines assessed against polluting industries went unpaid, especially in the industrial Katowice District. The Ecofund, an arrangement by which part of debts forgiven by Western banks would be channeled into environmental programs, received little funding in its early stages in 1993. And environmental agencies remained cautious about strangling vital industries, especially in the power generation sector, by levying excessive fines.

Poland's rate of population growth was among the highest in Europe throughout the postwar period. It reached a postwar low in 1992, however, because of lower birth rates and the continuing decline in average life expectancy. Poland was expected to retain its place at the top of European growth rates, however, when the larger next generation of women reached childbearing age in the 1990s.

By early 1993, Poland had moved ahead of its East European neighbors in several economic measurements. Major economic indicators suggested that the worst fallout of Poland's ''shock therapy'' might be past; growth in exports and major expansion of the private enterprise sector were reasons for economic optimism. But the overall privatization rate still lagged behind government plans, and Polish workers remained alienated or skeptical of reforms that seemed to produce only lower employment and lower standards of living. The domestic price for more international aid and debt forgiveness, considered vital to pump capital into the economy, included additional painful stringency measures to satisfy international lenders. The main question was whether recognizable recovery could occur before the public abandoned its commitment to capitalist reform.

In politics, Hanna Suchocka emerged as a strong leader respected by most of the Polish public, even as the members of her fragile coalition fought bitterly over social issues such as abortion. As Suchocka's fortunes improved, however, the image of President Lech Wałęsa declined. In 1992 the pragmatic Little Constitution had clarified the main lines of government power, but agreement among political factions on a full constitution remained impossible in early 1993. Aside from the calming influence of Suchocka, Polish politics remained confrontational and coalitions tenuous. For that reason, the potential for solid, long-term political and economic reform was unclear; in spite of positive economic signs, Polish society reacted to the turmoil of postcommunist transition with increased restlessness as it approached the fourth anniversary of the end of communist rule.

June 1, 1993

*   *   *

In the months following preparation of this manuscript, significant events occurred in the process of political and economic reform in postcommunist Poland. The upturn of economic productivity that began at the end of 1992 continued through 1993 and brought Poland recognition as the best example of postcommunist progress toward a market economy among the nations that had been in the Soviet sphere. Despite economic improvement, however, the government of Hanna Suchocka, the fourth prime minister of Poland since the fall of the Jaruzelski regime in 1989, was rejected decisively in the parliamentary election of September 19, 1993. Through the remainder of 1993, a new governing coalition negotiated toward workable approaches to the programs already in progress.

By midsummer the simmering test of wills between President Wałęsa and the Sejm had erupted in a parliamentary no-confidence vote toppling the Suchocka government, which Wałęsa had supported strongly. Ironically, the initial no-confidence vote was proposed by Solidarity deputies as a bargaining ploy to gain wage increases for public employees. With no agreement on a successor to Suchocka, Wałęsa dissolved parliament and called for a new election.

An important result of the ensuing election was rejection of the political elite that had dominated the political scene since 1989. In fact, all parties favoring rapid transition to a full-scale market economy met defeat in 1993. Also defeated were the most radical advocates of a return to the state central planning of the communist era. The representation thresholds in the election law of May 1993 were the main cause of this upheaval. The law succeeded in reducing fragmentation, because only six parties or coalitions gained one or more seats in the National Assembly. The main beneficiaries of the change were the Alliance of the Democratic Left (Sojusz Lewicy Demokratycznej—SLD), direct heir to the PZPR, and the Polish Peasant Party (Polskie Stronnictwo Ludowe—PSL), which had been a figurehead opposition party in the communist era.

The election also reduced the influence of the two most prominent political figures in Poland, Suchocka and Wałęsa, both of whom had pushed market reform at a rate judged by some as harmful to employment and social stability. Wałęsa, not due to stand for reelection until 1995, was expected to lose considerable influence on policy making because of declining support for the Solidarity-based parties. His newly restructured pro-reform coalition was second to Suchocka's Democratic Union (Unia Demokratyczna—UD) among opposition groups pressing for reform in the new Sejm. Wałęsa was also damaged by renewed allegations of connections with the communist-era internal security agencies. Suchocka, who had weathered major crises and gained unexpected personal popularity in 1993, easily retained her seat in the Sejm.

After the election, the shape of the Polish government and the fate of economic reform remained unclear for some time. Despite its historical connections with communist regimes, by 1993 the constituency of the SLD had changed markedly, and the party's triumph did not threaten a return to centralized state planning. The SLD now included substantial support from private entrepreneurs, together with part of the structure remaining from the communist days. New diversity and unforeseen growth complicated formation of a ruling-party platform, but a majority of the SLD favored continuing most of the Suchocka program. The PSL continued to represent mostly agricultural interests, many of which contradicted SLD's more urban economic priorities. Under pressure from Wałęsa, the two groups agreed to compromise their differences on financial policy, privatization, agricultural policy, trade, and other key issues to form a new government.

The SLD and the PSL formed a loose, pragmatic, majority coalition that backed Waldemar Pawlak of the PSL as prime minister and SLD members as heads of key economic ministries and speaker of the Sejm. The new Polish cabinet did not take shape until late October 1993. Although Pawlak technically headed the Council of Ministers, Wałęsa and SLD leader Aleksandr Kwasniewski both used their positions to control parts of Pawlak's cabinet. At the end of 1993, this arrangement promised a new struggle for power involving personalities as much as policy. The last months of the year included debate about which policies of the previous government should be retained, which modified, and which rejected. Domestic policies under dispute included the rate and emphasis of privatization activity; improvement of tax revenues and application of taxes more fairly to minimize the suffering of the transition process; subsidies for Polish exporters to enhance competitiveness in West European agricultural markets; and the need for a more autonomous, streamlined system of local and regional government, including reestablishment of the *powiat* (county) level of local government.

Also unresolved between Wałęsa and the Sejm was official authority for national security policy making. In November 1993, the National Defense Committee (renamed the National Security Council by the Little Constitution but unchanged in membership or unofficial nomenclature since that time) resolved to cede its authority to a restructured National Security Council. The Sejm refused to pass legislation for the change, however, because Wałęsa would then control the agency whose national security decisions were binding on the Sejm.

The election of September 1993 sent signals in other directions as well. After receiving strong criticism for its activism in the 1991 election, the Polish Catholic Church limited itself to quietly advocating a conservative coalition in the 1993 election. When the right-of-center parties most closely identified with church positions gained no seats in the new parliament, the strong showing of the SLD brought warnings from church officials about Poland's leftward swing. Experts predicted that the moral issues that church-affiliated parties had pushed in the previous parliament would receive much less attention in 1994.

In the first two months of its operation, parliament impressed most observers as more competent and less given to procedural wrangling than its predecessor. In November 1993, the National Assembly established a new constitutional committee charged with drafting the full constitution that had eluded previous legislation. A six-month period was fixed for the committee to create its own text and consider other constitutional bills submitted by the major political parties or by Wałęsa.

In 1993 Poland also suffered increased ethnic tensions in Silesia. In the 1991 treaty of friendship and cooperation with Germany, Poland had recognized several hundred thousand citizens of Poland as ethnic Germans with separate cultural identities and political rights. Nevertheless, in 1993 the new freedoms of the postcommunist era continued to breed expression of animosity from parts of the Silesian German population toward the Poles. Encouraged by ultranationalist groups in Germany, an expanded Germanization movement included replacing Polish place-names in Silesia with the German form applied by the Nazis during their occupation of Poland.

According to a report on the state of the nation by outgoing Prime Minister Suchocka, in late 1993 economic indicators were more favorable than at any previous point since 1989. At that time, about 60 percent of the work force and half of the gross domestic product (GDP—see Glossary) was in the private sector, and an estimated 1.1 million new jobs had appeared in that sector since 1990. Projected GDP growth for 1994 was 4 to 4.5 percent, the highest estimate in all of Europe. Still, 2.8 million Poles, over 15 percent of the work force, were unemployed at the end of 1993. Economic growth was hindered by scarce credit, which stemmed from low bank reserves and a frequent failure to repay loans. The cost of social welfare continued to be high in 1993, and no change was forecast. In late 1993, some 6.5 million pensioners were supported by the social security payments of about 13 million working Poles. Meanwhile, the new government increased retirement pensions for 1994 by an average of 40 percent.

The 1994 budget, which the cabinet passed and presented to parliament at the the end of December 1993, featured a deficit of about US$4.1 billion. On the one hand, although this amount was less than the 5 percent of GDP stipulated for credit approval by international lenders, it was criticized for failing to set a long-term budgetary structure while it substantially increased state debt. On the other hand, the final figure was reached under protest from several of the larger ministries, which demanded a bigger share. Major funding increases were to go to the Ministry of National Defense (for purchase of domestically produced equipment), to agricultural subsidies, to the Ministry of Justice (to hire more judges, among other purposes), and to the Ministry of Internal Affairs for improved public security. The main revenue sources were to be value-added and personal income taxes and excise duties.

Although Poland maintained its diversified foreign-trade policy through the end of 1993, it met obstacles in expanding partnerships. Trade with former partners to the East, notably Russia and Ukraine, remained meager. To the West, a combination of general recession and protective trade barriers discouraged Polish initiatives and created resentment among Polish exporters. As an alternative, the Pawlak government sought improved trade with the five-member nations of the European Free Trade Agreement (EFTA) in

1994. Under these circumstances, a final trade deficit of at least US$2 billion was forecast for 1993, and domestic producers called for limitation of consumer goods imports in 1994 to improve the trade balance. Meanwhile, the new government took up negotiations with the London Club (see Glossary), to whose European member banks Poland owed over US$12 billion at the end of 1993, to gain more favorable repayment terms and protect Poland's image as a responsible borrower. Prime Minister Pawlak identified foreign and internal debt among the most urgent problems that Poland would face in 1994.

Political unrest in Russia in the fall of 1993 and the very strong showing of militant nationalists in the Russian elections of December 1993 increased Polish worries about Russia's long-term intentions toward the lost empire of Eastern Europe. In response to pressure from the members of the Visegrád Group (known as the Visegrád Triangle before the split of Czechoslovakia) for immediate full membership in the North Atlantic Treaty Organization (NATO—see Glossary), that organization offered a compromise, gradual admission procedure. The program, dubbed the Partnership for Peace, would set up a system of joint military planning, maneuvers, and eventual operations of NATO forces and forces of the Visegrád Group and the other East European nations. The proposal did not promise full membership, nor did it guarantee specifically the security of the new democracies in the region, however. The proposal did require participating nations to divert additional defense funds to joint activities.

Poland's official response was a warning that, although Russian military domination was not an immediate threat, nationalist forces within the East European countries could push those countries back to anti-Western positions if the people viewed overtures to the West as unproductive. Thus the insecurities of the Cold War could resume if NATO did not make immediate security guarantees and integrate those nations speedily into the European Union (formerly the European Community). When the other members of the Visegrád Group accepted the partnership readily, however, Wałęsa reluctantly accepted the arrangement at a meeting with President William J. Clinton in Prague in January 1994.

Elsewhere, in December 1993 Poland concluded a treaty with Ukraine setting procedures for solving border issues. And the sensitive issue of rights for Lithuania's Polish minority calmed somewhat in the second half of 1993; negotiations with Lithuania, the only neighbor with whom Poland had achieved no major treaty in the postcommunist era, thus offered hope for a 1994 treaty of friendship and cooperation.

Although no direct military threat existed at the end of 1993, internal conditions remained a vital concern to Poland's national security. Although the outburst of crime that had accompanied the fall of communism in 1990 had stabilized, banditry, financial scandals, and organized crime continued to rise. Improvements in the equipment and methods of police and internal security agencies (including better communications technology and stricter licensing and regulation of commercial activities) promised a long-range reduction in street crime and white-collar crime.

Among the chief obstacles facing Poland in 1994 were the following: the threat of labor unrest caused by continued unemployment and low wages; continued resistance to reform from former communists entrenched in influential policy-making positions; doubts among potential Western investors about Poland's long-term economic and political health; continued ambiguity in Russian policy toward Eastern Europe; and the collapse of Eastern markets combined with protectionist tendencies among trade partners in the West. Although skeptics saw the economic success of 1993 as a short-term anomaly, the ever-expanding private sector remained a vigorous support for the entire economic system. The efficiency of the political system, depending at the end of 1993 on a tenuous parliamentary alliance of two quite diverse parties and an unproven prime minister, remained the chief unknown factor as 1994 began.

January 14, 1994   Glenn E. Curtis

Chapter 1. Historical Setting

Clio, the muse of history, from a sculpture in Warsaw's Saxon Gardens

THE POLES POSSESS one of the richest and most venerable historical traditions of all European peoples. Convention fixes the origins of Poland as a nation near the middle of the tenth century, contemporaneous with the Carolingians, Vikings, and Saracens, and a full hundred years before the Norman conquest of Britain in 1066. Throughout the subsequent centuries, the Poles managed despite great obstacles to build and maintain an unbroken cultural heritage. The same cannot be said of Polish statehood, which was notoriously precarious and episodic. Periods of independence and prosperity alternated with phases of foreign domination and disaster. Especially in more recent centuries, frequent adversity subjected the Poles to hardships scarcely equaled in European history.

Many foreign observers perceive Poland as a perennial victim of history, whose survival through perseverance and a dogged sense of national identity has left a mixed legacy of indomitable courage and intolerance toward outsiders. To Poles, their history includes brighter recollections of Poland as a highly cultured kingdom, uniquely indulgent of ethnic and religious diversity and precociously supportive of human liberty and the fundamental values of Western civilization. The contrast between these images reflects the extremes of fortune experienced by Poland. The two visions of history combine in uneasy coexistence in the Polish consciousness. One striking feature of Polish culture is its fascination with the national past; the unusual variety and intensity of that past defy tidy conclusions and produce energetic debate among Poles themselves on the meaning of their history.

Early History until 1385

In the first centuries of its existence, the Polish nation was led by a series of strong rulers who converted the Poles to Christendom, created a strong Central European state, and integrated Poland into European culture. Formidable foreign enemies and internal fragmentation eroded this initial structure in the thirteenth century, but consolidation in the 1300s laid the base for the dominant Polish Kingdom that was to follow.

The Origins of Poland

According to Polish myth, the Slavic nations trace their ancestry to three brothers who parted in the forests of Eastern Europe, each moving in a different direction to found a family of distinct but related peoples. Fanciful elements aside, this tale accurately describes the westward migration and gradual differentiation of the early West Slavic tribes following the collapse of the Roman Empire. About twenty such tribes formed small states between A.D. 800 and 960. One of these tribes, the Polanie or Poliane ("people of the plain"), settled in the flatlands that eventually formed the heart of Poland, lending their name to the country. Over time the modern Poles emerged as the largest of the West Slavic groupings, establishing themselves to the east of the Germanic regions of Europe with their ethnographic cousins, the Czechs and Slovaks, to the south.

In spite of convincing fragmentary evidence of prior political and social organization, national custom identifies the starting date of Polish history as 966, when Prince Mieszko (r. 963–92) accepted Christianity in the name of the people he ruled. In return, Poland received acknowledgment as a separate principality owing some degree of tribute to the German Empire (later officially known as the Holy Roman Empire—see Glossary). Under Otto I, the German Empire was an expansionist force to the West in the mid-tenth century. Mieszko accepted baptism directly from Rome in preference to conversion by the German church and subsequent annexation of Poland by the German Empire. This strategy inaugurated the intimate connection between the Polish national identity and Roman Catholicism that became a prominent theme in the history of the Poles.

Mieszko is considered the first ruler of the Piast Dynasty (named for the legendary peasant founder of the family), which endured for four centuries. Between 967 and 990, Mieszko conquered substantial territory along the Baltic Sea and in the region known as Little Poland to the south. By the time he officially submitted to the authority of the Holy See in Rome in 990, Mieszko had transformed his country into one of the strongest powers in Eastern Europe.

Mieszko's son and successor Bolesław I (r. 992–1025), known as the Brave, built on his father's achievements and became the most successful Polish monarch of the early medieval era. Bolesław continued the policy of appeasing the Germans while taking advantage of their political situation to gain territory wherever possible. Frustrated in his efforts to form an equal partnership with the Holy Roman Empire, Bolesław gained some non-Polish territory in a series of wars against his imperial overlord in 1003 and 1004. The Polish conqueror then turned eastward, extending the boundaries of his realm into present-day Ukraine. Shortly before his death in

Cathedral at Gniezno, where Poland's first Roman Catholic archbishopric was established circa A.D. 1000
Courtesy Ronald D. Bachman

1025, Bolesław won international recognition as the first king of a fully sovereign Poland (see fig. 2).

The Medieval Era

During the eleventh century and the first half of the twelfth century, the building of the Polish state continued under a series of successors to Bolesław I. But by 1150, the state had been divided among the sons of Bolesław III, beginning two centuries of fragmentation that brought Poland to the brink of dissolution.

Fragmentation and Invasion, 1025–1320

The most fabled event of the period was the murder in 1079 of Stanisław, the bishop of Kraków. A participant in uprisings by the aristocracy against King Bolesław II, Stanisław was killed by order of the king. This incident, which led to open rebellion and ended the reign of Bolesław, is a Polish counterpart to the later, more famous assassination of Thomas à Becket on behalf of King Henry II of England. Although historians still debate the circumstances of the death, after his canonization the martyred St. Stanisław entered national lore as a potent symbol of resistance to illegitimate state authority—an allegorical weapon that proved especially effective against the communist regime.

During the eleventh and twelfth centuries, Poland lost ground in its complex triangular relationship with the German Empire to

5

the west and the kingdom of Bohemia to the south. New foreign enemies appeared by the thirteenth century. The Mongol invasion cut a swath of destruction through the country in 1241; for fifty years after their withdrawal in 1242, Mongol nomads mounted devastating raids into Poland from bases in Ruthenia to the southeast. Meanwhile, an even more dangerous foe arrived in 1226 when a Polish duke invited the Teutonic Knights (see Glossary), a Germanic crusading order, to help him subdue Baltic pagan tribes. Upon completing their mission with characteristic fierceness and efficiency, the knights built a stronghold on the Baltic seacoast, from which they sought to enlarge their holdings at Polish expense. By that time, the Piasts had been parceling out the realm into ever smaller units for nearly 100 years. This policy of division, initiated by Bolesław II to appease separatist provinces while maintaining national unity, led to regional governance by various branches of the dynasty and to a near breakdown of cohesiveness in the face of foreign aggression. As the fourteenth century opened, much Polish land lay under foreign occupation (two-thirds of it was ruled by Bohemia in 1300). The continued existence of a united, independent Poland seemed unlikely.

The Later Piasts

In the fourteenth century, after a long period of instability and growing menace from without, the Polish state experienced a half century of recovery under the last monarchs of the house of Piast. By 1320 Władysław Łokietek (r. 1314–33), called the Short, had manipulated internal and foreign alignments and reunited enough territory to win acceptance abroad as king of an independent Poland. His son Kazimierz III (r. 1333–70) would become the only Polish king to gain the sobriquet "great." In foreign policy, Kazimierz the Great strengthened his country's position by combining judicious concessions to Bohemia and the Teutonic Knights with eastward expansion.

While using diplomacy to win Poland a respite from external threat, the king focused on domestic consolidation. He earned his singular reputation through his acumen as a builder and administrator as well as through foreign relations. Two of the most important events of Kazimierz's rule were the founding of Poland's first university in Kraków in 1364, making that city an important European cultural center, and his mediation between the kings of Bohemia and Hungary at the Congress of Kraków (also in 1364), signaling Poland's return to the status of a European power. Lacking a male heir, Kazimierz was the last ruler in the Piast line. The extinction of the dynasty in 1370 led to several years of renewed political uncertainty. Nevertheless, the accomplishments of the fourteenth century began the ascent of the Polish state toward its historical zenith.

Integration into European Civilization

Without question the most significant development of the formative era of Poland's history was the gradual absorption of the country into the culture of medieval Europe. After their relatively late arrival as pagan outsiders on the fringes of the Christian world, the Western Slavs were fully and speedily assimilated into the civilization of the European Middle Ages. Latin Christianity came to determine the identity of that civilization and permeate its intellect and creativity. Over time the Central Europeans increasingly patterned their thought and institutions on Western models in areas of thought ranging from philosophy, artistic style, literature, and architecture to government, law, and social structure. The Poles borrowed especially heavily from German sources, and successive Polish rulers encouraged a substantial immigration of Germans and Jews to invigorate urban life and commerce. From its beginning, Poland drew its primary inspiration from Western Europe and developed a closer affinity with the French and Italians, for example, than with nearer Slavic neighbors of Eastern Orthodox and Byzantine (see Glossary) heritage. This westward orientation, which in some ways has made Poland the easternmost outpost of Latinate and Catholic tradition, helps to explain the Poles' tenacious sense of belonging to the ''West'' and their deeply rooted antagonism toward Russia as the representative of an essentially alien way of life.

The Jagiellon Era, 1385–1572

The next major period was dominated by the union of Poland with Lithuania under a dynasty founded by the Lithuanian grand duke Jagiello. The partnership proved profitable for the Poles, who played a dominant role in one of the most powerful empires in Europe for the next three centuries.

The Polish-Lithuanian Union

Poland's unlikely partnership with the adjoining Grand Duchy of Lithuania, Europe's last heathen state, provided an immediate remedy to the political and military dilemma caused by the end of the Piast Dynasty. At the end of the fourteenth century, Lithuania was a warlike political unit with dominion over enormous stretches of present-day Belarus and Ukraine. Putting aside their previous hostility, Poland and Lithuania saw that they shared common enemies, most notably the Teutonic Knights; this situation

7

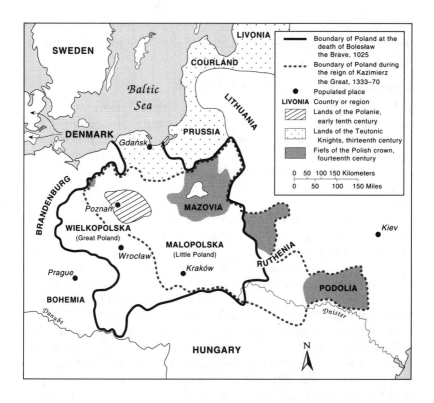

Figure 2. Piast Poland, 966 to 1370

was the direct incentive for the Union of Krewo in 1385. The compact hinged on the marriage of the Polish queen Jadwiga to Jagiello, who became king of Poland under the name Władysław Jagiello. In return, the new monarch accepted baptism in the name of his people, agreed to confederate Lithuania with Poland, and took the name Władysław II. In 1387 the bishopric of Wilno was established to convert Władysław's subjects to Roman Catholicism. (Eastern Orthodoxy predominated in some parts of Lithuania.) From a military standpoint, Poland received protection from the Mongols and Tatars, while Lithuania received aid in its long struggle against the Teutonic Knights.

The Polish-Lithuanian alliance exerted a profound influence on the history of Eastern Europe (see fig. 3). Poland and Lithuania would maintain joint statehood for more than 400 years, and over the first three centuries of that span the "Commonwealth of Two Nations" ranked as one of the leading powers of the continent.

Fortress of Malbork, seat of grand masters of the Teutonic
Knights in fourteenth and fifteenth centuries
Courtesy Jean R. Tartter
Part of the old city wall of Kraków, established in the fourteenth century
Courtesy Ronald D. Bachman

The association produced prompt benefits in 1410 when the forces of Poland-Lithuania defeated the Teutonic Knights in battle at Grunwald (Tannenberg), at last seizing the upper hand in the long struggle with the renegade crusaders. The new Polish-Lithuanian dynasty, called "Jagiellon" after its founder, continued to augment its holdings during the following decades. By the end of the fifteenth century, representatives of the Jagiellons reigned in Bohemia and Hungary as well as Poland-Lithuania, establishing the government of their clan over virtually all of Eastern Europe and Central Europe. This far-flung federation collapsed in 1526 when armies of the Ottoman Empire (see Glossary) won a crushing victory at the Battle of Mohács (in Hungary), wresting Bohemia and Hungary from the Jagiellons and installing the Turks as a menacing presence in the heart of Europe.

The "Golden Age" of the Sixteenth Century

The Jagiellons never recovered their hegemony over Central Europe, and the ascendancy of the Ottomans foreshadowed the eventual subjection of the entire region to foreign rule; but the half century that followed the Battle of Mohács marked an era of stability, affluence, and cultural advancement unmatched in national history and widely regarded by Poles as their country's golden age.

Poland-Lithuania as a European Power

The Teutonic Knights had been reduced to vassalage, and despite the now persistent threats posed by the Turks and an emerging Russian colossus, Poland-Lithuania managed to defend its status as one of the largest and most prominent states of Europe. The wars and diplomacy of the century yielded no dramatic expansion but shielded the country from significant disturbance and permitted significant internal development. An "Eternal Peace" concluded with the Ottoman Turks in 1533 lessened but did not remove the threat of invasion from that quarter.

A lucrative agricultural export market was the foundation for the kingdom's wealth. A population boom in Western Europe prompted an increased demand for foodstuffs; Poland-Lithuania became Europe's foremost supplier of grain, which was shipped abroad from the Baltic seaport of Gdańsk. Aside from swelling Polish coffers, the prosperous grain trade supported other notable aspects of national development. It reinforced the preeminence of the landowning nobility that received its profits, and it helped to preserve a traditionally rural society and economy at a time when Western Europe had begun moving toward urbanization and capitalism.

The Government of Poland-Lithuania

In other respects as well, the distinctive features of Jagiell
Poland ran against the historical trends of early modern Europ
Not the least of those features was its singular governmental stru
ture and practice. In an era that favored the steady accumulatic
of power within the hands of European monarchs, Poland-Lithuan
developed a markedly decentralized system dominated by a land
ed aristocracy that kept royal authority firmly in check. The Polis
nobility, or *szlachta,* enjoyed the considerable benefits of landowner
ship and control over the labor of the peasantry. The *szlachta* in
cluded 7 to 10 percent of the population, making it a very large
noble class by European standards. The nobility manifested an impressive group solidarity in spite of great individual differences in
wealth and standing. Over time, the gentry induced a series of royal
concessions and guarantees that vested the noble parliament, or
Sejm, with decisive control over most aspects of statecraft, including exclusive rights to the making of laws. The Sejm operated on
the principle of unanimous consent, regarding each noble as ir-
reducibly sovereign. In a further safeguard of minority rights, Polish
usage sanctioned the right of a group of gentry to form a confederation, which in effect constituted an uprising aimed at redress of
grievances. The nobility also possessed the crucial right to elect
the monarch, although the Jagiellons were in practice a hereditary
ruling house in all but the formal sense. The prestige of the Jagiellons and the certainty of their succession supplied an element of
cohesion that tempered the disruptive forces built into the state
system.

In retrospect historians frequently have derided the idiosyncratic,
delicate governmental mechanism of Poland-Lithuania as a recipe
for anarchy. Although its eventual breakdown contributed greatly
to the loss of independence in the eighteenth century, the system
worked reasonably well for 200 years while fostering a spirit of civic
liberality unmatched in the Europe of its day. The host of legal
protections that the nobility enacted for itself prefigured the rights
generally accorded the citizens of modern democracies, and the
memory of the ''golden freedoms'' of Poland-Lithuania is an important part of the Poles' present-day sense of their tradition of
liberty. On the other hand, the exclusion of the lower nobility from
most of those protections caused serious resentment among that
largely impoverished class, and the aristocracy passed laws in the
early sixteenth century that made the peasants virtual slaves to the
flourishing agricultural enterprises.

Figure 3. Jagiellon Poland-Lithuania, Fifteenth Century

Poland-Lithuania in the Reformation Era

In modern eyes, the most saliently liberal aspect of Jagiellon Poland is its relative toleration of religious dissent. This tolerance prevailed in Poland even during the religious upheavals, war, and atrocities associated with the Protestant Reformation (see Glossary) and its repercussions in many parts of sixteenth-century Europe. The Reformation arrived in Poland between 1523 and 1526. The small Calvinist, Lutheran, and Hussite groups that sprang up were harshly persecuted by the Roman Catholic Church in their early years. Then in 1552 the Sejm suspended civil execution of

ecclesiastical sentences for heresy. For the next 130 years, Poland remained solidly Roman Catholic while refusing to repress contending faiths and providing refuge for a wide variety of religious nonconformists.

Such broad-mindedness derived as much from practical necessity as from principle, for Poland-Lithuania governed a populace of remarkable ethnic and religious diversity, embracing Roman Catholics, Eastern Orthodox, Protestants, and numerous non-Christians. In particular, after the mid-sixteenth century the Polish lands supported the world's largest concentration of Jews, whose number was estimated at 150,000 in 1582. Under the Jagiellons, Jews suffered fewer restrictions in Poland-Lithuania than elsewhere in Europe while establishing an economic niche as tradesmen and managers of noble estates.

The Polish Renaissance

The sixteenth century was perhaps the most illustrious phase of Polish cultural history. During this period, Poland-Lithuania drew great artistic inspiration from the Italians, with whom the Jagiellon court cultivated close relations. Styles and tastes characteristic of the late Renaissance were imported from the Italian states. These influences survived in the renowned period architecture of Kraków, which served as the royal capital until that distinction passed to Warsaw in 1611. The University of Kraków gained international recognition as a cosmopolitan center of learning, and in 1543 its most illustrious student, Nicolaus Copernicus (Mikołaj Kopernik), literally revolutionized the science of astronomy.

The period also bore the fruit of a mature Polish literature, once again modeled after the fashion of the West European Renaissance. The talented dilettante Mikołaj Rej was the first major Polish writer to employ the vernacular, but the elegant classicist Jan Kochanowski (1530–84) is acknowledged as the genius of the age. Accomplished in several genres and equally adept in Polish and Latin, Kochanowski is widely regarded as the finest Slavic poet before the nineteenth century.

The Eastern Regions of the Realm

The population of Poland-Lithuania was not overwhelmingly Catholic or Slavic. This circumstance resulted from the federation with Lithuania, where ethnic Poles were a distinct minority. In those days, to be Polish was much less an indication of ethnicity than of rank; it was a designation largely reserved for the landed noble class, which included members of Polish and non-Polish origin alike. Generally speaking, the ethnically non-Polish noble families

13

Figure 4. Polish-Lithuanian Commonwealth from the Union of Lublin, 1569 to 1667

of Lithuania adopted the Polish language and culture. As a result, in the eastern territories of the kingdom a Polish or Polonized aristocracy dominated a peasantry whose great majority was neither Polish nor Catholic. This bred resentment that later grew into separate Lithuanian, Belorussian, and Ukrainian nationalist movements.

In the mid-sixteenth century, Poland-Lithuania sought ways to maintain control of the diverse kingdom in spite of two threatening circumstances. First, since the late 1400s a series of ambitious tsars of the house of Rurik had led Russia in competing with Poland-Lithuania for influence over the Slavic territories located between the two states. Second, Sigismund II Augustus (r. 1548–72) had no male heir. The Jagiellon Dynasty, the strongest link between the halves of the state, would end after his reign. Accordingly, the Union of Lublin of 1569 transformed the loose federation and personal union of the Jagiellonian epoch into the Polish-Lithuanian Commonwealth, deepening and formalizing the bonds between Poland and Lithuania (see fig. 4).

The Noble Republic, 1572–1795

Although most accounts of Polish history show the two centuries after the end of the Jagiellon Dynasty as a time of decline leading to foreign domination, Poland-Lithuania remained an influential player in European politics and a vital cultural entity through most of the period.

The Elective Monarchy

The death of Sigismund II Augustus in 1572 was followed by a three-year interregnum during which adjustments were made in the constitutional system. The lower nobility was now included in the selection process, and the power of the monarch was further circumscribed in favor of the expanded noble class. From that point, the king was effectively a partner with the noble class and constantly supervised by a group of senators. Once the Jagiellons passed from the scene, the fragile equilibrium of the commonwealth government began to go awry. The constitutional reforms made the monarchy electoral in fact as well as name. As more and more power went to the noble electors, it also eroded from the government's center.

In its periodic opportunities to fill the throne, the *szlachta* exhibited a preference for foreign candidates who would not found another strong dynasty. This policy produced monarchs who were either totally ineffective or in constant debilitating conflict with the nobility. Furthermore, aside from notable exceptions such as the able Transylvanian Stefan Batory (r. 1576–86), the kings of alien origin were inclined to subordinate the interests of the commonwealth to those of their own country and ruling house. This tendency was most obvious in the prolonged military adventures waged by Sigismund III Vasa (r. 1587–1632) against Russia and his native Sweden. On occasion, these campaigns brought Poland near to conquest of Muscovy and the Baltic coast, but they compounded the military burden imposed by the ongoing rivalry with the Turks, and the Swedes and Russians extracted heavy repayment a few decades later.

The Deluge, 1648–67

Although Poland-Lithuania escaped the ravages of the Thirty

15

Years' War (see Glossary), which ended in 1648, the ensuing two decades subjected the country to one of its severest trials. This colorful but ruinous interval, the stuff of legend and the popular historical novels of Nobel laureate Henryk Sienkiewicz (1846–1916), became known as the *potop,* or deluge, for the magnitude of its hardships. The emergency began with an uprising of Ukrainian Cossacks that persisted in spite of Warsaw's efforts to subdue it by force. After the rebels won the intervention of Muscovy on their behalf, Tsar Alexis conquered most of the eastern half of the country by 1655. Taking advantage of Poland's preoccupation, Charles X of Sweden rapidly overran much of the remaining territory of the commonwealth in 1655. Pushed to the brink of dissolution, Poland-Lithuania rallied to recover most of its losses to the Swedes. Swedish brutality raised widespread revolts against Charles, whom the Polish nobles had recognized as their ruler in the meantime. Under Stefan Czarniecki, the Poles and Lithuanians drove the Swedes from their territory by 1657. Further complicated by noble dissension and wars with the Ottoman Turks, the thirteen-year struggle over control of Ukraine ended in the Truce of Andrusovo in 1667. Although Russia had been defeated by a new Polish-Ukrainian alliance in 1662, Russia gained eastern Ukraine in the peace treaty.

Despite the improbable survival of the commonwealth in the face of the *potop,* one of the most dramatic instances of the Poles' knack for prevailing in adversity, the episode inflicted irremediable damage and contributed heavily to the ultimate demise of the state. When Jan II Kazimierz abdicated in 1668, the population of the commonwealth had been nearly halved by war and disease. War had destroyed the economic base of the cities and raised a religious fervor that ended Poland's policy of religious tolerance. Henceforth, the commonwealth would be on the strategic defensive facing hostile neighbors. Never again would Poland compete with Russia as a military equal.

Decay of the Commonwealth

Before another 100 years had elapsed, Poland-Lithuania had virtually ceased to function as a coherent and genuinely independent state. The commonwealth's last martial triumph occurred in 1683 when King Jan Sobieski drove the Turks from the gates of Vienna with a cavalry charge. Poland's important role in aiding the European alliance to roll back the Ottoman Empire was rewarded with territory in western Ukraine by the Treaty of Karlowicz (1699). Nonetheless, this isolated success did little to mask the internal weakness and paralysis of the Polish-Lithuanian political system. For the next quarter century, Poland was often a pawn in Russia's campaigns against other powers. Augustus II of Saxony (r. 1697–1733), who succeeded Jan Sobieski, involved Poland in Peter the Great's war with Sweden, incurring another round of invasion and devastation by the Swedes between 1704 and 1710.

In the eighteenth century, the powers of the monarchy and the central administration became purely trivial. Kings were denied permission to provide for the elementary requirements of defense and finance, and aristocratic clans made treaties directly with foreign sovereigns. Attempts at reform were stymied by the determination of the *szlachta* to preserve their "golden freedoms" as well as the rule of unanimity in the Sejm, where any deputy could exercise his veto right to disrupt the parliament and nullify its work. Because of the chaos sown by the veto provision, under Augustus III (r. 1733–63) only one of thirteen Sejm sessions ran to an orderly adjournment.

Unlike Spain and Sweden, great powers that were allowed to settle peacefully into secondary status at the periphery of Europe at the end of their time of glory, Poland endured its decline at the strategic crossroads of the continent. Lacking central leadership and impotent in foreign relations, Poland-Lithuania became a chattel of the ambitious kingdoms that surrounded it, an immense but feeble buffer state. During the reign of Peter the Great (1682–1725), the commonwealth fell under the dominance of Russia, and by the middle of the eighteenth century Poland-Lithuania had been made a virtual protectorate of its eastern neighbor, retaining only the theoretical right to self-rule.

The Three Partitions, 1764–95

During the reign of Empress Catherine the Great (1762–96), Russia intensified its manipulation of Polish affairs. Prussia and Austria, the other powers surrounding the republic, also took advantage of internal religious and political bickering to divide up the country in three partition stages. The third partition in 1795 wiped Poland-Lithuania from the map of Europe.

First Partition

In 1764 Catherine dictated the election of her former favorite, Stanisław August Poniatowski, as king of Poland-Lithuania. Confounding expectations that he would be an obedient servant of his mistress, Stanisław August encouraged the modernization of his realm's ramshackle political system and achieved a temporary moratorium on use of the individual veto in the Sejm (1764–66). This turnabout threatened to renew the strength of the monarchy and brought displeasure in the foreign capitals that preferred an

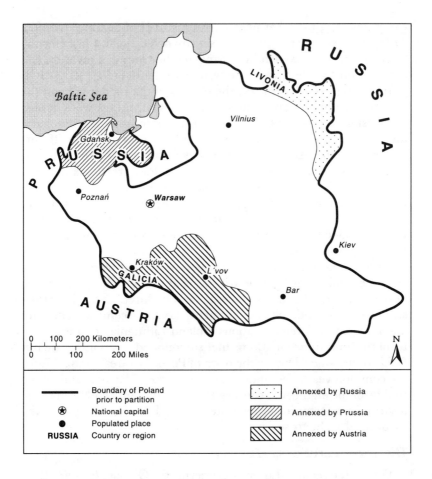

Figure 5. The First Partition of Poland, 1772

inert, pliable Poland. Catherine, among the most displeased by Poniatowski's independence, encouraged religious dissension in Poland-Lithuania's substantial Eastern Orthodox population, which earlier in the eighteenth century had lost the rights enjoyed during the Jagiellon Dynasty. Under heavy Russian pressure, the Sejm restored Orthodox equality in 1767. This action provoked a Catholic uprising by the Confederation of Bar, a league of Polish nobles that fought until 1772 to revoke Catherine's mandate.

The defeat of the Confederation of Bar again left Poland exposed to the ambitions of its neighbors. Although Catherine initially opposed partition, Frederick the Great of Prussia profited from Austria's threatening military position to the southwest by pressing a long-standing proposal to carve territory from the commonwealth. Catherine, persuaded that Russia did not have the resources to continue unilateral domination of Poland, agreed. In 1772 Russia, Prussia, and Austria forced terms of partition upon the helpless commonwealth under the pretext of restoring order in the anarchic Polish situation (see fig. 5).

National Revival

The first partition in 1772 did not directly threaten the viability of Poland-Lithuania. Poland retained extensive territory that included the Polish heartland. In fact, the shock of the annexations made clear the dangers of decay in government institutions, creating a body of opinion favorable to reform along the lines of the European Enlightenment (see Glossary). King Stanisław August supported the progressive elements in the government and promoted the ideas of foreign political figures such as Edmund Burke and George Washington. At the same time, Polish intellectuals discussed Enlightenment philosophers such as Montesquieu and Rousseau. During this period, the concept of democratic institutions for all classes was accepted in Polish society. Education reform included establishment of the first ministry of education in Europe. Taxation and the army underwent thorough reform, and government again was centralized in the Permanent Council. Landholders emancipated large numbers of peasants, although there was no official government decree. Polish cities, in decline for many decades, were revived by the influence of the Industrial Revolution, especially in mining and textiles.

Stanisław August's process of renovation reached its climax on May 3, 1791, when, after three years of intense debate, the "Four Years' Sejm" produced Europe's first written constitution. Conceived in the liberal spirit of the contemporaneous document in the United States, the constitution recast Poland-Lithuania as a hereditary monarchy and abolished many of the eccentricities and antiquated features of the old system. The new constitution abolished the individual veto in parliament; provided a separation of powers among the legislative, executive, and judicial branches of government; and established "people's sovereignty" (for the noble and bourgeois classes). Although never fully implemented, the Constitution of May 3 gained an honored position in the Polish political heritage; tradition marks the anniversary of its passage as the country's most important civic holiday.

Destruction of Poland-Lithuania

Passage of the constitution alarmed nobles who stood to lose

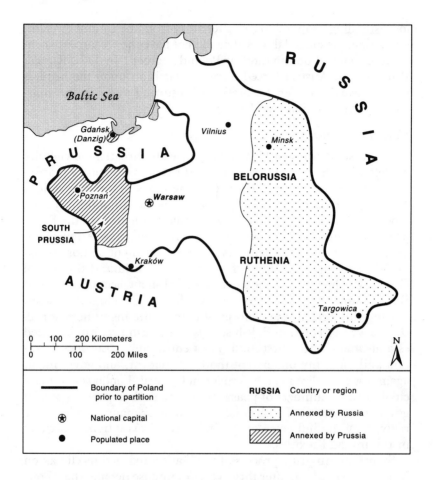

Figure 6. The Second Partition of Poland, 1793

considerable stature under the new order. In autocratic states such as Russia, the democratic ideals of the constitution also threatened the existing order, and the prospect of Polish recovery threatened to end domination of Polish affairs by its neighbors. In 1792 domestic and foreign reactionaries combined to end the democratization process. Polish conservative factions formed the Confederation of Targowica and appealed for Russian assistance in restoring the status quo. Catherine gladly used this opportunity; enlisting Prussian support, she invaded Poland under the pretext of defending Poland's ancient liberties. The irresolute Stanisław August capitulated, defecting to the Targowica faction. Arguing that Poland had fallen prey to the radical Jacobinism (see Glossary) then at high tide in

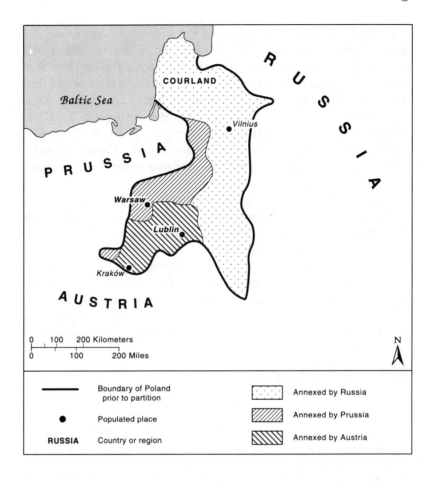

Figure 7. The Third Partition of Poland, 1795

France, Russia and Prussia abrogated the Constitution of May 3, carried out a second partition of Poland in 1793, and placed the remainder of the country under occupation by Russian troops.

The second partition was far more injurious than the first (see fig. 6). Russia received a vast area of eastern Poland, extending southward from its gains in the first partition nearly to the Black Sea. To the west, Prussia received an area known as South Prussia, nearly twice the size of its first-partition gains along the Baltic, as well as the port of Gdańsk (then renamed Danzig). Thus, Poland's neighbors reduced the commonwealth to a rump state and plainly signaled their designs to abolish it altogether at their convenience.

In a gesture of defiance, a general Polish revolt broke out in 1794 under the leadership of Tadeusz Kościuszko, a military officer who had rendered notable service in the American Revolution. Kościuszko's ragtag insurgent armies won some initial successes, but they eventually fell before the superior forces of Russian General Alexander Suvorov. In the wake of the insurrection of 1794, Russia, Prussia, and Austria carried out the third and final partition of Poland-Lithuania in 1795, erasing the Commonwealth of Two Nations from the map and pledging never to let it return (see fig. 7).

Much of Europe condemned the dismemberment as an international crime without historical parallel. Amid the distractions of the French Revolution and its attendant wars, however, no state actively opposed the annexations. In the long term, the dissolution of Poland-Lithuania upset the traditional European balance of power, dramatically magnifying the influence of Russia and paving the way for the Germany that would emerge in the nineteenth century with Prussia at its core. For the Poles, the third partition began a period of continuous foreign rule that would endure well over a century.

Partitioned Poland

Although the majority of the *szlachta* was reconciled to the end of the commonwealth in 1795, the possibility of Polish independence was kept alive by events within and outside Poland throughout the nineteenth century. Poland's location in the very center of Europe became especially significant in a period when both Prussia/Germany and Russia were intensely involved in European rivalries and alliances and modern nation states took form over the entire continent.

The Napoleonic Period

At the turn of the nineteenth century, Europe had begun to feel the impact of momentous political and intellectual movements that, among their other effects, would keep the "Polish Question" on the agenda of international issues needing resolution. Most immediately, Napoleon Bonaparte had established a new empire in France in 1804 following that country's revolution. Napoleon's attempts to build and expand his empire kept Europe at war for the next decade and brought him into conflict with the same East European powers that had beleaguered Poland in the last decades of the previous century. An alliance of convenience was the natural result of this situation. Volunteer Polish legions attached themselves to

Bonaparte's armies, hoping that in return the emperor would allow an independent Poland to reappear out of his conquests.

Although Napoleon promised more than he ever intended to deliver to the Polish cause, in 1807 he created a Duchy of Warsaw from Prussian territory that had been part of old Poland and was still inhabited by Poles (see fig. 8). Basically a French puppet, the duchy did enjoy some degree of self-government, and many Poles believed that further Napoleonic victories would bring restoration of the entire commonwealth.

In 1809, under Józef Poniatowski, nephew of Stanisław II Augustus, the duchy reclaimed the land taken by Austria in the second partition. The Russian army occupied the duchy as it chased Napoleon out of Russia in 1813, however, and Polish expectations ended with the final defeat of Napoleon at Waterloo in 1815. In the subsequent peace settlement of the Congress of Vienna, the victorious Austrians and Prussians swept away the Duchy of Warsaw and reconfirmed most of the terms of the final partition of Poland.

Although brief, the Napoleonic period occupies an important place in Polish annals. Much of the legend and symbolism of modern Polish patriotism derives from this period, including the conviction that Polish independence is a necessary element of a just and legitimate European order. This conviction was simply expressed in a fighting slogan of the time, "for your freedom and ours." Moreover, the appearance of the Duchy of Warsaw so soon after the partitions proved that the seemingly final historical death sentence delivered in 1795 was not necessarily the end of the Polish nation. Instead, many observers came to believe that favorable circumstances would free Poland from foreign domination.

The Impact of Nationalism and Romanticism

The intellectual and artistic climate of the early nineteenth century further stimulated the growth of Polish demands for self-government. During these decades, modern nationalism took shape and rapidly developed a massive following throughout the continent, becoming the most dynamic and appealing political doctrine of its time. By stressing the value and dignity of native cultures and languages, nationalism offered a rationale for ethnic loyalty and resistance to assimilation. The associated principle of the nation state, or national homeland, provided a rallying cry for the stateless peoples of Europe.

Romanticism was the artistic element of nineteenth-century European culture that exerted the strongest influence on the Polish national consciousness. The Romantic movement was a natural partner of political nationalism, for it echoed the nationalist sympathy

Figure 8. Duchy of Warsaw, 1807–13, and Congress Poland, 1815

for folk cultures and manifested a general air of disdain for the conservative political order of post-Napoleonic Europe. Under this influence, Polish literature flourished anew in the works of a school of nineteenth-century Romantic poets, led by Adam Mickiewicz (1798–1855). Mickiewicz concentrated on patriotic themes and the glorious national past. Frédéric Chopin (1810–49), a leading composer of the century, also used the tragic history of his nation as a major inspiration.

Nurtured by these influences, nationalism awoke first among the intelligentsia and certain segments of the nobility, then more gradually in the peasantry. At the end of the process, a broader definition of nationhood had replaced the old class-based ''gentry patriotism'' of Poland.

The Era of National Insurrections

For several decades, the Polish national movement gave priority to the immediate restoration of independence, a drive that found expression in a series of armed rebellions. The insurgencies arose mainly in the Russian zone of partition to the east, about three-quarters of which was formerly Polish territory. After the Congress of Vienna, St. Petersburg had organized its Polish lands as the Congress Kingdom of Poland, granting it a quite liberal constitution, its own army, and limited autonomy within the tsarist empire. In the 1820s, however, Russian rule grew more arbitrary, and secret societies were formed by intellectuals in several cities to plot an overthrow. In November 1830, Polish troops in Warsaw rose in revolt. When the government of Congress Poland proclaimed solidarity with the insurrectionists shortly thereafter, a new Polish-Russian war began. The rebels' requests for aid from France were ignored, and their reluctance to abolish serfdom cost them the support of the peasantry. By September 1831, the Russians had subdued Polish resistance and forced 6,000 resistance fighters into exile in France, beginning a time of harsh repression of intellectual and religious activity throughout Poland. At the same time, Congress Poland lost its constitution and its army.

After the failure of the November Revolt, clandestine conspiratorial activity continued on Polish territory. An exiled Polish political and intellectual elite established a base of operations in Paris. A conservative group headed by Adam Czartoryski (leader of the November Revolt) relied on foreign diplomatic support to restore Poland's status as established by the Congress of Vienna, which Russia had routinely violated beginning in 1819. Otherwise, this group was satisfied with a return to monarchy and traditional social structures.

The radical factions never formed a united front on any issue besides the general goal of independence. Their programs insisted that the Poles liberate themselves by their own efforts and linked independence with republicanism and the emancipation of the peasants. Handicapped by internal division, limited resources, heavy surveillance, and persecution of revolutionary cells in Poland, the Polish national movement suffered numerous losses. The movement sustained a major setback in the 1846 revolt organized in Austrian Poland by the Polish Democratic Society, the leading radical nationalist group. The uprising ended in a bloody fiasco when the peasantry took up arms against the gentry rebel leadership, which was regarded as potentially a worse oppressor than the Austrians. By incurring harsh military repression from Austria, the failed revolt left the Polish nationalists in poor position to participate in the wave of national revolution that crossed Europe in 1848 and 1849. The stubborn idealism of this uprising's leaders emphasized individual liberty and separate national identity rather than establishment of a unified republic—a significant change of political philosophy from earlier movements.

The last and most tenacious of the Polish uprisings of the mid-nineteenth century erupted in the Russian-occupied sector in January 1863. Following Russia's disastrous defeat in the Crimean War, the government of Tsar Alexander II enacted a series of liberal reforms, including liberation of the serfs throughout the empire. High-handed imposition of land reforms in Poland aroused hostility among the landed nobles and a group of young radical intellectuals influenced by Karl Marx and the Russian liberal Alexander Herzen. Repeating the pattern of 1830–31, the open revolt of the January Insurrection by Congress Poland failed to win foreign backing. Although its socially progressive program could not mobilize the peasants, the rebellion persisted stubbornly for fifteen months. After finally crushing the insurgency in August 1864, Russia abolished the Congress Kingdom of Poland altogether and revoked the separate status of the Polish lands, incorporating them directly as the Western Region of the Russian Empire. The region was placed under the dictatorial rule of Mikhail Muravev, who became known as the Hangman of Wilno. All Polish citizens were assimilated into the empire. When Russia officially emancipated the Polish serfs in early 1864, it removed a major rallying point from the agenda of potential Polish revolutionaries.

The Time of "Organic Work"

Increasing oppression at Russian hands after failed national uprisings finally convinced Polish leaders that insurrection was premature at best and perhaps fundamentally misguided and counterproductive. During the decades that followed the January Insurrection, Poles largely forsook the goal of immediate independence and turned instead to fortifying the nation through the subtler means of education, economic development, and modernization. This approach took the name Organic Work for its philosophy of strengthening Polish society at the grass roots. For some, the adoption of Organic Work meant permanent resignation to foreign rule, but many advocates recommended it as a strategy to combat repression while awaiting an eventual opportunity to achieve self-government.

Not nearly as colorful as the rebellions nor as loftily enshrined in national memory, the quotidian methods of Organic Work proved well suited to the political conditions of the later nineteenth century. The international balance of forces did not favor the recovery of statehood when both Russia and Germany appeared bent on the eventual eradication of Polish national identity. The German Empire, established in 1871 as an expanded version of the Prussian state, aimed at the assimilation of its eastern provinces inhabited by Poles. At the same time, St. Petersburg attempted to Russify the former Congress Kingdom, joining Berlin in levying restrictions against use of the Polish language and cultural expression. Poles under Russian and German rule also endured official campaigns against the Roman Catholic Church: the Cultural Struggle (Kulturkampf) of Chancellor Otto von Bismarck to bring the Roman Catholic Church under state control and the Russian campaign to extend Orthodoxy throughout the empire.

The Polish subjects under Austrian jurisdiction (after 1867 the Habsburg Empire (see Glossary) was commonly known as Austria-Hungary) confronted a generally more lenient regime. Poles suffered no religious persecution in predominantly Catholic Austria, and Vienna counted on the Polish nobility as an ally in the complex political calculus of its multinational realm. In return for loyalty, Austrian Poland, or Galicia, received considerable administrative and cultural autonomy. Galicia gained a reputation as an oasis of toleration amidst the oppression of German and Russian Poland. The Galician provincial Sejm acted as a semiautonomous parliamentary body, and Poles represented the region in the empire government in Vienna. In the late 1800s, the universities of Kraków and L'vov (Lwów in Polish) became the centers of Polish intellectual activity, and Kraków became the center of Polish art and thought. Even after the restoration of independence, many residents of southern Poland retained a touch of nostalgia for the days of the Habsburg Empire.

Social and Political Transformation

Throughout the later nineteenth century, profound social and economic forces operated on the Polish lands, giving them a more modern aspect and altering traditional patterns of life. Especially in Russian Poland and the Silesian regions under German control, mining and manufacturing commenced on a large scale. This development sped the process of urbanization, and the emergence of capitalism began to reduce the relative importance of the landed aristocracy in Polish society. A considerable segment of the peasantry abandoned the overburdened land. Millions of Poles emigrated to North America and other destinations, and millions more migrated to cities to form the new industrial labor force. These shifts stimulated fresh social tensions. Urban workers bore the full range of hardships associated with early capitalism, and the intensely nationalistic atmosphere of the day bred frictions between Poles and the other peoples remaining from the old heterogeneous Commonwealth of Two Nations. The movement of the former noble class into cities created a new urban professional class. Mirroring a trend visible throughout Central Europe, antisemitic sentiment mounted visibly, fed by Poles competing for the urban livelihoods long regarded as Jewish specialties.

These transformations changed the face of politics as well, giving rise to new parties and movements that would dominate the Polish landscape for the next century. The grievances of the lower classes led to the formation of peasant and socialist parties. Communism gained only a marginal following, but a more moderate socialist faction led by Józef Piłsudski (1867–1935) won broader support through its emphatic advocacy of Polish independence. By 1905 Piłsudski's party, the Polish Socialist Party, was the largest socialist party in the entire Russian Empire. The National Democratic Party of Roman Dmowski (1864–1939) became the leading vehicle of the right by espousing a doctrine that combined nationalism with mistrust of Jews and other minorities. By the turn of the century, Polish political life had emerged from the relative quiescence of Organic Work and entered a stage of renewed assertiveness. In particular, Piłsudski and Dmowski had initiated what would be long careers as the paramount figures in the civic affairs of Poland. After 1900 political activity was suppressed only in the Prussian sector.

Independence Won and Lost, 1914–45

Beginning in 1914, the newly invigorated Polish political scene combined with cataclysmic events on the European continent to offer both new hope and grave threats to the Polish people. By the end of World War II, Poland had seen the defeat or retreat of all three occupying powers, establishment of a shaky independent government, world economic crisis, then occupation and total domination by the resurgent Germans and Russians.

World War I

The first general European conflict since the Napoleonic Wars exerted a huge impact on the Poles, although their position in

Europe was not an issue among the combatants. Again, however, Poland's geographical position between Germany and Russia meant much fighting and terrific human and material losses for the Poles between 1914 and 1918.

War and the Polish Lands

The war split the ranks of the three partitioning empires, pitting Russia as defender of Serbia and ally of Britain and France against the leading members of the Central Powers, Germany and Austria-Hungary. This circumstance afforded the Poles political leverage as both sides offered pledges of concessions and future autonomy in exchange for Polish loyalty and recruits. The Austrians wanted to incorporate Congress Poland into their territory of Galicia, so they allowed nationalist organizations to form there. The Russians recognized the Polish right to autonomy and allowed formation of the Polish National Committee, which supported the Russian side. In 1916, attempting to increase Polish support for the Central Powers, the German and Austrian emperors declared a new kingdom of Poland. The new kingdom included only a small part of the old commonwealth, however.

As the war settled into a long stalemate, the issue of Polish self-rule gained greater urgency. Roman Dmowski spent the war years in Western Europe, hoping to persuade the Allies to unify the Polish lands under Russian rule as an initial step toward liberation. In the meantime, Piłsudski had correctly predicted that the war would ruin all three of the partitioners, a conclusion most people thought highly unlikely before 1918. Piłsudski therefore formed Polish legions to assist the Central Powers in defeating Russia as the first step toward full independence for Poland.

Much of the heavy fighting on the war's Eastern Front took place on the territory of the former Polish state. In 1914 Russian forces advanced very close to Kraków before being beaten back. The next spring, heavy fighting occurred around Gorlice and Przemyśl, to the east of Kraków in Galicia. By the end of 1915, the Germans had occupied the entire Russian sector, including Warsaw. In 1916 another Russian offensive in Galicia exacerbated the already desperate situation of civilians in the war zone; about 1 million Polish refugees fled eastward behind Russian lines during the war. Although the Russian offensive of 1916 caught the Germans and Austrians by surprise, poor communications and logistics prevented the Russians from taking full advantage of their situation.

A total of 2 million Polish troops fought with the armies of the three occupying powers, and 450,000 died. Several hundred thousand Polish civilians were moved to labor camps in Germany. The scorched-earth retreat strategies of both sides left much of the war zone uninhabitable.

Recovery of Statehood

In 1917 two separate events decisively changed the character of the war and set it on a course toward the rebirth of Poland. The United States entered the conflict on the Allied side, and a process of revolutionary upheaval in Russia weakened and then removed the Russians from the Eastern Front, finally bringing the Bolsheviks (see Glossary) to power in that country. After the last Russian advance into Galicia failed in mid-1917, the Germans went on the offensive again, the army of revolutionary Russia ceased to be a factor, and the Russian presence in Polish territory ended for the next twenty-seven years.

The defection of Russia from the Allied coalition gave free rein to the calls of Woodrow Wilson, the American president, to transform the war into a crusade to spread democracy and liberate the Poles and other peoples from the suzerainty of the Central Powers. Polish opinion crystallized in support of the Allied cause. Piłsudski became a popular hero when Berlin jailed him for insubordination. The Allies broke the resistance of the Central Powers by autumn 1918, as the Habsburg monarchy disintegrated and the German imperial government collapsed. In November 1918, Piłsudski was released from internment in Germany, returned to Warsaw, and took control as provisional president of an independent Poland that had been absent from the map of Europe for 123 years.

Interwar Poland

Piłsudski's first task was to reunite the Polish regions that had assumed various economic and political identities since the partition in the late eighteenth century, and especially since the advent of political parties. Piłsudski took immediate steps to consolidate the Polish regions under a single government with its own currency and army, but the borders of the Second Polish Republic were not established until 1921 (see fig. 9). Between 1921 and 1939, Poland achieved significant economic growth despite world economic crisis. The Polish political scene remained chaotic and shifting, however, especially after Piłsudski's death in 1935.

Formative Years, 1918–21

From its inception, the Second Polish Republic struggled to secure and maintain its existence in difficult circumstances. The extraordinary complications of defining frontiers preoccupied the state in its infancy. To the southwest, Warsaw encountered boundary disputes with Czechoslovakia. More ominously, an embittered Germany begrudged any territorial loss to its new eastern neighbor. The 1919 Treaty of Versailles (see Glossary) settled the German-Polish borders in the Baltic region. The port city of Danzig, a city predominantly German but as economically vital to Poland as it had been in the sixteenth century, was declared a free city. Allied arbitration divided he ethnically mixed and highly coveted industrial and mining district of Silesia between Germany and Poland, with Poland receiving the more industrialized eastern section. These terms would be a primary incentive to the German aggression that ignited World War II.

Military force proved the determinant of Poland's frontiers in the east, a theater rendered chaotic by the repercussions of the Russian revolutions and civil war. Piłsudski envisioned a new federation with Lithuania and Polish domination of western Ukraine, centered at Kiev, forming a Polish-led East European confederation to block Russian imperialism. Vladimir I. Lenin, leader of the new communist government of Russia, saw Poland as the bridge over which communism would pass into the labor class of a disorganized postwar Germany. When Piłsudski carried out a military thrust into Ukraine in 1920, he was met by a Red Army counterattack that drove into Polish territory almost to Warsaw. Although many observers marked Poland for extinction and Bolshevization, Piłsudski halted the Soviet advance before Warsaw and resumed the offensive. The Poles were not able to exploit their new advantage fully, however; they signed a compromise peace treaty at Riga in early 1921 that split disputed territory in Belorussia and Ukraine between Poland and Soviet Russia. The treaty avoided ceding historically Polish territory back to the Russians.

From Democracy to Totalitarianism

Reborn Poland faced a host of daunting challenges: extensive war damage, a ravaged economy, a population one-third composed of wary national minorities, and a need to reintegrate the three zones kept apart forcibly during the era of partition. Under these trying conditions, the experiment with democracy faltered. Formal political life began in 1921 with adoption of a constitution that designed Poland as a republic modeled after the French example, vesting most authority in the legislature. The postwar parliamentary system proved unstable and erratic. In 1922 disputes with political foes caused Piłsudski to resign his posts as chief of state and commander of the armed forces, but in 1926 he assumed power in a coup that followed four years of ineffectual government. For the next decade, Piłsudski dominated Polish affairs as strongman

Figure 9. Independent Poland, 1921–39

of a generally popular centrist regime. Military in character, the government of Piłsudski mixed democratic and dictatorial elements while pursuing *sanacja,* or national cleansing. After Piłsudski's death in 1935, his protégé successors drifted toward open authoritarianism.

In many respects, the Second Republic fell short of the high expectations of 1918. As happened elsewhere in Central Europe, the attempt to implant democracy did not succeed. Minority peoples became increasingly alienated, and antisemitism rose palpably in the general population. Nevertheless, interwar Poland could justifiably claim some noteworthy accomplishments: economic advances, the revival of Polish education and culture after decades of official curbs, and, above all, reaffirmation of the Polish nationhood that had been disputed so long. Despite its defects, the Second Republic retained a strong hold on later generations of Poles as a genuinely independent and authentic expression of Polish national aspirations.

Poland's International Situation

By far the gravest menace to Poland's longevity came from abroad, not from internal weaknesses. The center of Poland's postwar foreign policy was a political and military alliance with France, which guaranteed Poland's independence and territorial integrity. Although Poland attempted to join the Little Entente, the French-sponsored alliance of Czechoslovakia, Romania, and Yugoslavia, Czechoslovak suspicions of Polish territorial ambitions prevented Polish membership. Beginning in 1926, Piłsudski's main foreign policy aim was balancing Poland's still powerful neighbors, the Soviet Union and Germany. Piłsudski assumed that both powers wished to regain the Polish territory lost in World War I. Therefore, his approach was to avoid Polish dependence on either power. Above all, Piłsudski sought to avoid taking positions that might cause the two countries to take concerted action against Poland. Accordingly, Poland signed nonaggression pacts with both countries in the early 1930s. After Piłsudski's death, his foreign minister Józef Beck continued this policy.

The failure to establish planned alliances in Eastern Europe meant great reliance on the French, whose enthusiasm for intervention in the region waned markedly after World War I. The Locarno Pact, signed in 1926 by the major West European powers with the aim of guaranteeing peace in the region, contained no guarantee of Poland's western border. Over the next ten years, substantial friction arose between Poland and France over Polish refusal to compromise with the Germans and French refusal to resist Adolf Hitler's rise to power in the early 1930s. The Polish nonaggression treaties with Germany and the Soviet Union resulted from this bilateral deterioration of confidence.

The Polish predicament worsened in the 1930s with the advent of Hitler's openly expansionist Nazi regime in Germany and the obvious waning of France's resolve to defend its East European allies. Piłsudski retained the French connection but had progressively less faith in its usefulness. As the decade drew to an end, Poland's policy of equilibrium between potential enemies was failing. Complete Nazi occupation of Czechoslovakia in early 1939 encircled Poland on three sides (East Prussia to the northeast had remained German). Hitler's next move was obvious. By 1939 Hitler had shattered the continental balance of power by a concerted campaign of armed diplomatic extortion that brought most of Central Europe into his grasp.

World War II

Profiting from German national resentment of World War I peace terms and international aversion to new armed conflict, Hitler began driving a new German war machine across Europe in 1939. His invasion of Poland in September 1939 was the tripwire that set off World War II, the most devastating period in the history of the Polish state. Between 1939 and 1945, 6 million people, over 15 percent of Poland's population, perished, with the uniquely cruel inclusion of mass extermination of Jews in concentration camps in Poland. Besides its human toll, the war left much of the country in ruins, inflicting indelible material and psychic scars.

The Outbreak of War

The crisis that led directly to renewed European conflict in 1939 commenced with German demands against Poland, backed by threats of war, for territorial readjustments in the region of Danzig and the Baltic coast to connect East Prussia with the rest of Germany. When Warsaw refused, correctly reading Hitler's proposal as a mere prelude to further exactions, it received only hesitant promises of British and French backing. Hitler overcame the deterrent effect of this alliance on August 23 when Nazi Germany and the Soviet Union signed a nonaggression treaty that ended their interwar hostility. A secret provision of the treaty essentially divided all of Eastern Europe into Soviet and German spheres of domination. This provision signified the blessing of Soviet dictator Joseph V. Stalin for Berlin to attack Poland without fear of Soviet interference.

The Hitler-Stalin pact sealed Poland's fate and put the country in an indefensible position. On September 1, Germany hurled the bulk of its armed forces at its eastern neighbor, touching off World War II. Based on existing guarantees of security, Britain and France declared war two days later, but they gave no effective assistance to their ally. By mid-September, Warsaw was surrounded in spite of stout resistance by outnumbered Polish forces. As Poland reeled under the assault from the west, the Soviet Union administered the coup de grace by invading from the east on September 17. By the end of the month, the "September campaign" was over, Hitler and Stalin had reached terms defining their respective

*Memorial sculpture on
site of Warsaw Ghetto
Courtesy Sam and Sarah
Stulberg*

*Gate of Auschwitz
concentration
camp, later made into
a national museum
Courtesy Sam and Sarah
Stulberg*

gains, and the Polish lands had been subjected once more to occupation.

German and Soviet Rule

For the next five years, Poland endured the most severe wartime occupation conditions in modern European history. Initially, Germany annexed western Poland directly, establishing a brutal colonial government whose expressed goal was to erase completely the concept of Polish nationhood and make the Poles slaves of a new German empire. About 1 million Poles were removed from German-occupied areas and replaced with German settlers. An additional 2.5 million Poles went into forced labor camps in Germany.

Until mid-1941, Germany and the Soviet Union maintained good relations in the joint dominion they had established over Poland. Moscow had absorbed the eastern regions largely inhabited by Ukrainians and Belorussians. By 1941 the Soviets had moved 1.5 million Poles into labor camps all over the Soviet Union, and Stalin's secret police had murdered thousands of Polish prisoners of war, especially figures in politics and public administration. The most notorious incident was the 1940 murder of thousands of Polish military officers; the bodies of 4,000 of them were discovered in a mass grave in the Katyń Forest near Smolensk in 1943. Because Soviet authorities refused to admit responsibility until nearly the end of the Soviet Union in 1991, Polish opinion regarded the Katyń Massacre as the ultimate symbol of Soviet cruelty and mendacity (see Soviet Union and Russia, ch. 4).

After Germany invaded the Soviet Union in June 1941, all the Polish lands came under control of the Third Reich, whose occupation policies became even more bloodthirsty as the war continued (see fig. 10). Hitler considered Poland to be an integral part of German Lebensraum, his concept of German domination of the European continent. Eastern Europe would be purged of its population of putative racial inferiors and prepared as the hinterland of a grandiose Germanic empire. This vision fueled the genocidal fanaticism of the conquerors. Reduced to slave status, the Poles lived under severe restrictions enforced with savage punishment. As the principal center of European Jewry, Poland became the main killing ground of the Nazi Holocaust; several of the most lethal death camps, including Auschwitz, Majdanek, and Treblinka, operated on Polish soil. The Germans annihilated nearly all of Poland's 3 million Jews. Roughly as many Polish gentiles also perished under the occupation.

Resistance at Home and Abroad

Poland was the only country to combat Germany from the first day of the Polish invasion until the end of the war in Europe. After the disaster of September 1939, a constitutionally legitimate Polish government-in-exile established a seat in London under the direction of General Władysław Sikorski. In the early years of the war, Stalin maintained a strained cooperation with the Polish government-in-exile while continuing to demand retention of the eastern Polish territories secured by the Hitler-Stalin pact and assurances that postwar Poland would be "friendly" toward the Soviet Union.

Shortly after Germany invaded the Soviet Union, the Kremlin sought to organize Polish forces to aid in repelling the Nazis on the Eastern Front. Although 75,000 Polish troops were amassed on Soviet soil from Soviet camps, they never were deployed on the Soviet front because of disagreements about their utilization. Instead, the forces under the command of the "London Poles" fought with great distinction in the British Eighth Army in North Africa and Italy. The armored Polish I Corps played an important role in the Normandy invasion. Although some Polish units fought with the Red Army on the Eastern Front in the early years of the war, by 1943 Stalin had broken relations with the Sikorski government, and the Soviet Union formed a rival front group, the Union of Polish Patriots, led by Polish communists in the Soviet Union. That group formed an entire field army that aided the Red Army in the last year of the war.

Polish intelligence personnel also made a major contribution to the Allied side. In the 1930s, Polish agents had secured information on the top-secret German code machine, Enigma, and in the war émigré Polish experts aided the British in using this information to intercept Hitler's orders to German military leaders.

In Poland itself, most elements of resistance to the German regime organized under the banner of the Home Army (Armia Krajowa), which operated under direction of the London government-in-exile. The Home Army became one of the largest and most effective underground movements of World War II. Commanding broad popular support, it functioned both as a guerrilla force, conducting a vigorous campaign of sabotage and intelligence gathering, and as a means of social defense against the invaders. The Home Army became the backbone of a veritable underground state, a clandestine network of genuine Polish institutions and cultural activities. By 1944 the Home Army claimed 400,000 members. Acting independently of the overall Polish resistance, an

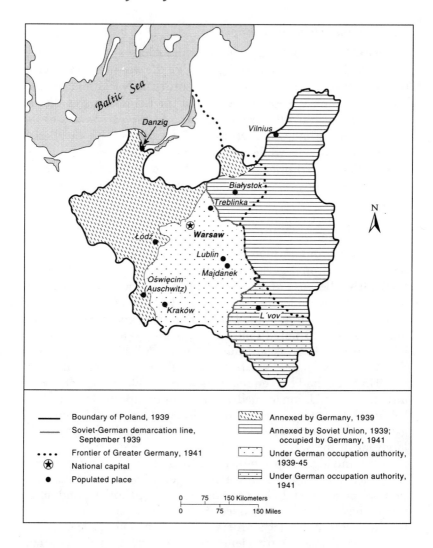

Figure 10. Occupied Poland in World War II

underground Jewish network organized the courageous but unsuccessful 1943 risings in the ghettos of Warsaw, Białystok, and Vilnius.

Soviet Liberation of Poland

Later in the war, the fate of Poland came to depend on the Soviet Union, which was initially the agent of deliverance from Nazi tyranny but later was the bearer of a new form of oppression. Stalin responded to Polish indignation over the Katyń Massacre by establishing an alternative Polish government of communists. The underground Polish Workers' Party (Polska Partia Robotnicza) had already been active in German-occupied Poland for over a year. In 1943 it established a small military arm, the People's Army (Armia Ludowa). The Home Army and the Polish Workers' Party acted separately throughout the war.

As the tide of war turned in favor of the Allies, the Soviet shadow over Poland and Central Europe loomed larger. When Soviet forces neared Warsaw in the summer of 1944, the Home Army, anticipating imminent Red Army assistance, launched a rebellion against the German garrisons in the capital. Instead, the Soviets halted their advance just short of Warsaw, isolating the uprising and enabling the Germans to crush it after two months of intense fighting. In retaliation against the Poles, the Germans demolished Warsaw before retreating westward, leaving 90 percent of the city in ruins.

Just before the Home Army uprising, the communist factions had formed the Polish Committee of National Liberation, later known as the Lublin Committee, as the official legal authority in liberated territory. In January 1945, the Lublin Committee became a provisional government, was recognized by the Soviet Union, and was installed in Warsaw. From that time, the Polish communists exerted primary influence on decisions about the restoration of Poland. Given this outcome, there is a strong suspicion that the Soviet failure to move on Warsaw in 1944 was an intentional strategy used by Stalin to eliminate the noncommunist resistance forces. The Red Army expelled the last German troops from Poland in March 1945, several weeks before the final Allied victory in Europe.

The Polish People's Republic

Soviet success in liberating Poland began an entirely new stage in Polish national existence. With the reluctant blessing of the Allies, the communist-dominated government was installed in 1945. During the next seven years, Poland became a socialist state modeled on the Soviet Union. Although Poland remained within this political structure through the 1980s, open social unrest occurred at intervals throughout the communist period. Protests in 1980 spawned the Solidarity (Solidarność) labor movement, which forced fundamental compromise in the socialist system.

Consolidation of Communist Power

The shattered Poland that emerged from the rubble of World

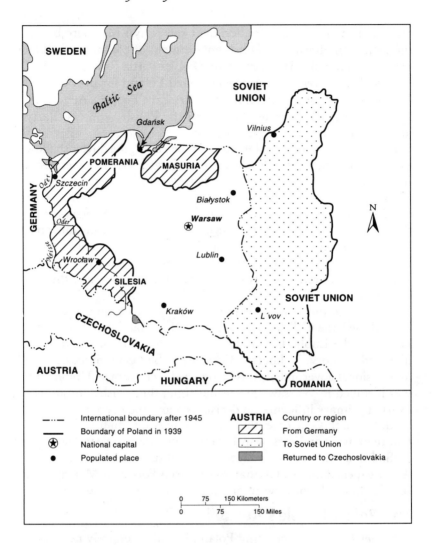

Figure 11. Postwar Territorial Adjustments, 1945

War II was reconstituted as a communist state and incorporated within the newly formed Soviet sphere of influence in Eastern Europe, despite the evident wishes of the overwhelming majority of the Polish nation. The deciding factor in this outcome was the dominant position gained by the victorious Red Army at the end of the war. At the conferences of Yalta and Potsdam in 1945, United States presidents and Britain's prime minister, Winston Churchill, met with Stalin to determine postwar political conditions, including the disposition of Polish territory occupied by the Red Army. At Yalta in February, Stalin pledged to permit free elections in Poland and the other Soviet-occupied countries of Eastern Europe. At Potsdam in July–August, the Allies awarded Poland over 100,000 square kilometers of German territory, west to the Oder and Neisse rivers, commonly called the Oder-Neisse Line (see fig. 11). In turn, about 3 million Poles were removed from former Polish territory awarded to the Soviet Union and resettled in the former German lands; similarly about 2 million Germans had to move west of the new border.

The Yalta accords sanctioned the formation of a provisional Polish coalition government composed of communists and proponents of Western democracy. From its outset, the Yalta formula favored the communists, who enjoyed the advantages of Soviet support, superior morale, control over crucial ministries, and Moscow's determination to bring Eastern Europe securely under its thumb as a strategic asset in the emerging Cold War. The new regime in Warsaw subdued a guerrilla resistance in the countryside and gained political advantage by gradually whittling away the rights of their democratic foes. By 1946 the coalition regime held a carefully controlled national referendum that approved nationalization of the economy, land reform, and a unicameral rather than bicameral Sejm. Rightist parties had been outlawed by that time, and a progovernment Democratic Bloc formed in 1947 included the forerunner of the communist Polish United Workers' Party (Polska Zjednoczona Partia Robotnicza—PZPR) and its leftist allies.

The first parliamentary election, held in 1947, allowed only opposition candidates of the now-insignificant Polish Peasant Party, which was harassed into ineffectiveness. Under these conditions, the regime's candidates gained 417 of 434 seats in parliament, effectively ending the role of genuine opposition parties. Within the next two years, the communists ensured their ascendancy by restyling the PZPR as holder of a monopoly of power in the Polish People's Republic.

From Stalinism to the Polish October

Communist social engineering transformed Poland nearly as much as did the war. In the early years of the new regime, Poland became more urban and industrial as a modern working class came into existence. The Polish People's Republic attained its principal accomplishments in this initial, relatively dynamic phase of its existence. The greatest gains were made in postwar reconstruction and in integration of the territories annexed from Germany. Imposition of the Soviet model on the political, economic, and social aspects of Polish life was generally slower and less traumatic than in the other East European countries following World War II. The PZPR took great care, for example, to limit the pace of agricultural collectivization lest Soviet-style reform antagonize Polish farmers (see Agriculture, ch. 3).

Nevertheless, in the late 1940s and early 1950s, PZPR rule grew steadily more totalitarian and developed the full range of Stalinist features then obligatory within the Soviet European empire: ideological regimentation, the police state, strict subordination to the Soviet Union, a rigid command economy, persecution of the Roman Catholic Church, and blatant distortion of history, especially as it concerned the more sensitive aspects of Poland's relations with the Soviet Union. Stringent censorship stifled artistic and intellectual creativity or drove its exponents into exile. At the same time, popular restiveness increased as initial postwar gains gave way to the economic malaise that would become chronic in the party-state (see System Structure, ch. 3).

Soviet-style centralized state planning was introduced in the First Six-Year Plan, which began in 1950. The plan called for accelerated development of heavy industry and forced collectivation of agriculture, abandoning the previous go-slow policy in that area. As the earlier policy had cautioned, however, collectivization met stubborn peasant resistance, and the process moved much more slowly than anticipated. The state also took control of nearly all commercial and industrial enterprises. Leaving only family-run shops in the private sector, the government harassed such independent shopkeepers with bureaucratic requirements.

In its relations with the Roman Catholic Church, the communist government carefully avoided open intervention, seeking rather to foment anticlerical sentiment in society. Polish Catholic clergy denounced the atheism and materialism in the regime; in 1949 the Vatican's excommunication of Catholics belonging to the PZPR brought open hostility from both sides, including state control of church institutions and propaganda against them and church officials. By 1954 nine high Polish churchmen, including Stefan Cardinal Wyszyński, had been imprisoned (see Religion, ch. 2).

A brief liberalizing "thaw" in Eastern Europe followed the death of Stalin in early 1953. In Poland this event stirred ferment, calls for systemic reform, and conflict in the ranks of the PZPR. The de-Stalinization of official Soviet dogma left Poland's Stalinist regime in a difficult position, especially following Nikita S. Khrushchev's 1956 attack on Stalin's cult of personality. In the same month as Khrushchev's speech, the death of hard-liner Bolesław Bierut exacerbated an existing split in the PZPR. In 1951 Bierut had won a struggle with Władysław Gomułka for the top position in the party. In June 1956, scores of demonstrators died when army troops quelled street riots in Poznań, inaugurating a recurrent phenomenon of Polish worker protest against the self-proclaimed workers' state.

Realizing the need for new leadership, the PZPR chose Gomułka as first secretary in October 1956. This decision was made despite Moscow's threats to invade Poland if the PZPR picked Gomułka, a moderate who had been purged after losing his battle with Bierut. When Khrushchev was reassured that Gomułka would not alter the basic foundations of Polish communism, he withdrew the invasion threat. On the other hand, Gomułka's pledge to follow a "Polish road to socialism" more in harmony with national traditions and preferences caused many Poles to interpret the dramatic "Polish October" confrontation of 1956 as a sign that the end of the dictatorship was in sight.

The Gathering Crisis of People's Poland, 1956–80

Although Gomułka's accession to power raised great hopes, the 1956 incident proved to be a prelude to further social discontent when those hopes were disappointed. The 1960s and 1970s saw Gomułka's decline in power and his eventual ouster; spectacular economic reforms without long-term results; widespread dissent, often including open confrontations, from intellectuals, the church, and the workers; and, finally, the near-collapse of the Polish economy.

The Gomułka Years

The elevation of Gomułka to first secretary marked a milestone in the history of communist Poland. Most importantly, it was the first time that popular opinion had influenced a change at the top of any communist government. Gomułka's regime began auspiciously by curbing the secret police, returning most collective farmland to private ownership, loosening censorship, freeing political prisoners, improving relations with the Catholic Church, and pledging democratization of communist party management. In general, Gomułka's Poland gained a deserved reputation as one of the more open societies in Eastern Europe. The new party chief disappointed many Poles, however, by failing to dismantle the fundamentals of the Stalinist system. Regarding himself as a loyal communist and striving to overcome the traditional Polish-Russian enmity, Gomułka came to favor only those reforms necessary to secure public toleration of the party's dominion. The PZPR was to be both the defender of Polish nationalism and the keeper of communist ideology. By the late 1960s, Gomułka's leadership had grown more orthodox and stagnant as the memory of the Poznań uprising faded. In 1968 Gomułka encouraged the Warsaw Pact (see Glossary) military suppression of the democratic reforms in Czechoslovakia.

Gomułka's hold on power weakened that year when Polish students, inspired by the idealism of the Prague Spring (see Glossary), demonstrated to protest suppression of intellectual freedom. Popular disenchantment mounted as police attacked student demonstrators in Warsaw. The PZPR hardliners, who had been alarmed by Gomułka's modest reforms, seized the opportunity to force the first secretary into purging Jews from party and professional positions, exacerbating discontent among the most vocal elements of Polish society.

The downfall of the Gomułka regime in December 1970 was triggered by a renewed outbreak of labor violence protesting drastic price rises on basic goods. When strikes spread from the Lenin Shipyard in Gdańsk to other industrial centers on the Baltic coast, Gomułka interpreted the peaceful stoppages and walkouts as counterrevolution and ordered them met with deadly force. The bloodshed claimed hundreds of victims and inflamed the entire coastline before the party annulled the price increases and pushed Gomułka into retirement. The Baltic slayings permanently embittered millions of workers, while the events of the later Gomułka period convinced Polish progressives that enlightened communist rule was a futile hope. Many of the future leaders of Solidarity and other opposition movements gained their formative political experiences in 1968 and 1970.

Consolidation of the Opposition in the 1970s

In the wake of the Baltic upheavals, Edward Gierek was selected as party chief. A well-connected party functionary and technocrat, Gierek replaced all of Gomułka's ministers with his own followers and blamed the former regime for all of Poland's troubles. Gierek hoped to pacify public opinion by administering a dose of measured liberalization coupled with a novel program of economic stimulation. The center of the program was large-scale borrowing from the West to buy technology that would upgrade Poland's production of export goods. Over the long term, the export goods would pay for the loans and improve Poland's world economic position. The program paid immediate dividends by raising living standards and expectations, but it quickly soured because of worldwide recession, increased oil prices, and the inherent weaknesses and corruption of communist planning and administration. By the mid-1970s, Poland had entered a seemingly irreversible economic nosedive compounded by a crushing burden of external debt.

Another attempt to raise food prices in 1976 failed after an additional round of worker protests (see Reliance on Technology in the 1970s, ch. 3).

Domestic economic problems were accompanied by increased pressure from the Soviet Union for closer Polish cooperation with the other members of the Council for Mutual Economic Assistance (Comecon—see Glossary). In 1971 Poland abandoned Gomułka's strict opposition to closer economic integration, and a series of long-term agreements committed Polish resource and capital investment to Soviet-sponsored projects. Such agreements guaranteed Poland access to cheap Soviet raw materials, especially oil and natural gas. Nonetheless, in the 1970s Poland experienced shortages of capital goods such as computers and locomotives because Comecon obligations moved such products out of Poland.

Meanwhile, the Helsinki Accords (see Glossary) of 1975 inspired open dissent over human rights issues. The immediate objects of dissent were the regime's proposal of constitutional amendments that would institutionalize the leading role of the PZPR, Poland's obligations to the Soviet Union, and the withholding of civil rights pending obedience to the state. In 1976 a group of intellectuals formed the Committee for Defense of Workers (Komitet Obrony Robotników—KOR), and students formed the Committee for Student Solidarity. Together those organizations intensified public pressure on Gierek to liberalize state controls, and many publications emerged from underground to challenge official dogma.

By the end of the 1970s, the hard-pressed Gierek regime faced an implicit opposition coalition of disaffected labor, dissident intelligentsia, and Roman Catholic clergy and lay spokespeople sympathetic to dissident activities. Democratically oriented activists grew more adept at defending workers' interests and human rights, a strategy that paid off handsomely in 1980. Under the stellar leadership of its longtime primate Cardinal Stefan Wyszyński, the Catholic Church attained unrivaled moral authority in the country. The prestige of the church reached a new peak in 1978 with the elevation to the papacy of the archbishop of Kraków, Cardinal Karol Wojtyła. As John Paul II, Wojtyła became the first non-Italian pope since the sixteenth century. The election of the Polish pope sparked a surge of joy and pride in the country, and John Paul's triumphant visit to his homeland in 1979 did much to precipitate the extraordinary events of the next year.

The Birth of Solidarity

When the government enacted new food price increases in the

summer of 1980, a wave of labor unrest swept the country. Partly moved by local grievances, the workers of the Lenin Shipyard in Gdańsk went on strike in mid-August. Led by electrician and veteran strike leader Lech Wałęsa, the strikers occupied the shipyard and issued far-reaching demands for labor reform and greater civil rights. The workers' top priority was establishment of a trade union independent of communist party control and possessing the legal right to strike. Buoyed by a wave of popular support and formally acknowledged by other striking enterprises as their leader, the Gdańsk workers held out until the government capitulated. The victorious strikers hailed the Gdańsk Agreement (see Glossary) of August 31 as a veritable social contract, authorizing citizens to introduce democratic change to the extent possible within the confines of the communist system.

Solidarity, the free national trade union that arose from the nucleus of the Lenin Shipyard strike, was unlike anything in the previous experience of Comecon nations. Although primarily a labor movement led and supported by workers and represented by its charismatic chairman Wałęsa, Solidarity attracted a diverse membership that quickly swelled to 10 million people, or more than one of every four Poles. Because of its size and massive support, the organization assumed the stature of a national reform lobby. Although it disavowed overtly political ambitions, the movement became a de facto vehicle of opposition to the communists, who were demoralized but still in power. With the encouragement of Pope John Paul II, the church gave Solidarity vital material and moral support that further legitimized it in the eyes of the Polish population.

In the sixteen months following its initial strike, Solidarity waged a difficult campaign to realize the letter and spirit of the Gdańsk Agreement. This struggle fostered an openness unprecedented in a communist East European society. Although the PZPR ousted Gierek as first secretary and proclaimed its willingness to cooperate with the fledgling union, the ruling party still sought to frustrate its rival and curtail its autonomy in every possible way. In 1980–81, repeated showdowns between Solidarity and the party-state usually were decided by Solidarity's effective strikes. The movement spread from industrial to agricultural enterprises with the founding of Rural Solidarity, which pressured the regime to recognize private farmers as the economic foundation of the country's agricultural sector.

Meanwhile, the persistence of Solidarity prompted furious objections from Moscow and other Comecon members, putting Poland under constant threat of invasion by its Warsaw Pact allies.

This was the first time a ruling communist regime had accepted organizations completely beyond the regime's control. It was also the first time an overwhelming majority of the workers under such a regime were openly loyal to an organization fundamentally opposed to everything for which the party stood. In 1981 an estimated 30 percent of PZPR members also belonged to an independent union.

In late 1981, the tide began to turn against the union movement. In the midst of the virtual economic collapse of the country, many Poles lost the enthusiasm that had given Solidarity its initial impetus. The extremely heterogeneous movement developed internal splits over personality and policy. Wałęsa's moderate wing emphasized nonpolitical goals, assuming that Moscow would never permit Poland to be governed by a group not endorsed by the Warsaw Pact. Wałęsa sought cooperation with the PZPR to prod the regime into reforms and avoid open confrontation with the Soviet Union. By contrast, the militant wing of Solidarity sought to destabilize the regime and force drastic change through wildcat strikes and demonstrations.

In 1981 the government adopted a harder line against the union, and General Wojciech Jaruzelski, commander in chief of the Polish armed forces, replaced Stanisław Kania as party leader in October. Jaruzelski's very profession symbolized a tougher approach to the increasingly turbulent political situation. At the end of 1981, the government broke off all negotiations with Solidarity, and tension between the antagonists rose sharply.

The Jaruzelski Interlude

The Jaruzelski regime marked another historic turning point in governance of the Polish state. Beginning with repressive measures to silence all opposition, Jaruzelski eventually presided over the popular rejection of Polish communism.

Martial Law

In December 1981, Jaruzelski suddenly declared martial law, ordering the army and special police units to seize control of the country, apprehend Solidarity's leaders, and prevent all further union activity. In effect, Jaruzelski executed a carefully planned and efficient military coup on behalf of the beleaguered and paralyzed PZPR. The motives of this act remain unclear. The general later claimed that he acted to head off the greater evil of an imminent Soviet invasion; detractors dismissed this explanation as a pretext for an ironfisted attempt to salvage party rule. In any case, the junta suppressed resistance with a determination that cost the lives of several protesters, and by the new year the stunned nation was again under the firm grip of a conventional communist regime.

Under martial law, Jaruzelski's regime applied draconian restrictions on civil liberties, closed the universities, and imprisoned thousands of Solidarity activists, including Wałęsa. During the succeeding months, the government undid much of Solidarity's work and finally dissolved the union itself. Official pressure overcame repeated attempts by Solidarity sympathizers to force the nullification of the December coup. By the end of 1982, the junta felt sufficiently secure to free Wałęsa, whom it now characterized as the "former leader of a former union." After gradually easing the most onerous features of the state of emergency, Warsaw lifted martial law in July 1983, but Jaruzelski and his generals continued to control the most critical party and government posts.

Poland at an Impasse

From the viewpoint of the regime, implementing martial law efficiently extinguished the immediate challenge posed by Solidarity. It did nothing, however, to resolve the long-standing crisis of "People's Poland," which in many ways originated in the very foundation of communist rule and the shadow of illegitimacy and ineptitude from which it never escaped. Jaruzelski presented himself as a realistic moderate, a proponent of reform who nevertheless insisted on the leading role of the party. Polish society remained sullenly unresponsive to his appeals, however. At the same time, he encountered resistance from the PZPR conservatives. These so-called hardheads, held in contempt by the public, regarded the party chief as too conciliatory and resented the interference of Jaruzelski's fellow generals in the affairs of the civilian party apparatus.

Time proved that Jaruzelski's coup had staggered Solidarity but not killed it. Adherents of the union operated underground or from jail cells, advocating a waiting game to preserve the principles of the Gdańsk Agreement. Wałęsa in particular refused to fade into obscurity; he gained added luster by his receipt of the Nobel Prize for Peace in 1983. In the next year, the Jaruzelski government suffered embarrassment when secret policemen were discovered to have abducted and murdered Father Jerzy Popiełuszko, a priest who had gained recognition as the spiritual adviser of the repressed Solidarity. At that juncture, Poland seemed mired in frustrating deadlock, with no reasonable prospect of resuscitating the stricken economy or achieving political harmony.

Collapse of the Communist Regime

The deadlock was broken chiefly by events elsewhere in the Soviet alliance. The birth of Solidarity proved to be a precursor of forces of change across all of Eastern Europe and the Soviet Union. Once again Poland was in the midst of cataclysmic European events, but in this case Poland had a decisive influence on events in neighboring countries. Beginning with the liberalization programs of Mikhail S. Gorbachev in the Soviet Union and continuing with the unforeseen and sudden demise of Poland's communist regime, decades of tension had been released throughout the region by the end of 1989.

Toward the Round-Table Talks

The first break in the Polish logjam occurred in 1985 when Gorbachev assumed leadership of the Soviet Union. Although Gorbachev in no way willed the demolition of the communist order in Poland and elsewhere in Eastern Europe, his policies of *glasnost'* (see Glossary) and *perestroika* (see Glossary) inadvertently accelerated the indigenous systemic rot in those countries. As the literal and figurative bankruptcy of East European communism became obvious, apologists resorted more frequently to the Brezhnev Doctrine—the understanding that Moscow would use force to prevent ceding any territory once under its control—as the ultimate justification of the status quo. But the sustained liberalism of the Gorbachev era undermined the credibility of this last-ditch argument. The inhibiting fear of Soviet Army retaliation, which had blocked reform in Poland and elsewhere in earlier years, gradually faded. Hastening to identify itself with Gorbachev, the Jaruzelski team welcomed the spirit of reform wafting from the east and cautiously followed suit at home. By 1988 most political prisoners had been released, unofficial opposition groups were flourishing, and Solidarity, still nominally illegal, operated quite openly.

In the meantime, however, economic malaise and runaway inflation had depressed Polish living standards and deepened the anger and frustration of society. In early 1988, strikes again were called in Gdańsk and elsewhere, and a new generation of alienated workers called for representation by Solidarity and Wałęsa. Amid widespread predictions of a social explosion, Jaruzelski took the momentous step of beginning round table talks with the banned trade union and other opposition groups. This measure was taken over the objections of the still-formidable hard-line faction of the PZPR.

The 1989 Elections and Their Aftermath

After months of haggling, the round table talks yielded a historic compromise in early 1989: Solidarity would regain legal status and the right to post candidates in parliamentary elections (with the outcome guaranteed to leave the communists a majority of seats). Although to many observers the guarantee seemed a foolish concession by Solidarity at the time, the election of June 1989 swept communists from nearly all the contested seats, demonstrating that the PZPR's presumed advantages in organization and funding could not overcome society's disapproval of its ineptitude and oppression.

Solidarity used its newly superior position to broker a coalition with various small parties that until then had been silent satellites of the PZPR. The coalition produced a noncommunist majority that formed a cabinet dominated by Solidarity. Totally demoralized and advised by Gorbachev to accept defeat, the PZPR held its final congress in January 1990. In August 1989, Tadeusz Mazowiecki became prime minister of a government committed to dismantling the communist system and replacing it with a Western-style democracy and a free-market economy. By the end of 1989, the Soviet alliance had been swept away by a stunning succession of revolutions partly inspired by the Polish example. Suddenly, the history of Poland, and of its entire region, had entered the post-communist era.

* * *

The list of English-language literature on the history of Poland, formerly sparse, has improved considerably in recent years, stimulated in great part by the dramatic events of contemporary times. The leading survey is Norman Davies's two-volume *God's Playground.* Davies covers the same territory in a single volume, *Heart of Europe,* recommended despite its confusing reverse chronological organization. The older, two-volume *Cambridge History of Poland* and Oskar Halecki's *The History of Poland* are standard but dated. Adam Zamoyski's *The Polish Way* is a popular account aimed at the general reader. One of the most significant and controversial topics arising from the Polish tradition of heterogeneity receives sound and balanced coverage in the composite work *The Jews in Poland,* edited by Chimen Abramsky and others.

For the medieval period, *Eastern and Western Europe in the Middle Ages,* edited by Geoffrey Barraclough, discusses Poland in its regional context. Pawel Jasienica's *The Commonwealth of Both Nations* addresses the early modern era in colorful style. The nineteenth century is best summarized in *The Lands of Partitioned Poland, 1795–1918* by Piotr S. Wandycz.

Recommended general sources for the modern period include M.K. Dziewanowski's *Poland in the Twentieth Century, The History of Poland since 1863,* edited by R.F. Leslie, and Hans Roos's *A History of Modern Poland* (all of which predate the upheavals of the 1980s).

Monographic treatment has not caught up with the collapse of East European communism, and no complete English survey of the rise and fall of the Polish People's Republic yet exists. The most perceptive commentator on contemporary Central Europe, the journalist Timothy Garton Ash, covers the developments of the decade from the rise of Solidarity to the end of communist rule in his three works *The Polish Revolution, The Uses of Adversity,* and *The Magic Lantern.* (For further information and complete citations, see Bibliography.)

Chapter 2. The Society and Its Environment

Monument to Poland's greatest classical composer, Frédéric Chopin, in Łazieńki Park, Warsaw

THE SEVENTH-LARGEST country in Europe, Poland is located in the middle of the North European Plain that extends from the Netherlands to the Ural Mountains of Russia. Although its topography is broken by some terrain variations, especially in the south, most of Poland lacks significant changes of elevation. The combination of geographic location and topography has strongly influenced Polish society and the country's relations with surrounding nations.

In the years following World War II, Poland, like other East European countries, underwent a rapid, planned transition from a predominantly agrarian to a predominantly industrial society. When the country came under communist control in 1945, Polish society also was subjected to a set of rigid ideological tenets. Communist dogma failed to change the intellectual or spiritual outlook of most Poles, however, because traditional institutions such as the Roman Catholic Church and the family remained strong support structures for alternative viewpoints. On the other hand, the institutions created by the communist regimes fundamentally influenced the day-to-day functions of Polish society. This influence was especially pervasive in areas such as health and education, where state programs made services accessible to more of the population, albeit in a homogenized and regimented form.

Among the permanent results of communist ideology was the disappearance of the landed aristocracy, which had played an especially large role in governance and in preserving Polish culture and national consciousness, especially during the more than 100 years when Poland was partitioned. The disruption of traditional social hierarchies and barriers also brought substantially more upward mobility as the urban population came into direct contact with the peasants. Within a decade of the communist takeover, however, the initial benefits of this social engineering had faded, and in 1956 the first of several waves of unrest swept the country. Subsequent social and economic stagnation mobilized intellectuals and workers to stage increasingly widespread and effective protests. These protests eventually overthrew communism and ended its suppression of social diversity. Nevertheless, the forty-four-year postwar communist period left permanent marks on the Polish way of life even after the state control structures crumbled in 1989.

World War II resulted in a marked homogenization of the Polish population, which previously had been ethnically and religiously rather diverse. Massive relocations of ethnic populations resulting from boundary changes and the destruction of most of Poland's Jewish population in the Holocaust meant that a country previously two-thirds ethnically Polish and spiritually Roman Catholic entered the postwar era with a population over 90 percent Catholic and over 98 percent ethnically Polish.

Demographically, Poland in 1992 was a young country, more than 64 percent of whose population was under forty years of age. The country also had one of Europe's highest birth rates. By 1980 nearly half of employed Poles belonged to a socioeconomic group different from that of their parents, showing the mobility of the younger generations across traditional class lines. By 1980 less than one-quarter of working Poles remained in agriculture, and about two-thirds were either manual or white-collar workers in urban areas. About one-third of the postwar intelligentsia came from worker families, while about one-quarter came from peasant families. These numbers represented a drastic change from the predominance of the aristocracy in the intelligentsia before World War II.

Both by cultural tradition and by recent social policy, Poles are relatively well educated. The 1990 literacy rate was 98 percent. At that time, more than 17 percent of Poles had postsecondary education, and 4 percent had achieved advanced college degrees.

The end of communist rule in 1989 presented new challenges to Polish society and to government policy makers. The concept of universal, state-guaranteed protection from unemployment, sickness, and poverty was challenged as Poland turned toward privatization and opened its economy to market forces. Although society had retained a healthy skepticism about the benefits of total socialization, postcommunist governments could not devise replacement social programs fast enough to avoid bitter social dissatisfaction when the security of the old system disappeared.

Physical Setting

Generally speaking, Poland is an unbroken plain reaching from the Baltic Sea in the north to the Carpathian Mountains in the south. Within that plain, terrain variations generally run in bands from east to west. The Baltic coast lacks natural harbors except for the Gdańsk-Gdynia region and Szczecin in the far northwest. The northeastern region, called the Lake District, is sparsely populated and lacks agricultural and industrial resources. To the south and west of the lake district, a vast region of plains extends to the Sudeten (Sudety) Mountains on the Czech border to the southwest and to the Carpathians on the Slovak and Ukrainian borders to the southeast. The country extends 649 kilometers from

north to south and 689 kilometers from east to west. Poland's total area is 312,683 square kilometers, including inland waters—a
slightly smaller area than that of New Mexico. The neighboring
countries are Germany to the west, the Czech and Slovak Federative Republic (see Glossary) to the south, Ukraine and Belarus to
the east, and Lithuania and the Russian province of Kaliningrad
to the northeast.

Topography

The average elevation of Poland is 173 meters, and only 3 percent of Polish territory, along the southern border, is higher than
500 meters. The highest elevation is Mount Rysy, which rises 2,499
meters in the Tatra Range of the Carpathians, 95 kilometers south
of Kraków. About 60 square kilometers along the Gulf of Gdansk
are below sea level. Poland is traditionally divided into five topographic zones from north to south (see fig. 12). The largest, the
central lowlands, is narrow in the west, then expands to the north
and south as it extends eastward. Along the eastern border, this
zone reaches from the far northeast to within 200 kilometers of the
southern border. The terrain in the central lowlands is quite flat,
and earlier glacial lakes have been filled by sediment. The region
is cut by several major rivers, including the Oder (Odra), which
defines the Silesian Lowlands in the southwest, and the Vistula
(Wisła), which defines the lowland areas of east-central Poland.

To the south of the lowlands are the lesser Poland uplands, a
belt varying in width from ninety to 200 kilometers, formed by
the gently sloping foothills of the Sudeten and Carpathian mountain ranges and the uplands that connect the ranges in south-central
Poland. The topography of this region is divided transversely into
higher and lower elevations, reflecting its underlying geological
structure. In the western section, the Silesia-Kraków Upthrust contains rich coal deposits.

The third topographic area is located on either side of Poland's
southern border and is formed by the Sudeten and Carpathian
ranges. Within Poland, neither of these ranges is forbidding enough
to prevent substantial habitation; the Carpathians are especially
densely populated. The rugged form of the Sudeten range derives
from the geological shifts that formed the later Carpathian uplift.
The highest elevation in the Sudeten is 1,602 meters, in the Karkonosze Mountains. The Carpathians in Poland, formed as a discrete topographical unit in the relatively recent Tertiary Era, are
the highest and most picturesque mountains in the country. They
are the northernmost edge of a much larger range that extends
into Slovakia, Ukraine, Hungary, and Romania. Within Poland

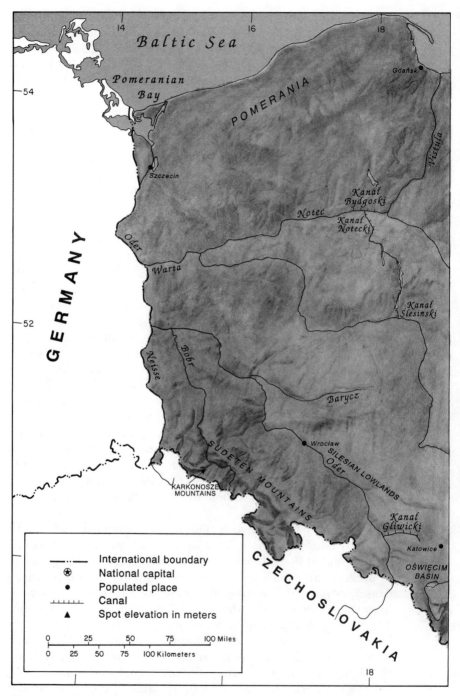

Figure 12. Topography and Drainage

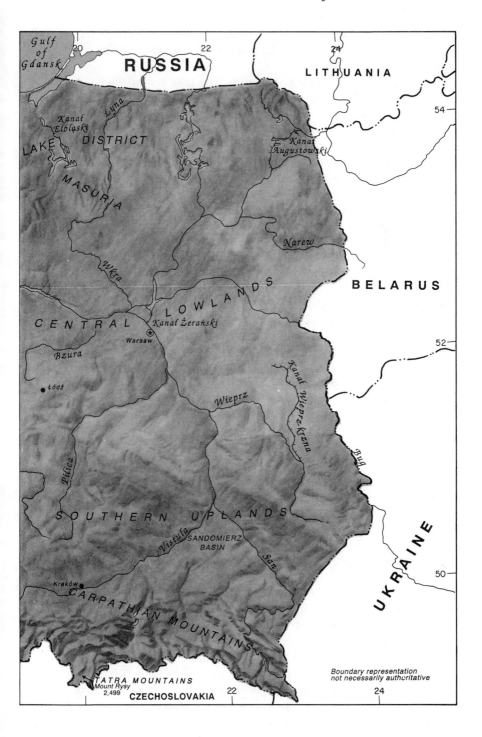

the range includes two major basins, the Oświęcim (Auschwitz) and Sandomierz, which are rich in several minerals and natural gas (see Fuels and Energy, ch. 3).

To the north of the central lowlands, the lake region includes the only primeval forests remaining in Europe and much of Poland's shrinking unspoiled natural habitat. Glacial action in this region formed lakes and low hills in the otherwise flat terrain adjacent to Lithuania and the Baltic Sea. Small lakes dot the entire northern half of Poland, and the glacial formations that characterize the lake region extend as much as 200 kilometers inland in western Poland. Wide river valleys divide the lake region into three parts. In the northwest, Pomerania is located south of the Baltic coastal region and north of the Warta and Noteć rivers. Masuria occupies the remainder of northern Poland and features a string of larger lakes. Most of Poland's 9,300 lakes that are more than one hectare in area are located in the northern part of the lake region, where they occupy about 10 percent of the surface area.

The Baltic coastal plains are a low-lying region formed of sediments deposited by the sea. The coastline was shaped by the action of the rising sea after the Scandinavian ice sheet retreated. The two major inlets in the smooth coast are the Pomeranian Bay on the German border in the far northwest and the Gulf of Gdansk in the east. The Oder River empties into the former, and the Vistula forms a large delta at the head of the latter. Sandbars with large dunes form lagoons and coastal lakes along much of the coast.

Drainage

Nearly all of Poland is drained northward into the Baltic Sea by the Vistula, the Oder, and the tributaries of these two major rivers. About half the country is drained by the Vistula, which originates in the Tatra Mountains in far south-central Poland. The Vistula Basin includes most of the eastern half of the country and is drained by a system of rivers that mainly join the Vistula from the east. One of the tributaries, the Bug, defines 280 kilometers of Poland's eastern border with Ukraine and Belarus. The Oder and its major tributary, the Warta, form a basin that drains the western third of Poland into the bays north of Szczecin. The drainage effect on a large part of Polish terrain is weak, however, especially in the lake region and the inland areas to its south. The predominance of swampland, level terrain, and small, shallow lakes hinders large-scale movement of water. The rivers have two high-water periods per year. The first is caused by melting snow and ice dams in spring adding to the volume of lowland rivers; the second is caused by heavy rains in July.

Climate

Poland's long-term and short-term weather patterns are made transitional and variable by the collision of diverse air masses above the country's surface. Maritime air moves across Western Europe, Arctic air sweeps down from the North Atlantic, and subtropical air arrives from the South Atlantic. Although the Arctic air dominates for much of the year, its conjunction with warmer currents generally moderates temperatures and generates considerable precipitation, clouds, and fog. When the moderating influences are lacking, winter temperatures in mountain valleys may drop to − 40°C.

Spring arrives slowly in April, bringing mainly sunny days after a period of alternating wintry and springlike conditions. Summer, which extends from June to August, is generally less humid than winter. Showers alternate with dry sunny weather that is generated when southern winds prevail. Early autumn is generally sunny and warm before a period of rainy, colder weather in November begins the transition into winter. Winter, which may last one to three months, brings frequent snowstorms but relatively low total precipitation.

The range of mean temperatures is 6°C in the northeast to 8°C in the southwest, but individual readings in Poland's regions vary widely by season. On the highest mountain peaks, the mean temperature is below 0°C. The Baltic coast, influenced by moderating west winds, has cooler summers and warmer winters. The other temperature extreme is in the southeast along the border with Ukraine, where the greatest seasonal differences occur and winter temperatures average 4.5°C below those in western Poland. The growing season is about forty days longer in the southwest than in the northeast, where spring arrives latest.

Average annual precipitation for the whole country is 600 millimeters, but isolated mountain locations receive as much as 1,300 millimeters per year. The total is slightly higher in the southern uplands than in the central plains. A few areas, notably along the Vistula between Warsaw and the Baltic and in the far northwest, average less than 500 millimeters. In winter about half the precipitation in the lowlands and the entire amount in the mountains falls as snow. On the average, precipitation in summer is twice that in winter, providing a dependable supply of water for crops.

Environment and Pollution

Poland suffered as heavily as any other East European country from the environmental negligence inherent in the central planning approach to resource development. Although some warnings reached the public during the 1980s, the communist regimes typically had portrayed economic activity in the capitalist countries as the true enemy of the environment. Investigations after 1989 revealed that enormous damage had been inflicted on water, air, and soil quality and on forests, especially surrounding the industrial centers in Upper Silesia and the Kraków region. But because the economy had depended for over forty years on unrestrained abuse of Poland's natural resources, environmental planners in the early 1990s faced the prospect of severe economic disruption if they abruptly curtailed the industrial practices causing pollution.

Environmental Conditions and Crises

In 1991 Poland designated five official ecological disaster areas. Of the five, the densely concentrated heavy industry belt of Upper Silesia had suffered the most acute pollution. In that area, public health indicators such as infant mortality, circulatory and respiratory disease, lead content in children's blood, and incidence of cancer were uniformly higher than in other parts of Poland and dramatically higher than indicators for Western Europe (see Health Conditions, this ch.). Experts believed that the full extent of the region's environmental damage was still unknown in 1992. The situation was exacerbated by overcrowding; 11 percent of Poland's population lived in the region. With 600 persons per square kilometer, Upper Silesia ranked among the most densely populated regions of Europe. In 1991 the region's concentrated industrial activity contributed 40 percent of Poland's electrical power, more than 75 percent of its hard coal, and 51 percent of its steel.

A variety of statistics reflect the effects of severe environmental degradation in Upper Silesia. In 1990 the infant mortality rate was over 30 deaths per 1,000 births, nearly five times the levels in some countries of Western Europe; some 12,000 hectares of agricultural land had been declared permanently unfit for tillage because of industrial waste deposition; and between 1921 and 1990 the average number of cloudy days per year had increased from ten to 183. Average life expectancy in southern Poland was four years less than elsewhere in the country (see Health and Welfare, this ch.).

Water and air pollution affect the entire country, however. A 1990 report found that 65 percent of Poland's river water was so contaminated that it corroded equipment when used in industry. After absorbing contaminants from the many cities on its banks, the Vistula River was a major polluter of the Baltic Sea. River water could not be used for irrigation. In 1990 about half of Poland's lakes had been damaged by acid rain, and 95 percent of the country's river water was considered undrinkable. Because Polish forests are dominated by conifers, which are especially vulnerable to acid rain, nearly two-thirds of forestland had sustained some damage from air pollution by 1990. In 1989 Polish experts estimated total economic losses from environmental damage at over US$3.4 billion, including soil erosion, damage to resources and equipment from air and water pollution, and public health costs.

In 1988 about 4.5 million hectares, or 14.3 percent of Poland's total area, were legally protected in national and regional parks and reserves. But all fourteen national parks were exposed to heavy air pollution, and half of them received substantial agricultural, municipal, and industrial runoff.

A special environmental problem was discovered when Polish authorities began inspecting the military bases occupied by Soviet troops for forty-six years. Uncontrolled fuel leakage, untreated sewage release, noise pollution from air bases, and widespread destruction of vegetation by heavy equipment were among the most serious conditions observed when inspections began in 1990. The government of Prime Minister Tadeusz Mazowiecki was late in pursuing the issue with the Soviet government, however, and in 1991 the Soviet Union continued its longstanding refusal to pay fines and natural resource usage fees required by Polish law. In 1992 the Poles dropped all demands for compensation as part of the withdrawal protocol (see Threat Perception, ch. 5).

Environmental Groups

The burst of political activity in the late 1980s and the early 1990s included establishment of over 2,000 organizations with environmental agendas. A precedent for such groups was set in 1980, however, when the Green Solidarity movement forced closure of an aluminum plant in Kraków. The diverse groups that appeared in the next decade achieved some additional successes, but lack of cohesion and common goals deprived the movement of political influence. No environmental group or party was represented in the Polish legislative branch in 1992.

Among the objects of protest in the 1980s were Poland's lack of a national plan for dealing with ecological disasters; construction of a Czechoslovak coking plant near the Polish border; continued reliance on high-sulfur and high-ash coal in electric power plants; and the severe environmental damage caused by Soviet troops stationed in Poland. In 1986 the explosion and resulting fallout from the Soviet Union's Chernobyl' nuclear power plant galvanized environmental activism, which in Poland was dominated by the professional classes. But environmental groups faced several obstacles. Volunteer recruitment, a critical aspect of organizational development, was hindered by the necessity for many Poles to work two jobs to survive. Refining practical operational priorities proved difficult for organizations whose initial inspiration came from broad statements of environmental ethics. And the agendas of the many activist groups remained fragmented and dissimilar in 1992. Meanwhile, the most influential political parties were split between advocates of preserving jobs ahead of protecting the environment and those who saw unchanged economic activity as the paramount danger to the health of workers and society (see Solidarity, ch. 4). Public attitudes toward environmental problems also were divided. In a 1992 nationwide survey, only 1 percent of Poles cited the environment as the country's most serious problem, although 66 percent rated environmental issues "very serious." By contrast, 72 percent cited economic issues as the country's most serious problem.

Government Environmental Policy

Poland established a Ministry of Environmental Protection and Natural Resources in 1985, but the new department exerted little authority. Between 1987 and 1988, for example, government investment in environmental protection increased by only 6 percent. In 1990 the initial postcommunist environmental timetable was to achieve "substantial" reduction of extreme environmental hazards in three years and to reach the level of European Community (EC—see Glossary) requirements in seven to ten years. In early 1991, the ministry drafted a new state ecological policy, the core of which eliminated the communist rationale of "social interest" in the arbitrary consumption of natural resources. Instead, the new policy fixed responsibility for the negative results of resource consumption at the source. The Ministry of Environmental Protection and Natural Resources officially identified the eighty enterprises causing the most pollution and promised to shut them down if pollution were not reduced. The role of nongovernmental environmental organizations in policy making was recognized officially for the first time. In late 1991, a State Environmental Protection Inspectorate was established, with broad powers to regulate polluting industries. Penalties for environmental damage also were increased at that time.

At the same time, government policy steered carefully away from measures that would sacrifice economic development, and policy makers debated the appropriate standards for comparing immediate economic growth with the estimated longer-term gains of beginning a rigorous cleanup program. Accordingly, in 1990 the Ministry of Environmental Protection and Natural Resources adopted a policy of "ecodevelopment" emphasizing modernization and restructuring measures that theoretically would curtail pollution while they streamlined production operations. The policy included distribution of information to the public to gain acceptance of economic sacrifice for environmental improvement; linkage of environmental law to the new market mechanism slowly being created; promotion of an awareness in Western Europe of the transnational impact of Poland's air and water pollution; and application of foreign capital and technology to environmental cleanup problems. At the end of 1990, Western banks began opening credit lines for Polish environmental protection, and plans for some multinational ecological enterprises included Poland. In 1991 the United States government agreed to forgive part of Poland's debt in exchange for domestic investment in pollution control.

Demography

Between 1939 and 1949, the population of Poland underwent two major changes. The deaths, emigration, and geopolitical adjustments resulting from World War II reduced the 1939 population of about 35 million to about 24 million by 1946. Only in the 1970s did Poland again approach its prewar population level. In addition, the ethnic composition of the country was drastically homogenized by the mass annihilation of Polish Jews and the loss of much of the non-Polish Slavic population through the westward shift of the borders of the Ukrainian and Belorussian republics of the Soviet Union.

Languages

Beginning with the early postwar years, Polish has been the language of all but a very few citizens. Grouped with Czech and Slovak in the West Slavic subgroup of the Slavic linguistic family, Polish uses a Latin alphabet because the Roman Catholic Church has been dominant in Poland since the tenth century (see The Origins of Poland, ch. 1). Documents written in Polish survive from the fourteenth century; however, the literary language largely developed during the sixteenth century in response to Western religious and humanistic ideas and the availability of printed materials. In the eighteenth century, the Enlightenment stimulated a second period of advances in the literary language. When the Polish state fell at the end of the eighteenth century, the language played an important role in maintaining the Polish national identity (see The Three Partitions of Poland, 1764–95, ch. 1).

Although modern Polish was homogenized by widespread education, distribution of literature, and the flourishing of the mass media, several dialects originating in tribal settlement patterns survived this process in the late twentieth century. Among the most significant are Greater Polish and Lesser Polish (upon a combination of which the literary language was based), Silesian, Mazovian, and Kashubian, which is sometimes classified as a separate language.

Population Growth and Structure

In the immediate postwar period, Poland's birth rate surged upward and many Poles were repatriated from military duty or imprisonment abroad. This population increase was tempered, however, by continued emigration of ethnic groups such as the Jews and non-Polish Slavs after the war ended. The annual growth rate peaked in 1953 at more than 1.9 percent; between 1955 and 1960, it averaged 1.7 percent before dropping to 0.9 percent in 1965. The growth rate then remained fairly steady through 1980. In the early 1980s, however, Poland's growth rate of 1.0 percent placed it behind only Albania, Ireland, and Iceland among European countries. The population increase in the early 1980s was attributed to childbearing by women born in the postwar upswing as well as to lower death rates.

Later in the 1980s, as many women passed their peak childbearing years, growth rates again dropped. From 1985 through 1991, the actual population increase was smaller every year. The actual increase in 1991 was 122,000. Nevertheless, in 1988 one in five persons added to the population of Europe outside the Soviet Union was a Pole. Experts forecast that in the year 2000 Poland would be contributing virtually all the natural growth in Europe's employed population. In 1990 the shape of Poland's population pyramid was expected to remain relatively constant; it was composed of a relatively small base of young people, with a wider component of citizens over age sixty and a bulge in the cohort born during the postwar upswing. In 1990 this group ranged in age from thirty-five to forty-four. At the end of 1991, the total population was estimated at 38.3 million; projected population in the year 2000 was 39.5 million.

In 1988 about 51 percent of Poland's population was female, a statistic reflecting the fact that average life expectancy was about nine years greater for women (66.5 years for men, 75.5 for women). The ratio of men to women was significantly higher (as much as five to two) in rural areas, from which many women migrated to

*Man in traditional
local costume, Kraków
Courtesy Sam and Sarah Stulberg*

escape poor conditions on private farms (see The Working Classes; The Role of Women, this ch.). Over a period of years, a lower rural birth rate led to a smaller agricultural work force. Already in 1981, only 55 percent of the rural population was of working age, compared with 63 percent of the urban population. (Working age was defined as eighteen to fifty-nine for women, eighteen to sixty-four for men.) In 1991 some 29.4 percent of the overall population was below working age, and 13 percent was past working age. The former figure had fallen since the mid-1980s, while the latter rose in the same period. The 547,000 live births in Poland in 1991 equaled 14.3 births per 1,000 people (see Health Issues, this ch.). However, the 74 deaths versus 100 births recorded that year was a higher ratio than in any recent year. (In the early 1980s, the ratio was less than 50 to 100.)

In the late 1980s, emigration from Poland was stimulated mainly by poor economic conditions. The 1989 total of 26,000 émigrés dropped to 18,500 in 1990, but the slow progress of economic reform caused the rate to increase again in 1991. In this period, the group most likely to emigrate was healthy men between the ages of twenty-six and thirty who had completed high school or trade school. The majority in this group came from regions of high unemployment and had experience working abroad. In 1991 polls showed that as much as one-third of the Polish population viewed emigration as at least a theoretical option to improve their standard of living.

Population Density and Distribution

The most important change in postwar Poland's population distribution was the intense urbanization that took place during the first two decades of communist rule. The priorities of central economic planning undoubtedly hastened this movement, but experts hypothesize that it would have occurred after World War II in any case (see Establishing the Planning Formula, ch. 3). In 1931 some 72.6 percent of the population was classified as rural, with nearly 60 percent relying directly on agriculture for their livelihood. By 1978 those figures had diminished to 42.5 and 22.5 percent, respectively. In the next ten years, the share of rural population dropped by only 3.7 percent, however, indicating that the proportions had stabilized.

In 1989 Poland had twenty-four cities with populations of at least 150,000 people. Major urban centers are distributed rather evenly through the country; the most concentrated urban region is the cluster of industrial settlements in Katowice District (see fig. 13). In 1990 overall population density was 121 persons per square kilometer, up from 115 per square kilometer in 1981. The most densely populated places are the cities of Łódź (over 3,000 persons per square kilometer) and Warsaw (about 2,000 persons per square kilometer). Urban areas, which contain over 60 percent of Poland's population, occupy about 6 percent of the country's total area. In 1990 average population density in rural areas was fifty-one persons per square kilometer, a small increase over the 1950 figure of forty-seven persons per square kilometer.

The Social Order

The dislocations during and after World War II changed Poland's class structure and ethnic composition. Important parts of the Polish middle class—which between the world wars had become the foundation of industrial and commercial activity—were annihilated or forced to emigrate, and those that survived the war lost their social status with the advent of state socialism. Nazi and Soviet occupation also decimated the intelligentsia that had supplied expertise to the legal, medical, and academic professions. Under the postwar communist regimes, leaders of the ruling Polish United Worker's Party (Polska Zjednoczona Partia Robotnicza—PZPR) formed a new elite class by combining workers, peasants, and members of the intelligentsia in their ranks. Then in the late 1970s, the intelligentsia began to carry greater weight in the social structure by

Legend:

District boundary — ⊛ National capital

PERSONS PER SQUARE KILOMETER

- Over 700
- 500-700
- 300-499
- 175-299
- 125-174
- 100-124
- 75-99
- 50-74
- Under 50

0   50   100 Kilometers
0   50   100 Miles

*Boundary representation
not necessarily authoritative*

Source: Based on information from *The Statesman's Year-Book, 1991–1992*, New York, 1991, 1012.

Figure 13. Population Density by District, 1992

leading an intermittent, long-term protest movement. That movement culminated in the overthrow of the communist elite and re-emergence of the dormant entrepreneurial segments of society.

Ethnic Groups

During most of its history, Poland was a multiethnic society that included substantial numbers of Belarusians (prior to 1992 known as Belorussians), Germans, Jews, and Ukrainians. This ethnic diversity was reduced sharply by World War II and the migrations that followed it. The Jewish population, which in the interwar period was over 10 percent of Poland's total and over 30 percent of Warsaw's, was reduced by about 3 million in the Holocaust. Postwar resettlement and adjustment of borders sent about 2 million Germans from Polish territory westward and awarded the Polish territory inhabited by 500,000 Ukrainians, Belarusians, and Lithuanians to the Soviet Union. These multiethnic émigrés were replaced by an estimated 3 million ethnic Poles repatriated from the Soviet Union and by thousands of others who returned from emigration or combat in the West. (Poland's communist governments, which consistently emphasized ethnic homogeneity, did not differentiate ethnic groups in official census statistics.) As a result of this process, in 1990 an estimated 98 percent of Poland's population was ethnically Polish.

Jews

Although an estimated 200,000 Polish Jews survived the Holocaust, only about 10,000 remained in Poland in 1991, and that population was mostly elderly. As the postcommunist era began, relations with the now very small Jewish community retained an ambiguous but prominent place in the consciousness of Polish society. Beginning in the late 1970s, public interest in past Polish-Jewish relations increased significantly despite the dwindling of the Jewish population. Social observers attributed this partly to nostalgia for prewar times, when the Jews had made a dynamic contribution to Poland's diverse urban cultural environment. Another source of renewed interest was a need to finally understand the long and tangled historical connection of the Poles and the Jews. That connection was formed most prominently by the Holocaust, which had wrought havoc upon both Poles and Jews, and by the role of antisemitic elements in Polish society before and after World War II. In the early 1990s, these issues still provoked deep emotional responses as well as intellectual contemplation.

When communist rule ended, the phenomenon of "antisemitism without Jews" came under renewed scrutiny. In the first national elections of postcommunist Poland, candidates frequently exchanged charges of antisemitism and, conversely, of undue Jewish influence in policy making. In 1991 Solidarity leader Lech Wałęsa apologized personally before the Israeli parliament, the Knesset, for antisemitic statements by some of his supporters during the presidential campaign. According to a 1992 survey, 40 percent of Poles estimated the current Jewish population in Poland at above 750,000 people; 16 percent believed the Jews were a threat to Poland's political development in the 1990s; and 26 percent said the Jews exerted too much influence in Polish society. On the other hand, 81 percent said that the memory of the Holocaust should be preserved indefinitely to prevent a recurrence. Extreme right-wing parties with antisemitic platforms gained no seats in the parliamentary elections of 1991.

Germans

The German population of Poland is centered in the southern industrial region of Silesia, but a small population remains in the northeastern region that had been East Prussia in the nineteenth century. As was the case with other ethnic minorities, only approximate estimates of numbers were available in 1991. Definition and quantification of the German population of Polish Silesia vary greatly according to the time and the source of statistics. The communist regimes of Poland counted only 2,500 Germans through 1989. In 1992 German minority organizations, whose activities increased markedly after 1990, claimed that over 300,000 Silesians, concentrated in Opole District, were ethnic Germans (see fig. 1). The official Polish estimate at that time, however, was 100,000 ethnic Germans. The constant shifting of Silesia between Polish and German control during several centuries created a unique ethnic amalgam and regional self-consciousness. Whatever the original ethnic composition of the region, the Silesians themselves developed a separate culture that borrowed liberally from both Polish and German. The predominant spoken language is a heavily Germanized dialect of Polish.

Although the Silesians retained close traditional ties with their locality and their own group, in the early 1990s they could not ignore the difference between their standard of living and that of nearby Germany. Many non-German Silesians very likely declared themselves ethnic Germans to receive preferential treatment from the German government; this practice played a major role in the diversity of minority population estimates.

Some Silesians were bitter over the resettlement policy of the postwar communist governments and other forms of anti-German discrimination. Immediately following the end of Polish communist rule, a well-organized German faction in Silesia demanded that dual citizenship and other privileges be guaranteed the German minority in Poland by the forthcoming Polish-German friendship treaty (see Foreign Relations, ch. 4). In this demand they were joined by German citizens who had been expelled from the German territory awarded Poland after World War II. Ratification of the Polish-German treaty of friendship and cooperation in 1991 blunted the impact of radicals, however, and promoted pragmatic local cooperation rather than confrontation between Poles and Germans in Silesia.

Postcommunist Polish governments established no firm criteria for proving German nationality; in most cases, oral declarations were accepted as sufficient proof. Beginning in 1989, the Social Cultural Association began propagating German culture in Silesia. By 1992 the group had initiated German instruction in 260 schools, stocked libraries with German materials, and arranged technical instruction in Germany for Silesian health and education workers. The special ties with Germany make Opole one of the most prosperous regions in Poland; the Silesian Germans provide important resources to the local economy, and the lifestyle of many Silesian communities resembles that of Germany more than that of Poland. Although many non-German Silesians feared that the spread of German economic and cultural influences would erase the unique ethnic qualities of their region and the idea of German dominance retained some negative historical associations, in the early 1990s postcommunist aspirations for the prosperity promised by German connections remained an important factor in public opinion on the German ethnic issue.

A smaller concentration of Germans became active and visible for the first time in 1990 in Olsztyn District in northeastern Poland, although the resettlement of the 1950s and ongoing emigration had reduced the German population there substantially between 1956 and 1980. In 1992 estimates of the group's size ranged from 5,000 to 12,000. Beginning in 1990, several German cultural associations appeared in the region with the aims of preventing discrimination and preserving German culture. Association members received transportation to and employment opportunities in Germany, and the German government contributed money to support association activities in the early 1990s.

Ukrainians and Belarusians

Before World War II, the Ukrainian population, concentrated in the far southeast along the Carpathian Mountains, constituted

13.8 percent of interwar Poland's total, making the Ukrainians by far the largest ethnic minority. Postwar border changes and resettlement removed most of that ethnic group, whose persistent demands for autonomy in the 1930s had become a serious worry for the postwar communist government. In 1947 most remaining Ukrainians were resettled from their traditional centers in Rzeszów and Lublin districts in southeastern Poland to northern territory gained from Germany in the peace settlement. State propaganda designed to further isolate the Ukrainians reminded Poles of wartime atrocities committed by Ukrainians. In 1991 some 130,000 Ukrainians remained in the resettlement regions, while the rest of the Ukrainian population was widely dispersed and assimilated.

Beginning in 1989, Ukrainians in Poland sought redress for the abuses they had endured under communist regimes. The Union of Ukrainians in Poland demanded that the postcommunist government condemn the postwar deportation policy and compensate Ukrainians and their churches for state confiscation of property in the resettlement period. In 1992 all such claims awaited approval by parliament. Property claims by the Greek Catholic (Uniate) Church aroused controversy for two reasons. First, the Polish Catholic Church had occupied many former Greek Catholic churches and refused to return or share them. Second, conflicting claims between Greek Catholic Ukrainians and the Ukrainians of the Polish Autocephalous Orthodox Church threatened the minority with a major rift along religious lines (see Other Churches, this ch.).

In 1992 estimates of the Ukrainian population in Poland ranged from 200,000 to 700,000. Of that number, roughly one-third belonged to the Polish Autocephalous Orthodox Church, a branch of the Greek Orthodox Church. The remainder belonged to the Greek Catholic Church, which recognizes the authority of the Vatican. Orthodox Ukrainians are especially visible in Poland because they compose nearly the entire population of the Polish Orthodox Church. Because of the importance of religion in Polish society, the relations of the Roman Catholic Church in Poland with the two major minority religions influence the status of Ukrainian communities in areas other than religion. In the communist era, the government attempted to minimize the danger of Ukrainian nationalism by shifting its support as the two Ukrainian churches sought recognition. The Ukrainian Social and Cultural Society, founded in 1956, published a weekly newspaper in Ukrainian and supported several schools in Warsaw, with the purpose of preventing the assimilation of Ukrainians into Polish society.

The size of the Belarusian population also was disputed in the early 1990s. In 1991 the official figure was 250,000, but minority spokesmen claimed as many as 500,000 people. Although concentrated in a smaller area (nearly all live in the Białystok District adjoining the Belarusian border), the Belarusian minority has been less assertive of its national identity than have been the Ukrainians. Białystok is one of Poland's least prosperous and most sparsely populated regions. Mainly composed of peasants, the minority includes few educated citizens, and the group has received little support from Belarus itself. Therefore, low national self-awareness has led to easy assimilation into Polish society. The Belarusian Social and Cultural Society, founded in 1956 as the minority's official mouthpiece in Poland, remained under the control of former communists in 1991 because of Belarusian distrust of Solidarity's ties with the Polish Catholic Church. Since 1989, however, some new ethnic organizations have appeared. A weekly newspaper is published in Belarusian, and a few new student, political, and social organizations have brought a modest revival of Belarusian ethnic community in the early postcommunist years.

Gypsies

The Gypsies (Rom, in the preferred vernacular term), a major sociopolitical issue in most other East European countries, are much less numerous and less controversial in Poland. Estimates of the Gypsy population in Poland range from 15,000 to 50,000. Czechoslovakia's Gypsy population, by contrast, numbered 500,000 in the 1980s, when Poland became a transit point on the illegal migration route from Romania to Germany. Emigration of Polish Gypsies to Germany in the late 1980s reduced Poland's Gypsy population by as much as 75 percent. Nevertheless, negative stereotypes remain strong in Polish society, and acts of violence and discrimination against this most visible minority are common in Poland. In 1991 a mob destroyed a wealthy Gypsy neighborhood in central Poland. The Polish government has adopted no comprehensive policy on Gypsies but instead has treated violent acts against them as isolated incidents.

The Intelligentsia

The Polish intelligentsia played a unique and vital role in several phases of Polish history. During the partition period of the nineteenth century, the intelligentsia was the chief repository of national consciousness. Containing the last vestiges of the landed gentry that had led the country during its heyday as an independent commonwealth, the intelligentsia was the chief means by which new and progressive ideas entered the fabric of partitioned Poland's society. As such, the class became the chief repository of a romanticized, idealistic concept of Polish nationhood (see The Elective Monarchy; The Impact of Nationalism and Romanticism, ch. 1). Well into the twentieth century, the roughly 50 percent of the intelligentsia that had roots in the landowning class maintained the aristocratic values of their ancestors. Although those values conferred a distinctly higher social status on the intelligentsia in everyday life, they also included the cultural heritage that all Poles recognized.

In the first part of the twentieth century, the intelligentsia was diversified and enriched as more middle- and lower-class Poles attained education and upward mobility. At this point, the intelligentsia divided philosophically into conservative idealists of the past (whose landholdings gave them a vested interest in maintaining the status quo) and liberal reformers advocating development of capitalism. In the interwar period, Poland's social structure was further complicated by the rise of a vigorous, practical upper middle class. After the war, however, socialism drastically reduced the influence of this entrepreneurial class.

Facing a severe shortage of educated citizens, in 1945 the communists expanded opportunities for political loyalists to advance through education into the professions and the bureaucracy (see Education, this ch.). Of the 300,000 college graduates produced by the education system between 1945 and 1962, over 50 percent were from worker or peasant families. The introduction of these groups sharply diversified the class basis of the postwar intelligentsia. In the late 1960s, however, the policy of preferential treatment in education ended. The percentage of working-class university admissions dropped to below 25 percent. Because the chief means of entry into the professional classes remained educational achievement, the drop in university admissions drastically slowed mobility from the working classes into the intelligentsia. In the postwar years, the intelligentsia diversified into several categories of employment: highly educated professionals, government and party officials, senior civil servants, writers and academics, and top-level economic managers.

Especially in the 1970s, many members of the intelligentsia established careers in the ruling party or its bureaucracy, joining the cause of the socialist state with varying degrees of commitment. By 1987 all but one of the forty-nine provincial PZPR first secretaries had at least a bachelor's degree. The strong presence of the intelligentsia in the party influenced the policy of the ruling elite away from standard Soviet practice, flavoring it instead with pragmatic nationalism (see PZPR and Successor Parties, ch. 4). Then, as that force exerted subtle influence within the establishment, other elements of the intelligentsia joined with worker and student groups to express open dissent from the system. They objected to the system as a whole and decried the increasingly stressful conditions it imposed on Polish society in the 1970s and 1980s. The most salient result of this class alliance was the Solidarity movement, nominally a workers' movement that achieved broad support in the intelligentsia and finally toppled the last communist regime.

In the 1980s, the activist elements of the intelligentsia resumed the traditional role as protectors of national ideals from outside political interference. In this role, the Polish intelligentsia retained and gradually spread the values it had inherited from its nineteenth-century predecessors: admiration for Western society, disdain for contact with and reliance on Russia and the Soviet Union, and reverence for the prepartition commonwealth of the nobility and the romantic patriotism of the partition era.

As it had after Poland regained its independence in 1918, however, the intelligentsia reverted to its naturally fragmented state once the common enemy fell. In the early 1990s, the official communist leadership elite had disappeared (although in reality that group continued to control powerful economic positions), and no comparably identifiable and organized group had taken its place. In this atmosphere, a wide variety of social and political agendas competed for attention in the government, reflecting the diverse ideas proposed by the intelligentsia, the source of most of Poland's reformist concepts in the early 1990s.

The Working Classes

In the years following World War II, the composition of the Polish working classes changed significantly. Agriculture, which underwent several major changes in government policy during this period, consistently lost stature as an occupation and as a life-style in competition with expanded urban industrial opportunities. The postwar rural exodus left an aging farm population, split apart the traditional multigenerational families upon which rural society had been based, and fragmented landholdings into inefficient plots. In the same period, the augmented Polish industrial work force struggled to achieve the social gains promised in Marxist-Leninist ideology. In the early days, the central planning system yielded impressive gains in the education level and living standards of many industrial workers. Later in the communist era, this group made less tangible gains in social status and began actively opposing the regressive government policies that prevented its further progress. In the early postcommunist era, industrial workers faced high unemployment as privatization and the drive for efficiency restructured their enterprises. By the early 1980s, the working population reached a stable proportion of 40 percent in industry, 30 percent in agriculture, and 30 percent in the service sector (which, like industry, had tripled in size in the postwar era).

Agricultural Workers

Although the communist leadership's economic agenda was the immediate cause of large-scale shifts from agriculture to industry, prewar conditions also contributed to this trend. Contrary to the nineteenth-century romanticization of the Polish peasant class as a homogeneous repository of national virtue, agricultural workers in the interwar period were stratified economically. A few peasants had large farms, many more farmed small plots, and fully 20 percent of peasants did not own the land they farmed. In 1921 only 43 percent of peasants owned their own house. The depression of the 1930s hit the peasants especially hard because much of their income depended on world commodity prices. By the late 1930s, Poland had several million superfluous agricultural workers, but industry had not developed sufficiently to offer alternative employment.

At the close of World War II, little had changed in the society of rural Poland. At that time, Poland's peasants made up 60 percent of the population. Although many villages were wrecked or diminished and 500,000 farms were destroyed, war dead included a much higher proportion of urban Poles. After the war, the large estates owned by former noblemen and rich peasants and worked by rural proletarians still dominated the rural social structures. The first step of the postwar communist regime was confiscation of the largest estates. Those lands were redistributed to private owners, although to avoid alienating the peasants, plots smaller than fifty hectares were allowed to remain with their original owners. At this point, rapidly expanding local industry began to offer peasants supplementary income, and industrial expansion in urban centers relieved prewar overpopulation and starvation in many rural areas. After the war, rural life increasingly was transformed by electrification, improved roads, and state-supplied equipment and materials. Nevertheless, on most Polish farms the fundamental relationship of the peasant to the land remained as it was before World War II.

Although Soviet-style collectivization remained a nominal state goal until 1956, early attempts caused precipitous declines in production and an estimated 1 million farmers to leave the land. As a result of the decollectivization program of the late 1950s, only 6 percent of farms remained collectivized. In the long term, the state's attempts at collectivization fostered a permanent resistance among peasants to direct state interference. In the next thirty years,

Haystacks at the foot of the Tatra Mountains
Highlanders guiding their sheep to pasture in the Tatra Mountains
Courtesy Sam and Sarah Stulberg

the peasant family farm, whose value system made distribution of farm products to the rest of society clearly subordinate to immediate household needs, continued to be the dominant form of agricultural organization. Improved communications and agricultural education programs gradually broke the isolation of rural existence, however; as more contact with the outside world brought new values, it weakened the family cohesion and the inherited patterns of life that were the foundations of the purely domestic farm.

Immediately after the collectivization drive ended in 1956, mid-sized farms (those between five and fifteen hectares) predominated in the private sector, but in the next decades farms of that size were split repeatedly. By 1986 nearly 60 percent of private farms were smaller than five hectares. Furthermore, the holdings of individual farmers often were scattered across considerable distances. In the late 1980s, state efforts to stimulate reconcentration were stalled by peasant suspicion and by ideological disagreements among communist policy makers over the solution to agricultural problems. Prevented by government inertia and distribution policies from obtaining tractors and other equipment, many small landowners used horses for cultivation or simply ignored portions of their land. Frequent reliance on nonagricultural employment for a livelihood further reduced peasants' concentration on improving the use of their rural plots.

In the mid-1980s, only 50 percent of Poland's rural population was involved in agriculture. The other 50 percent commuted to jobs in towns. Of the private farmers in the first group, 33 percent were full-time farmers, 34 percent earned most of their income from agricultural employment, and more than 21 percent earned most of their income from nonagricultural sources. The remaining 11 percent worked for institutions with land allotments smaller than 0.5 hectare. The large group of landless rural laborers of the interwar years had virtually disappeared by 1980.

In the postcommunist era, experts projected large numbers of peasants would continue their split lifestyles unless major investments were made to upgrade Poland's rural infrastructure. In the late 1980s, new housing units and water mains were still extremely rare and sewage lines virtually nonexistent in rural areas. Only half of Polish villages were accessible by paved roads, and many poorer villages lacked a retail store of any type. An important failure of the collectivization effort had been the exclusion of peasants from the broad social welfare benefits instituted by the socialist state for urban workers. Although the peasantry received nominal coverage under the state medical system beginning in 1972, rural education and health services remained far behind those in the cities for the next twenty years.

The lack of rural amenities caused the most promising young Poles from rural families to move to the cities. As the traditional rural extended family began to collapse, the aging population that remained behind further strained the inadequate rural social services. The communist state modified its pension and inheritance policies in the 1970s to encourage older peasants to pass their rural plots to the next generation, but the overall disparity in allocation of benefits continued through the 1980s. In the early postcommunist era, however, urban unemployment and housing shortages began to drive workers back to rural areas. Experts predicted that as many as 1 million people might return to rural areas if urban employment continued to fall.

Industrial Workers

Between 1947 and 1958, the number of agricultural workers moving to industrial jobs increased by 10 percent each year. In those years, most industrial jobs did not require even basic education. Therefore, over 40 percent of recruits from agriculture were basically illiterate in 1958. From that time, however, the level of education among Polish industrial workers rose steadily. By 1978 only 5 percent of workers lacked a complete elementary education. A fundamental change in the social status of workers was heralded by the first workers' councils, founded in the late 1950s to voice opinions on industrial policy. Those increasingly articulate leadership groups, dominated by the 5 percent of the work force that had a secondary education at that time, led to the formidable labor organizations that shook Poland's political structure in the 1980s.

In the 1980s, workers age thirty-five and younger were better educated and more likely to come from urban families than their elders. Also, unlike their elders, the young workers had been raised under a communist regime and were accustomed to the social status conferred by membership in workers' organizations. Many saw their laborer status as an intermediate social step between their agricultural past and anticipated advancement to white-collar employment. Conversely, association with the working class was an important qualification for advancement into social leadership positions both during and after the communist era. Labor's active role in the political and social life of the 1980s revived the self-esteem and prestige of workers. On the other hand, a 1985 study showed that 70 percent of workers did not wish their children to pursue a manual occupation.

In the late 1980s, some 45 percent of industrial workers had second jobs. Increasing numbers of moonlighting workers sharply stratified the working class, as workers without supplementary income were less able to maintain their living standard. Major inequities were inherent in the wage system as well. In 1986 the best-paid workers earned nearly five times the pay of the average Polish worker, while 33 percent of workers received less than 65 percent of the average wage. Postcommunist reforms brought new financial risk to industrial workers by lowering the upper end of the pay scale. That change, combined with the scarcity of supplementary jobs, pulled a significant new section of Polish workers below the official poverty line in the early 1990s.

In 1992 workers in many industries, including coal and copper mining, aviation, and automobiles, organized strikes to protest lower wages and the displacement caused by economic reform. Outside the jurisdiction of Solidarity, which advocated negotiation with the government, the strikes escalated under the leadership of radical labor leaders. Coal miners, who had enjoyed the highest pay and the best perquisites throughout the communist era because of coal's importance as a hard-currency export, played a central role in the strikes as they sought to protect their privileges.

Social Relationships

In the forty-four years of their rule, the communists built a monocentric society whose social and political fabric was dominated by a new elite of loyal government functionaries. In the 1950s, social institutions such as political groups, voluntary organizations, youth and professional organizations, and community associations lost their autonomy and were forced into a hierarchical state-controlled network. Only the Polish Catholic Church retained some degree of independence during this period (see Religion, this ch.). At the same time, however, smaller groups, initially isolated and fragmented, developed informal, pragmatic networks for economic supply, mediation of interests, and expression of antiestablishment views. Such groups functioned both within state-sanctioned institutions and among families, groups of friends, and small communities. In this context, *dojście* (informal access to useful connections) was the means by which ordinary citizens remained above subsistence level.

The family, the traditional center of Polish social life, assumed a vital role in this informal system. In this respect, everyday urban life assumed some characteristics of traditional rural life. For both professional and working classes, extended families and circles of friends helped when a family or individual was not self-sufficient.

Private exchange arrangements eased the chronic scarcities of the official supply system (see Reform Failure in the 1980s, ch. 3). Especially important within the family structure were parental support of grown children until they became self-sufficient and care by the children for their aging parents and grandparents. In the economic slump of the 1980s, urban food shortages often were alleviated by exchanges with rural relatives.

The inventive and independent networking process formed a distinct tier within Polish society. Seen by its participants as the repository of Polish nationhood and tradition, the world of *dojście* increasingly contrasted with the inefficient, rigid, invasive, and corrupt state system. The emergence of Solidarity was a first step toward restoring the variety of social structures and independent cultural activities present in interwar Poland. In 1980 the phenomenon of public figures rising to tell the truth about Poland's problems began to break the wall between private and public morality, although the subsequent declaration of martial law temporarily dampened its effect (see The Birth of Solidarity, ch. 1).

The second tier involved illegal and quasi-legal actions as well as the pragmatic rearrangement of social relationships. Especially in the 1980s, the relationships between work performed and official wages and between job qualification and salary level (which for "ideological" reasons was higher for many classes of unskilled workers) were objects of general ridicule in Polish society. Under these circumstances, Poles increasingly saw the second tier, rather than the official economy, as the more rewarding investment of their initiative and responsibility. By the 1980s, this allocation of energy led some sociologists to argue that the second tier was necessary in order for communist societies such as Poland's to function.

The end of communism brought no rapid change in social attitudes. In the early postcommunist period, many Poles retained a deep-seated cynicism toward a state long perceived as an untrustworthy privileged elite. Direct and indirect stealing from such a state was at worst an amoral act that could never match the hypocrisy and corruption of high authorities who claimed to govern in the name of all the Polish people. But society's habit of separating "us" from "them" became a major obstacle to enlisting widespread public cooperation and sacrifice or large-scale economic and political reform. Between October 1990 and January 1992, public confidence in the national government declined from 69 percent to 27 percent, according to a national poll.

The Role of Women

By the mid-1970s, nearly half the Polish work force was made up of women. On a purely statistical basis, Poland, like the rest of the Soviet alliance in Eastern Europe, offered women more opportunities for higher education and employment than did most West European countries. Between 1975 and 1983, the total number of women with a higher education doubled, to 681,000 graduates. Many professions, such as architecture, engineering, and university teaching, employed a considerably higher percentage of women in Poland than in the West, and over 60 percent of medical students in 1980 were women (see table 2, Appendix). In many households in the 1980s, women earned more than their husbands. Yet the socialist system that yielded those statistics also uniformly excluded women from the highest positions of economic and political power. In the mid-1980s, only 15 percent of graduates in technical subjects were women, while more than 70 percent of jobs in health, social security, finance, education, and retail sales were filled by women. During the 1980s, very few women occupied top positions in the PZPR (whose 1986 membership was 27 percent women). Similar statistics reflected the power relationships in Solidarity, the diplomatic corps, and the government. By definition, women were excluded completely from the other great center of power, the Catholic Church. In mid-1992, Poland elected its first woman prime minister, Hanna Suchocka (see The Suchocka Government, ch. 4). Her coalition government included no other women. In 1992 the head of the National Bank of Poland, a very powerful position, was a woman, and Ewa Lętowska, former commissioner of citizens' rights, was prominently mentioned as a presidential candidate.

Some experts assert that the male power structure protects its dominance by limiting the opportunities for the advancement of Polish women to those that fill an existing need in the male-dominated society. Another factor in the role of women, however, is the high priority that Polish society continues to give to their role within the family and in raising children (see table 3, Appendix). In the 1980s, one in ten Polish mothers was single, and many single mothers had never been married. In 1991 over 6 percent of Polish families consisted of a single mother caring for one or more children. The extended family provided support for such unconventional arrangements. During the 1980s, both the state (by adjusting school schedules and providing nurseries and substantial paid maternity leave) and the church (by its influential emphasis on the sanctity of the family) successfully promoted the traditional role of women in raising the next generation. In the early 1980s, a very small women's liberation movement began at Warsaw University, but in the years following it failed to expand

Musicians at the Żywiec Folk Festival
Courtesy Sam and Sarah Stulberg

its membership significantly. In 1990 women in Warsaw set a precedent by demonstrating against church-inspired legislation making abortion illegal.

Even with the support of state institutions, however, during the communist era working women with families often had the equivalent of two full-time jobs because their husbands did not make major contributions to household work. According to one study, working women averaged 6.5 hours per day at their jobs and 4.3 hours per day on household duties. In the times of scarcity in the 1980s, standing in line to make purchases occupied a large part of the latter category. Women without jobs, by contrast, spent an average of 8.1 hours per day on household duties. The increased unemployment of the early 1990s generally affected more women than men. According to official figures, in 1992 forty women were jobless for every vacancy they were qualified to fill, while the ratio for men was fourteen to one. Women made up 52.4 percent of the total unemployed, a higher percentage than their overall share of the work force.

In 1992 women ran about 20 percent of Polish farms, a much higher percentage than in Western countries. In most cases, such arrangements reflected necessity rather than choice. Nearly 70 percent of these women were single, and over 40 percent were over age sixty. In most cases, grown children had left the farm for better opportunities and the husband had died or become incapacitated.

The end of communist government brought a new debate about women's role in Polish society. After 1989 many Poles began to associate women's rights with the enforced equality of the discredited communist past. A significant part of society saw the political transformation as an appropriate time for women to return full-time to the home after communism had forced them into the workplace and weakened the Polish family.

The rights of women were central to the controversy over state abortion law that escalated sharply in 1991 and 1992, although few women had policy-making roles and no major women's groups took advocacy positions (see The Polish Catholic Church and the State, this ch.). Some of the social policies of the postcommunist governments complicated the situation of working mothers. A 1992 national study revealed discrimination against women in hiring practices and payment of unemployment benefits, and no law prohibited such sex discrimination. Because child-support payments were not indexed to the cost of living, the payments many women received became nearly worthless in periods of high inflation. In the communist system, daycare for the children of working mothers had been cheap and widely available, but by 1992 more than half the Polish daycare centers had closed. Striving to become self-supporting, the remaining centers raised their prices sharply in the reform period.

Housing

At the end of the communist era, housing was a major social problem. Although the postwar era saw steady growth in housing quality and quantity, that growth fell far short of demand in both geographic distribution and total availability. In 1990 the disparity between available dwellings and number of households requiring housing was estimated at between 1.6 million and 1.8 million units. The causes of this enduring shortage were complex. They included the failures of the communist centralized approach to housing policy before 1989 and the economic downturns that occurred in the 1980s and after the reform era began in 1990.

Communist Housing Policy

As in most other economic and social areas, postwar Polish housing policy followed the Soviet model. The principle behind that model was that housing should be public property and a direct tool of the state's social policy. Accordingly, the Soviet model eliminated private ownership or construction of multifamily residential buildings. Except for single-family units, the government had the legal power to take over private houses and land required for building. Private construction firms were turned into state enterprises that did contract building for central state organizations. State housing policy disregarded supply and demand in favor of administrative space allocation norms, standardized design and construction practices, and central rent control. Maintaining rents at a very low level was supposed to ensure that housing was available to even the poorest citizens. However, housing policy was subordinate to the requirements of central economic planning, so resources for housing construction were directed to industrial areas critical to fulfilling plans and advancing state policy. Materials distribution for housing also was subject to delays or disruption caused by the urgency of other types of construction projects. Although rural and small-town housing nominally escaped direct control, materials rationing and deliberate state hindrance of private construction limited the availability of new housing in such areas.

Polish Housing in Practice

In practice the housing policy of Polish communist regimes was more pragmatic than the Soviet model. In some regions, high housing demand inspired locally controlled cooperatives that pooled state and private resources. State housing construction actually was halted in the 1960s to create demand for cooperative housing, for which rents were much higher. Thereafter, however, the cooperatives gradually became centralized national monopolies, and construction in the 1970s was dominated again by large state enterprises. The monopoly status of the builders and the cooperatives insulated those groups from market competition and enabled them to pass along the costs of inefficient operations to the tenant or to the state.

Under these conditions, housing construction was extremely wasteful and inefficient. The economic crisis of 1980 combined with existing weaknesses in industrial policy to begin a housing shortage that lasted through most of the decade. Between 1978 and 1988, annual housing completions dropped by nearly 45 percent, and investment in housing dropped by nearly 20 percent. At the same time, the Polish birth rate added pressure to the housing situation. By the late 1980s, the average waiting time to buy a house was projected at between fifteen and twenty years if construction continued at the same rate. The housing shortage was a primary cause of social unrest; however, the structural flaws of Polish building continued unchanged. Construction remained of low quality, builders maintained the monopoly control granted by centralized planning, labor productivity dropped, and distribution and transport remained centralized and inefficient.

Housing also remained subordinate to industrial goals. In the 1980s, this meant that new workplaces were the center of housing construction activity, which produced dormitories for workers. By 1988 Poland ranked last in Europe in housing with only 284 dwellings per 1,000 persons; 30 percent of Polish families did not have their own housing accommodations; and the average number of persons per dwelling was 20 percent above the European average. In addition, the average usable area per dwelling in Poland was 10 to 15 percent below the average for other socialist countries and 30 percent below the average for Western Europe (see table 4, Appendix).

Private housing revived somewhat in the 1980s, although independent cooperatives still faced critical materials shortages in the construction stage. An easing of tax regulations and other economic changes raised the profitability of private property in that period. In 1988 the percentage of housing construction projects in which individuals invested had risen to nearly 34 percent from its 1978 level of 26 percent. Although state investment also rose slightly in that period, both increases were at the expense of cooperative investment, which dropped by 10 percent. Nevertheless, in towns privately owned properties remained insignificant until 1989, mainly because high inflation in the 1980s devalued the long-term, low-interest loans offered on state property. In 1989 the new government's anti-inflation measures realigned such loans with present currency values and raised interest rates, stimulating conversion of two-thirds of cooperative flats into private property by early 1990. At the same time, the monopolistic Central Cooperatives Association was split into numerous genuine cooperatives, the state housing administration was abolished, and new incentives were introduced to stimulate private building and rentals.

Housing after 1989

In 1990 Poland's traditionally low rents rose drastically when government subsidies of fuel, electricity, and housing maintenance ended. The long-term goal of housing reform was to let rents rise to market levels. A housing benefits program was to help the poorest groups in society, and new rules were put in place for financing housing purchases. In the transitional period that followed the end of communist government, however, the gap between demand and supply grew. Rising rental and purchase prices, the new obstacles created for housing construction firms by competitive conditions, and the economic downturn that began in 1990 also contributed to this gap. To function efficiently, the housing industry also required more substantial investment in modern technology, particularly in chronically wasteful areas such as cement production and building assembly.

In 1989 and 1991, new housing legislation concentrated on privatizing the ownership of housing units. Of the 2.7 million cooperative apartments in Poland, 57 percent were still tenant-occupied rather than owner-occupied in 1991. An additional 1.5 million apartments were owned by enterprises, which continued the uneconomical communist system of subsidizing as much as 80 percent of the property upkeep for their tenant workers. Beginning in 1989, private owners of multifamily houses could receive subsidies for maintenance, for which they had paid in full under the old system. The 1991 legislation set financial and legal conditions under which renters of cooperative-owned and enterprise-owned housing could assume ownership, creating individual property units from the larger units formerly administered by a central agency.

Religion

World War II essentially transformed Poland into a state dominated by a single religion. According to a 1991 government survey, Roman Catholicism was professed by 96 percent of the population. The practice of Judaism declined more dramatically than any other religion after the war, but the numbers of adherents of Greek Orthodox, Protestant, and other groups also fell significantly. Although the claim of religious affiliation signified different levels of participation for different segments of society (80.6 percent of professed Catholics described themselves as attending mass regularly), the history of Roman Catholicism in Poland formed a uniquely solid link between nationality and religious belief. As a result of that identity, Poland is the only country where the advent of communism had very little effect on the individual citizen's practice of organized religion. During the communist era, the Catholic Church enjoyed varying levels of autonomy, but the church remained the primary source of moral values, as well as an important political force. Of the 4 percent of Poles who were not Roman Catholic, half belonged to one of forty-two other denominations in 1991, and the rest professed no religion. The largest of the non-Catholic faiths is the Polish Autocephalous Orthodox Church. Although Poland returned to its tradition of religious tolerance after the communist era, jurisdictional issues have complicated relations between the Orthodox and Roman Catholic churches.

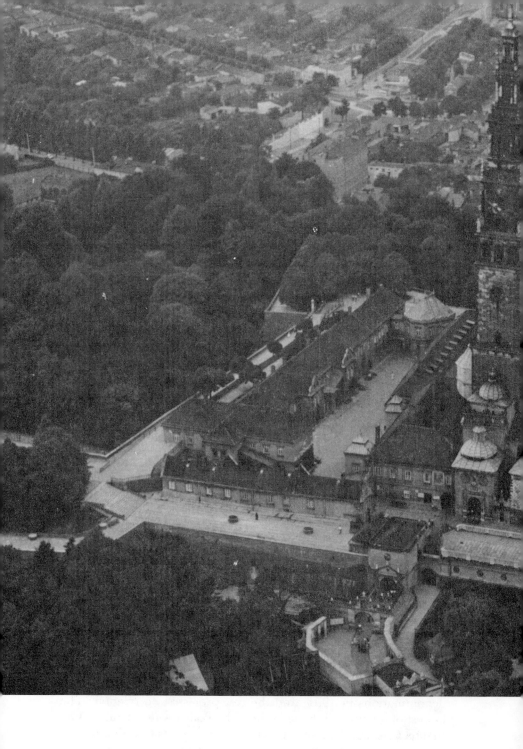

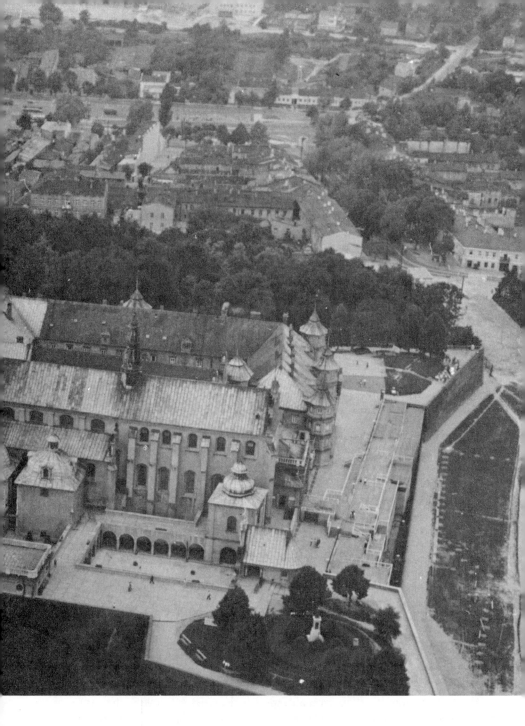

Monastery and basilica of Jasna Góra at Częstochowa
Courtesy Consulate General of Polish People's Republic, New York

The Polish Catholic Church and the State

Throughout the 1800s and 1900s, the Catholic Church was not only a spiritual institution but also a social and political force. The dynamics of church-state relations in Poland after the communist era were shaped by the multifaceted identity the church had assumed during many decades when conventional social and political institutions were suppressed. That identity, called by one scholar a "civil religion," combined religious and political symbols in Poles' conception of their national history and destiny. Important aspects of this social and political role remained intact after 1989, fueling a controversial new drive for church activism.

Church and State Before 1945

The first impetus for an expanded church role was the social repression Poles experienced during the era of the third partition, from 1795 to 1918. In this period, the partitioning nations severely limited freedom of organization, education, and publication in Polish territory (see The Era of Partitioned Poland, ch. 1). With the exception of the post-1867 Austrian-occupied sector, public use of the Polish language was also forbidden. These restrictions left religious practice as the only means of national self-expression and the preservation of social bonds among lay Catholics. From that situation came a strong new sense of national consciousness that combined nineteenth-century literary, philosophical, and religious trends within the formal structure of the church. In 1925 the newly independent Polish state signed a concordat that prescribed separate roles for church and state and guaranteed the church free exercise of religious, moral, educational, and economic activities.

Although Poland enjoyed fourteen years of independence between the signing of the concordat and the Nazi invasion, the special role of the church continued and intensified when postwar communist rule again regimented other forms of self-expression. During the communist era, the church provided a necessary alternative to an unpopular state authority, even for the least religious Poles. Between 1945 and 1989, relations between the Polish Catholic Church and the communist regimes followed a regular pattern: when the state felt strong and self-sufficient, it imposed harsh restrictions on church activities; in times of political crisis, however, the state offered conciliatory measures to the church in order to gain popular support.

The Early Communist Decades

The Polish Catholic Church suffered enormous losses during the

Nazi occupation of Poland in World War II. Its leadership was scattered or exterminated, its schools were closed, and its property was destroyed. Ironically, in the war years this destruction fostered the church's conversion from an aloof hierarchy with feudal overtones to a flexible, socially active institution capable of dealing with the adversity of the postwar years. In the first two postwar years, the church enjoyed considerable autonomy. In 1947, however, consolidation of the East European nations under the hegemony of the Stalinist Soviet Union led to the closing of Polish seminaries and confiscation of church property in the name of the state. The state abolished the concordat and assumed legal supremacy over all religious organizations in 1948.

In the decades that followed, the church adapted to the new constraints, pragmatically reaching compromise agreements with the state and avoiding open confrontation over most issues. Between 1948 and 1981, the church was led by Cardinal Stefan Wyszyński, an expert on Catholic social doctrine whose commanding personality augmented the power of the church hierarchy as a direct conduit from the Vatican to the people of Poland. As a general policy in the early communist decades, Wyszyński avoided fruitless direct campaigning against communist oppression. Instead, he stressed the church's role as advocate of Christian morality. Nevertheless, the cardinal's criticism of PZPR party leader Bolesław Bierut earned Wyszyński three years under house arrest (1953–56), as well as international stature as a spokesman against communism. During this period, a total of 1,000 priests and eight bishops were imprisoned, and convents were raided by the police in the communist drive to destroy completely the authority of the church in Polish society.

Wyszyński was released in 1956 as a result of severe social unrest that forced a change in party leadership. The release was followed by a church-state agreement significantly relaxing restrictions in such areas as religious teaching and jurisdiction over church property. This agreement marked a general softening of state religious policy at the end of the period of hard-line Stalinism. Ten years later, the church's lavish celebration of the millennium of Polish Christianity strengthened the identification of Polish national consciousness with the church and, in the process, the state's respect for the church as representative of national opinion.

Relations in the 1970s and 1980s

When the "reform" regime of Edward Gierek came to power in 1970, it took conciliatory measures to enlist church support. The 1970s were a time of bargaining and maneuvering between a state increasingly threatened by social unrest and a church that was increasingly sure of its leadership role but still intent on husbanding its political capital. Between 1971 and 1974, the church demanded the constitutional right to organize religious life and culture in Poland, using education institutions, religious groups, and the mass media. Major protest documents were issued in 1973 and 1976 against the weakening or withdrawal of state guarantees of such a right.

In 1976 church support for workers' food price riots began a new phase of political activism that would endure until the end of communist rule. In late 1977, a meeting of Gierek and Wyszyński, prompted by continuing social unrest, promised a new reconciliation, but the church continued its harsh criticism of state interference in religious affairs. In 1978 the selection of Cardinal Karol Wojtyła of Kraków as pope opened vital new lines of communication between Polish Catholics and the outside world and gave the Poles a symbol of hope in a period of economic and political decay. In 1979 the triumphal visit of Pope John Paul II to Poland boosted the Polish cultural self-image and turned international attention to Poland's political and spiritual struggles. The next year, the church lent vital moral support to the Solidarity labor movement while counseling restraint from violence and extreme positions. In 1981 the government requested that the church help it to establish a dialog with worker factions. Needing church approval to gain support among the people, the government revived the Joint Episcopal and Government Commission, through which the church gradually regained legal status in the early 1980s. In 1981 the Catholic University of Lublin reopened its Department of Social Sciences, and in 1983 clubs of the Catholic intelligentsia reopened in sixty cities. Twenty-three new church-oriented periodicals appeared in the 1980s, reaching a total printing of more than 1.2 million copies in 1989. Nevertheless, state censorship, paper rationing, and restriction of building permits provoked serious conflicts with the Polish government in the last decade of communist rule (see Politics and the Media, ch. 4).

Wyszyński died in 1981. He was replaced as primate by the less dynamic Cardinal Józef Glemp, who attempted to continue the dual policy of conciliation and advancement of religious rights.

By 1983 several activist bishops and priests had broken with an official church policy they saw as too conciliatory toward the regime. In a 1984 meeting with Prime Minister Wojciech Jaruzelski, Glemp again attempted to obtain official recognition of the church's legal status as well as freedom for imprisoned dissidents. Later that year, the murder of dissident priest Jerzy Popiełuszko by Polish security agents fueled a new confrontation between church and state. The Jaruzelski government, which had met with Glemp seeking the legitimacy that would come from renewed diplomatic relations with the Vatican, abandoned its conciliatory tone and returned to the pre-1970 demand that the church limit itself to purely spiritual matters and censure politically active priests. During 1985 and 1986, the church hierarchy replied with renewed demands for the release of political prisoners and for constitutional guarantees of free assembly. By the end of 1986, 500 political prisoners had received amnesty, and Pope John Paul II's second visit to Poland included a meeting with Jaruzelski—signals that relations were again improving.

The last two years of communist rule brought intensified bargaining as social unrest continued to weaken the government's position. The church demanded that the government open dialogs with opposition organizations, arguing that social and economic problems could not be solved without considering all views. When national strikes hit Poland in mid-1988, the church attempted to arbitrate between labor organizations and the government and to prevent labor from adopting radical positions. The Polish Episcopate, the administrative body of the Polish Catholic Church, took part in the talks that began in September 1988 between Solidarity representatives and the Ministry of Internal Affairs. Those talks ultimately led to restoration of Solidarity's legal status. In early 1989, round table discussions between church and state representatives yielded a new law on church-state relations passed by the Sejm (the lower legislative house) in May 1989. The religious freedom guaranteed by that law allowed the church to resume officially its role as intermediary between the state and society. The law also set the stage for organized activity by the Catholic laity never permitted in the communist era. The Vatican resumed full diplomatic relations with the Polish government two months later.

Church and State after 1989

The approach of the Polish Catholic Church to the Polish state changed drastically after 1989. The church's influential role in promoting opposition views, its close relationship with Solidarity, and its mediation between factions in the tumultuous 1980s brought it enhanced political power in the postcommunist system. In 1989 virtually every significant public organization in Poland saw the church as a partner in its activities and decisions. One result of this identification was that when the Sejm began deliberations on a new constitution in 1990, the Episcopate requested that the document virtually abolish the separation of church and state. Such a change of constitutional philosophy would put the authority of the state behind such religious guarantees as the right to religious education and the right to life beginning at conception (hence a ban on abortion). Throughout the communist era, the separation of church and state had been the basis of the church's refusal to acknowledge the authority of atheistic political regimes over ecclesiastical activities. In justifying its new approach to the separation doctrine, the Episcopate explained that the communist regimes had discredited the doctrine as a constitutional foundation for post-communist governance by using the separation of church and state to defend their totalitarian control of society against church interference.

As a political matter, however, the unleashing of stronger church influence in public life began to alienate parts of the population within two years of the passage of the bill that restored freedom of religion. Catholic intellectuals, who had shared opposition sympathies with the church in the communist era, also had opposed the autocratic rule of Cardinal Wyszyński. Many people feared that compromise between the church and the communist state might yield an alliance that in effect would establish an official state church. Once the common opponent, the communist system, disappeared in 1989, these fears revived and spread to other parts of Polish society.

In the period that followed, critical issues were the reintroduction of religious instruction in public schools—which happened nationwide at church insistence, without parliamentary discussion, in 1990—and legal prohibition of abortion. Almost immediately after the last communist regime fell, the church began to exert pressure for repeal of the liberal communist-era abortion law in effect since 1956. Between 1990 and 1992, church pressure brought three progressively tighter restrictions on birth control and abortion, although surveys showed that about 60 percent of Poles backed freedom of individual choice on that issue. By 1991, the proper boundary of church intervention in social policy making was a divisive social and political issue. At that point, only 58 percent of citizens polled rated the church the most-respected institution in Polish public life—second behind the army. By contrast, one year before 90 percent of citizens polled had rated the church as most respected.

The church responded to the conditions of the reform era in other ways as well. It campaigned vigorously (but unsuccessfully) to prevent dissemination of pornographic materials, which became quite abundant in all East European nations after 1989 and were viewed as a moral threat. The church strongly defended aid for the poor, some aspects of which were suspended in the period of austerity

*The "Black Madonna,"
Poland's most significant
religious relic
Courtesy Reverend Edward
Mroczynski, S. Ch.*

that accompanied Poland's drive toward capitalism, although some
policy makers saw welfare programs as remnants of the communist
state (see The Welfare System, this ch.). Following the issuance
of a papal encyclical on the condition of the poor, Cardinal Glemp
stressed the moral dangers of the free market.

After 1989 the church had to cut its highly professional publication operations drastically. In 1992 the church discussed improving
access to the lay community, however, by publishing a mass-cir-
culation newspaper and establishing a Catholic press agency. Glemp
also considered decentralization of the church hierarchy and establishment of more dioceses to reach the faithful more directly.

The Polish Catholic Church and the People

Throughout the 1970s and 1980s, more than 90 percent of Polish children were baptized in the Catholic Church, showing that
the younger generation shared loyalty to traditional religion. Surveys of young people in the 1980s showed an increase in professed
religious belief over the decade, from 74 percent to 96 percent. Also,
the number of men preparing for the priesthood rose from 6,285
to 8,835 between 1980 and 1986. The church's influence extended far beyond the limits of a traditional predominant religion,
however. Especially in rural areas and among the less-educated
urban population, religion permeated everyday life, and church
attendance was higher in the communist era than it had been before

World War II. As other forms of social affiliation were repressed or reorganized, churches continued as the de facto arbiters of a wide range of moral and ethical problems in their communities, a role they had assumed initially during the war. Although church affiliation was less prevalent among the educated elite, over 60 percent of that group (which included most of the nominally atheistic communist ruling class) professed belief in Catholicism in 1978.

Experts point to certain characteristics of Polish Catholicism to explain its unique resilience in a population bombarded for decades with state-sponsored atheistic propaganda. Polish Catholic religiosity focuses more strongly on the Virgin Mary and the saints than on the direct relationship of the individual to God or on abstract religious doctrine. The most important pilgrimage destination for Polish Roman Catholics is the image of the Virgin (called the Black Madonna) at Jasna Góra Monastery in Częstochowa. The image is believed to have rescued Poland miraculously from invasions by the Tatars and the Swedes, and some Solidarity leaders wore replicas of the icon.

Especially for less-educated Poles, Mary represents a tangible yet mystical connection with God much preferable to contemplation of abstract theological doctrine. During the communist era, this more immediate and anthropocentric religiosity seemed uniquely resistant to replacement by the intellectual doctrine of atheism. On the other hand, in the early 1990s, once the specter of state-sponsored atheism had disappeared, this immediacy promoted individual expression of beliefs in ways that questioned the church's authority over secular social ethics. Thus, the official church that had protected the spiritual interests of all Poles under communism risked separation from the everyday religious practice that retained great meaning for the average Polish Catholic.

Other Churches

A total of forty-two non-Catholic church groups existed in Poland in 1989, accounting for about 2 percent of the population. In the communist era, the legal status of these communities was severely restricted. In March 1988, the Polish Ecumenical Council, which represented the major non-Catholic groups, began participating in a commission with government representatives to restore unrestricted freedom of religion. The 1989 law on freedom of conscience and creed redefined the state's relationship to all religions, conferring equal status on the Roman Catholic and the minority churches.

The Greek Catholic Church

The Greek Catholic Church (also called the Uniate Church) was established in 1596 by the Union of Brest-Litovsk. That agreement brought several million Eastern Orthodox Belorussians and Ukrainians under the authority of the Roman Catholic Church, although they preserved Orthodox religious rites. From the outset, many in the Orthodox Church strongly opposed Latinization and what they perceived as the compromise of tradition, and conflict between the Greek Catholic Church and both the Polish Catholic Church and the Orthodox Church flared periodically into the early 1990s. In Poland the tense relations between proponents of the Latin and the Greek Catholic rites had relaxed significantly in the 1980s, although serious issues remained unsolved. Among the foremost of those issues was Catholic occupation of Greek Catholic Church property confiscated by the state in the late 1940s.

In 1947 the resettlement of the Ukrainian population from southeastern Poland substantially reduced the practice of Greek Catholicism in Poland. In 1949 Pope Pius XII appointed Wyszyński as the papal delegate to the Greek Catholic congregations of Poland. In 1956 Wyszyński named sixteen Ukrainian priests as the clerical body of the Greek Catholic Church, and a vicar general was also named and installed in Przemyśl. In 1981 Glemp named two vicars general for Warsaw and Legnica to improve the church's ministry to the dispersed Ukrainian Greek Catholic communities. Beginning at that time, church administration was divided into northern and southern districts. In 1989 the total membership of the Greek Catholic Church in Poland was estimated at 300,000, with eighty-five centers of worship and fifty-five priests. Twelve candidates were preparing for the Greek Catholic priesthood at the Catholic University of Lublin in 1989; five monasteries and three orders of nuns were active.

The Evangelical Church of the Augsburg Confession

The largest Protestant church in Poland, the Evangelical Church of the Augsburg Confession, or Old Lutheran Church, had about 90,000 members in six dioceses in 1989, figures substantially reduced by postwar resettlement of the German minority that made up a large part of the church's membership (see Ethnic Groups, this ch.). Services were conducted in Polish. The membership was concentrated in the Cieszyn Diocese, on the Czechoslovak border southwest of Kraków. Of the original twenty-six parishes founded in German communities of Silesia and Pomerania, nineteen remained in 1985. Despite its name, the church was not a formal member of the Germany-based Evangelical Church of the Augsburg Confession.

The Old Catholic Churches

The Polish National Catholic Church, one of a number of so-called Old Catholic churches worldwide, had about 50,000 members in 1989, organized in dioceses centered in Katowice, Warsaw, Kraków, and Wrocław. The church claims to retain all genuine Roman Catholic doctrine, while rejecting mainstream Roman Catholic tenets such as the infallibility of the pope and the immaculate conception and assumption of the Virgin Mary. The thrust of the Polish National Catholic Church's beliefs is a return to "original" doctrine untainted by the addition of any new belief. The church belongs to the Union of Utrecht, which includes Old Catholic churches from many countries and is overseen from the Netherlands by the archbishop of Utrecht.

The Mariavite Catholic Church of Poland is a schismatic Old Catholic group excluded from the Union of Utrecht because of unorthodox beliefs. In 1989 its membership in Poland was about 25,000, divided into three dioceses administered from Płock. About thirty priests were active in 1989.

The Polish Ecumenical Council

Founded in 1946 to promote interchurch cooperation, the Polish Ecumenical Council includes nearly all churches except the Polish Catholic Church. In 1989 member churches included the Orthodox, Lutheran, Methodist, Baptist, Reformed (Calvinist), Old Catholic, and Evangelical churches of Poland. Cooperation with the Polish Catholic Church began in 1974 when the council established a Combined Ecumenical Commission to deal with the analogous ecumenical commission of the Polish Catholic Bishops' Conference. In 1977 the council named a subcommittee for discussion of individual theological questions; by 1980 bilateral dialogs had begun among members sharing similar doctrine. Given Poland's history of religious tolerance, the restoration of religious freedom in 1989 was expected to expand the tentative ecumenical contacts achieved during the communist era.

Education

Throughout the modern history of Poland, education has played a central role in Polish society. Together with the church, formal and informal education helped to preserve national identity and prepare society for future independence during the partition period.

In the communist era, education was the chief mode of restructuring society and improving the social mobility of hitherto unprivileged workers. The postcommunist era brought an extensive debate over the goals of restructuring the system and the role of the church in secular education.

The Education Tradition

The education of Polish society was a goal of rulers as early as the twelfth century, when monks were brought from France and Silesia to teach agricultural methods to Polish peasants. Kraków University, founded in 1364 by Kazimierz the Great, became one of Europe's great early universities and a center of intellectual tolerance (see The Medieval Era, ch. 1). Through the eighteenth century, Poland was a refuge for academic figures persecuted elsewhere in Europe for unorthodox ideas. The dissident schools founded by these refugees became centers of avant-garde thought, especially in the natural sciences. The Renaissance and Enlightenment periods in Western Europe brought advanced educational theories to Poland. In 1773 King Stanisław August established his Commission on National Education, the world's first state ministry of education. This body set up a uniform national education system emphasizing mathematics, natural sciences, and language study. The commission also stressed standardizing elementary education, integrating trade and agricultural skills into the elementary school curriculum, and improving textbooks at all levels.

Eras of Repression

Partition challenged the work of the Commission on National Education because Germany, Austria, and Russia sought to destroy Polish national consciousness by Germanizing or Russifying the education system. During the 123-year partition, pockets of resistance continued teaching and publishing in Polish, and some innovations such as vocational training schools appeared. In general, the Austrian sector had the least developed education system, whereas the least disruption in educational progress occurred in the Prussian sector (see fig. 7).

Between 1918 and 1939, the newly independent Poland faced the task of reconstructing a national education system from the three separate systems imposed during partition. Although national secondary education was established in the 1920s, the economic crisis of the 1930s drastically decreased school attendance. Among the educational accomplishments of the interwar period were establishment of state universities in Warsaw, Wilno (Vilnius), and Poznań (available only to the upper classes), numerous specialized secondary schools, and the Polish Academy of Learning.

Between 1939 and 1944, the Nazi occupation sought to annihilate the national Polish culture once again. All secondary and higher schools were closed to Poles, and elementary school curricula were stripped of all national content during this period. In response, an extensive underground teaching movement developed under the leadership of the Polish Teachers' Association and the Committee for Public Education. An estimated 100,000 secondary students attended classes in the underground system during the Nazi occupation.

Under communist regimes, the massive task of postwar education reconstruction emphasized opening institutions of secondary and higher education to the Polish masses and reducing illiteracy. The number of Poles unable to read and write had been estimated at 3 million in 1945. In harmony with the principles of Marxism-Leninism, wider availability of education would democratize the higher professional and technical positions previously dominated by the gentry-based intelligentsia and the wealthier bourgeoisie. Because sweeping industrialization goals also required additional workers with at least minimum skills, the vocational school system was substantially expanded. At least in the first postwar decade, most Poles welcomed the social mobility that these policies offered. On the other hand, Poles generally opposed Marxist revision of Polish history and the emphasis on Russian language and area studies to the detriment of things Polish—practices especially stringent in the first postwar decade, when Stalinist doctrine was transferred wholesale from the Soviet Union and dominated pedagogical practice. During this period, all levels of Polish education were plagued by shortages of buildings and teachers. Capital investment lagged far behind the grandiose goals of centralized planning.

Education reform was an important demand of widespread Polish demonstrations against Stalinism in 1956. Under the new PZPR first secretary, Władysław Gomułka, government education policy rejected the dogmatic programs of Stalinism and in their place began the first period of (fragmentary) postwar education reform. Religious instruction was restored, at the option of parents; by 1957 over 95 percent of schools had resumed offering such instruction. In the vocational program, agricultural training schools were added, and technical courses were restructured to afford greater contact with actual industrial operations. By 1961, however, state doctrine followed the generally conservative turn of Polish politics by again describing the goal of education as preparing workers to build the socialist state.

The Law on the Development of Education Systems, passed in 1961, established four formal principles that reiterated the goals of the pre-1956 system and endured through the rest of the communist era. The education system was to prepare qualified employees for industry, to develop proper attitudes of citizenship in the Polish People's Republic, to propagate the values of the working classes everywhere, and to instill respect for work and national values. Education was specifically described as a function of the state, and schools were to be secular in nature. Religious institutions could sponsor schools under strict limitations, however, and the church was permitted to establish a network of separate religious education centers to compensate for this restriction. In 1968 the return of strict communist dogma to school curricula was an important stimulus for a national wave of student demonstrations. Although the Gierek regime sought broad education reform when it took power in 1970, the uneven progress of reform programs in the 1970s led to further unrest and diminished the role of education in state control of society.

In the communist era, two levels of education management existed. At the central level, the Ministry of National Education was the chief organ of state administration. That agency prescribed course content, textbooks, principles of school operation, standards for admissions and scholarship awards, examination procedures, and interschool relations throughout the country. At the local level, superintendents established personnel policy, hired and trained personnel, and oversaw other local institutions having educational functions. The daily functioning of each individual school was administered by a headmaster and a pedagogical council.

The Drive for Education Reform

In the Solidarity movement of 1980, student and teacher organizations demanded a complete restructuring of the centralized system and autonomy for local educational jurisdictions and institutions. In response, the Jaruzelski government issued sympathetic statements and appointed committees, but few meaningful changes ensued in the 1980s. Although an education crisis was recognized widely and experts advised that education could not be viewed in isolation from Poland's other social problems, the PZPR continued making cosmetic changes in the system until the party was voted out of office in 1989. The political events of that year were the catalyst for fundamental change in the Polish education system.

The round table discussions of early 1989 between the government and opposition leaders established a special commission on education questions, which was dominated by the Solidarity view that political dogma should be removed from education and the heavily bureaucratized state monopoly of education should end (see The Round Table Agreement, ch. 4). That view also required autonomy for local school administrations and comprehensive upgrading of material support. Accordingly, the Office of Innovation and Independent Schools was established in 1990 to create the legislative basis for government support of private schools established by individuals and civic organizations. In a compromise with communists remaining in parliament, state subsidies were set at 50 percent of the state's per-student cost. The new private schools featured smaller classes of ten to fifteen students, higher teacher salaries, and complete freedom for educational innovation. Tuition was to be high, from 40,000 to 50,000 zloty per month (for value of the zloty—see Glossary), with scholarships available for poorer students with high grades. In the first eighteen months, about 250 new private schools appeared, 100 of which were affiliated with the Catholic Church. In 1990 the total enrollment of 15,000 reflected parental caution toward the new system, but the figure rose steadily in 1992. The Ministry of National Education viewed the alternative schools as a stimulus for reform of the public school system.

In 1990 Minister of National Education Henryk Samsonowicz established interim national minimum requirements while offering teachers maximum flexibility in choosing methodology. The drafts of new education laws to replace the 1961 law called for the "autonomy of schools as societies of students, teachers, and parents," with final responsibility for instructional content and methods. Controversy over the laws centered not on their emphasis on autonomy and democracy, but on the relative status of interest groups within the proposed system. Disagreements on such issues postponed the effective date of the new Polish education laws until September 1991.

The most controversial aspect of the new law was the status of religious education in public schools (see table 5, Appendix). A 1991 directive from the Ministry of National Education required that every student receive a grade in religion or ethics. For many Poles, this meant an invasion of the constitutional right to keep silent about religious convictions as well as recognition of a church education authority rivaling secular authority. Many other Poles, however, considered separation of the church from education to be a continuation of communist policies and a weakening of the national moral fabric.

Structure of the Education System

Poland's postcommunist education legislation left intact the public structures established by the 1961 education law. In that system, the first stage was kindergarten, attended by children between three and seven years of age. City kindergarten schools were open from seven to eleven hours per day and designed their programs to accommodate the schedules of working parents. Schools in rural areas were open from five to eight hours, depending on the season and on agricultural requirements. The level of education and auxiliary services was generally much lower in rural schools, and kindergarten attendance there was roughly half that in the cities. Some primary schools also had kindergarten sections, whose graduates continued to the next level in the same institution. The cost of kindergarten education was shared by the government and parents. Under the communist system, the cost of kindergarten education had been paid wholly by the parents. In 1992 the 23,900 kindergartens in operation included 11,000 separate kindergartens and 12,900 kindergarten sections.

Eight years of primary school were obligatory in both the communist and the postcommunist systems (see table 6, Appendix). Children entered this phase at age seven and remained until they completed the program or until they turned seventeen. Foreign-language instruction was widely available (see table 7, Appendix). Some special schools were available for students gifted in the arts or sports, and special courses were designed for physically or mentally handicapped students.

Poland's acute shortage of classroom space required double shifts and large classes (thirty to forty students) in most primary schools. Some schools provided after-school programs for students in grades one to three whose parents both worked; older students, however, were released at the end of the school day, regardless of their home situation. In 1992 some 5.3 million children were in primary school; new enrollments dropped 2.9 percent from the previous year.

In 1991 over 95 percent of primary-school graduates continued to some form of secondary education. Admission to the secondary level was by examination and overall primary-school records. In general, the students with the highest primary achievement went into a college preparatory track, those with the lowest into a trade-school track. Of pupils completing primary school in 1991, about 43 percent went to three-year trade schools (specializing in various trades, from hairdressing to agriculture), 25 percent to four-year vocational lycea and to technical schools, and 26 percent to college preparatory schools. The last category grew by 3.2 percent between 1990 and 1991, while the other two fell slightly. Of the three categories, only the first provides a trade immediately upon graduation. Students in the other two categories require further education at a university or at a two-year postsecondary school to prepare them for employment. Some college preparatory schools combine a variety of nontechnical subjects in their curricula; others specialize in humanities, mathematics and physical sciences, biology and chemistry, sports, or classical subjects. In 1987 these schools enrolled more than twice as many girls as boys; about 11 percent of secondary-school students received scholarships. Students passing final exams in the college preparatory program are permitted to take university entrance exams.

Most technical programs are five years in length. Such programs are offered in economics, art, music, theater production, and teacher training (a six-year track). Many students live at secondary technical schools because some districts have only one such school. The government and parents share board and room expenses; tuition is free. The Polish Catholic Church also operates fourteen high schools, whose curricula were state-mandated until 1989.

To enroll at the university level, students have to pass entrance exams. Institutions at this level include full universities (of which Poland had twelve in 1990), polytechnical schools, academies, and specialized colleges. In 1988 the largest of these were Warsaw University (23,300 students), Marie Curie-Skłodowska University in Lublin (12,900), Adam Mickiewicz University at Poznań (12,100), the Warsaw Technical School (12,000), and the Silesian University at Katowice (11,400).

The polytechnical schools offer theoretical and applied training in such fields as electronics, engineering, computer science, and construction. Academies specialize in medicine, fine arts, economics, agriculture, sports, or theology; thirty-four academies were in operation in 1990. In that year, twenty-nine specialized colleges were training students in pedagogy, oceanography, and art. College enrollment increased each year between 1989 and 1992. In 1992 some 430,000 persons attended college, 330,000 as full-time students; initial enrollment for the 1991–92 school year was 17.7 percent higher than for the previous year.

As a rule, students pursue postgraduate degrees as members of an academic team working under a single professor. Continued progress through the academic ranks depends on regular evaluation of scholarly activity and publications, and failure to meet requirements means removal from the program. Polish postgraduate studies programs, which culminate in doctoral degrees, suffer from lack of material support, low salaries, and low demand for individuals with advanced degrees in the job market. In the late 1980s, these factors made the dropout rate very high and forced cancellation of several programs. Between 1982 and 1992, Poland suffered a serious "brain drain" in higher education and the sciences as more than 15,000 scientists emigrated or changed their profession.

Health and Welfare

The fall of centralized state planning and the onset of massive economic and social reform put new strains on Poland's health and welfare systems, whose nominally full and equal coverage had been increasingly faulty in the 1980s. In the last decade of communist rule, national health care suffered from poor material support, inaccessible medical personnel and facilities, and poor organization. At the same time, critical national health indicators for the 1970s and 1980s showed many negative trends. Likewise, access to social services, nominally equal for all workers, was limited by the availability of welfare funds in individual enterprises during the communist era. Because no national standards existed, some enterprises offered their employees no social services at all, while others offered a wide range. By 1989 the material position of low-income families and pensioners was especially desperate. The economic "shock therapy" begun in 1990 by the Balcerowicz Plan further reduced the level of guaranteed health and welfare services, to which a large part of Polish society had become accustomed under communist regimes (see Marketization and Stabilization, ch. 3).

Health Conditions

In the two decades after World War II, the health of Poland's people improved overall, as antibiotics became available and the standard of living rose in most areas. In the 1970s and 1980s, however, alarming trends appeared in certain national health statistics. Between 1970 and 1986, the mortality rate rose from 8.1 to 10.1 persons per 1,000, and from 8.8 to 10.9 males per 1,000. The increase was sharpest among males between the ages of forty-five and fifty-four. For the same period, working days lost because of illness or accidents increased by 45 percent (see table 8, Appendix). Between 1988 and 1991, the incidence of newborns requiring intensive care rose from 2.9 to 4.5 percent. Experts listed the major contributing factors as high levels of air and water pollution, unsatisfactory working conditions, overcrowded housing, psychological depression because of deteriorating economic conditions, poorly balanced diets, alcoholism, and deterioration of health services, especially in prenatal and postnatal care. (see Environmental Conditions and Crises; Housing, this ch.).

The Health Care System

The constitution of 1952 guaranteed universal free health care.

In the last two decades of the communist era, however, such care became progressively less dependable for those without informal support networks or enough money to buy health care outside the official system (see Social Relations, this ch.). As early as 1970, Polish governments recognized the need to reform the cumbersome, inefficient national health care system, but vested interests in the central planning system prevented meaningful change. From the beginning, administration of the system was inefficient. The structure of the medical profession did not supply enough general practitioners, and medical personnel such as dentists and nurses were in short supply (see table 9; table 10, Appendix). Treatment facilities were too few and crowded, preventive medicine received little attention, and the quality of care was generally much poorer in rural areas. As in other communist countries, the finest medical facilities were reserved for the party elite.

In the postcommunist reform period, constriction of the state budget and fragmentary privatization of medical practices made the availability of health care unpredictable for many Poles. After inheriting a deteriorating health care system, Polish policy makers placed their near-term hopes on reducing bureaucracy, encouraging self-government in the medical profession, shifting resources to more efficient departments, and streamlining admissions and diagnosis procedures.

In 1992 Poland had fifty-seven hospital beds per 10,000 citizens, about half the ratio of beds available in France and Germany. The ratio had been declining since the 1960s; in 1991 alone, however, over 2,500 beds and nearly 100 clinics and dispensaries were eliminated in the drive for consolidation and efficiency. Already in the mid-1980s, about 50 percent of the medicines officially available could not be obtained by the average Pole, and the average hospital had been in service sixty-five years. Because the reform budgets of the early 1990s included gradual cuts in the funding of the Ministry of Health and Social Welfare, additional targeted cuts of 10 to 20 percent were expected in clinics and hospital beds by 1994. The long-term goal of Polish health policy was a complete conversion of state budget-supported socialized medicine to a privately administered health system supported by a universal obligatory health insurance fee. Under such a system, fees would be shared equally by workers and enterprises. Before introduction of that system, which was not expected until at least 1995, interim funding was to depend heavily on a patchwork of voluntary contributions and local and national health-care taxes. Even after 1995, however, planners projected that the state budget would continue contributing to the national health care fund until the insurance system became self-sufficient. The state would now contribute directly, however, bypassing the old health care bureaucracy.

Health Issues

In 1991 Poland's overall mortality rate increased to 10.6 deaths per 1,000 persons, from the 1990 figure of 10.2 per 1,000 (see table 11, Appendix). In the same period, infant mortality remained constant at 15.9 per 1,000. About 50 percent of the 405,000 deaths in 1991 were attributed to circulatory diseases, and another 20 percent were caused by malignant tumors. Poland's communist regimes partially or completely ignored a number of major health problems, including acquired immune deficiency syndrome (AIDS), drug addiction, and alcoholism. Only with the open discussion that began in 1989 did the extent of these problems become clear. Solutions, on the other hand, were often blocked in the postcommunist years by popular distrust of state authority, controversy between church and state, and lack of resources.

AIDS

AIDS emerged as an issue in Poland later than in the West— partly because of communist suppression of statistics, partly because the epidemic apparently reached Poland later. In 1991 the government officially estimated that 2,000 Poles had been infected with the human immunodeficiency virus (HIV), whereas an independent health expert put the figure at 100,000. This statistical discrepancy reflects Poland's late start in testing the groups at highest risk of infection. Narcotics addicts are endangered particularly because the drug in widest use in Poland is administered and distributed by syringe, one of the most potent means of HIV transmission. Early efforts to control the spread of HIV were hampered by public ignorance and superstition; in 1992 about 70 percent of Poles believed they could not be infected, while many believed that water and mosquitoes were carriers. The total lack of sex education programs in the schools (the Polish Catholic Church forced their removal after the communist era) and the disinclination of political and religious leaders to address the issue publicly have further hindered prevention efforts.

Twice in 1991, World Health Organization (WHO) teams evaluated the Polish situation and proposed a program to combat the spread of AIDS. The teams advised that, to prevent the disease from spreading from high-risk groups to society at large, information on the epidemic be given maximum dissemination to certain less visible groups that were likely victims of the second phase of the disease. The most urgent target groups were the prostitute community—whose numbers in 1992 were estimated to be as high as 180,000—and their potential customers. At that point, however, a comprehensive information program was impossible because the country lacked trained workers and money for training programs. Other obstacles were lack of modern diagnostic technology and poor hygiene in public health facilities. In 1991 WHO allocated a small fund for a three-year education and prevention program in Poland.

Narcotics

As in the case of AIDS victims, communist regimes denied the existence of drug addicts. The first private drug treatment center opened in 1970, and in the 1970s health and legal professionals discussed the drug problem guardedly. Not until the 1980s were organizations founded to combat drug addiction, and they were harassed and limited by government agencies until 1989. In 1992 between 4,000 and 5,000 Poles dependent on narcotics were being treated at facilities of the national health service or social organizations. The Ministry of Health and Social Welfare estimated that 200,000 to 250,000 persons were taking drugs at that time, however. In 1991 some 190 deaths were attributed to drug overdoses. Addicts under treatment were predominantly from the working class and the intelligentsia, male, and younger than thirty years of age (nearly half were under twenty-four). The most commonly abused substance, *kompot,* is a powerful and physically devastating drug readily produced from the poppy plants grown widely in Poland. The drug is injected intravenously. *Kompot* moves through society via informal networks operating independently of the international drug market.

In the period from 1986 to 1992, drug abuse in Poland remained stable despite declining standards of living, rising unemployment, and a rising overall crime rate. As barriers to the West fell, however, amphetamine manufacture and trafficking introduced a new threat. By 1992, amphetamines from Poland were considered as serious a threat in Germany and Scandinavia as imported cocaine and heroin; at that time, an estimated 20 percent of amphetamines in Western Europe originated in Polish laboratories. The confiscation of 150 kilograms of cocaine in Poland in 1991 also indicated that domestic narcotics production was diversifying, and local authorities feared that Colombian drug cartels were investing in that activity. To counter criminal drug producers, who also were involved in other types of crime, Poland established a National Drug Bureau in 1991. Because *kompot* remained much cheaper and more accessible in the early 1990s, however, the Polish market for amphetamines remained very small. Meanwhile, a 1990 law made illegal the cultivation of poppies without a government permit, and a new, morphine-free poppy species was introduced in 1991 to enable farmers to continue poppy cultivation.

In 1992 nineteen of Poland's drug rehabilitation centers were operated by the Young People's Movement to Combat Drug Addiction (known by its Polish acronym, MONAR). Although hundreds of people were cured in such centers in the 1980s, the severe treatment methods of MONAR's two-year program caused controversy in the Polish health community. For that reason, in 1990 the Ministry of Health and Social Welfare began opening clinics that emphasized preparing individuals for life after treatment.

Alcoholism

The older generations of Poles escaped narcotics addiction, but alcoholism is a problem in all generations. Alcohol consumption is an integral part of Polish social tradition, and nondrinkers are relatively rare. Per capita consumption increased significantly after World War II, however, and consumption remained above the European average throughout the communist period. Children often began drinking when still in primary school. Government programs nominally discouraged excessive drinking, but the importance of revenue from the Polish alcohol industry restricted their activity. Throughout the 1980s, the percentage of strong alcoholic beverages in overall consumption rose steadily, putting Poland near the top among nations in that statistic. In 1977 an estimated 4.3 million Poles consumed the equivalent of more than 48 liters of pure alcohol per person per year; of that number, about 1 million were believed to be clinically alcohol-dependent. In 1980 the average male Pole over sixteen years of age consumed the equivalent of 16.6 liters of pure alcohol per year.

The Welfare System

The communist central planning system made a wide variety of payments to subsidize citizens in certain categories and encourage or discourage the activities of citizens in other categories. By the mid-1980s, the planning labyrinth created by such payments was such a fiscal burden that severe cuts were made in some payments. Like the health system, Poland's welfare system underwent substantial decentralization and restructuring, and all parts of the system suffered from limited funding in the transition period that began in 1989. Although a higher percentage of the population needed welfare services because of high unemployment in that period, the need to reduce the government's budget deficit caused drastic cuts in many services. Eventual reversal of this trend depends upon the speed with which Poland's economy rebounds from its transition crisis and upon the efficiency of the new welfare bureaucracies.

Structural Change

Until 1989 social policy making was centralized in the Planning Commission of the Council of Ministers. The postcommunist reforms placed social policy responsibility in the Ministry of Labor and Social Policy and the Ministry of Health and Welfare, with the aim of liberating social policy from its communist-era linkage with economic policy considerations. The social welfare policy of the postcommunist governments was planned in two phases. The first stage included short-term measures to offset the income losses of certain groups resulting from government anti-inflation policy. These measures varied from the setting up of soup kitchens and partial payment of heating bills to reorganization of the social assistance system. The second, long-term policy aims at rebuilding the institutions of the system to conform with the future market economy envisioned by planners. Communal and regional agencies are to assume previously centralized functions, and authority is to be shared with private social agencies and charities.

Welfare Benefits

In the late 1980s, Poland spent about 22 percent of its gross national product (GNP—see Glossary) on social benefits in the form of monetary payments or services. At that time, over 5 million Poles received retirement or disability pensions, and about 100,000 were added yearly in the latter category. In the years of labor shortage, government incentives encouraged pensioners to continue to work past retirement age (sixty-five for men, sixty for women). In the early 1980s, the number of invalids receiving benefits increased from 2.5 million to 3.6 million, straining the welfare system. The communist system also paid benefits to single mothers with preschool children, sickness benefits for workers, income supplements and nonrepayable loans to the poor, and education grants to nearly 75 percent of students, in addition to providing nominally free health care, cultural and physical education facilities. By the mid-1980s, however, all the free, state-funded services were being considered for privatization, fees, or rationing.

In the first postcommunist years, social support programs for the unemployed underwent important changes. The initial postcommunist policy guaranteed unemployment benefits and retraining regardless of the reason for a person's unemployed status. Benefits were to be paid indefinitely and were based on previous pay or on the national minimum wage for those who had never worked. Benefits included old-age, disability, and survivors' pensions and compensation for work injuries, sickness, maternity, and family-related expenses. Although the system covered both industry and agriculture, enterprises in the industrial sector paid much higher surcharges (usually 45 percent of the worker's salary) to the benefit fund than did either the agriculture or housing sectors.

In 1991 and early 1992, a series of laws drastically reduced the coverage of the unemployment program. Under the modified policies, benefits no longer went to those who had never been employed; a twelve-month limit was placed on all payments; and benefit levels were lowered by pegging them to income the previous quarter rather than to the last salary received. This reform immediately disqualified 27 percent of previous beneficiaries, and that percentage was expected to rise in ensuing years.

In 1992 the Warsaw welfare office divided its benefit payments among 4,500 recipients of permanent benefits, 8,500 recipients of temporary benefits, and 25,500 recipients of housing assistance. The public assistance law entitled one person per family to permanent benefits at the official minimum subsistence level. Throughout Poland, the demand for welfare assistance grew steadily between 1990 and 1992, well beyond the financial and organizational capabilities of the state system. The shortage affected a wide range of social categories: the homeless and unemployed, AIDS victims, families of alcoholics, and the elderly. According to a 1991 study, 18 percent of Polish children lived in poverty. Thus, the postcommunist conversion of a state-sponsored and state-controlled economy reverberated strongly in the "social security" that communism had promised but very often failed to deliver in the 1980s.

* * *

Numerous useful monographs cover all or parts of Poland's society and environment. *The Poles* by Stewart Steven and Janine Wedel's *The Private Poland* are anecdotal treatments of the general fabric of Polish society. *Länderbericht Polen* is a collection of essays in German edited by Wilhelm Wöhlke covering religion, ethnic groups, health and welfare, and geography. *Economic Reforms and Welfare Systems in the USSR, Poland, and Hungary,* edited by Jan Adam, includes treatment of the postcommunist welfare structure. Kenneth R. Wulff's *Education in Poland* is a detailed description of the subject before, during, and after the communist regimes. *Poland into the 1990s,* edited by George Blazyca and Ryszard Rapacki, contains informative chapters on social structure in the communist era and on the condition of the environment after communism.

Aleksander Gella's *Development of Class Structure in Eastern Europe* relates the evolution of social classes in Poland to those found in surrounding countries. And George Kolankiewicz and Paul G. Lewis's *Poland: Politics, Economics, and Society* treats a number of social issues in the context of the country's political and economic structure. (For further information and complete citations, see Bibliography.)

Chapter 3. The Economy

Polish coin from the early eleventh-century reign of Bolesław I the Brave

POLAND'S ECONOMIC GROWTH was favored by relatively rich natural resources for both agriculture and industry. Eastern Europe's largest producer of food, Poland based its sizeable and varied industrial sector on ample coal supplies that made it the world's fourth largest coal producer in the 1970s. The most productive industries, such as equipment manufacturing and food processing, were built on the country's coal and soil resources, respectively, and energy supply still depended almost entirely on coal in the early 1990s.

After World War II, Poland's new communist rulers reorganized the economy on the model of state socialism established by Joseph V. Stalin in the Soviet Union. The result was the predominance of heavy industry, large enterprises, and a topheavy centralized bureaucracy controlling every aspect of production. Considerations such as consumer demand and worker job satisfaction, familiar in Western capitalist systems, were ignored. Isolated from the processes of the marketplace, pricing and production levels were set to advance the master plans of the ruling party. The socioeconomic disproportions that resulted from this isolation were a burdensome legacy to the reform governments in the early postcommunist era.

Poland's abundant agricultural resources remained largely in private hands during the communist period, but the state strongly influenced that sector through taxes, controls on materials, and limits on the size of private plots. Many small industries and crafts also remained outside direct state control.

The Polish economy also was isolated from the international economy by the postwar nationalization of foreign trade. Reforms in the 1970s and 1980s gradually gave individual enterprises more direct control over their foreign trade activities, bypassing much of the state planning machinery. But until 1990 Polish trade policy remained severely limited by its obligations to the Council for Mutual Economic Assistance (Comecon—see Glossary), which was dominated by the Soviet Union. Although price supports helped Poland's balance of trade within the system, they also encouraged inefficient and low-quality production that discouraged trade with the rest of the world.

Failure of central state planning to yield economic growth inspired social unrest and official policy reform in the 1970s and the early 1980s, but no real change occurred until the installation of a noncommunist government in mid-1989 (see The 1989 Elections and Their Aftermath, ch. 1). With massive public support, the first noncommunist government imposed a shock-therapy reform program in 1990. This program included privatization of all parts of the Polish economy and a rapid shift from the unrealistic state planning system to a Western-style market economy. The momentum of the early reform days flagged in the next two years, however. In 1992 signs of economic progress were very uneven. Consumer goods became much more available, but the continued existence of inefficient state enterprises lowered productivity significantly, unemployment rose, and inflation became a serious threat after initially being reduced to virtually zero.

In its efforts to westernize its economy after 1989, Poland relied heavily on expertise and financial support from international financial institutions. Although its substantial hard-currency debt was partially forgiven in 1991, the remains of the communist management system hindered efficient use of foreign capital and discouraged the foreign investment that Poland vigorously sought. Thus, by 1992 what was initially planned as a brief period of painful economic adjustment had become a much longer ordeal that had brought mixed results.

Natural Resources

Poland's rapid postwar industrialization was supported by a combination of readily available natural resources, especially economically important minerals. After the era of communist economics and politics ended in 1989, however, industrial policy makers contemplated major changes in the balance of resource consumption.

Minerals and Fuels

Coal is Poland's most important mineral resource. In 1980 total reserves were estimated at 130 billion tons. The largest coal deposits are located in Upper Silesia in the southwestern part of the country, where large-scale mining began in the nineteenth century. Silesian deposits, generally of high quality and easily accessible, accounted for about 75 percent of the country's hard coal resources and 97 percent of its extraction in the 1980s. The Lublin region of eastern Poland was exploited in the 1980s as part of an expansion program to supplement Silesian hard coal for industry and export. But development of this relatively poor, geologically difficult, and very expensive field ended in 1990. A number of unprofitable Upper Silesian mines also were to be closed in the early 1990s.

Poland also has significant quantities of lignite in the district of Zielona Góra in the west and in two districts located in the central part of the country between the Vistula and the Oder rivers. This low-quality fuel has been used on a large scale for the production of electricity, despite its very damaging effect on the environment (see Environment and Pollution, ch. 2). Plans called for gradual reduction of lignite extraction and use in the 1990s (see Fuels and Energy, this ch.).

Natural gas is extracted mostly in Upper Silesia, Lower Silesia, and the southeastern part of the country. Production expanded in the 1960s and 1970s, then declined in the next decade. In 1989 domestic production covered 43 percent of the country's total requirement.

A major offshore oilfield was discovered in the Baltic Sea in 1985. Including that field and the older fields in the Carpathian Mountains in southeastern Poland, total oil reserves were estimated at 100 million tons in 1990. Poland remained heavily dependent on the Soviet Union for petroleum throughout the 1980s.

Large reserves of sulfur at Tarnobrzeg and Staszów in the south-central region make that material Poland's most important nonmetallic export mineral. Favorable geological conditions have supported large-scale operations in three mines yielding about 5 million tons annually. About 3 million tons of sulfuric acid, along with several other chemicals, are produced each year.

Poland has limited deposits of some nonferrous metal ores. The most significant is copper, which is extracted in large quantities at ten mines in Lower Silesia in southwestern Poland. Copper production expanded greatly after discovery of major new deposits in the 1960s and 1970s. In 1990 annual copper ore output was about 26 million tons, and 51 percent of electrolytic copper was exported. In 1982 Poland had the world's fifth-largest deposits of lead and zinc (which occur in association). The annual output of lead and zinc ores was about 5 million tons, supporting annual production of 164 thousand tons of zinc and 78,000 tons of lead. In 1990 about 76 percent of Poland's zinc and nearly all its lead were used by domestic industry.

Although Poland has some fairly large iron ore deposits, this ore requires enrichment before processing. Until the 1970s, the main source of iron ore was the district of Częstochowa; but output there declined sharply in the early 1980s, and other deposits are of poor quality or provide such small quantities that exploitation is unprofitable. The country depended on iron imports from the Soviet Union and Sweden to support the rapid expansion of the steel industry that is a high priority in the communist era.

Rich deposits of salt provide an important raw material for the chemical industry. Salt mining, which began in the Middle Ages, was concentrated in the Wieliczka-Bochnia area near Kraków until the middle of the twentieth century; then the major salt-mining operations moved to a large deposit running northwest from Łódź in central Poland. Salt is extracted in two ways: by removing it in solid form and by dissolving it underground, then pumping brine to the surface. Annual output declined from 6.2 million tons in 1987 and 1988 to 4.7 million tons in 1989. Other mineral resources include bauxite, barite, gypsum, limestone, and silver (a byproduct of processing other metals).

Agricultural Resources

Poland's climate features moderate temperatures and adequate rainfall that enable cultivation of most temperate-zone crops, including all the major grains, several industrial crops, and several varieties of fruit (see Agriculture, this ch.; Climate, ch. 2). Crops are distributed according to the substantial regional variations in soil and length of growing season (see Topography, ch. 2). The sandy soils of the central plains are most suitable for rye, the richer soil in the south favors wheat and barley, and the poorer soil of the north is used for oats. All parts of Poland favor potato cultivation; sugar beets, the most important industrial crop, grow mainly in the west and southeast.

Labor Force

At the end of 1991, about 30.7 percent of Poland's estimated population of 38.3 million lived in urban centers with populations of 100,000 or more. The priority given urbanization and industrialization in postwar Poland caused the urban working class to grow dramatically and the rural working class to shrink proportionately in the first decade of communist rule. This process slowed considerably over the next three decades (see Demography, ch. 2).

In 1989 nearly 22 million Poles were of working age: 11.3 million men between the ages of eighteen and sixty-four years and 10.6 million women between ages eighteen and fifty-nine. The population was relatively well educated. In 1988 about 1.8 million people had a postsecondary education, another 7.0 million had a secondary education, and 6.7 million had a basic trade education (see Education, ch. 2).

In 1989 the total labor force of 18.4 million included 36.8 percent employed in manufacturing, mining, and construction; 25.7 percent in agriculture, forestry, and fishing; and 7.1 percent in transport and communications. About 12 million workers, or 70 percent of the work force, worked in the state sector in 1990 (see table 12, Appendix).

The communist system was marked by major inequality of labor allocation. In spite of considerable overstaffing in both production and administrative units, labor shortages were a perennial problem in other areas of the economy. Unemployment began to grow in January 1990, partly as the result of the reform policies of the post-communist governments and partly because of the collapse of markets in the Soviet Union and the German Democratic Republic (East Germany), which were Poland's most important trading partners in Comecon. At the end of 1991, unemployment had reached 11.4 percent. Unemployment benefits, an unemployment insurance system, and some retraining were introduced in early 1990.

Wage increases in the state sector were controlled by a very steep tax on wages that exceeded prescribed levels. In the private sector, the labor market operated without such restrictions, however. Wages generally were low in the first reform years. In 1991 the average monthly wage was 2,301,200 zloty (for value of the zloty— see Glossary), not including agricultural labor and positions in education, health and social services, culture, law and order, national defense, and public administration. At that time, however, rents were low, electricity, gas, and fuels remained partly subsidized, and medical services were free (see The Welfare System, ch. 2).

In 1992 two nationwide labor unions existed. The Solidarity labor union (Solidarność) was internationally known for the decade of strikes and efforts to achieve reform that finally thrust it into a central political role in 1989. The National Coalition of Labor Unions, originally established by the communist government after the suppression of Solidarity in the early 1980s, became independent of state control in 1990 and began to compete with Solidarity for members.

The Economy under the Communist System

After World War II, a centrally planned socialist system was transplanted to Poland from the Soviet Union without any consideration for the differences in the level of development of the country, or its size, resource endowment, or cultural, social, and political traditions. The inadequacies of that system left Poland in an economic crisis in the late 1980s.

System Structure

The new system was able to mobilize resources, but it could not ensure their efficient use. High but uneven rates of growth of the net material product (NMP—see Glossary), also called "national income" in Marxist terminology, were recorded over a rather long period. However, these gains were made at the expense of large investment outlays. Lacking support from foreign capital, these outlays could be financed only by severe restriction of consumption and a very high ratio of accumulation (forced saving) in the NMP.

During the communist period, the same cycle of errors occurred in Poland as in the other state-planned economies. The political and economic system enabled planners to select any rate of accumulation and investment; but, in the absence of direct warning signals from the system, accumulation often exceeded the optimum rate. Investment often covered an excessively broad front and had an over-extended gestation period; disappointingly low growth rates resulted from diminishing capital returns and from the lowering of worker incentives by excessive regulation of wages and constriction of consumption. Planners reacted to these conditions by further increasing the rate of accumulation and the volume of investment.

Investment funds mobilized in this wasteful way then were allocated without regard to consumer preference. Planners directed money to projects expected to speed growth in the economy. Again, considerable waste resulted from overinvestment in some branches and underinvestment in others. To achieve the required labor increases outside agriculture, planners manipulated participation ratios, especially of women, and made large-scale transfers of labor from rural areas. Shortages of capital and labor became prevalent despite government efforts to maintain equitable distribution.

An example of inefficient state planning was the unpaid exchange of technical documentation and blueprints among Comecon members on the basis of the Sofia Agreement of 1949. The countries of origin had no incentive to make improvements before making plans available to other members of Comecon, even when improved technology was known to be available. For this reason, new factories often were obsolete by the time of completion. In turn, the machines and equipment these factories produced froze industry at an obsolete technological level.

The institutional framework of the centrally planned economy was able to insulate it to some extent from the impact of world economic trends. As a result, domestic industry was not exposed to foreign competition that would force improvements in efficiency or to foreign innovations that would make such improvements possible. Above all, the isolation of the system kept domestic prices totally unrelated to world prices.

Prices were determined administratively on the basis of costs plus a fixed percentage of planned profit. Because every increase in production costs was absorbed by prices, the system provided no incentive for enterprises to reduce costs. On the contrary, higher costs resulted in a higher absolute value of profit, from which the enterprise hierarchy financed its bonuses and various amenities. When the price was fixed below the level of costs, the government provided subsidies, ensuring the enterprise its planned rate of profit. Enterprises producing the same types of goods belonged to administrative groups, called associations in the 1980s. Each of these groups was supervised by one of the industrial ministries. The ministry and the association controlled and coordinated the activities of all state enterprises and defended the interests of a given industry. The enterprises belonging to a given industrial group were not allowed to compete among themselves, and the profit gained by the most efficient was transferred to finance losses incurred by the least efficient. This practice further reduced incentives to seek profits and avoid losses.

In this artificial atmosphere, prices could not be related to market demand; and without a genuine price mechanism, resources could not be allocated efficiently. Much capital was wasted on enterprises of inappropriate size, location, and technology. Furthermore, planners could not identify which enterprises contributed to national income and which actually reduced it by using up more resources than the value added by their activities. The inability to make such distinctions was particularly harmful to the selection of products for export and decisions concerning import substitution, i.e., what should be produced within the country rather than imported.

Development Strategy

In the postwar years, all East European countries including Poland adopted a fundamentally similar inward-looking development strategy following the Soviet model of accelerated industrialization and collectivization of agriculture. Planners attempted to enforce excessively high rates of growth and to achieve a relatively high degree of self-sufficiency. Strong autarkic tendencies were modified only by the shifting import requirements of the Soviet Union and by specialization agreements within Comecon; those agreements were limited, however, by their insulation from the factors of real profitability and comparative advantage.

In 1945 the Polish economy was completely disorganized and urgently needed reestablishment of its prewar industrial base. The initial central planning organization that began work in Poland in late 1945 stressed socialist rather than communist economic goals: relative decentralization, increased consumer goods production to raise the standard of living, and moderate investment in production facilities. In 1949, however, that approach was scrapped in favor of the completely centralized Soviet planning model. During the 1950s, planners followed Stalin's requirements for a higher growth rate in heavy industry than the overall industrial rate and a higher growth rate in the steel industry than that of heavy industry as a whole. This approach neglected the other economic sectors: agriculture, infrastructure, housing, services, and consumer goods. The sectors that were emphasized were all capital-, fuel-, and material-intensive. Materials shortages had developed already in the Comecon group by the 1960s. In response, Poland was required to expand its extraction of coal, copper, and sulfur, as well as its production of steel and other basic industrial materials without considering costs.

Stalinist planning also forcibly redirected foreign economic relations. Poland's extensive interwar commercial links with Western Europe were reduced, and some important prewar markets were lost as trade with the Soviet Union expanded rapidly. For Poland this trade was based mainly on export of coal and manufactured goods primarily from the rapidly growing heavy industries. In return, Poland became dependent on the supply of Soviet oil, natural gas, iron ore, and some other raw materials. This arrangement meant that Poland's industrial structure adjusted to Soviet needs and specifications, yielding many products that could be sold only to the Soviet Union or its allies. Thus exports became heavily dependent on markets in Comecon.

Development of the Centrally Planned Economy

This development strategy brought about a specific pattern of economic growth in Poland. As in the other centrally planned economies, rates of growth depended on increases in the quantity of inputs rather than on improvements in productivity. Material production remained high as long as greater quantities of inputs were available. This pattern of growth priorities and the emerging industrial structure left no possibility of raising wages significantly. Wages had been reduced during the first industrialization drive of the early 1950s. For this reason, the Polish standard of living lagged behind that of Western Europe as the continent recovered from World War II. Already in the first postwar decade, awareness of this disparity began to cause social unrest, a situation that became a tradition during the next thirty-five years.

Establishing the Planning Formula

Centralized planning ranged from broad, long-range statements of fundamental future development to guidance on the operation

A family harvesting potatoes on a private farm
Courtesy Polish Information Agency, Warsaw

of specific enterprises. The basic planning unit for transformation of the Polish economy was the five-year plan, the first of which began in 1956. Within that framework, current production goals were established in an annual operational plan, called the National Economic Plan. As the years passed, these plans contained more and more specific detail; because requirements and supplies could not be forecast in advance, plans were inconsistent and constantly needed revision.

The Soviet system had already encountered difficulties, however, in the overly ambitious Six-Year Plan of 1950–55. Maladjustments, shortages, and bottlenecks appeared in the implementation of that plan, which was intended to create the infrastructure for the industrial future: heavy industry, mining, and power generation. In 1956, after workers' riots in Poznań, a general uprising was averted only by a change in the leadership of the communist party, the Polish United Workers' Party (Polska Zjednoczona Partia Robotnicza—PZPR). The new government of Władysław Gomułka promised modification of the system and changes in the development strategy. Consumer goods received a larger share of the national product, and some quantities of grain and food were imported from the West. State control was mitigated by giving limited policy input to enterprises, and the rate of investment was reduced. Although a lively debate occurred on so-called "market socialism," actual systemic reforms were limited and short-lived. Among the reform measures of 1956, the only significant lasting change was the decollectivization of agriculture.

Retrenchment and Adjustment in the 1960s

By the early 1960s, economic directives again came only from the center, and heavy industry once more received disproportionate investment. At that point, the government began a new industrialization drive, which was again far too ambitious. Rates of investment were excessive, the number of unfinished industrial projects increased, and the time required for project completion was considerably extended. Structural distortions increased, and the rates of growth in high-priority sectors were adversely affected by the slower than expected growth in low-priority sectors. Bottlenecks and shortages increased inefficiency. By the late 1960s, the economy was clearly stagnant, consumer goods were extremely scarce, and planners sought new approaches to avoid repetition of the social upheavals of 1956. At this point, suppression of consumption to its previous levels had become politically dangerous, making a high rate of accumulation problematic at a time when demand for investment funds was growing rapidly. Because of these factors, additional investment funds were allocated to the neglected infrastructure and to the production of consumer goods.

Modernization efforts stressed technological restructuring rather than fundamental systemic reforms. However, a policy of "selective development," introduced in 1968, required another acceleration of investments at the expense of consumption. Selective development and a new system of selectively applied financial incentives ended in the worker riots of December 1970 and a second forced change in the communist leadership in Poland. Meanwhile, no funds were invested in remedying the environmental crisis already being caused by excessive reliance on "dirty" lignite in the drive for heavy industrialization.

These conditions necessitated a switch from an "extensive" growth pattern (unlimited inputs) to an "intensive" pattern of growth that would ensure high rates of growth through improvements in productivity rather than in the amount of inputs. The new emphasis helped drive another reorganization of industry in the early 1970s. State enterprises were combined into a number of huge conglomerates called Big Economic Organizations. They were expected to increase efficiency by economies of scale. Wage increases were tied to net increases in the value of outputs as an incentive to labor productivity. In practice, however, central planners could now control a smaller number of industrial units and regulate their activities more intensely. The system was never implemented fully, and no improvement in efficiency resulted. The failure of the 1973 reform demonstrated that the technological level of industrial products was still too low to permit significant increases in efficiency.

Reliance on Technology in the 1970s

In the early 1970s, East-West detente, the accumulation of petrodollars in Western banks, and a recession in the West created an opportunity for Eastern Europe to import technology and capital from the West to restructure and modernize its industrial base. Poland was relatively late in introducing this so-called "new development strategy," but it eventually went farther in this direction than its Comecon allies. The share of trade with Comecon declined, and trade with other countries increased quite dramatically during the first half of the 1970s.

The technology import strategy was based on the assumption that, with the help of Western loans, a large-scale influx of advanced equipment, licenses, and other forms of technology transfer would automatically result in efficient production of modern, high-quality manufactured goods suitable for export to the West. Under those conditions, repayment of debts would not be difficult. Expansion of exports encountered considerable difficulties, however, partly because of the oil crisis and stagflation in the West, but mainly because the central planners remained unable to effect the required changes in the structure of production. The investment drive, financed by foreign borrowing, exceeded the possibilities of the economy. Removed from direct contact with the foreign markets, centralized selection of exportables was ineffective in expanding the markets for Polish goods. At the same time, the dependence of the economy on imported Western materials, components, and machines inevitably increased. By the middle of the 1970s, large trade deficits had been incurred with the Western countries. The negative balance of payments in convertible currencies increased from US$100 million in 1970 to US$3 billion in 1975. During the same period, the gross convertible currency debt increased from US$1.2 billion to US$8.4 billion. Unable to expand exports to the West at the necessary pace, Polish planners began centralized restriction of imports. This policy in turn had an adverse effect on domestic production, including the production of exportables.

Reform Failure in the 1980s

By 1980 it had become clear that the large-scale import of capital and technology from the West could not substitute for economic reform. On the contrary, systemic reforms were needed to ensure satisfactory absorption and diffusion of imported technology. Significant expansion of profitable exports to the world markets was impossible for an inflexible and overly centralized economic system. On the other hand, without an increase in exports, reducing or even servicing Poland's rapidly increasing international debt was extremely difficult.

Meanwhile, the enormous investment drive of the early 1970s had destabilized the economy and developed strong inflationary pressure. Rates of NMP growth dropped throughout the second half of the decade, and the first absolute decline took place in 1979. Although planners should have been adjusting the level of aggregate demand to the declining aggregate supply, they found this task politically and administratively difficult. The authorities also feared major price revisions, especially after workers' riots forced withdrawal of a revision introduced in 1976. In the late 1970s, some prices were increased gradually whereas other increases were concealed by designating them for new, higher quality, or luxury items. The rest of the inflationary gap was suppressed by fixing prices administratively.

By the late 1970s, the shortage of consumer goods was acute. Nominal income increases continued as a "money illusion" to minimize social discontent and provide a work incentive. This strategy increased the "inflationary overhang," the accumulated and unusable purchasing power in the hands of the population. At the same time, suppressed inflation spurred maladjustments and inequities in the production processes, further reducing the supply of goods. The deteriorating situation in the consumer goods market resulted in a series of watershed events: a wave of strikes that led to the formation of the Solidarity union in August 1980, a third enforced change in the communist leadership in September 1980, and the imposition of martial law in December 1981.

Between 1978 and 1982, the NMP of Poland declined by 24 percent, and industrial production declined by 13.4 percent. The decline in production was followed by prolonged stagnation. Recognizing a strong grass-roots resistance to the existing system, the new government of Stanisław Kania, who had replaced Edward Gierek, established the Commission for Economic Reform in late 1980. This body presented a weakened version of drastic reforms recommended by the independent Polish Economic Society, an advisory board of economists formed earlier in 1980. Implemented hastily in mid-1981, the reforms nominally removed the PZPR from day-to-day economic management and gave the enterprises responsibility for their own financial condition and for planning. These decentralizing reforms were distorted by the constraints of martial law that had been imposed nationally in December 1981, however, and they failed to improve the economic situation (see The Jaruzelski Interlude, ch. 1). Internally inconsistent and insufficiently far-reaching, the reforms reduced central administrative control without establishing any of the fundamentals of an alternative market system. Thus, in effect, the economy operated from 1981 to 1989 in a systemic vacuum.

After 1985 the foreign trade situation further complicated Poland's economic crisis. The relative importance of Comecon trade declined yearly, necessitating expanded trade with the West, particularly the European Community (EC—see Glossary). This shift was a policy change for which neither the communist regime nor the economic system was prepared in the late 1980s.

After the Fall of the Communist System

In 1989 the NMP declined by 0.2 percent to a level 1 percent below the 1978 figure, and industrial production also declined slightly. Despite price controls, inflation increased from 25.3 percent in 1987 to 343.8 percent in 1989. As the scarcity of goods rose sharply, lines in front of stores lengthened and social unrest grew.

Shortages of materials and fuels, unreliable supply, and administrative disarray caused frequent shutdowns of industrial production lines.

Disequilibrium also increased rapidly in the external economy. The balance of payments deficit in hard currency (denominations exchanged on the world market) increased from US$392 million in 1987 to US$1,922 million in 1989, and the national debt grew from US$39.2 billion to US$40.8 billion during that period. In the last years of communist rule, hard-currency deficits were exacerbated by the priority still given to economic relations within Comecon. In its Comecon transactions between 1987 and 1989, Poland converted a current account deficit of 424 million transferable rubles (the artificial currency used in Comecon transactions but unrecognized outside the trading bloc) to a positive balance of 1,104 million transferable rubles as its ruble debt declined from 5.8 billion to 0.6 billion (see table 13; table 14, Appendix). These transactions meant that Poland was ignoring the catastrophic condition of its domestic economy to help alleviate the general shortages within Comecon by supporting a net outflow of capital (more exports than imports), most of which went to the Soviet Union.

In 1989 new policies in the Soviet Union made clear that Soviet retaliation against liberalization in Poland was no longer a real possibility. Under a new set of international conditions, the long history of riots and strikes by workers and students, criticism by the intellectual classes, and general lack of cooperation by society with the economic programs of successive communist governments ended in the collapse of the communist regime of Wojciech Jaruzelski in May 1989. The proximate cause of its fall, however, was deepening economic crisis. Although the crisis was a very effective political weapon for Polish noncommunist parties, the underlying structural defects of the national economy became a legacy of persistently intractable problems for the noncommunist governments that followed Jaruzelski.

Marketization and Stabilization

The first noncommunist government in Eastern Europe was formed in Poland by Tadeusz Mazowiecki after Solidarity won an overwhelming victory in the parliamentary election of June 1989. The government came to office on September 12 and within one month announced an ambitious program of economic reforms. The objective was not to improve the socialist system, as had been the case in previous reforms, but to accomplish a rapid and complete transformation from the Soviet-type economy into a capitalist system and to reintegrate the Polish economy into the world economy.

Under the best of circumstances, accomplishing such a transformation would be an enormous task. But, like other Comecon countries, Poland had an inefficient industrial structure that was fuel- and material-intensive and a foreign trade mechanism incompatible with expansion of exports to the West. The inherited system did not support greater supply of consumer goods, nor was it any longer appropriate for trade with Poland's Comecon partners, all of which were now restructuring their economies according to national requirements and resources. Without fundamental restructuring, the economy faced further declines in production, high unemployment, and strong inflationary pressure. Therefore, the first postcommunist Polish governments pursued economic reform with great urgency, although they had limited success.

Required Short-Term Changes

Modernization was a fundamental requirement. Because a considerable part of Poland's capital stock was obsolete or in poor condition, a very large share of the country's industrial products was of poor quality. The system lacked a well-developed modern infrastructure, particularly in financial institutions, transportation and telecommunications, and housing (see Transportation and Communications, this ch.; Housing, ch. 2). Without major improvement of infrastructure, the economy's overall efficiency could not be raised significantly. Reform was further hampered by a shortage of well-trained managers and enterprise staff who understood the workings of the modern free-enterprise economy and could function efficiently in such a system. Expenditures necessary to meet these needs were restricted or delayed, however, by simultaneous requirements to reduce inflation and the balance of payments disequilibrium.

The Shock Strategy

The gravity of the economic crisis and the immediate threat of hyperinflation caused the Mazowiecki government to choose a "shock strategy." Called the Balcerowicz Plan after its chief architect, Minister of Finance Leszek Balcerowicz, the program received approval and financial support from the International Monetary Fund (IMF—see Glossary). On January 1, 1990, a program for marketization was introduced together with harsh stabilization measures, a restructuring program, and a social program to protect the poorest members of the society. The program included liberalizing controls on almost all prices, eliminating most subsidies, and abolishing administrative allocation of resources in favor of trade, free establishment of private businesses, liberalization of the system of international economic relations, and introduction of internal currency convertibility with a currency devaluation of 32 percent.

At the same time, a very strict income policy was introduced. Although prices were allowed to rise suddenly to equalize supply and demand, nominal wage increases were limited to a fraction of the overall price increase of the previous month. Very heavy tax penalties were imposed on state enterprises whose wages exceeded these ceilings. This policy reduced real incomes and the real value of accumulated balances that, combined with inadequate supplies of goods and services, had caused prolonged inflationary pressure. Together with the lifting of restrictions on private economic activity, import policy reform and internal convertibility, the wage-and-price policy reestablished market equilibrium.

Initial Results

Within one month, stores were well stocked, and the long lines in front of them had disappeared. Individual budgets rather than the availability of goods became the primary determinant of buying patterns. A large number of street vendors appeared, contributing to the supply of consumer goods and competing with established stores. This new type of enterprise often was the starting point for launching more established business units.

Besides income policy, the new government used highly restrictive monetary and fiscal policies to reduce aggregate demand. The reorganized central bank drastically limited the quantity of money by imposing a positive real rate of interest, introducing and subsequently increasing obligatory reserve ratios for the commercial banks, and imposing caps on credits (see Banking and Finance, this ch.). The budgetary deficit in 1989 had been equal to 11 percent of expenditures. In 1990 this deficit was converted into a surplus of 1.3 percent of expenditures. The surplus then began to decline, however, in the second half of the year, and by the spring of 1991 negative economic factors had again created a large deficit. The government eliminated most enterprise subsidies from its budget and introduced specific tax reductions to force state enterprises to depend on their revenues. In the many cases where the government action threatened their operations, state enterprises gained time by developing a system of interenterprise credits, selling some extra equipment and materials, and obtaining extensions for the payment of taxes and debts.

Long-Term Requirements

These rapidly introduced short-term policies quickly and

Wine caves, traditional part of local economy and culture in Tatra Mountains
Courtesy Sam and Sarah Stulberg

fundamentally changed the workings of the Polish economy. Establishment of a full market system has other requirements, however, that take more time and are more problematic. The new Polish economy required a reorganized legal and institutional framework. Financial institutions, capital and labor markets, the taxation system, and contract laws required revision. Establishing systems for protection of consumers and of the environment was another priority. For these institutional changes, legislation had to be prepared, considered, and enacted by the government; then key personnel had to be trained to gradually bring the system to full efficiency. Because many flaws in new legislation or regulations were only detectable after implementation, policy making took on an unstable, trial-and-error quality. Reform and stabilization measures did not meet expectations, and the country's economic situation deteriorated in 1990–91.

Macroeconomic Indicators for 1990–91

Postcommunist economic reform initially brought both positive and negative results in the key areas of prices, productivity, inflation, and wages (see table 15, Appendix). In general, early indicators showed that the adjustment to a market economy would require more time and greater social discomfort than was anticipated in 1989.

133

Price Increases

Sudden liberalization of prices brought an average price increase of 79.6 percent in the program's first month. The high prices were intended to eliminate some major distortions in pricing and begin to adjust demand to the existing limited supply. Price liberalization stopped hyperinflation but, unexpectedly, inflation remained high.

Annual price increases were 250 percent in 1990 and 70.3 percent in 1991. Except for the first quarter, however, average quarterly price increases in 1990 were considerably smaller than the equivalent increases in 1989, when the administrative system of price determination and controls still dominated. The average quarterly price increases were lower in 1991 than in 1990.

Impact on Productivity and Wages

Experts predicted that the highly restrictive stabilization policy would suppress production, but the extent of the decline exceeded all projections. Industrial output declined by 24 percent in 1990 and by another 12 percent in 1991. In 1990 all branches of industry registered a substantial decline. In 1991 only the food industry showed a modest increase in output. In agriculture the situation was somewhat better. Gross agricultural production declined by 2.2 percent in 1990 and by 2.4 percent in 1991. In both years, however, the grain harvest was a very robust 28 million tons.

Gross domestic product (GDP—see Glossary) declined by 12 percent in 1990 and by 8 percent in 1991. Gross fixed investment, after declining by 2.4 percent in 1989, decreased by 10.6 percent in 1990 and by 7.5 percent in 1991. Consumption declined by 11.7 percent in 1990 but increased by 3.7 percent in 1991. The decline in investment meant that no significant modernization and restructuring could take place, which in turn jeopardized future growth. The number of unemployed people reached 1.1 million, or 6.1 percent of the labor force, at the end of 1990 and 2.2 million people, or 11.4 percent, at the end of 1991 (see table 16, Appendix).

Real personal incomes decreased by 22.3 percent in 1990, but they increased by 12.7 percent in January–September 1991. Real wages, excluding agriculture and jobs financed directly from the state budget, declined by 29.2 percent in 1990 and increased by 2.0 percent in 1991. The average real value of pensions decreased by 14 percent in 1990, then increased by 15 percent in 1991.

Statistical Distortions

Comparative statistics for this period, which generally caused overstatement of the 1990 decline, must be understood in their context. Two factors contributed to this faulty estimate. First, 1989 figures provided the basis for evaluating the economy's 1990 performance. Traditionally, output statistics in centrally planned economies were inflated to show success in every case. Also, the 1989 figures did not reflect the low-quality, unprofitable goods produced by subsidized state enterprises. Unprofitable production was shown as a statistical increase in NMP even as it reduced national income in the real world. Furthermore, until 1989 personal income and real wage calculations used the artificial official price index, so they were not a true measure of consumer purchasing power.

On the other hand, official statistics for 1990 and 1991 reflected a downward bias. Revenues and incomes deliberately were underestimated in order to avoid higher taxes. Because of these distortions, decentralized economic activity in the state sector and rapid growth in the private sector clearly required new methods of collecting and presenting statistics. In 1992, however, the Central Statistical Office in Poland had not yet removed the distortions of the previous system from its statistical formats. Unemployment statistics also failed to keep pace with the actual economic situation. The rapid expansion of private enterprise in 1990 provided jobs for many people who had registered for benefits established at the beginning of the reform period. Meanwhile, legislation was slow to reform the accounting system. Even after statistical adjustment, however, the first three years of economic reform brought Poland genuine, deep decline in industrial production, in GDP, and in real personal incomes and wages.

Agricultural Imbalances

A serious political problem developed in the agricultural sector during this period. Reduced domestic demand for food, the loss of Comecon markets, a rapid increase in imports, and relatively good harvests led to oversupply of agricultural products. Agricultural prices lagged behind the prices of goods and services purchased by Polish farmers. As a result, incomes fell farther than incomes in other sectors in 1990 and 1991. This situation made farmers one of the most dissatisfied groups in Poland; although traditionally not politically active, farmers demonstrated en masse to improve their situation. In 1992 they demanded that government policy include higher tariffs, guaranteed minimum prices, and cheap credits to protect them from economic hardship.

Causes of Decline

No single factor was responsible for Poland's large-scale decline in production and incomes in 1990 and 1991. The very restrictive stabilization policy caused some of the decline in economic indicators as well as increased unemployment. But when some fiscal and monetary restrictions were eased and real incomes increased late in 1990, inflation again increased. A similar succession of events in 1991 indicated that under prevailing conditions any increase in aggregate demand would lead to an increase in prices (hence inflation) rather than to an increase in output that would match the demand generated by higher wages.

An important reason for the unresponsiveness of supply was the inherited industrial structure, especially the poor condition of capital stock and shortages of various components and materials only available on the import market. But other factors also played a role. In many cases, enterprise managers failed to make responses and decisions appropriate to reform goals. The reform of 1981 had called for election of most managers by the workers' councils of their enterprises. Under the communist system, the political leverage of this relationship meant that managers sought to satisfy the councils by raising wages and avoiding layoffs through whatever strategy was available. Beginning in January 1990, however, the enterprises suddenly found themselves in a buyer's market instead of the traditional seller's market. Substantial and rapid adjustments within the enterprises were needed to cope with a decline in the domestic demand caused by a drastic reduction in personal incomes, cuts in government expenditures, and rapidly increasing imports. At the same time, the sudden elimination of the formerly secure Comecon markets, especially those in the Soviet Union and East Germany, made establishment of new markets in the West a condition of survival for many enterprises.

Few managers were prepared by training or experience to deal with this new requirement. No consulting or foreign trade brokerage firms were available to provide assistance, and the banking system that succeeded the old structure under the National Bank of Poland (Narodowy Bank Polski—NBP) had no experience in this respect. Although the elimination of price distortions and the introduction of an economically meaningful rate of exchange finally made profit and loss projections meaningful, the system of internal accounting within the enterprises still required considerable adjustment in 1992. At that point, however, major changes in the product mix and improvements in quality were unlikely because anti-inflationary macroeconomic policy had caused a scarcity of investment funds for modernization and restructuring.

Another inhibiting factor was the persistent concentration of the postcommunist Polish industrial structure, which in 1992 was still dominated by huge state-owned enterprises. In many cases, one enterprise monopolized an entire group of products. Antimonopoly legislation and an antimonopoly office established in 1990 had limited effect in the early postcommunist years. Some large enterprises were split, and some monopolistic practices were stopped. Rapidly increasing imports provided new competition, but imports also reduced the market for domestic products and created an adverse trade balance despite a surprisingly strong performance by Polish hard-currency exports.

Closing bankrupt or unprofitable state- or municipally owned enterprises proved especially difficult when the livelihood of entire communities or regions was based on one or two such plants. Powerful workers' councils lobbied for continuation of the status quo. In 1992 thousands of bankrupt state enterprises survived on loans from other enterprises or from banks, which were not capable of enforcing repayment under the financial conditions of the time.

The External Balance of the Economy

The collapse of Comecon put all former member countries in a state of economic crisis by completely changing the terms of trade among them. Those disturbances seriously damaged the Polish economy. Polish imports from the Comecon partners declined by 34 percent in 1990 and by 45 percent in the first three quarters of 1991, whereas exports declined by 13 percent and 44 percent during the same periods.

Beginning January 1, 1991, the former Comecon countries ceased using transferable rubles in most trade among themselves. In 1991 imports paid for in rubles declined by 83.0 percent, and ruble exports declined by 84.9 percent. At the end of the year, this category accounted for only 14.4 percent of Poland's overall imports and 9.8 percent of its overall exports. Only five years earlier, these proportions were 51.9 and 46.1 percent, respectively.

Particularly influential was the collapse of the Soviet Union's economic and geopolitical structure, an event that undermined that country's international commitments. Drastic declines in imports from the republics of the former Soviet Union rapidly eroded Poland's supply of fuels and raw materials critically needed for production. At the same time, Polish exports to the Soviet republics also declined dramatically. In the general chaos of economic restructuring, potential importers in Russia, Belarus, Ukraine, and other republics could pay in foreign currencies in amounts only up to 18 percent of their own trade earnings, and barter transactions were prohibited by their governments. Under these conditions, the overall share of Comecon partners and the former Soviet Union in Polish trade fell precipitously in 1990 and again in 1991.

Polish enterprises that traditionally had supplied the Soviet market suffered particularly strong losses as the Comecon system shattered. Before 1990 about 300 Polish enterprises exported a large proportion of their output to the Soviet Union, and more than thirty of them produced exclusively for the Soviet market. Producers of metalworking machinery, light airplanes, construction equipment, electronics, medical equipment, ships, textiles, clothing, and pharmaceuticals found themselves with little opportunity to adapt their product mix or shift exports to new markets before most or all of their traditional market was lost (see Foreign Trade, this ch.).

Especially in light industries, entire enterprises became idle and contributed heavily to Poland's unemployment problem. Particularly hard hit was Łódź, the main textile center and second largest city. Łódź experienced 16.3 percent unemployment in 1991, the third highest figure in the country. The metallurgical industry experienced the second biggest export decline in 1990. Ironically, this industry had received the largest share of investments in the 1970s drive for new technology. In 1990 declining demand led to worker layoffs at the giant Katowice Steel Mill and other centers.

The Privatization Process

Transformation of more fundamental aspects of the economy have proceeded much more slowly than did the reforms undertaken in 1990 and 1991. The most important feature of the longer-term transformation is the privatization of the means of production. The end of the communist system brought an immediate and dynamic growth in new privately owned businesses, most of which were small retailing, trade, and construction enterprises. In 1990 about 516,000 new businesses were established, while 154,000 were liquidated, a net increase of 362,000. Another 100,000 small businesses formerly owned by local government agencies were sold to private investors in the initial rush to privatization. By September 1991, an additional 1.4 million one-person businesses and 41,450 new companies had been registered since the beginning of the year. Overall, in 1990 and 1991 about 80 percent of Polish shops went into private hands, and over 40 percent of imports went through private traders.

Legal and administrative preparations for privatization of state-owned enterprises took much longer than expected. The "small privatization" of shops, restaurants, and other service establishments was a relatively simple process, but privatization of large enterprises proved much more difficult. By October 1991, some 227 larger enterprises had been converted into stock exchange-listed companies, and twenty of them had been privatized by offering them for public or private sale. Some of these transactions involved foreign capital. To speed the process, the government of Prime Minister Jan Bielecki, which came to power in late 1990, had made capital vouchers available without charge to all adult citizens. The vouchers were to be exchangeable for shares in mutual investment funds. At first these funds were to be managed under contract with foreign and domestic management firms. Voucher holders would be allocated 27 percent of shares of the enterprises selected for "mass privatization" and would be able to purchase any 33 percent share of the privatized enterprises sold by auction. Because of their configuration, the vouchers were expected to give their holders effective control of these enterprises. Various technical problems delayed implementation of this program, as did the change of government at the beginning of 1992. At that point, vouchers for fewer than ten major enterprises were being traded.

Already in 1990, the private sector had emerged as the most dynamic part of the economy. The economy's overall GDP declined in 1990 by 12 percent, but it increased by 17 percent in the private sector. Total industrial production dropped by 23 percent, but the private sector production increased by 8 percent. At the end of 1991, the private sector provided about 38 percent of employment; it was responsible for 22.1 percent of total industrial production, 43.9 percent of construction output, 70 percent of retail sales, and 16.3 percent of transportation services. Surprising growth occurred in private foreign trade activity, which accounted for 28 percent of foreign transactions in the first three quarters of 1991.

By early 1992, some form of privatization had occurred in 17.4 percent of state enterprises. At that point, plans called for conversion of half of Poland's state enterprises to private ownership by 1995. The rate of privatization had already slowed in 1992, however, partly because of reduced government outlays and continual alteration of program goals. Enterprises were restructured in several ways: medium-sized firms typically were liquidated, and large enterprises were transformed into stock companies and limited liability companies.

Economic Policy Making in the 1990s

The presidential election at the end of 1990 and the completely free parliamentary election one year later revealed widespread dissatisfaction among the population about the hardships caused by the process of transformation, but not about its main direction.

Campaigning politicians criticized the stabilization policy severely and promised a better alternative to the approach taken by Finance Minister Leszek Balcerowicz. Election results, however, showed continued strong support for privatization and wide acceptance of the principles of the stabilization program. The government of Prime Minister Jan Olszewski came to office in December 1991 promising to ease the burden the austerity program had imposed on society. A particularly thorny political issue was the threat that the communist-installed system of social services such as health care and pensions, to which Poles had become accustomed, would go unfunded at reformed government spending levels. Olszewski's proposals of higher spending were rejected by the Sejm (the lower chamber of the parliament), however, on the grounds that such spending would cause an excessive budgetary deficit whose effects would overshadow any revival of economic activity. Shortly thereafter the IMF warned that a proposed return to agricultural subsidies and price supports would increase the deficit and jeopardize the financial aid package of US$2.5 billion that the IMF had offered on condition of economic reform. IMF disapproval of the budget would also have ended aid in reduction of the national debt (over half of which was to be forgiven by terms of a 1991 agreement) and cut off foreign credits.

Because foreign funding was considered necessary to counteract capital flight from Poland and finance the national deficit while encouraging private enterprise, the government revised its budget proposal. Its new austerity budget, containing a deficit of only 5 percent of GDP, was approved by parliament in early 1992, and the IMF expressed approval as well. On a visit to the United States in spring 1992, Olszewski reassured the United States government, the IMF, and the World Bank (see Glossary) that his government remained determined to transform and stabilize the Polish economy.

Whatever the form of the coalition government, in 1992 effective political leadership was the most important requirement in dealing with the more intractable aspects of economic reform and balancing negative short-term effects with the long-term goals upon which most of Polish society still agreed. The Olszewski government did not pursue vigorously the expansion of its coalition or full-speed economic reform. Olszewski's fall provided an opportunity for Hanna Suchocka, his successor, to reinvigorate the reform program in the second half of 1992.

Structure of the Economy

Although Poland possessed abundant supplies of some natural resources, the structure and administration of the centrally planned

Coal vendor on a Kraków street
Courtesy Sam and Sarah Stulberg

Coal miner in the
Andaluzja Mine, Silesia
Courtesy Polish Information
Agency, Warsaw

system had long caused misallocation of those resources and of investment funds among the economic sectors. In addition, the cutoff of critical industrial inputs from the Soviet Union required major restructuring and rebalancing of all sectors.

Fuels and Energy

Poland's fuel and energy profile is dominated by coal, the only fuel in abundant domestic supply. Because of lopsided and uneconomical dependence on this single fuel, the fuels and energy sector of the economy was a primary target for reorganization and streamlining in the early 1990s. In 1989 production of coke and extraction and refining of gas and oil accounted for 4.9 percent of Poland's total industrial base. Electric power generation accounted for 2.9 percent. However, these statistics were downward biased by the very low, heavily subsidized prices of the products of those industries. Higher, market-established prices of fuels and electricity were expected to induce more economical fuel consumption, as were modern fuel-saving technologies in industry, construction, and transportation and gradual elimination of the most heavily fuel-intensive industries. By 1991 official policy had recognized that making such changes was less expensive than continuing the cycle of higher energy demand and production characteristic of the centrally planned economy.

Coal

In 1992 coal continued to play a central role in the Polish economy, both in support of domestic industry and as an export commodity. In 1990 about 90 percent of the country's energy production was based on hard coal and lignite. The two largest mines extracted over six million tons each in 1991, but the average mine produced between one million and three million tons. Compared with coal mines in Western Europe, Polish mining was quite inefficient because of isolation from technical advances made in the 1980s and, more recently, lack of investment funds for modernization.

Because the communist regimes ignored profitability in establishing quantitative output targets, coal output was expanded irrespective of costs, and inefficient mines were heavily subsidized. At the same time, the extensive type of mineral exploitation called for by central planning caused a very high ratio of waste (about 24 percent of output) as well as heavy environmental damage. Under the new planning system, a lower annual output is expected, but production operations are to be justified by profitability.

At the end of the 1980s, some eighty-four shaft mines and four large open-cast lignite mines were in operation. Plans for the 1990s call for closing many of those mines. In 1991 annual coal output declined from the 193 million tons mined in 1988 to 140 million tons, and output was expected to remain at the lower level in 1992. During the same period, extraction of lignite declined from 73 million tons to 69 million, with 70 million tons the maximum annual output expected for the next few years. In 1989 about 16 percent of Poland's coal and 19 percent of its coke were exported. In 1990 these shares increased to 19 percent and 26.6 percent, respectively, because a recession reduced domestic demand for coal.

The postcommunist governments abolished centralized allocation of coal and partially liberalized prices. By 1992 a relatively free coal market had been created, and subsidies were gradually reduced. This process also abolished the central administrations for coal mining and for electricity generation that had ensured state monopoly of those industries and perpetuated wasteful resource management. The reform program made both coal mines and power generation plants autonomous state enterprises fully competitive among themselves. To offset the loss of subsidies, price increases of as much as 13 percent were contemplated, although the planned rise of 5 percent had already aroused strong objections from industrial customers. The 1991 economic restructuring program of the Bielecki government envisaged establishment of ten independent and competing coal-mining companies, several wholesalers, and one export agency. Following the World Bank's advice, a holding company for lignite mines was also considered.

By the end of 1991, however, the Polish coal industry was in serious economic trouble. Fifty-six of sixty-seven mines ended 1991 showing losses, and only seven showed profits sufficient to cover all obligations. In 1991 government subsidies dropped from their 1990 total of 9.1 billion zloty to 5.9 billion zloty, but individual mines still received as much as 2.2 billion. Liquidation, already accomplished at six mines by 1992, cost between 0.6 and 1.5 billion zloty per mine, not counting the economic cost of added unemployment (coal mining in Poland is much more labor intensive than in the West). An alternative solution, combining individual mines into complexes, had been attempted in the 1970s efficiency campaign but did not have the expected impact. In mid-1992, mines and power plants had large coal surpluses that seemingly could not be alleviated by domestic consumption. At that point, the disparity between low domestic demand and continuing supply threatened to raise unemployment by forcing more mines to close.

Oil and Gas

After rising sharply in the early 1970s, domestic oil production dropped and remained at about 350,000 tons per year into the 1980s because no new deposits were discovered. Domestic oil had never accounted for more than 5 percent of total consumption, but even this figure had dropped sharply by 1980. Under these circumstances, the Soviet Union supplied between 80 percent and 100 percent of Poland's imported oil, with some purchases from the Middle East when market conditions permitted. Poland received Soviet oil through the Druzhba Pipeline, which remained the chief source of imported oil in early 1992. The line supplied the major refinery at Płock. Oil arriving by ship from other sources was processed at a refinery near Gdańsk (see fig. 14). In 1992, however, the pattern of Polish oil imports changed markedly. Because the Druzhba Pipeline was considered subject to political pressure and delivery taxes by the countries through which it passed, and because Russian crude oil was high in environmentally undesirable sulfur, Poland cut imports from that source from 63 percent in 1991 to 36 percent in 1992. The gap was to be filled by North Sea (British and Norwegian) oil imports, which rose from 19.5 to 26 percent in 1991, and by the Organization of the Petroleum Exporting Countries (OPEC) imports, which rose from 17.5 to 38 percent in 1992. To accommodate more North Sea oil, the transloading capacity of the North Harbor facility at Gdańsk was doubled in 1992.

Domestic natural gas provided a much higher percentage of national consumption than did domestic oil. Although pipeline imports of gas from the Soviet Union rose sharply in the 1970s and early 1980s, reaching 5.3 billion cubic meters in 1981, domestic output remained slightly ahead of that figure. Domestic natural gas exploration was pursued vigorously in the 1980s, but equipment shortages hampered the effort. By 1991, however, Polish experts declared the country potentially self-sufficient in natural gas; in 1990 and 1991, large-scale agreements with United States firms brought about new exploration in Silesia and made possible extraction of gas from Poland's many intact coal seams. New domestic gas sources opened the prospect of reducing reliance on coal and saving the hard currency spent on the 7 billion cubic meters of gas imported (mostly from the former Soviet Union) in 1991. No natural gas was imported from the West in 1991, nor did plans for 1992 call for such imports. At the end of 1991, a new agreement with Russia maintained both oil and gas deliveries from that country at approximately their previous levels. (Some 5 million tons of oil were delivered from Russia in 1991.) At the same time, plans called for linkage of Polish and German gas lines as early as 1993, making Poland's gas supply more flexible.

Power Generation

In 1989 the electric power generation industry comprised seventy enterprises. Between 1980 and 1991, the industry's power production increased from 122 billion kilowatt hours to 135 billion kilowatt hours. By 1990 a large proportion of obsolete or aging generation machines and equipment required replacement. Modernization was especially critical to achieve efficient utilization of fuels and to reduce transmission losses through the national power grid. A wide range of technical improvements and higher energy prices were expected to reduce losses and waste in 1992, making possible a subsequent reduction in annual power generation to 128 billion kilowatt hours. Estimates of energy price increases necessary to achieve conservation ranged as high as five times the subsidized levels of the late 1980s. Meanwhile, obstacles to energy conservation included the lack of meters to measure consumption, widespread use of central heating without charges proportional to consumption, and the high cost of new generating equipment, such as boilers, needed to upgrade generation efficiency.

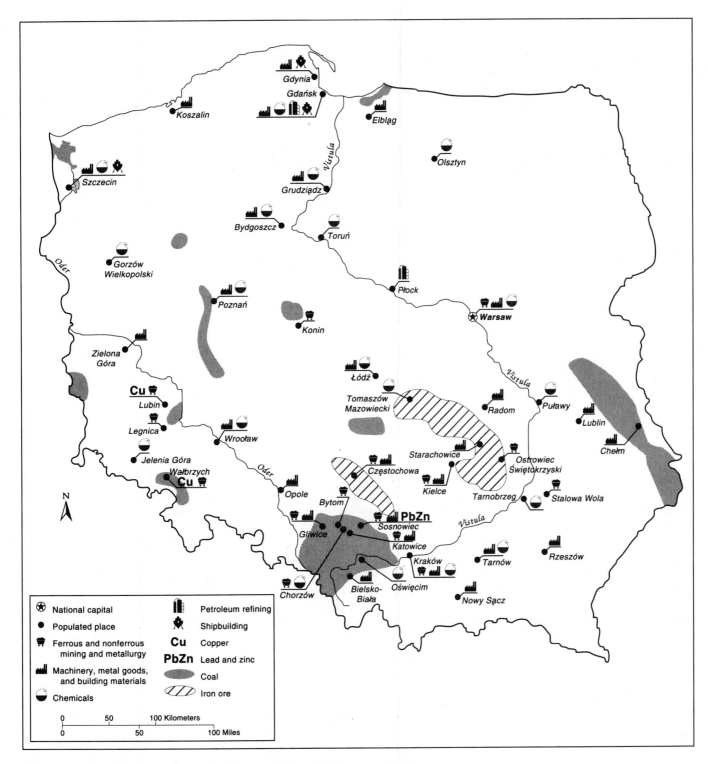

Figure 14. Distribution of Heavy Industry and Mineral Resources, 1990

During the communist period, hydroelectric power stations were not expanded because of the easy availability of the lignite burned in conventional thermoelectric plants. All hydroelectric stations existing in 1992 were built before World War II. Plans in the 1980s called for construction of three nuclear power stations. The first, at Żarnowiec in south-central Poland, was scheduled to open in 1991 and be at full production in 1993. After long years of construction and controversy, however, doubts about the safety of the station's Soviet-made equipment (similar to that used at Chernobyl') caused the first postcommunist government to abandon the project. Some 86 percent of participants in a 1990 referendum voted against completion. A second station had been started near Klempicz in west-central Poland, but work on it was stopped in 1989. The third station never passed the planning stage, and in 1992 Poland remained without any nuclear power capacity. It had, however, joined its Comecon partners in investing in large nuclear stations in Ukraine, from which Poland received power in the 1980s.

The World Bank's advice on restructuring Poland's power industry included reorganization into four or five companies with seventeen regional subsidiaries responsible for power distribution. All these companies initially would be state owned but eventually would be privatized.

Extractive and Manufacturing Industries

The range of products manufactured in Polish plants increased greatly in the postwar years, mostly through construction of new facilities in the period of accelerated industrialization. By the 1980s, heavy industry produced processed metals (mainly iron, steel, zinc, lead, and copper) and derivative products; chemicals; a wide variety of transportation equipment, including ships and motor vehicles; electrical and nonelectrical machines and equipment; and electronic and computer equipment. The most important light industry was textiles.

Under the central planning system, statistics on production by individual industries and on their relative shares in total industrial production through the communist period were distorted by administrative price fixing and unequal distribution of industrial subsidies (see table 17, Appendix). In general, however, between 1960 and 1989 the relative importance of food processing declined steadily while that of the engineering and chemical industries grew steadily. The share of light industry declined early in the period but then increased under the stimulus of expanded Soviet export markets. The relative importance of the metallurgical, mineral, and wood and paper industries remained basically unchanged. Within the engineering group, the machine building, transport equipment, and electrotechnical and electronic industries increased in relative importance between 1960 and 1989.

The engineering and chemical industries received a considerable injection of Western technology, including patents and licenses, under the technology import program of the 1970s (see Reliance on Technology in the 1970s, this ch.). In the late 1980s and early 1990s, however, economic crisis, recession, and postcommunist reform measures brought a drastic decline in output in those industries. For example, output of the artificial fertilizer industry dropped 32 percent between 1989 and 1990, mostly because rising fertilizer prices reduced domestic demand. A sharper drop was prevented by quadrupling fertilizer exports. In 1991 output of nitrogenous fertilizers remained stable, but output of phosphoric fertilizers again dropped sharply.

Some existing manufacturing facilities could support expansion of production, but others required modernization before they could be exploited efficiently to meet Poland's new economic priorities. Other facilities offered no possibility of expansion or modernization and were simply closed. In the Polish steel industry, which was second only to that of the Soviet Union in Comecon, only two plants had been built between 1945 and 1982. The Lenin Iron and Steel Plant at Nowa Huta, the largest in the country, was built near Kielce in 1954 with aid from the Soviet Union. Although some plants were modernized in the intervening years, most of the prewar Polish steel plants featured low productivity, low-quality metal, and poor working conditions, as well as very high pollution levels.

With the help of foreign experts, the Bielecki government undertook a number of sectoral studies. The objective was to draw attention to the existing obstacles to growth and to increase international competitiveness of industrial enterprises in various sectors. Four major restructuring programs were prepared in cooperation with United Nations experts. They included improving the management and modernization of the agricultural machinery industry, restructuring the production of fertilizers, improving management and technology in the pharmaceutical industry, and increasing the degree of automation in various branches of industry.

Light Industry

On behalf of the World Bank, United States experts assessed Polish light industry in early 1991. They found the critical difference between Polish and West European manufacturing systems to be computerization; the high degree of computerization utilized

Hungarian beer produced at the Okocim Brewery
Courtesy Polish Information Agency, Warsaw

by the latter systems enabled them to use short production series and make quick design changes. In textiles, Polish machinery was geared to produce intermediate-quality yarn that could not be made into exportable products. Polish finishing machinery was also outmoded. Although textile enterprises had been privatized quite early, they nevertheless remained too labor-intensive and used materials inefficiently, according to the report. On the other hand, Polish combed woolens and linen products were rated as potentially competitive in the European market.

Automotive Industry

In 1992 the Polish automotive industry was expecting to modernize through a series of joint ventures with Western firms. In 1992 Fiat Corporation, the pioneer of Western automobile production in Eastern Europe since 1973, invested in Polish production of a new model at its Bielsko-Biała plant. Fiat was to arrange for export of a large part of the output of that model. Also in 1992, General Motors Europe, the European branch of the United States automotive giant, was expected to begin assembling cars in Warsaw by agreement with the Warsaw-based Passenger Car Plant. Volvo of Sweden planned to produce buses, trucks, and tractors

149

at a plant near Wrocław following the signing of a joint venture agreement in early 1992.

Construction Machinery

The construction machinery industry, which expanded during the 1970s on the basis of Western licenses, traditionally exported a large proportion of its output to the Soviet Union, with which some joint ventures were established. Under license with Western firms, Polish machinery plants produced mobile cranes, heavy truck axles, hydraulic equipment, truck-mounted concrete mixers, and other construction machinery. In the 1980s, reduced Western investments in Poland curtailed demand for these products. In the 1990s, the highly centralized, bureaucratic construction machine industry was reorganized into a large number of small- and medium-sized private firms. The reorganization targeted expansion of the housing construction industry, which received high priority in reform planning. The second goal of this reorganization was to revive demand for the relatively modern and sophisticated construction machines that the Polish industry was able to produce.

Shipbuilding

Polish shipbuilding expanded rapidly in the 1960s and 1970s, spurred by the Soviet drive to become a maritime superpower. In the 1980s, the industry included six shipyards, twenty-one equipment factories, and three research and development centers, altogether employing about 57,000 people. In that decade, Poland became the fifth largest producer of ships in the world, exporting most of its products to the Soviet Union. Some 1,000 plants all over the country supplied materials to the shipbuilding industry. At the end of the 1980s, however, the industry suffered greatly from drastic reduction in orders from the Soviet Union and other customers, the loss of government subsidies in the midst of production, and a rapid rise in domestic material costs for ships already contracted. Nevertheless, the shipbuilding firms were able to attract many Western licenses, and they retained a highly skilled labor force. If modernized and restructured, the industry had the potential to significantly accelerate its production of modern ships, including fishing vessels, factory ships, trawlers, car ferries, container vessels, roll on-roll off ships, and tankers. The well-equipped Gdynia Shipyard was capable of building very large bulk cargo ships, but it operated at only 30 percent of capacity in 1991. Large new contracts were expected to more than double that level of production by 1994, however. In 1992 it seemed probable that the shipyard's very high debt would be eased by a two-step transition, first into

*Polonez cars come off the assembly line at the Passenger
Car Plant in Warsaw.*
Courtesy Polish Information Agency, Warsaw

a partnership with the State Treasury and ultimately into a private enterprise. In 1991 the Ministry of Industry completed a restructuring program for the entire shipbuilding industry in cooperation with Western experts.

Agriculture

Of Poland's 18,727,000 hectares of agricultural land (about 60 percent of the country's total area), 14,413,000 hectares were used for crop cultivation, 265,000 for orchards, and about 4,048,500 for meadows and pastures in 1989. In most areas, soil and climatic conditions favored a mixed type of farming. In 1990 the most important crops were grains, of which the highest yields came from wheat, rye, barley, and oats. Other major crops were potatoes, sugar beets, fodder crops, flax, hops, tobacco, and fruits (see table 18, Appendix). Cultivation of corn expanded during the 1980s but remained limited. The northern and east-central regions of the country mainly offered poorer sandy soils suitable for rye and potatoes. The richer soils of the central and southern parts of the country, excluding higher elevations, made those regions the centers of wheat, sugar beet, hops, and tobacco production. The more accessible land at higher elevations was used to cultivate oats or was left as meadow and pastureland. In 1989 almost half of Poland's arable land was used for the cultivation of the four major grains; another 13 percent grew potatoes. All regions of Poland raised dairy cows, beef cattle, pigs, and poultry, and cultivated fruit, usually as an integral part of mixed farming.

In 1989 Poland was the second largest producer of rye and potatoes in the world. The latter were used as vegetables, fodder for pigs, and production of industrial starch and alcohol. The country occupied sixth place in the world in sugar beet, milk, and pig production. The quantity and quality of agricultural land ensured self-sufficiency and considerable quantities of various agricultural products and processed foodstuffs available for export. In 1990 Poland exported 26 percent of the bacon it produced, as well as 63 percent of the ham, 16 percent of the tinned meat, 10 percent of the poultry, 17 percent of the sugar, and 67 percent of the frozen fruits and vegetables.

Organization under State Planning

Beginning with decollectivization in 1956, Poland was the only member of Comecon where the private sector predominated in agriculture. The state maintained indirect control, however, through the state agencies that distributed needed input materials and purchased agricultural produce. Compulsory delivery quotas were maintained for farms until the beginning of the 1970s. The state also retained significant influence on the process of cultivation, restrictions on the size of farms, and limitations on the buying and selling of land. Until the beginning of the 1980s, the allocation system for fertilizers, machines, building materials, fuels, and other inputs discriminated severely against private farmers. As a result of these policies, private farms remained inefficiently small and labor-intensive.

Private and State Farms

In 1987 about 2.7 million private farms were in operation. About 57 percent of them were smaller than five hectares. Of the remaining farms, 25 percent were between five and ten hectares and 11 percent were between ten and fifteen hectares. Only 7 percent of private farms were larger than fifteen hectares. Whereas the majority of the private farms were below optimum size, the majority of state farms were excessively large. Only 12 percent of the latter farms were below 200 hectares, and 60 percent were larger than 1,000 hectares.

In 1989 the private sector cultivated 76.2 percent of arable land and provided 79 percent of gross agricultural production. State

Construction at the
Szczecin Shipyard
Courtesy Polish Information
Agency, Warsaw

farms, the main institutional form in state ownership, cultivated 18.8 percent of the total arable land and produced 17.0 percent of gross output. Cooperative farms, the dominant form of state agricultural organization in other East European economies, were not important in Poland. In 1989 they cultivated only 3.8 percent of arable land and contributed 3.9 percent of gross production.

In the 1980s, grain yields and meat output per hectare were higher in the socialist sector than in the private sector. An important factor in this difference was the more intensive use of fertilizers in state farms. On the other hand, the milk yield per cow was higher in the private sector. From the standpoint of overall performance, the private sector was less material- and capital-intensive, and gross production per hectare and the value of product per unit of cost were higher in that sector. Besides being more efficient, private farms were also more flexible in adjusting production to obtain a higher product value.

Postcommunist Restructuring

Because of the predominance of private farms in communist Poland, privatization of agriculture was not a major necessity during the reform period, as it was in the other postcommunist countries. Excessively large state farms were to be split into more efficient units and sold; some state farms would be converted into modern agrobusinesses operating as limited stock companies; and a certain

153

number were to be retained as state experimental farms. In all cases, however, rapid modernization and improvement in agrotechnology were urgent requirements.

The streamlining of agriculture faced serious obstacles in the early 1990s, notably because of the existing agrarian structure. Private farm size had to increase to provide farmers a satisfactory level of income and investment. Drastic reduction in the agricultural labor force also was needed. Because unemployment outside agriculture rose in 1991 and 1992, however, only gradual reductions were possible. A satisfactory social safety net and retraining programs for displaced agricultural workers were prerequisites for further reductions in labor. Experts estimated that unemployment on former state farms would reach 70 to 80 percent, meaning about 400,000 lost jobs, once the farms were privatized and streamlined.

Considerable investment is needed to provide adequate agricultural infrastructure, including road improvement, telecommunications, water supply, housing, and amenities. Especially important is establishment of a well-developed, competitive network of suppliers of materials and equipment necessary for modern agricultural production. Equally necessary are commercial firms to purchase agricultural products and provide transportation and storage facilities. In particular, expansion and modernization of the food-processing industry are necessary to strengthen and stabilize demand for agricultural products. The first postcommunist governments prepared agricultural modernization programs, and some financial help was obtained from the World Bank and Western governments for this purpose. Modernization was expected to require several decades, however.

By 1992 nearly all the 3,000 remaining state farms had substantial unpaid bank loans and other liabilities. For this reason, and because the government had not devised usable privatization plans at that point, the Farm Ownership Agency of the State Treasury was authorized to take over all the state farms in 1992. The agency was authorized to lease state farm lands to either Polish or foreign renters, as a temporary measure to ensure continued productivity.

Fishing and Forestry

The fishing and forestry industries were important producers for both domestic consumption and the export market during the communist era. For both industries, however, the resource base had begun to shrink noticeably by the end of the 1980s.

Fishing

The fresh-water fishing industry is concentrated in the numerous

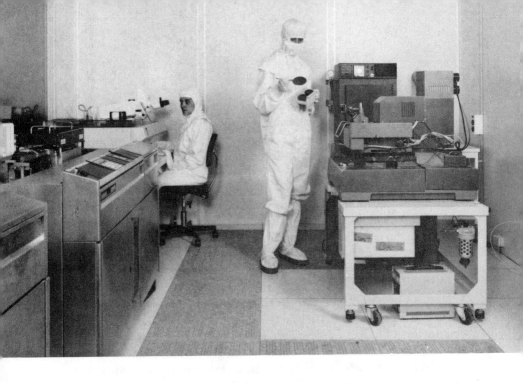

Clean room at Unitra-Cemi Electronics Plant, Warsaw
Courtesy Polish Information Agency, Warsaw

lakes of northern Poland. Fishing fleets also operate along the
528-kilometer Baltic coast and in the North Sea and the North Atlantic. The deep-sea fleet, developed in the 1970s to serve the new
official emphasis on fish as a cheap source of protein, had grown
to 101 trawler-factory ships and ten supply and service vessels by
1982. Besides fishing in the North Atlantic, Polish fleets fished off
Africa, South America, Alaska, Australia, and New Zealand. Activity in the more distant fisheries involved much higher expenses,
however, especially for fuel. In the 1980s, the Baltic fishery, which
provided about 25 percent of the total catch, was plagued by shortages of supplies and storage facilities. At the same time, pollution
in the lakes caused fresh-water catches to decline rapidly. In 1990
Poland exported about 123,000 tons of fish and fish products.

Forestry

Large forested areas are located in the western, northeastern,
and southeastern parts of Poland, but the only remaining stands
of old forest are in the northeast. Conifers dominate in the far north,
the northeast, and at higher elevations, and deciduous species
dominate elsewhere. Under the communist regimes, 82 percent
of forested land was state-owned, with the remainder held by individual farmers or groups of farmers. The 8,679,000 hectares of

155

forest supported total commercial lumber production of 22,675 cubic decameters in 1989. Already in the early 1980s, however, cutting rates exceeded replacement rates, and heavy demand for wood products prevented meaningful reduction of exploitation. A long-term afforestation program was initiated in the communist era to increase total forest cover to 30 percent of Poland's land surface. This increase would amount to slightly more than 1 percent more than the cover remaining in the 1980s. Poland's forests support the export of significant quantities of lumber, paper, and wood furniture.

Transportation and Communications

In 1989 Poland had 26,644 kilometers of railroads, including 11,016 adapted for electric traction. The country also had 159,000 kilometers of hard-surface public roads, 6,846 kilometers of oil and gas pipelines, and 3,997 kilometers of regulated inland waterways (see fig. 15). Polish State Railroads, a state monopoly, ran 1,920 electric locomotives, 2,567 diesel locomotives, and 198 steam locomotives, 136,128 freight cars, and 5,530 passenger cars. The main intercity lines were well serviced, and trains generally ran on schedule. In the postcommunist reform era, fares and freight rates were gradually increased and subsidies reduced accordingly.

In 1989 the Polish merchant fleet included 249 freight ships totaling 4 million deadweight tons and nine ferries totaling 18,000 deadweight tons. Regular international lines reached London, Asian ports, Australia, and some African and Latin American countries. The inland fleet included sixty-nine passenger ships, twenty-six tugboats, 387 motor units, 325 motor barges, and 1,055 barges. The major Baltic ports are Szczecin, Gdańsk, Gdynia, and Świnoujście, and the major inland ports are Gliwice on the Gliwice Canal (Kanał Gliwice), Wrocław on the Oder River, and Warsaw on the Vistula River.

The national airline, Polish Airlines (Polskie Linie Lotnicze, commonly known as LOT), flew forty-six Soviet-made airplanes in 1989. LOT purchased its first Boeing airliner in 1990 at the beginning of a modernization program that included replacement of a large part of the fleet, construction of a modern airport, Okęcie International, in Warsaw by contract with a German firm, and updating kitchens and cargo facilities. By 1992 the airline's transatlantic lines were served by Western-made jets, although LOT did not expect to meet overall Western standards of air travel for several years. In 1989 only eighty of Poland's 140 operating airports had permanent-surface runways. Five airports offered runways

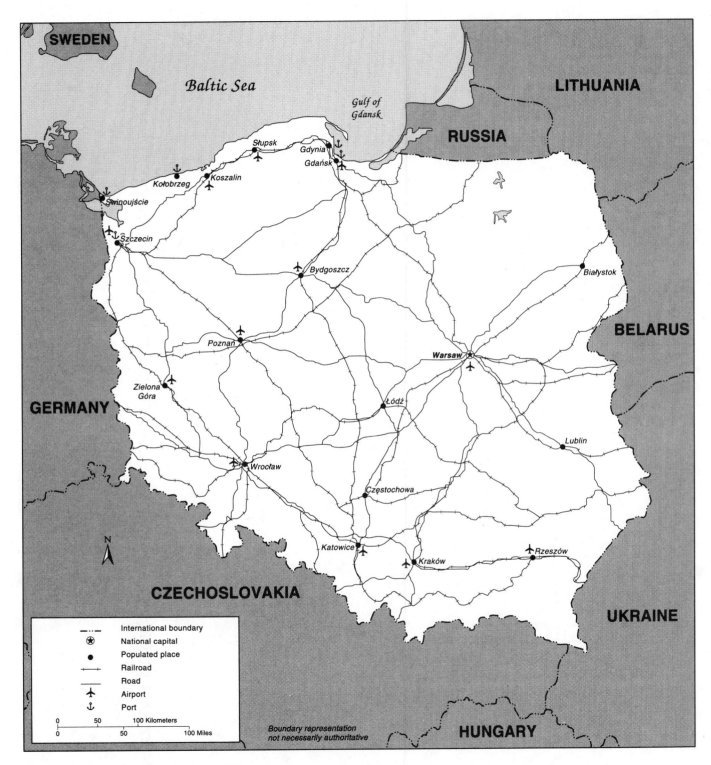

Figure 15. Transportation System, 1992

longer than 3,600 meters. The largest airports are at Warsaw, Rzeszów, Kraków, Koszalin, Słupsk, Zielona Góra, Gdańsk, Katowice, Poznań, and Bydgoszcz.

National telecommunications networks were neglected badly during the communist era. In 1989 Poland had only 5,039,000 telephones, of which 544,000 were in rural areas. Beginning in 1990, however, several major contracts with Western firms promised substantial improvement.

The national radio and television broadcast system was entirely state-owned and state-controlled until 1990. In the restructured telecommunications program developed in 1991 and 1992, part of the system remained under state control. But the new system also licensed private broadcast stations, whose programming received minimal state oversight. The first private television station began broadcasting in Wrocław in 1990. At that time, the state-run Polish Radio and Television Network was broadcasting over four radio and two television channels. Color television was broadcast through the Secam system, and the Eutelsat satellite system provided a hookup with Western Europe. About 10 million television sets and 11.1 million radio receivers were registered in 1988, and 3,500 licenses for satellite television receivers were current. Some eighty-two television transmitters were in operation in 1990. Radio programs were broadcast in English, Russian, German, Lithuanian, Finnish, and French as well as Polish.

Banking and Finance

In the reform programs of the early 1990s, major restructuring of Poland's financial infrastructure was a top priority in order to achieve more efficient movement of money through the domestic economy and to provide a secure environment for the foreign investment that was expected to carry Poland through its postcommunist economic slump.

The State Banking System

A highly concentrated state banking monopoly was a typical feature of East European economies in the communist period. In Poland the monopoly was composed of the National Bank of Poland (Narodowy Bank Polski—NBP), which had replaced the prewar Western-style Bank of Poland in 1945; the Commercial Bank (Bank Handlowy—BH), which had a monopoly in financing foreign trade; the Polish Savings Office, which controlled transactions with private international transfers; and about 1,600 small regional and specialized cooperative banks that jointly formed the Bank of Food Economy. To encourage private savings, a specialized savings bank, the General Savings Office, was established in 1987 by detaching designated departments from the NBP. In 1988 nine state-owned commercial banks were formed from regional branches of the NBP, and a state Export Development Bank was established.

Legislation was introduced in 1989 to allow private individuals, both Poles and foreigners, to form banks as limited stock companies. Between 1989 and 1991, a total of seventy licenses was issued to private banks, including seven banks funded by foreign capital, two cooperative banks, and three branches of foreign banks. In October 1991, privatization of the Export Development Bank began, and the nine state commercial banks (which until that time still operated as they had under the old NBP) were transformed into limited stock companies. The State Treasury owned and operated the banks for an intermediate period while they prepared for privatization.

Banking Reform, 1990-92

A fundamental reorganization of the banking sector took place between 1990 and 1992. The NBP lost all its central planning functions, including holding the accounts of state enterprises, making transfers among them, crediting their operations, and exercising financial control of their activities. The NBP thus became only a central bank, and state enterprises competed with other businesses for the scarce credits available from commercial banks. In its new form, the NBP exercised a considerable degree of autonomy in monetary policy and performed the same functions as the central banks in West European countries or the Federal Reserve System in the United States.

Nevertheless, the entire Polish banking system remained inefficient in the early 1990s because of backward banking technology and a very serious shortage of trained personnel in all branches. Considerable technical and financial aid from the World Bank, the IMF, and the central banks of Western countries was expected to improve the situation eventually.

Insurance and Securities Reform

In July 1990, the insurance system was reorganized. Abolished were the monopoly State Insurance Company, which had been responsible for all domestic insurance, and the Insurance and Reinsurance Company, which had been responsible for all foreign transactions. Domestic and foreign-owned private limited stock and mutual insurance companies were then allowed to begin operating. At the same time, procedures were introduced to maintain adequate financial reserves and legal protection for people and assets

A Boeing 767 of LOT at Okęcie International Airport, Warsaw
Courtesy Polish Information Agency, Warsaw

insured. At the end of 1991, twenty-two insurance companies were operating in Poland, six of which were foreign-owned.

In early 1991, important legislation was introduced to regulate securities transactions and establish a stock exchange in Warsaw. At the same time, a securities commission was formed for consumer protection. A year later, the shares of eleven Polish companies were being traded weekly on the new exchange. Restructuring the financial market not only was necessary for increasing the overall efficiency of the economy and accelerating privatization but also was a precondition for the rapid influx of Western capital critical to economic development.

New Financial Institutions

Several specialized financial institutions were established with direct or indirect help from the Polish government, international organizations, and foreign experts to facilitate economic restructuring. They include the Agency for Industrial Development, the Polish Development Bank, the Export Finance Insurance Corporation, the Enterprise Consulting Foundation, the Employment Fund, and a growing number of consulting firms. These institutions are expected to provide credit guarantees, help to establish new businesses, purchase a certain quantity of shares of the companies being converted to private enterprise, and facilitate leasing, financial restructuring, and bankruptcy processes. Some of the new institutions received designated funds from international financial organizations. The European Bank for Reconstruction and Development (EBRD—see Glossary) established a Joint Investment Fund in cooperation with the Polish Development Bank.

Foreign Loans and Money Supply

In April 1991, representatives of the seventeen major West European creditor governments collectively known as the Paris Club (see Glossary) agreed to a two-phase, 50 percent reduction of Poland's debt on government loans. The United States made a similar reduction of 70 percent. Terms for servicing of the debt were rearranged, with payments to escalate gradually from US$0.5 billion in 1992-93 to US$1.5 billion later in the decade. Negotiations with Western commercial banks, the so-called London Club (see Glossary), continued in 1992. The hard currency debt was reduced from US$48.5 billion at the end of 1990 to US$44.3 billion in August 1991, partly because of the debt relief of US$1.6 billion effected by the United States and partly as the revaluation of the dollar against other Western currencies reduced the debt in those currencies.

In 1991 the total money supply in Poland, counting both zlotys and convertible currency, increased by 83.9 trillion zlotys. Of this amount, over 90 percent belonged to private individuals or private enterprises, and about 6 percent belonged to state enterprises. The increase in the money supply came mainly from higher bank debts owed by economic units and the government. A midyear alteration of the exchange rate between the zloty and the United States dollar also played a major role. Foreign currency held in Polish bank accounts increased by 13.2 percent in 1991 because more accounts were opened in 1991. Although money in personal savings accounts grew by 250 percent in 1991, money held by enterprises in bank accounts grew by only 12.4 percent in the same period. Estimated total foreign currency resources declined by over 3 percent in 1991 to US$5.3 billion.

Foreign Trade

In the early 1990s, internal and external economic conditions forced a major reappraisal of Poland's export and import policies. The once-profitable export markets of the Soviet Union were a much less reliable source of income after that empire disintegrated and hard currency became the predominant medium of exchange among its former members. In this situation, increased trade with much more demanding Western partners became the primary goal of Polish trade policy.

The Foreign Trade Mechanism

Centrally planned economies typically minimized trade with free-trade markets because their central bureaucratic systems could not adjust quickly to changing situations in foreign markets. The high degree of self-sufficiency that was a declared economic objective of Comecon made trade with the West a difficult undertaking for an economy such as Poland's. On the other hand, the basically bilateral barter agreements that characterized trade within Comecon often had made expansion of trade within the organization problematic.

State monopoly of foreign trade was an integral part of centrally planned economic systems. Even after some decentralization of this field in Poland during the 1980s, the Ministry of Foreign Economic Relations maintained direct or indirect control of all foreign trade activities. Originally, trading activities in the communist system were conducted exclusively by the specialized foreign trade organizations (FTOs), which isolated domestic producers of exportables and domestic buyers of imported goods from the world market. Then, in the late 1980s, some state and cooperative production enterprises received licenses from the Ministry of Foreign Economic Relations to become directly involved in foreign trade, and by 1988 the number of economic units authorized to conduct foreign trade had nearly tripled. Nonetheless, many enterprises still preferred the risk-free, conventional approach to foreign trade through an FTO, relying on guaranteed Comecon markets and avoiding marketing efforts and quality control requirements.

Prior to 1990, the Polish foreign trade system included the following elements: a required license or concession to conduct any foreign transactions; allocation of quotas by planners for the import and export of most basic raw materials and intermediate goods; state allocation and control of exchange and transfer of most foreign currencies; an arbitrary rate of currency exchange lacking all relation to real economic conditions; and artificial leveling of domestic and foreign prices by transfers within a special account of the state budget. Even among Comecon countries, Poland's foreign trade had particularly low value. Its share of total world exports, 0.6 percent in 1985, dropped to 0.4 percent in 1989. The share of imports dropped even lower, from 0.5 to 0.3 percent, in the same period.

In early 1990, Poland entered a painful process of massive transformation for which reintegration into the world economy was a primary objective. The first postcommunist government dismantled the existing foreign trade mechanism and replaced it with a mechanism compatible with an open market economy. This change eliminated license and concession requirements for the conduct of foreign trade activities, eliminated quotas except in trade with the Soviet Union, introduced internal convertibility of the zloty and free exchange of foreign currencies, and accepted the rate of exchange as the main instrument of adjustment of exports and imports, supported by a liberal tariff system.

Postcommunist Policy Adjustments

In early 1990, the Mazowiecki government planned to maintain Poland's high export volume to the Soviet Union for an indefinite period. The goal of this plan was to ensure a long-term position for Poland in that important market and to protect domestic industry from a further decline in production and increased unemployment. Subsequently, however, an export limit became necessary to avoid accumulating an excessive surplus of useless transferable rubles. In 1992, after the Soviet Union split into a number of independent states, the Polish government had no indication whether existing balances would ever be exchanged into convertible currencies, or under what conditions that might happen.

In December 1991, Poland reached agreement on associate membership in the European Community (EC). Having taken this intermediate step, the Polish government set the goal of full EC membership by the year 2000. Among the provisions of associate membership were gradual removal of EC tariffs and quotas on Polish food exports; immediate removal of EC tariffs on most industrial goods imported from Poland and full membership for Poland in the EC free trade area for industrial goods in 1999; EC financial aid to restructure the Polish economy; and agreements on labor transfer, rights of settlement, cultural cooperation, and other issues. The agreement, which required ratification by the Polish government, all twelve member nations of the EC, and the European Parliament, went into interim operation as those bodies considered its merits. Both houses of the Polish parliament ratified the agreement in July 1992.

The End of the Soviet Era

In 1990 Poland's trade balance with the Soviet Union was almost 4.4 billion transferable rubles. At that point, some Polish exporters took the risk of continuing their exports to traditional Soviet

Canal in Baltic port of Gdańsk
Courtesy Ronald D. Bachman

markets, hoping that they would eventually be paid either by the importers in the Soviet Union, who were very anxious to get Polish goods, or by the Polish government. In the first quarter of 1991, the value of these exports was about US$130 million. Only about US$20 million was received, however, because the Soviet government was prepared to pay only for imported foodstuffs, which received highest priority in its import policy. The Soviet government refused to pay the bill for Soviet importers who had purchased machines, pharmaceuticals, electronics, textiles, and clothing from Poland.

The sudden collapse of Comecon in 1990 increased short-term obstacles and accelerated changes in the geographic direction of trade. The share of Poland's trade occupied by the Comecon group declined to 22.3 percent in 1990 and 14.4 percent in 1991. On the export side, its share declined to 21.4 and 9.8 in the respective years.

The Role of Currency Exchange

In this situation, expanded exports to the West provided the only alternative for the many enterprises whose survival depended on foreign trade. The government's stabilization policy had an impact that promised expansion of exports to hard-currency markets. In 1991 drastic limitation of domestic demand, devaluation of the zloty by 32 percent, and liberalization of access to foreign trade by private entrepreneurs resulted in significant expansion of export earnings in convertible currencies. In 1990 the volume of hard-currency exports increased by 40.9 percent to over US$12 billion, while hard-currency imports increased by 6.3 percent, securing a positive trade balance of US$2.6 billion.

The level of exports earning hard currency in 1990 was particularly impressive in comparison with the generally sluggish growth of that category in the late 1980s. In the last years of the communist era, fuel exports declined steadily, and metallurgical exports decreased in three of the last five communist years. Construction work in countries paying in hard currency declined in the first three years of the period, whereas exports from the wood and paper, engineering, and chemical industries behaved unevenly.

In 1990, by contrast, hard-currency exports increased in most sectors of the economy. The largest increases in that category were achieved in agricultural, metallurgical, and chemical products. In general, the share of manufactured products in Poland's export mix declined sharply with the sudden shift away from Comecon trade. In 1990 the largest major categories of manufactured exports were, respectively, machines and transport equipment, miscellaneous manufactured goods, and chemicals; their share of total exports was 42.4 percent, compared with 67.3 percent for the same categories in 1985. Growth in exports of food, raw materials, and fuels accounted for the difference.

Although the share of engineering products among exports declined, that group was the most important single earner of hard currency in 1990, followed by metallurgical, chemical, and food products. In 1992 all those industries possessed considerable capacity to expand their productivity, given appropriate investment in modernization and efficient marketing. However, both modernization and marketing depended heavily on cooperation with Western firms. Despite the remarkable increase in hard-currency exports in 1990, their overall impact on the national economy was limited by the strong effect of reduced transferable-ruble exports on the priority sectors. In 1990 Polish light industry led the general decline in ruble exports.

At the beginning of 1991, however, the growth rate of hard-currency exports declined, and imports increased very rapidly. Inflation remained high, and the advantage created by the 1990 devaluation slowly eroded. Another devaluation, this time 17 percent, was effected in May 1991. At the same time, the zloty was pegged to a combination of hard currencies instead of to the dollar alone. In October the fixed exchange rate was replaced by an adjustable rate that would be devalued automatically by 1.8 percent every month as a partial hedge against inflation. The final import figure for 1991 was 87.4 percent higher than that for 1990. In 1991 exports in convertible currencies were a little over US$14.6 billion and imports were nearly US$15.5 billion, creating a hard-currency trade deficit of about US$900 million.

Figures for the first five months of 1992 showed a reversal of the previous year's imbalance. The hard-currency trade surplus of US$340 million reported for that period was attributed to a combination of commodity turnover and cancellation of interest payments in Poland's debt reduction agreement with the Paris Club.

For years under the old system, Poland dispersed small amounts of its export and import trade to a large number of non-Comecon countries on all continents. Experts considered such dispersion a policy weakness because marginal suppliers and buyers usually trade at less favorable terms than high-volume partners, making the former expendable in hard times. This factor became even more important in the first postcommunist years; in 1990 Poland's fifteen top import customers absorbed only 81.3 percent of exports, while the fifteen top suppliers contributed 86.2 percent of Polish imports. Poland's traditional partners in the former Soviet Union and Germany (before and after their respective realignments) retained disproportionately high shares in both categories in 1990 (see table 18, Appendix).

Foreign Investment

By the end of 1991, Poland had obtained US$2.5 billion from the World Bank and other international financial organizations and US$3.5 billion in bilateral credits and guarantees of credit from Western governments. In 1992, however, the limited absorptive capacity of the country still restricted the amounts of foreign cash and credit that could be used. Only US$428 million was utilized in 1990, about US$800 million in 1991. A significant increase was expected in 1992.

Poland's net balance of payments deficit, calculated as the difference between credits used and the amount paid to service the national debt, was more than US$1.3 billion in 1989, US$312 million in 1990, and US$449 million in 1991. In the long run, even investment credits and continued growth of exports could not maintain a balance of payments equilibrium without a substantial inflow of direct foreign investments.

Cooperative enterprises with foreign firms also offered access to advanced technology, better export trade, improved management and training, and attractive job opportunities for younger members of the work force. The first year of postcommunist rule brought an initial surge of investment in which permits for formation of foreign companies more than doubled. A number of United States, British, French, Swiss, Swedish, Dutch, and Japanese firms started Polish enterprises. Significantly, the share of permits issued to German firms dropped from 60 percent in 1989 to 40 percent in 1990, and that figure was expected to remain at about 30 percent after 1991.

Despite the adoption of very liberal investment legislation in the middle of 1991, however, the year did not bring the anticipated investment increases. In 1991 and 1992, major inhibiting factors were real and perceived political instability, conflicting and slow changes in economic policy, a faulty system for taxation of foreign enterprises, and a steep decline in the GNP. In spite of the increase in registered foreign direct investment projects between 1989 and 1991, the registered foreign capital involved in these projects was only US$353 million in 1990 and US$670 million in 1991. The actual investment amounts were not more than 40 percent of those amounts. At the end of 1991, some 4,800 partnerships operated with foreign participation. Of these, 43 percent were in industry, 24 percent in trade, and 6.6 percent in agriculture; about two-thirds of foreign ventures were concentrated in the economic centers of

Warsaw, Poznań, Gdańsk, Szczecin, Katowice, and Łódź—meaning that foreign investment was not benefiting many of Poland's less prosperous regions. Altogether, the foreign partnerships generated less than 1 percent of Poland's total national income in 1991.

Economic Prospects

Poland was the first of the East European Comecon nations to initiate a move from a centrally planned economy to a Western-type market economy. In many ways, however, the economic crisis that the postcommunist governments inherited in Poland was more severe than that in other countries undergoing the same transition. The early stages of Poland's transformation proved more difficult, more painful, and took longer than expected. Nevertheless, the first three postcommunist years brought a number of important achievements: elimination of shortages in the domestic consumers' market; considerable reduction in the rate of inflation; the quick dismantling of the mechanism of the command economy; marketization and liberalization of economic life; internal convertibility of currency; a very rapid "small privatization" and a more uneven "large privatization"; the creation of some of the legal and institutional framework fundamental to a market economy; and an impressive expansion in hard-currency exports. The banking system had moved decisively away from the previous state monopoly system, but the seventy commercial banks operating in 1992 still did not constitute a full Western-style commercial system. The stock market established in 1990 awaited the impetus of faster privatization to expand beyond its initial modest scale. Overall, by 1992 these initial steps had built a rather sound base for further progress in the near term and provided reason for guarded optimism over the long term.

Geographic location, the cause of many tragic events in Poland's history, provides a potentially major advantage in the new context of a united Europe. Good commercial relations with neighbors on both sides—Germany, Ukraine, Belarus, and Russia—promise rapid recovery from the end of the Comecon era. The political aspects of economic policy making have been problematic in the early reform years, as factionalism has hindered government implementation of needed legislation. The impact of politics is especially noticeable in the privatization process, which was slowed dramatically by three changes in the privatization ministry between 1989 and 1992 and by attendant bickering over methodology and priorities. Nevertheless, possessing relatively favorable human and natural resources, and having taken some of the basic steps to repair the distortions of centralized management, the Polish economy showed signs in 1992 of becoming an open modern industrial system that could ensure a reasonable standard of living for its population.

* * *

A number of English-language sources provide an overview of the Polish economy before and after the fall of the central planning system. *Doing Business with Eastern Europe: Poland,* a publication of Business International, outlines trade conditions in the 1980s from the viewpoint of Western business. Dariusz Rosati's *Poland: Economic Reform and Policy in the 1980s* and *Poland: The Economy in the 1980s,* edited by Roger Clarke, describe the reforms attempted by the last communist regimes in response to the failure of the system and the social upheavals that resulted. *Poland: Politics, Economics, and Society* by George Kolankiewicz and Paul G. Lewis describes economic conditions in the 1980s as they interacted with social and political changes. Several journal articles written by Zbigniew Fallenbuchl between 1990 and 1992 describe in detail the mechanics of Poland's postcommunist economic transition, including trade policy, banking and finance, and privatization issues. The statistical yearbook published annually by the Central Statistical Office in Warsaw is the fundamental source of economic statistics; an abbreviated version is available in English. (For further information and complete citations, see Bibliography.)

Chapter 4. Government and Politics

Twelfth-century sword, the "Szczerbiec," used in the coronation of Polish kings

THE UNEXPECTED SPEED with which communist governance ended in Poland put the country's anticommunist opposition in charge of the search for appropriate new political institutions. The subsequent hectic experiment in democracy yielded mixed results between 1989 and 1992, when the restored Republic of Poland was still attempting to find its political bearings. In 1989 round table talks between the opposition and the communist government spawned a flurry of legislation and constitutional amendments that merged democratic reforms with institutions and laws inherited from four decades of communist rule.

At that point, the young democracy's centers of power had not yet been able to define their span of control and their relationship to one another. Institutional ambiguity was exacerbated by the outcome of the long-awaited parliamentary elections of October 1991, which seated twenty-nine political parties in the powerful lower house, the Sejm. To form a coalition government from such diverse parties, of which none held more than 14 percent of the total seats, was a daunting task in itself. The greater challenge, however, lay in creating a political culture of negotiation and compromise that would make stable democracy feasible over the long term.

A key element in the development of any Western-style democracy is the unrestricted dissemination of accurate information and diverse opinion. In this respect, Poland underwent a less abrupt transition than other postcommunist states. A prolific, independent press had evolved from modest beginnings in the early 1970s, surviving the setback of martial law, and expanding its activities as government censorship diminished after the mid-1980s. Following the Round Table Agreement of early 1989, the press gave voice to an ever-widening spectrum of political and social opinion. But the end of generous state subsidies in favor of a profit- and competition-based system bankrupted hundreds of Polish publishing enterprises. Radio and television adjusted less rapidly to the changed political environment and remained under closer government control than the print media.

Despite a constantly changing constellation of political parties and coalitions that produced five prime ministers in three years, Warsaw maintained a consistent and successful foreign policy during the transition period. By mid-1992, Poland had achieved many of its long-range policy goals, including sovereignty over its foreign affairs; a Russian commitment for complete withdrawal of Soviet/

Russian combat forces from Polish territory; bilateral friendship treaties with most of its neighbors; German recognition of the permanent Oder-Neisse border; associate membership in the European Community (EC); and observer status in the North Atlantic Treaty Organization (NATO). At that point, Warsaw already had traveled a considerable distance on its ''path back to Europe.'' The West responded to Poland's democratizing and marketizing reforms by granting trade concessions, debt relief, and a range of economic and technical assistance.

Political Setting

In August 1980, faced with an increasingly severe economic crisis and social unrest that had been building throughout the 1970s, the communist government reluctantly conceded legal status to an independent labor federation, Solidarity (Solidarność). After monopolizing power for thirty-five years without genuine sanction from Polish society, the communist Polish United Workers' Party (Polska Zjednoczona Partia Robotnicza—PZPR) found itself in contention with an alternative source of political power that had a valid claim to represent the country's working people. Under the threat of general strikes and facing economic and political chaos, the regime grudgingly reached a series of limited compromises with Solidarity in 1980 and early 1981.

After the government's initial concessions, however, Solidarity militants insisted on substantially broader concessions. In response, PZPR hard-liners used the memories of the Soviet Union's violent reaction to Czechoslovakia's moderate political reforms in 1968 to justify the imposition of martial law in December 1981. Solidarity was declared illegal. General Wojciech Jaruzelski, earlier that year named prime minister and then first secretary of the PZPR, appointed trusted military men to key government positions and deemphasized communist ideology. Through the rest of the decade, the government sought in vain to recover a degree of legitimacy with the people and to overcome the country's severe economic problems. The overtures of the Jaruzelski government failed, however, to win the support of the Polish people. In a key 1987 national referendum, voters refused to support the government's package of painful reforms needed to halt the economic slide. Eventually, the government came to realize that improvement of the economic situation was not possible without the explicit support of the Solidarity opposition. At that point, the government had no choice but to enter into negotiations with Solidarity.

The Round Table Agreement

When the government convened round table talks with the opposition in early 1989, it was prepared to make certain concessions, including the legalization of Solidarity. It had no intention, however, of granting Solidarity the status of an equal partner. The fifty-seven negotiators at the talks included representatives from the ruling PZPR, Solidarity, and various PZPR-sanctioned quasi-parties and mass organizations, such as the United Peasant Party, the Democratic Party, the Christian Social Union, the Association of Polish Catholics, and the All-Polish Alliance of Trade Unions (see PZPR and Successor Parties, this ch.). The talks were organized into three working groups, which examined the economy, social policy, and the status of trade unions. A spirit of cooperation and compromise characterized the two-month negotiations.

The document signed by the participants on April 6, 1989, laid the groundwork for a pluralistic society that in theory would enjoy freedom of association, freedom of speech, an independent judiciary, and independent trade unions. The Round Table Agreement legalized Solidarity as a labor union; restored the pre-World War II Senate as the upper house of parliament and granted it veto powers over the decisions of the Sejm; promised partially free Sejm elections; replaced the State Council with the new executive office of president of Poland; and called for the creation of an independent judiciary of tenured judges appointed by the president from a list submitted by the parliament (see Government Structure, this ch.).

Although election to the Senate was to be completely free and open, the PZPR and its traditionally subservient partners, the United Peasant Party and the Democratic Party, were assured of 60 percent of the seats in the 460-member Sejm; and religious organizations long associated with the regime were promised 5 percent of the seats. The remaining 161 seats were open to opposition and independent candidates who had obtained at least 3,000 nominating signatures. The agreement allowed a national slate of incumbents, including Prime Minister Mieczysław Rakowski, to run unopposed and be reelected with a simple majority of the ballots cast. But because voters exercised their option not to endorse candidates and crossed names off the ballot, only two of thirty-five unopposed national candidates received a majority. At the same time, only three of the government's candidates for contested seats received 50 percent of the votes cast. Consequently, a second round of voting was necessary to fill the seats originally reserved for the PZPR coalition.

With only days to organize, Solidarity waged an intense and effective national campaign. A network of ad hoc citizens' committees posted lists of Solidarity candidates, mobilized supporters, and in June executed an electoral coup. Solidarity candidates won all 161 Sejm seats open to them and ninety-nine of 100 seats in the Senate. This impressive electoral performance soon convinced the PZPR-allied parties in the Sejm to side with Solidarity and to form the first postcommunist coalition government in Eastern Europe.

The erosion of the old PZPR-led coalition was evident in the July 19 parliamentary voting for the new office of president of Poland. Thirty-one members of the coalition refused to support General Jaruzelski, the unopposed candidate for the post. The Solidarity leadership, however, believed that Jaruzelski was the best candidate for the presidency. Seemingly, he could best ensure that the PZPR would honor the concessions it had made in the Round Table Agreement. Also, he was the candidate least likely to alarm Moscow. Through careful polling, Solidarity was able to engineer a one-vote margin of victory for Jaruzelski.

The Mazowiecki Government

Although Jaruzelski had won the presidency, Solidarity was not willing to concede the leadership of the new government to the PZPR. Jaruzelski's choice for the position of prime minister, General Czesław Kiszczak, had won respect for his flexibility as the primary government representative during the round table talks. Kiszczak received the necessary simple majority of Sejm seats by the narrowest of margins. But repeated failures to form a coalition government forced the PZPR to face the reality of its diminished power. After consulting with Moscow, Jaruzelski nominated Tadeusz Mazowiecki, a respected intellectual and long-time Solidarity adviser, to become the first noncommunist Polish prime minister since 1944.

The coalition government gave representation to all of the primary political forces extant in August 1989. To secure Mazowiecki's nomination, Solidarity leader Lech Wałęsa had assured Jaruzelski that the PZPR would continue to control the key ministries of national defense and internal affairs. While entrusting fourteen ministries to Solidarity, Mazowiecki allocated four ministries to the United Peasant Party and three to the Democratic Party. A tone of reconciliation characterized the new administration. Determined not to engage in an anticommunist witch hunt, Mazowiecki pursued an evolutionary program of democratic reform.

*Lech Wałęsa, Solidarity
leader and first post-
communist president
Courtesy Committee
in Support of Solidarity,
New York*

*General Wojciech Jaruzelski,
last communist
leader of Poland
Courtesy United Press
International*

Popular Election of a President

Although Wałęsa had handpicked Mazowiecki to be prime minister and had played a key role in persuading the population to
grant the young government a grace period, tensions between
the two men emerged in early 1990. Perhaps regretting his deci-
on not to seek the office of prime minister himself, Wałęsa began
to criticize the Mazowiecki government. After the formal dissolution of the PZPR in January 1990, Wałęsa argued that the time
had come to discard the concessions from the Round Table Agreement that prolonged the influence of the old regime (see Political
Parties, this ch.). Sensing the depth of public discontent over falling living standards and rising unemployment, he leveled ever
harsher criticism at Mazowiecki. In return, the Mazowiecki circle
accused Wałęsa of destructive sloganeering. The acrimonious relations between the two camps led to the emergence of the first

post-Solidarity political groupings. The pro-Wałęsa Center Alliance (Porozumienie Centrum) called for accelerating the pace of reform and purging former communist appointees as rapidly as possible. The Mazowiecki forces set up the Citizens' Movement for Democratic Action.

The split grew more serious following President Jaruzelski's announcement that he would retire before the expiration of his term in 1995. With the support of both noncommunist factions, parliament enacted legislation to make possible the direct election of the president. Both Wałęsa and Mazowiecki ran for the office in the fall of 1990, together with four other candidates of widely varying political associations and experience.

The campaign was bitter and divisive. Despite the heated rhetoric of the campaign, the candidates differed relatively little on substantive issues. Their disagreements stemmed mostly from the different leadership styles of the men. Wounded by attacks on his intelligence, Wałęsa revealed a streak of anti-Semitism with remarks about the Jewish roots of the ruling clique in Warsaw (see Ethnic Groups, ch. 2). Meanwhile, falling living standards increased voters' disenchantment with the government's economic program. An uninspiring public speaker and a poor campaign organizer, Mazowiecki could not rally support during the short time remaining before the election.

Many voters apathetic toward the two front runners were attracted to the iconoclastic Stanisław Tymiński, a wealthy expatriate with no political experience. Tymiński's campaign made effective use of his outsider status. His wild accusations against the leading candidates found a receptive audience. Tymiński asserted that given a chance, he could make all Poles rich.

The election results were a stunning rejection of the Mazowiecki government. With only 18 percent of the total vote, Mazowiecki finished third behind Wałęsa (40 percent) and the maverick Tymiński (23 percent). The candidate of the Social Democracy of the Republic of Poland (SdRP), successor to the PZPR, received more than 9 percent of the vote, demonstrating the residual strength of the old party elite.

A runoff election between Tymiński and Wałęsa was necessitated by all candidates' failure to achieve a majority. Wałęsa sought the votes of Mazowiecki's supporters, promising to continue the basic course of economic transformation initiated by Mazowiecki's minister of finance, Leszek Balcerowicz (see Marketization and Stabilization, ch. 3). But the ad hominem attacks of the campaign made immediate reconciliation impossible. With the reluctant support of the Mazowiecki faction and the implicit endorsement of the Roman Catholic Church, Wałęsa won the runoff with almost 75 percent of the vote to become Poland's first popularly elected president. Although Wałęsa had prevailed, the bitter campaign had badly tarnished his image and worsened the splits in the old Solidarity coalition.

The Bielecki Government

Upon taking office in December 1990, Wałęsa offered the post of prime minister to Jan Olszewski, a respected attorney who had defended prominent dissidents in the 1960s and 1970s and who had a long association with Solidarity. When Olszewski rejected the offer because of Wałęsa's insistence on controlling key cabinet positions, Wałęsa offered the position to Jan Bielecki, the leader of a small reformist party, the Liberal-Democratic Congress. Believing that this would be a short-lived interim government, Bielecki accepted and conceded to Wałęsa the right to oversee cabinet selection. The new government retained several key members of the Mazowiecki cabinet. Leszek Balcerowicz continued to coordinate economic policy, and the widely respected Krzysztof Skubiszewski remained in charge of foreign affairs.

By his involvement in forming the Bielecki government, Wałęsa expanded the ill-defined powers of the presidency. His resolve to be an activist president caused alarm in the parliament, intellectual circles, and the press. Some people accused Wałęsa of harboring ambitions to attain the powers of Józef Piłsudski, the strong-willed leader in the interwar years (see Interwar Poland, ch. 1). Although he vigorously denied such charges, Wałęsa's popularity plunged in early 1991 as his prime minister failed to deliver the promised acceleration of economic reform and improvement of government services. During his tenure, Bielecki made little headway in privatizing large state enterprises and dismantling the managerial bureaucracy left by the communists.

By the summer of 1991, factionalism and the obstructionism of remaining communist legislators prevented the Sejm from enacting major legislation sponsored by the Bielecki government. Therefore, with Wałęsa's support, Bielecki asked the Sejm to revise the constitution and grant the prime minister authority to issue economic decrees with the force of law. The proposal was defeated, and the gridlock between executive and legislative branches continued.

Wałęsa grew increasingly resentful of the political, institutional, and legal constraints placed on his office. He felt especially encumbered by the composition of the Sejm, which opposed much of his economic agenda. Therefore, Wałęsa called for parliamentary elections in the spring of 1991 to install a fully democratic Sejm. Because his timetable could not be met, a long power struggle between the Sejm and the president over parliamentary election legislation ensued, and Wałęsa sustained a major political defeat. The president had favored an election law that would end the fragmentation of the Sejm by fostering large parties and coalitions. However, the parties formerly allied with the communists joined other anti-Wałęsa factions in the Sejm in enacting a system that allocated seats in strict proportion to candidates' percentages of the total vote in thirty-seven multimember electoral districts. Such a system, Wałęsa rightly feared, would enable dozens of minor and regional parties to win seats in the parliament by receiving only a few thousand votes.

The Parliamentary Elections of October 1991

Over Wałęsa's veto, the Sejm version of the parliamentary election bill became law in mid-1991. Elections were scheduled for the following October. During the months before the election, Wałęsa refused to endorse any of the numerous post-Solidarity parties and other parties that fielded slates of candidates. He remained noncommittal, distancing himself even from the Center Alliance, which had been his core of support during the presidential election. In fact, Wałęsa defended the Bielecki government from attacks by the Center Alliance. The president participated in the parliamentary campaign only by urging voters to defeat former communist candidates who had joined other parties after the dissolution of the PZPR.

As Wałęsa had predicted, the first election held under the new election law produced a badly fragmented parliament. Only 43 percent of the electorate voted in the first totally free parliamentary elections since 1928. Twenty-nine parties won seats in the new Sejm, but none received more than 14 percent of the vote. Both extremes of the political spectrum fared well, while the moderate post-Solidarity parties failed to win the expected majority of seats. This outcome promised a Sejm no less obstructionist than the one it replaced, and prospects for a coalition agreeing on a new prime minister were dim. At least five parties were needed to form a coalition holding a majority of seats in the Sejm. The Social Democracy of the Republic of Poland was essentially an ineligible party because of its roots in the PZPR. Meanwhile, the grave split of the two leading Solidarity factions made them incompatible in any coalition. This situation left a center-right coalition as the only practical option. Wałęsa's initial nominee for prime minister failed, however, because he lacked support from the Center Alliance and Bielecki's party, the Liberal-Democratic Congress.

The Olszewski Government

After five weeks of struggle, Wałęsa reluctantly acceded to a Sejm coalition of five center-right parties by nominating Jan Olszewski of the Center Alliance as prime minister. Relations between the two men had been strained in early 1991 by Olszewski's initial refusal of the position of prime minister and by Wałęsa's fear that Olszewski would abandon the Balcerowicz economic reforms. At that point, Wałęsa had even threatened to assume the duties of prime minister himself.

Although supported by a fragile, unlikely coalition that included the Confederation for an Independent Poland and the Liberal-Democratic Congress, Olszewski was confirmed as prime minister. Within days, however, the coalition began to disintegrate. Although the Liberal-Democratic Congress had been promised a decisive role in setting economic policy, the futility of that promise soon drove the party out of the coalition. Next to leave was the ultranationalist Confederation for an Independent Poland, which was alienated when it was denied control of the Ministry of National Defense (see Confederation for an Independent Poland, this ch.). A frustrated Olszewski submitted his resignation only two weeks after his nomination.

The Sejm rejected Olszewski's resignation, sensing that no other nominee was likely to form a more viable government at that time. The prime minister survived mainly because of unexpected support from a party outside the coalition, the Polish Peasant Party, which won several key ministerial appointments in the political bargain. Nevertheless, dissension within the coalition continued to weaken and isolate the prime minister at the same time that the two largest parties in the Sejm—Mazowiecki's Democratic Union and the Social Democracy of the Republic of Poland, heir to the PZPR—openly opposed the government.

Although condemning the previous two governments for the deep recession and budget crisis, Olszewski had very little room to maneuver and continued the austerity policies initiated by those governments. Far from easing the pain of economic transition, Olszewski was forced to impose steep energy and transportation price increases. Government spending could not be increased without jeopardizing crucial credit arrangements with the International Monetary Fund (IMF—see Glossary).

A critical vote in the Sejm in March 1992 rejected the government's economic program outline and revealed the untenable position of the prime minister. The program, constructed by the head of the Office of Central Planning, Jerzy Eysymontt, called for continued sacrifice, reduced government spending, and higher prices for traditionally subsidized goods and services. This program clearly conflicted with the government's promises for a rapid breakthrough and a reversal of Balcerowicz's austerity policies (see Economic Policy Making in the 1990s, ch. 3).

Efforts to bring the major opposition parties into the governing coalition began in 1992, but preliminary talks produced nothing and alienated coalition members who had not been consulted in advance. Some members objected to all compromises with the Liberal-Democratic Congress and the Democratic Union. One such member was the Christian National Union, a strong supporter of Olszewski, which dominated his cabinet and advanced a Roman Catholic agenda incompatible with the secular views of the two opposition parties. The most problematic issue upon which the parties disagreed was the state's position on abortion.

The Sejm's rejection of his economic program convinced Olszewski to push harder for expansion of his coalition. In the days following the vote, Olszewski personally offered economic compromise to Mazowiecki in exchange for support by the Democratic Union. Mazowiecki insisted on a dominant role in economic policy and inclusion of his allied parties in a restructured government. Several weeks of amicable negotiations failed to enlarge Olszewski's coalition.

Even as he sought potential coalition partners and proposed economic compromises, Olszewski alienated the opposition and, most importantly, President Wałęsa, by his partisan leadership style and personnel policies at all levels of administration. Two members of Olszewski's cabinet defied presidential prerogatives in highly publicized, politically destabilizing incidents. First, Minister of National Defense Jan Parys enraged Wałęsa by failing to consult him in making key personnel decisions, a failure that led to dismissal of Parys for making public accusations that members of the president's circle planned a coup. Then the circulation of an unsubstantiated list of sixty-two current and former government officials alleged to have collaborated with the communist secret police caused a major upheaval. Wałęsa charged that the list threatened the stability of the state and required the dismissal of the Olszewski government. The Sejm then voted Olszewski out of office in June 1992 by the substantial margin of 273 to 119 votes.

Olszewski and his cabinet did not leave office quietly. The outgoing government launched unprecedented personal attacks on Wałęsa, accusing him of presiding over the recommunization of Poland. Wałęsa replied that Olszewski had issued orders to place on alert security forces in Warsaw, including the presidential guard, as a prelude to a coup d'état.

The Pawlak Interlude

In June Wałęsa nominated Waldemar Pawlak, the thirty-two-year-old leader of the Polish Peasant Party, as Olszewski's replacement. The Sejm approved the nomination by a vote of 261 to 149. To calm the highly charged atmosphere in Warsaw and the persistent rumors of coup plots, the new prime minister immediately replaced ministers implicated in circulation of the controversial list. Despite Pawlak's reputation as a reasonable and competent politician, he could not surmount his membership in a party tainted by past accommodation to the communists; he was unable to assemble a cabinet acceptable to the splintered Sejm. The first prime minister without Solidarity connections since the Round Table Agreement, Pawlak failed to win the support of any major party linked to Solidarity. When talks with the major opposition parties broke down a month after his appointment, Pawlak asked Wałęsa to relieve him of the mission of forming a new government.

The Suchocka Government

Once again frustrated by an uncooperative Sejm, Wałęsa threatened to assume the duties of prime minister and form his own cabinet unless a governing coalition were assembled within twenty-four hours. In July two emerging coalitions in the Sejm (a four-party Christian and peasant block and the existing Little Coalition formed around the Democratic Union) surprised most observers by reaching agreement on the candidacy of Hanna Suchocka of the Democratic Union and on the allocation of cabinet positions. Despite misgivings, Wałęsa approved the cabinet with the warning that if Suchocka failed, he would assume the duties of chief executive in a French-style presidential government.

A relatively unknown political figure, Suchocka was acceptable to other parties that felt personal antipathy toward the more prominent leaders of the Democratic Union. To strengthen support for the new government, two deputy prime minister positions were created, one for economic affairs and one for politics. These posts went to members of the Christian National Union and the Party of Christian Democrats, respectively. Drawing heavily on the experience of the first three Solidarity governments, Suchocka's cabinet included such well-known figures as Jacek Kuroń and Janusz Onyszkiewicz (minister of national defense) of the Democratic Union, Bielecki of the Liberal-Democratic Congress, Eysymontt of the Polish Economic Program, and independent Krzysztof

Skubiszewski (minister of foreign affairs). Members of the Little Coalition received eleven ministerial posts, most of which were concerned with economic policy; the Christian National Union received five cabinet positions, ensuring it a prominent role in social policy issues such as abortion. Noticeably outside the coalition were the Center Alliance, the Social Democracy of the Republic of Poland, and the Confederation for an Independent Poland, all of which found their political fortunes declining in mid-1992.

The Constitution

Although significantly amended after the Round Table Agreement of April 1989, much of the constitution of 1952 remained in effect in mid-1992 (see The Round Table Agreement, this ch.). The symbolic target date of May 3, 1992, for adopting a new constitution proved unrealistic in light of Poland's political climate. That date would have commemorated the two-hundredth anniversary of the enactment of Poland's first written constitution, the Ustawa Rządowa of May 3, 1791—a widely hailed document intellectually rooted in the philosophy of the Enlightenment. But in 1990 and 1991, a new constitution was impossible because the Round Table Agreement had allowed the communists continued predominance in the Sejm and because of growing factionalism within Solidarity, the most powerful party. Even after free parliamentary elections in October 1991, however, political instability precluded the adoption of a new constitution in the near term.

The Constitution of 1952

With the adoption of the 1952 document, which replicated much of the Soviet Union's 1936 constitution, the Republic of Poland was renamed the Polish People's Republic, and the crown symbolizing national independence was removed from the country's flag. The constitution declared that power derived from the working people, who by universal suffrage and the secret ballot elected their representatives in the Sejm and the regional and local people's councils. Like its Soviet counterpart, the 1952 Polish constitution listed in exhaustive detail the basic rights and responsibilities of the population. All citizens, regardless of nationality, race, religion, sex, level of education, or social status, were guaranteed work, leisure, education, and health care. The constitution promised freedom of religion, speech, the press, assembly, and association, and it guaranteed inviolability of the person, the home, and personal correspondence. As in the Soviet Union, however, the idealistic Polish constitution did not deliver the promised individual rights and liberties.

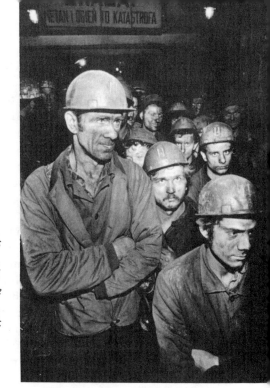

Striking coal miners in Katowice District, November 1981 Courtesy Committee in Support of Solidarity, New York

Instead, the constitution of 1952 provided a facade of legitimacy, behind which the PZPR concentrated real political power in its central party organs, particularly the Political Bureau, usually referred to as the Politburo, and the Secretariat. The document's ambiguous language concerning establishment of a state apparatus enabled the PZPR to bend the constitution to suit its purposes. The traditional tripartite separation of powers among governmental branches was abandoned. The constitution allowed the PZPR to control the state apparatus "in the interests of the working people." As a result, all levels of government were staffed with PZPR-approved personnel, and government in fact functioned as the party's administrative, subordinate partner.

Between 1952 and 1973, the PZPR-dominated Sejm approved ten constitutional amendments concerning the organization and function of central and local government bodies. In 1976, after four years of work by a Sejm constitutional commission, roughly one-third of the original ninety-one articles were amended. The new version described Poland as a socialist state, presumably signifying advancement from its earlier status as a people's democracy. For the first time, the constitution specifically mentioned the PZPR, which was accorded special status as the "guiding political force of society in building socialism." The document also recognized the Soviet Union as the liberator of Poland from fascism and as the innovator of the socialist state. More importantly, the 1976 amendments committed Poland to a foreign policy of friendly relations with the Soviet Union and its other socialist neighbors. These provisions, which in effect surrendered Polish national sovereignty, provoked such widespread protest by the intelligentsia and the Roman Catholic hierarchy that the government was forced to recast the amendments in less controversial terms (see The Intelligentsia; Religion, ch. 2).

In the decade preceding the Round Table Agreement, the PZPR endorsed a number of amendments to the 1952 constitution in a vain attempt to gain legitimacy with the disgruntled population. In the spirit of the Gdańsk Agreement of August 1980, which recognized workers' rights to establish free trade unions, the constitution was amended in October 1980. The amendments of that time promised to reduce PZPR influence over the Sejm. For that purpose, the Supreme Control Chamber (Najwyższa Izba Kontroli—NIK—chief agency for oversight of the government's economic and administrative activities) was transferred from the Council of Ministers to the Sejm. In December 1981, the imposition of martial law temporarily halted the erosion of the party's constitutional authority. But in March 1982, the Jaruzelski regime resumed its effort to appease the public by again amending the constitution.

The March 1982 amendments provided for the creation of two independent entities, the Constitutional Tribunal and the State Tribunal, which had the effect of reestablishing the traditional Polish constitutional principle of government by rule of law. The 1976 amendments had placed adjudication of the constitutionality of statutes with the Council of State (chief executive organ of the nation). Although the authority of the Constitutional Tribunal was strictly limited, beginning in 1982 that body issued a number of important decisions forcing the repeal of questionable regulations. The State Tribunal was established to adjudicate abuses of power by government officials. Although legally prevented from reviewing the activities of Sejm deputies, the State Tribunal represented yet another major step in the evolution of the democratic concept of government by the consent of the governed.

Shortly before the official lifting of martial law in July 1983, the Sejm enacted additional constitutional changes that held the promise of political pluralism. For the first time, the United Peasant Party and the Democratic Party officially were recognized as legitimate political parties, existing independently from the PZPR. The amendments also tacitly sanctioned the political activities of church organizations by stressing that public good can derive from "societal organizations."

Another important step toward meaningful constitutional guarantees in a civil society was the July 1987 decision to establish the
Office of the Commissioner for Citizens' Rights as a people's ombudsman. The office provided a mechanism for citizens to file
grievances against government organs for violations of constitutionally guaranteed civil rights. Receiving more than 50,000 peti-
tions in its first year, the office immediately proved to be more than
a symbolic concession.

Constitutional Revisions after April 1989

The Round Table Agreement brought a number of amendments
that substantially altered the 1952 constitution. The so-called April
Amendments resurrected the traditional Polish constitutional concept of separation of powers. The legislative branch would again
be bicameral after four decades of a single, 460-member Sejm. The
new body included a freely elected 100-member Senate and retained
the 460-member Sejm as its lower chamber. Power would be distributed among the houses of parliament and the newly established
Office of the President, which was to assume many of the executive powers previously held by the Council of State. The April
Amendments provided for election of the president by the two
houses of parliament.

In December 1989, the new parliament made several additional, highly symbolic amendments to the 1952 constitution to rid the
document of Marxist terminology. The PZPR lost its special status when its identification as the political guiding force in Polish
society was deleted from the constitution. The hated words "people's republic" would be discarded and the state's official name
would be restored to the prewar "Republic of Poland." Article
2 was revised to read "Supreme authority in the Republic of Poland
is vested in the People," amending the Marxist phrase "the working
people." The amendments of December 1989 also wrote into law
the equality of all forms of property ownership, the essential first
step in establishing a market economy.

Aware that piecemeal revision of the Stalinist 1952 constitution
would not meet the needs of a democratic Polish society, in December 1989 the Sejm created a Constitutional Commission to write
a fully democratic document untainted by association with Poland's
communist era. The next year, the National Assembly (the combined Sejm and Senate) prescribed the procedure by which the draft
would be enacted. The document would require approval by a two-
thirds vote of both assembly houses in joint session, followed by
a national referendum. Theoretically, this procedure would bolster

the constitution's legitimacy against doubts created by the dubious political credentials of some of its authors.

Chaired by one of the Solidarity movement's most brilliant intellectuals, Bronisław Geremek, the Sejm Constitutional Commission faced serious obstacles from the outset. The legitimacy of the Sejm itself was at issue because the Round Table Agreement had allowed Solidarity to contest only 35 percent of the Sejm seats. Claiming that its open election in 1989 made it more representative of the popular will, the Senate condemned the Sejm Constitutional Commission and began working on its own version of a new constitution. In reality, however the Senate was not an accurate cross section of Polish society because it lacked representatives from the peasants and the political left. Subsequent efforts to form a joint Sejm-Senate constitutional commission proved futile.

After his victory in the December 1990 presidential election, Wałęsa cast further doubt on the commission's activity by challenging the credentials of the existing Sejm. Nevertheless, the commission continued its work and presented a fairly complete draft constitution by the spring of 1991. The draft was based on the two series of amendments passed in 1989. It also borrowed heavily from various Western constitutions, most notably the constitution of the Federal Republic of Germany (West Germany). The draft was soon discarded, however, because of the Sejm's undemocratic constituency; for the same reason, the commission as such ceased to exist in 1991.

In the first half of 1992, attention shifted to the so-called Little Constitution, a document that used much of the 1991 draft in redefining the relationship between the legislative and executive branches of government and clarifying the division of power between the president and the prime minister. The Little Constitution was to be a compromise that would solidify as many democratic institutions as possible before all constitutional controversies could be resolved. Nevertheless, the new document would supersede all but a few provisions of the 1952 constitution and provide the basis for a full constitution when remaining points of dispute could be resolved. Its drafts retained the statement that Poland was a democratic state of law guided by principles of social justice. Agencies such as the Constitutional Tribunal, the State Tribunal, and the Office of the Commissioner for Citizens Rights were also retained (see Judicial System, this ch.).

Government Structure

The three years following the Round Table Agreement of 1989 were a period of dramatic but uneven change in the governmental structure of the Republic of Poland. The Round Table Agreement itself moved Poland decisively away from a Soviet-style unitary hierarchy in which the formal government was merely a bureaucracy to implement decisions made by the extraconstitutional organs of the PZPR. The Round Table Agreement created a tripartite structure in which power was distributed among the executive, legislative, and judicial branches. By mid-1992, the Polish government had evolved into a presidential and parliamentary democracy with an increasingly independent judiciary. The adoption of the Little Constitution promised to resolve ambiguities in the executive powers of the president and the prime minister and to clarify the scope of control of the bicameral National Assembly (see Constitutional Revisions after April 1989, this ch.).

Presidency

The presidency was established by the Round Table Agreement to replace the communist-era Council of State as the primary executive organ of government. According to the agreement, the president was to be elected by the National Assembly to a term of six years. Although not the head of government (that function was performed by the prime minister), the president was empowered to veto legislation and had control of the armed forces. The negotiators of the Round Table Agreement clearly crafted the presidency with the expectation that General Jaruzelski would be its first incumbent. A Jaruzelski presidency would have ensured PZPR compliance with the concessions the party had made in the agreement. Moreover, Jaruzelski was expected to be effective in protecting the new political arrangements from Soviet interference. After Solidarity succeeded in forming a noncommunist coalition government in mid-1989, however, Jaruzelski lost most of his powers, and the presidency became a largely ceremonial office. The office changed drastically when Wałęsa became Poland's first popularly elected president in late 1990 (see Political Setting, this chapter).

A constitutional amendment in the spring of 1990 provided for direct popular election of the president to a five-year term with a limit of one reelection. Any Polish citizen at least thirty-five years of age was eligible to appear on the ballot after obtaining 100,000 nominating signatures.

If accused of violating the constitution and Polish law, the president could be indicted before the State Tribunal if two-thirds of the National Assembly so voted. Upon indictment, the president would be relieved temporarily of the duties of office. A guilty verdict from the State Tribunal would bring expulsion from office. The presidency also could be vacated because of physical unfitness

189

to hold the office, as determined by the National Assembly. In such circumstances, the Sejm speaker would temporarily assume the duties of the presidency until a new president could be sworn in.

The president's duties include protecting the constitution; safeguarding the sovereignty, security, and territorial inviolability of the Polish state; and overseeing adherence to international agreements and treaties. The constitution authorizes the president to call for elections to the Sejm, Senate, and county councils (see Regional and Local Government, this ch.). The president also appoints diplomatic representatives and officially receives foreign diplomats; acts as commander in chief of the armed forces; calls and presides over emergency sessions of the Council of Ministers; and performs other duties assigned the chief of state by the constitution or by law.

A critical duty of the president is naming the head of government, the prime minister. The Little Constitution amends the procedure prescribed for this function. Originally, the president nominated the prime minister, but the Sejm had to approve both that nomination and the prime minister's cabinet choices that followed. The Little Constitution specifies that the president designate the prime minister and appoint the cabinet upon consultation with the prime minister. Within two weeks, however, the new government must receive the Sejm's confirmation (by a simple majority of the deputies present voting in favor). If the government is not confirmed, the Sejm then has the responsibility to nominate and confirm its own candidate, again by a majority vote. If the Sejm fails in this attempt, the president has another chance, this time with the lesser requirement that more votes be cast for approval than for nonapproval. Finally, if the president's choice again fails, the Sejm would attempt to confirm its own candidate by the lesser vote. If no candidate can be confirmed, the president has the option of dissolving parliament or appointing a six-month interim government. During the interim period, if the Sejm does not confirm the government, or one of its own choosing, parliament automatically would be dissolved.

The constitution grants the president certain legislative prerogatives, including the right to propose legislation; to veto acts of the National Assembly (the Sejm could overrule such a veto with a two-thirds majority); to ask the Constitutional Tribunal to judge the constitutionality of legislation; and to issue decrees and instructions on the implementation of laws. The president ratifies or terminates international agreements but needs prior approval from the Sejm to ratify agreements involving sizable financial liability on the state or changes in legislation.

If national security were threatened, the president could declare martial law and announce a partial or full mobilization. He or she could also introduce a state of emergency for a period of up to three months in case of a threat to domestic tranquility or natural disaster. A one-time extension of a state of emergency, not to exceed three months, could be declared with the approval of both houses of the National Assembly.

Sejm

The lower house of the bicameral National Assembly, the Sejm, is the more powerful of the two chambers. The Sejm has the constitutional responsibility of initiating and enacting laws that "set the basic direction of the state's activity" and of overseeing "other organs of power and state administration." The constitution specifies election of the 460 Sejm deputies to a term of four years. The 1991 election was conducted by a system that awarded seats in the Sejm in strict proportion to the number of votes each party or coalition garnered nationally (see table 20, Appendix). This system was blamed for the extreme fragmentation that plagued Polish politics in 1991–92. The new Sejm is required to convene within one month after national parliamentary elections.

Upon taking the oath of office, the Sejm deputies immediately elect a permanent marshal, who serves as Sejm speaker. The marshal and three vice marshals constitute the Presidium of the Sejm, the chief duties of which are to oversee accomplishment of the Sejm agenda, to coordinate the activities of the parliamentary commissions, and to represent the Sejm in external affairs. The marshal, vice marshals, and leaders of parliamentary caucuses (called "clubs") form an advisory organ to the Sejm Presidium known as the Council of Elders (Konwent Seniorów), which assists in scheduling.

The constitution empowers the president to declare a three-month state of emergency in the event of parliamentary paralysis. During this period, the president may perform the duties of the prime minister, but the Sejm cannot be dismissed, and changes cannot be made to the constitution or electoral law.

Among the most important agencies of the Sejm in mid-1992 were twenty-one permanent committees, which enjoyed considerable autonomy in deliberating issues and in referring their findings to the entire Sejm for action. The committees set their own agendas in analyzing the performance of individual sectors of the economy or units of state administration. The Sejm could also create special committees to study specific issues. Committee appointments were highly partisan and reflected the numerical representation of the various parties and factions within the Sejm.

The National Assembly has exclusive responsibility to pass a central state budget and to finance the entire range of state activities, including foreign monetary payments, and to approve a domestic credit plan and balance sheet of incomes and expenditures. The budget bill and financial plans passed by the Sejm are sent to the Senate, which may propose changes. The Little Constitution specifies that the Sejm can overturn the Senate's changes with an absolute majority vote. Previously, overriding Senate changes had required a two-thirds majority, with a quorum of at least 50 percent of the Sejm deputies. The president can dismiss parliament for failing to pass a budget within three months.

Senate

The upper house of the National Assembly, the Senate, was reestablished by the Round Table Agreement more than four decades after being abolished by the communist government. The Round Table Agreement provides for the direct popular election of all 100 senators—two from each of the forty-nine districts (*województwa;* sing., *województwo,* sometimes seen in English as voivodship) with the exception of Warsaw and Katowice, which elect three senators each. The senators' four-year terms of office coincide with those of Sejm deputies.

The Senate sets its own agenda and committee structure. As in the Sejm, committee appointments are dictated by the numerical strength of the parties and factions represented in the chamber. Besides its budget review function, the Senate also reviews Sejm legislation and may approve, amend, or reject within thirty days. The Senate also confirms key appointments, including the commissioner for citizens' rights and the chairperson of the Supreme Control Chamber, both of whom are nominated by the Sejm.

Within one month after parliamentary elections, the president is required to call the first session of the new Senate. The Senate Presidium consists of the permanent marshal and six other prominent senators. The Sejm and Senate presidia occasionally meet to coordinate agendas and create joint committees as required.

Supreme Control Chamber

The Supreme Control Chamber, often referred to as the NIK, was established during the communist period to monitor the economic, financial, and administrative activities of state organs, their subordinate enterprises, and other organizational units. The chairperson of the NIK was appointed or recalled by the Sejm with the concurrence of the Senate. The chamber gained a reputation for incorruptability in the communist era, exerting some control over inefficiency and budgetary excesses. The office has retained its watchdog role in the democratic system. Among other activities, the NIK submits reports on the performance, abuses, and failures of enterprise funds, customs offices, and currency exchanges.

Council of Ministers

The highest administrative organ of state authority, the Council of Ministers (commonly called the cabinet), and its chairperson, the prime minister, constitute the acting government. The Council of Ministers answers to the Sejm or, between Sejm sessions, to the president. Prior to the adoption of the Little Constitution, the Sejm could dismiss individual ministers or the entire Council of Ministers on its own initiative. The Little Constitution restricts this prerogative by requiring the Sejm to nominate an alternative candidate supported by an absolute majority of Sejm deputies. If the Sejm produces no such candidate, no vote for dismissal may be taken. The Little Constitution also eliminates the president's power to move for the government's dismissal.

The authority of the Council of Ministers is quite broad. The council coordinates the activities of the ministries and their subordinate entities. Among its other legally specified functions is compiling an annual state budget and presenting it to the Sejm and the Senate for approval. The Council of Ministers also presents an annual report on the previous year's budgetary implementation. Other constitutional functions include ensuring public order; protecting the interests of the state and the rights of individual citizens; guiding foreign policy and national defense; and organizing the armed forces and setting induction quotas. In running the Council of Ministers, the prime minister is assisted by one or more deputy prime ministers and a director of the Office of the Council of Ministers. In mid-1992, the government consisted of seventeen ministries, the Office of Central Planning, and three ministers without portfolio (see The Suchocka Government, this ch.).

The jurisdiction of the ministries is defined by statute, on the basis of which the ministries issue decrees and regulations. Under secretaries of state and vice ministers provide managerial support to the ministers. For certain ministries with exceptionally broad responsibilities, the position of secretary of state was established. The prime minister has authority to appoint and dismiss secretaries and under secretaries of state.

Regional and Local Government

The territory of Poland is administered through a system of forty-nine districts established in 1975 to replace the previous system of twenty-two districts. In addition, three city councils—Warsaw, Łódź, and Kraków—enjoy special administrative status. Each district is managed by a government-appointed *wojewoda* (typically a professional administrator) and a district assembly whose members are chosen by the popularly elected local government units, the community (*gmina;* pl., *gminy*) councils. Both the district and community levels of government enjoy far greater autonomy than they did under the highly centralized communist system of administration.

According to the amended constitution in use in mid-1992, local self-rule is the basic organizational form of public life in the community. The community possesses legal status and acts on behalf of the public interest in accordance with the law. The residents of the community directly elect a standing council of their peers to a four-year term by universal secret ballot. A community or town of fewer than 40,000 residents elects council members in single-seat districts on a simple majority basis. Cities with more than 40,000 people use multiseat districts, and seats are allocated on a proportional basis. The executive organ of the community is the municipal government (*zarząd*), which consists of a "chief officer" (*wojt;* pl., *wojtowie*) or mayor, his or her deputies, and other members. Communities may form intercommunity unions to coordinate projects of mutual interest.

Community councils in a given district elect delegates from their membership to a self-governing regional council (*sejmik samorządowy*), which approves formation of intercommunity unions and works closely with district authorities through mandatory reports moving in both directions. The prime minister and district authorities monitor community activity, but they may interfere only in instances of obvious incompetence or violation of law.

Judicial System

The constitution of 1952 reflected the communists' disdain for the concept of judicial independence. As in the Soviet system, the Polish judiciary was viewed as an integral part of the coercive state apparatus. The courts were not allowed to adjudicate the constitutionality of statutes. Instead, the function of constitutional review was within the purview of the legislative branch until 1976, when it passed to the Council of State. A key provision of the Round

Table Agreement was the reemergence of an independent judiciary, a concept rooted in the Ustawa Rządowa, the constitution of 1791. By 1992 most of the communist political appointees had left the Supreme Court, and at all levels new judges had been recruited from among qualified academic and courtroom barristers. On the other hand, in 1992 Poland's body of laws still contained a motley assortment of Soviet-style statutes full of vague language aimed at protecting the communist monopoly of power rather than the rule of law itself. A complete overhaul of the legal system was a universally recognized need.

National Judicial Council

A critical step in establishing the autonomy of the judicial branch was the Sejm's vote in December 1989 to create the National Judicial Council. The twenty-four member council, consisting of judges from the national, district, and local levels, serves a four-year term and has the primary function of recommending judgeship candidates to the president. Another basic function of the body is to oversee the entire judiciary and establish professional standards.

Supreme Court

Reform of the appointment mechanism for justices was a necessity to ensure an independent judiciary. In the communist era, the Council of State appointed Supreme Court justices to five-year terms, making selections on purely political grounds. Because the Supreme Court had jurisdiction over all other courts in the land, the political reliability of its members was an important consideration in appointment decisions. Judicial reform after the Round Table Agreement provided that the president appoint Supreme Court justices from a list prepared by an independent National Judicial Council, and that justices be appointed for life terms. The presiding officer of the Supreme Court, called the first chairman, is appointed from among the Supreme Court justices by the National Assembly upon the recommendation of the president. Dismissal from the chairmanship follows the same procedure.

The Supreme Court reviews the decisions of all lower courts; hears appeals of decisions made by the district courts, along with appeals brought by the minister of justice (who simultaneously serves as the prosecutor general) and the first chairman of the Supreme Court; and adopts legal interpretations and clarifications. The court is organized into four chambers: criminal, civil, labor and social insurance, and military. Because of its heavy case load, the Supreme Court is a large body, employing 117 judges and a staff of 140 persons in late 1990.

Lower Courts

In 1990 the system of lower courts included forty-four district and 282 local courts. These numbers were scheduled to be increased to forty-nine and 300, respectively, in 1991. Thereafter the local courts were to concentrate on minor, routine offenses, and the district courts were to take on more serious cases and consider appeals of local court verdicts. Misdemeanors generally are handled by panels of "social adjudicators," who are elected by local government councils. In 1991 these panels heard about 600,000 cases, of which about 80 percent were traffic violations. To relieve the heavy appeals case load of the Supreme Court, ten regional appeals courts were set up in late 1990 to review verdicts of the district courts.

Supreme Administrative Court

The Supreme Administrative Court was established in 1980 to review and standardize administrative regulations enforced by government agencies and to hear citizens' complaints concerning the legality of administrative decisions. In 1991 the court heard some 15,600 cases, mostly dealing with taxes, social welfare issues, and local government decisions. As of late 1990, the court employed 105 judges and 163 staff members.

Constitutional Tribunal

The Constitutional Tribunal was established by the Jaruzelski regime in early 1982 to adjudicate the constitutionality of laws and regulations. The Sejm appoints the tribunal's members to four-year terms. Initially, the body did not have authority to review laws and statutes enacted before 1982. Findings of unconstitutionality could be overruled by the Sejm with a two-thirds majority vote. Selected by the Sejm for their superior legal expertise, the members of the Constitutional Tribunal are independent and bound only by the constitution (see The Constitution of 1952, this ch.). In 1992 the tribunal made controversial findings that government plans to control wages and pensions retroactively violated rights constitutionally guaranteed to citizens.

State Tribunal

The Jaruzelski regime created the State Tribunal in 1982, by the same law that formed the Constitutional Tribunal, in response to instances of high official corruption in 1980. The State Tribunal passes judgment on the guilt or innocence of the highest office holders in the land accused of violating the constitution and laws. The body's twenty-seven members are appointed by the Sejm from outside its membership for a term coinciding with that of the Sejm. Judges in the State Tribunal are independent and bound only by the law. The chairperson of the State Tribunal is the president of the Supreme Court. As of mid-1992, the State Tribunal had never heard a case.

Prosecutor General

The communist-era Office of the Chief Prosecutor was abolished following the Round Table Agreement. Thereafter, the minister of justice has served as the prosecutor general. The mission of the prosecutor general is to safeguard law and order and ensure prosecution of crimes. Since 1990 the prosecutors on the district and local levels have been given autonomy from the police and are subordinated to the minister of justice, who has assumed the role of the defunct prosecutor general. In 1992 many prosecutors remained from the rubber-stamp judicial system of the communist era, however. Because they had no understanding of democratic judicial practice, these officials seriously inhibited the new legal system in dealing with the wave of crime that accompanied the transition to a market economy.

Commissioner for Citizens' Rights

The concept of a people's ombudsman to safeguard individual civil rights and liberties was first proposed by the Patriotic Movement for National Rebirth (Patriotyczny Ruch Odrodzenia Narodowego—PRON) in 1983. Four years later, the Sejm enacted legislation establishing the Office of the Commissioner for Citizens' Rights. Appointed to a four-year term by the Sejm with Senate approval, the commissioner is independent of other state agencies and answers only to the Sejm. The commissioner's mandate is to investigate on behalf of individual citizens or organizations possible infractions of Polish law or basic principles of justice by public officials, institutions, or organizations. Although the commissioner may review the administration of the courts, he or she may intercede only in matters such as scheduling of cases. In military or internal security matters, the commissioner does not investigate evidence but channels cases to the appropriate jurisdiction. As a public ombudsman, the commissioner confronts the accused party and conveys official displeasure at a given action or policy. The commissioner also may request the initiation of civil, criminal, or administrative proceedings and appeal to the Constitutional

197

Tribunal to review a law's constitutionality or consistency with a higher statute.

The public greeted the creation of the Office of the Commissioner for Citizens' Rights with enthusiasm. Lacking an established screening mechanism, the new office received more than 55,000 complaints in 1988 alone. The commissioner also conducts systematic inspections of prisons in response to inmates' complaints. Following the inspections, the commissioner issues a comprehensive report. This practice has resulted in a more humane, less congested prison system. In 1990 a national opinion poll revealed that at that point the ombudsman enjoyed the highest popularity of any Polish politician.

Political Parties

For four decades before the historic Round Table Agreement, Poland had three legal political parties: the ruling communist PZPR and its two subservient coalition partners, the United Peasant Party and the Democratic Party. The first communist regime to gain power had outlawed the major pre-World War II parties—National Democracy, the Labor Party, and the Polish Peasant Party (see Consolidation of Communist Power, ch. 1). The PZPR was formed in 1948 with the merger of the Polish United Workers' Party and the Polish Socialist Party. Realizing the lack of popular support for communism and public fears of Soviet domination, the Polish communists eschewed the term *communist* in their official name.

In return for acknowledging the leading role of the PZPR, the two major coalition partners and three smaller Catholic associations received a fixed number of seats in the Sejm. Although one of the latter category, Znak, was technically an independent party, its allotment of five seats gave it very limited influence. Typically, the United Peasant Party held 20 to 25 percent of the Sejm seats and the Democratic Party received about 10 percent. Despite the nominal diversity of the Sejm, the noncommunist parties had little impact, and the Sejm was essentially a rubber-stamp body that enacted legislation approved by the central decision-making organs of the PZPR. Following the Soviet model, political parties and religious associations, as well as all other mass organizations, labor unions, and the press only transmitted policy and programs from the central PZPR hierarchy to Polish society.

The years 1956, 1968, 1970, 1976, and 1980 were turning points in the evolution of organized political opposition in Poland. With the death of the Stalinist Bolesław Bierut in 1956, Poland entered a brief period of de-Stalinization. The PZPR relaxed its intimidation of the intelligentsia, artists, and the church (see The Polish

Catholic Church and the State, ch. 2). The Znak group emerged and experimented as a semiautonomous vehicle of dialog between the PZPR and society. But with the Soviet-organized invasion of Czechoslovakia in 1968, the PZPR again suppressed dissent and expelled outspoken Znak delegates from the Sejm. The 1970 ship-yard strikes, which claimed hundreds of victims, brought down the regime of Władysław Gomułka (1956–70) and demonstrated the potential of workers to oppose unpopular PZPR policies (see The Gathering Crisis of People's Poland, 1956-80, ch. 1). In 1976 the arrest of striking workers convinced a group of intellectuals, led by Jacek Kuroń and Adam Michnik, to form the Committee for Defense of Workers (Komitet Obrony Robotników—KOR), the most successful opposition group until Solidarity.

Solidarity

The breakthrough in ending the political monopoly of the PZPR came in 1980 with the emergence of the Interfactory Strike Committee, which rapidly evolved into the Solidarity mass movement of some 10 million Poles (see The Birth of Solidarity, ch. 1). Guided by Lech Wałęsa, the Interfactory Strike Committee won historic concessions from the communists in the Gdańsk Agreement of August 31, 1980. The PZPR granted recognition of the basic right of workers to establish free trade unions, but in return the strike committee agreed not to function as a political party. The workers promised to abide by the constitution and conceded the leading role in state affairs to the PZPR.

Despite the pledges of the Gdańsk Agreement, Solidarity did not remain simply a trade union movement. It rapidly changed into an umbrella organization under which a broad range of political and social groups united in opposition to the communist regime. At Solidarity's first national congress in the fall of 1981, the political nature of the movement became explicit. The congress adopted a program calling for an active Solidarity role in reforming Poland's political and economic systems. In the following months, outspoken radicals urged their leaders to confront the communist authorities, to demand free elections, and to call for a national referendum to replace the communist government. The radical challenge precipitated the imposition of martial law on December 13, 1981. Solidarity, now illegal, was forced underground until the late 1980s (see The Jaruzelski Interlude, ch. 1). Within six months after the start of the Round Table talks in February 1989, Solidarity not only had regained its legal status as a trade union, but also had become an effective political movement that installed Eastern Europe's first postcommunist government.

199

During its underground phase, Solidarity lost much of its original cohesion as tactical and philosophical disagreements split the movement into factions. The radical elements, convinced that an evolutionary approach to democratization was impossible, created the organization Fighting Solidarity in 1982. Ultimately, however, Wałęsa's moderate faction prevailed.

Favoring negotiation and compromise with the PZPR, the moderates created the Citizens' Committee, which represented Solidarity at the talks in 1989 and engineered the overwhelming election triumph of June 1989. Led by Bronisław Geremek, a prominent intellectual, the newly elected Solidarity deputies in parliament formed the Citizens' Parliamentary Club to coordinate legislative efforts and advance the Solidarity agenda.

The stunning defeat of the PZPR in the June 1989 parliamentary elections removed Solidarity's most important unifying force—the common enemy. By the time of the local elections of May 1990, Solidarity had splintered, and a remarkable number of small parties had appeared. Because any individual with fifteen nominating signatures could be placed on the ballot, an astounding 1,140 groups and "parties" registered for the elections. In the local elections, the new groups' lack of organization and national experience caused them to fare poorly against the Solidarity-backed citizens' committees that sponsored about one-third of the candidates running for local office.

Despite the success of the Solidarity candidates in the local elections, serious divisions soon emerged within the Citizens' Parliamentary Club concerning the appropriateness of political parties at so early a stage in Poland's democratic experiment. The intellectuals who dominated the parliamentary club insisted that the proliferation of political parties would derail efforts to build a Western-style civil society. But deputies on the right of the political spectrum, feeling excluded from important policy decisions by the intellectuals, advocated rapid formation of strong alternative parties.

Center Alliance

An outspoken Wałęsa supporter determined to end the political dominance of the intellectual elite in the Citizens' Parliamentary Club, Jarosław Kaczyński formed the Center Alliance in May 1990. The Center Alliance supported a strong political center embodying the ideals of Solidarity and Christian ethics. With the election of its candidate for president, Wałęsa, and the appointment of Kaczyński as the president's chief of staff, the Center Alliance became one of the most influential political organizations in the country.

The Center Alliance platform for the parliamentary elections of October 1991 called for accelerated economic reform, privatization, rapid decommunization, and a strongly pro-Western foreign policy, including full membership in NATO. Considering its prominent position in the government and media and its large national membership, the party fared rather poorly in the 1991 elections. Its popular vote total yielded forty-four Sejm and nine Senate seats. The Center Alliance made its last show of political power in engineering the selection of its candidate, Jan Olszewski, to lead the coalition government in December 1991. By mid-1992, however, the influence of the party had waned because of a bitter personal rift between Kaczyński and Wałęsa, the demise of the Olszewski government, and the party's decision not to participate in the ruling coalition of Hanna Suchocka.

Democratic Union

The Democratic Union (Unia Demokratyczna—UD) held its unification congress in May 1991 to integrate three Solidarity splinter groups and to adopt a platform for the parliamentary elections. The UD counted among its members such luminaries of the Solidarity movement as Jacek Kuroń, Adam Michnik, Bronisław Geremek, and Tadeusz Mazowiecki. The party sought political and economic reform through the rule of law. Rejecting extremism of any stripe, it pursued policies of economic pragmatism. Although its registered membership ranked only fifth numerically among political parties, the UD was a well-organized national party with branches in all forty-nine districts.

In October 1991, with the UD expected to win more than a quarter of the Sejm seats in the parliamentary election, party chairman Mazowiecki indicated his availability to reassume the duties of prime minister. But the UD took only sixty-two Sejm and twenty-one Senate seats, paying dearly for its refusal to renounce the Balcerowicz Plan of economic shock therapy and for opposing the Roman Catholic Church on the issue of abortion.

During the first half of 1992, relations between the UD and Wałęsa improved considerably. Wałęsa offered to appoint the two former prime ministers, Mazowiecki and Bielecki, as his senior advisers. He repeatedly urged the inclusion of the UD in an expanded governing coalition, but negotiations toward that end failed. Instead, the UD joined forces with two other economic reformist parties outside the Olszewski government to form the Little Coalition. After the collapse of the Olszewski government, the coalition failed to reach an agreement with the new prime minister, Waldemar Pawlak, on the composition of a new cabinet. According

201

to Pawlak, the coalition insisted on total control over the economy, a concession he was not willing to make. With the election of Hanna Suchocka as the new prime minister in mid-1992, the Democratic Union regained the leadership of the government and held four of the key cabinet positions, including director of the Office of the Council of Ministers and the ministries of finance, defense, and labor and social affairs.

Liberal-Democratic Congress

The Liberal-Democratic Congress (Kongres Liberalno-Demokratyczny—KLD) arose in 1983 as a loose organization of businessmen dedicated to a philosophy of small government and free enterprise. The KLD was registered as a party in October 1990 and supported the presidential candidacy of Wałęsa, who selected KLD leader Jan Krzysztof Bielecki as his nominee to be prime minister. Another prominent party member, Janusz Lewandowski, headed the Ministry of Ownership Transformation in the Bielecki cabinet. Donald Tusk, chairman of the KLD executive board, led an unsuccessful attempt to form a broad coalition to support candidates in the 1991 Senate race. The party foreswore ideological sloganeering and backed rational, pragmatic policies. In the parliamentary elections, the KLD finished seventh in popular vote, winning thirty-seven Sejm and six Senate seats.

Beer-Lovers' Party

Registered as a political party in December 1990, the Polish Beer-Lovers' Party (Polska Partia Przyjaciół Piwa—PPPP) may have started as a prank. But with time, its members developed a serious platform, for which the humorous stated goals of the party— lively political discussion in pubs serving excellent beer—were a symbol of freedom of association and expression, intellectual tolerance, and a higher standard of living. Its humorous name probably helped the party win votes from a politically disenchanted populace in the 1991 parliamentary elections, in which the PPPP captured sixteen Sejm seats. In early 1992, following a split within the PPPP into the Big Beer and Little Beer parties, the former assumed the name Polish Economic Program. Losing its image of quirkiness, the Polish Economic Program became associated with the UD and KLD in the Little Coalition of liberal promarket parties and supported the candidacy of Hanna Suchocka as prime minister.

Peasant Alliance

In mid-1992, the party of the Rural Solidarity farmers' union,

*Cardinal Józef Glemp,
leader of the Polish
Roman Catholic Church
Courtesy Reverend
Edward Mroczynski, S.Ch.*

the Peasant Alliance (Porozumienie Ludowe—PL) held two prominent positions in the Suchocka government, the Ministry of Agriculture and the Ministry of Environmental Protection and Natural Resources. The party also controlled the post of minister without portfolio for parliamentary liaison. In mid-1992 the Peasant Alliance and the Polish Peasant Party (Polskie Stronnictwo Ludowe—PSL) were still divided by their political backgrounds although they both represented Poland's large rural sector (see Polish Peasant Party, this ch.). The PL, still distrusting the PSL for its past accommodation with the communists, opposed the selection of PSL leader Waldemar Pawlak as prime minister. The PL supported import tariffs to protect domestic farmers, state subsidies to maintain farm commodity prices, and easy credit for farmers.

Christian National Union

Socially conservative but economically to the left, the Christian National Union (Zjednoczenie Chrześcijańsko-Narodowe—ZChN) was the dominant member of a short-lived electoral alliance known as Catholic Action. The alliance finished third in the 1991 parliamentary elections and earned ZChN forty-nine Sejm and nine Senate seats. The ZChN supported the involvement of the Roman Catholic Church in politics and government, religious instruction in the schools, a generous social welfare program, and trade protectionism. The party played a large role in both the Olszewski

203

and Suchocka governments. Under Suchocka, the ZChN held five cabinet positions and the post of deputy prime minister for economic affairs.

Party of Christian Democrats

Founded in December 1990, the small Party of Christian Democrats (Partia Chrześcijańskich Demokratów—PChD) used the political experience of its membership to gain success disproportionate to its size. Its most prominent member, Paweł Łączkowski, became deputy prime minister for political affairs in the Suchocka government. On social issues, the PChD supported a more pragmatic, centrist brand of Christian democracy than that advocated by the larger ZChN. On economic issues, the PChD supported rapid economic transformation and privatization.

Confederation for an Independent Poland

Founded in 1979 by military historian Leszek Moczulski, the Confederation for an Independent Poland (Konfederacja Polski Niepodległej—KPN) claimed with some justification to be the first true opposition party of the communist era. Years before the emergence of Solidarity, Moczulski was defying the authorities with calls for the restoration of Polish sovereignty and the replacement of the communist system; he was imprisoned repeatedly from the late 1970s through the mid-1980s. The KPN did not participate in the talks leading to the Round Table Agreement and refused to compromise with the PZPR.

Because of its reputation for radicalism and violence, the KPN fared poorly in its first electoral tests: the parliamentary elections of 1989, the local elections of May 1990, and the presidential election in the autumn of 1990. But by 1991 Polish voters had grown disenchanted with the seeming impotence of the postcommunist political establishment in the face of the country's worsening economic problems. As a result, the KPN was among the extremist groups and individuals that fared well in the 1991 parliamentary elections. The KPN won forty-six seats in the Sejm, two more than the mainstream Center Alliance.

Following its success in the parliamentary elections, the KPN sought to moderate its image by joining four center-right parties in a coalition supporting the candidacy of Jan Olszewski as prime minister. Moczulski took the KPN out of the short-lived coalition, however, when Olszewski failed to name him minister of national defense. Outraged at the government's charges that Moczulski had been a collaborator with the communist secret service, the KPN voted for Olszewski's removal in June 1992. The KPN then withdrew its initial support of Pawlak as Olszewski's replacement. The seven-party alliance in support of Suchocka in mid-1992 seemingly ended the KPN's participation in coalition politics and returned it to the role of the uncompromising outsider.

PZPR and Successor Parties

During the 1980s, the Marxist underpinnings of the PZPR steadily eroded, and, long before the round table talks, the ruling party had lost its ideological fervor. Official PZPR documents compiled in May 1987 revealed that only about 25 percent of the membership were politically active, more than 60 percent paid their dues but were inactive, and 15 percent did not even pay their dues. By that time, protecting the national interest had replaced Marxist doctrine as the guiding principle of the government's actions. For example, the Jaruzelski regime characterized its imposition of martial law in 1981 not as an attempt to restore Marxist purity but as a preemptive measure to avoid Soviet military intervention in Poland. The PZPR had accepted the necessity of economic decentralization, privatization, and price liberalization, realizing that to regain political legitimacy it had to win the cooperation of the opposition.

Despite its enormous advantage in institutional and monetary resources, control of the electronic media and most print media, and a slate of reformist, nonideological candidates, the PZPR suffered an overwhelming defeat in the parliamentary elections of June 1989. Once the parties that were its traditional allies had repositioned themselves with Solidarity to install a noncommunist government, the PZPR had become a political relic. In January 1990, at its final congress (the eleventh), the PZPR patterned itself after Western social democratic parties and adopted the name Social Democracy of the Republic of Poland (Socjaldemokracja Rzeczypospolitej Polski—SdRP).

The SdRP, which inherited the assets and infrastructure of the PZPR, was a political force that could not be ignored in the reform era. During the 1990 presidential elections, for example, the SdRP candidate received 9 percent of the vote. At its first national convention in May 1991, the party adopted a platform supporting pluralistic democracy, a parliamentary form of government, strict separation of church and state, women's rights, environmental protection, the right to work, a generous social safety net, and good relations with all of Poland's neighbors. In July 1991, preparing for the October parliamentary elections, the SdRP invited other groups with a communist lineage to join it in a broad coalition, the Alliance of the Democratic Left (Sojusz Lewicy Demokratycznej—SLD). The most important of these groups was the All-Polish

Alliance of Trade Unions (Ogólnopolskie Porozumienie Związków Zawodowych—OPZZ), which Jaruzelski had created in 1984 to co-opt Solidarity's influence among the working people. By the time of the 1991 elections, the OPZZ had a larger membership than Solidarity. Of the 390 SLD candidates for the parliamentary elections of October 1991, 45 percent were members of the SdRP and about one-third belonged to the OPZZ. The SLD surprised most political observers by finishing a close second to the Democratic Union and winning sixty Sejm and four Senate seats. Its failure to expand its membership, however, made the SLD a political outcast in the coalition-building efforts that followed the 1991 election.

Polish Peasant Party

The rebirth of the moderate interwar Polish Peasant Party (PSL) began in the summer of 1989, when the United Peasant Party (Zjednoczone Stronnictwo Ludowe—ZSL) joined forces with Solidarity and Democratic Party deputies in the new Sejm to usher in a noncommunist government. The ZSL adopted the name Polish Peasant Party "Renewal" to distance itself from its past in the communist coalition; then it united with the largest existing opposition peasant party and resumed its original name. In the May 1990 local elections, the PSL garnered 20 percent of the rural vote. In September 1990, the PSL withdrew support for the Mazowiecki government, citing its disapproval of current agricultural policy and Mazowiecki's failure to appoint a PSL member as the minister of agriculture. As it continued to seek legislative relief for farmers, the PSL also became a vocal critic of the Bielecki government that followed Mazowiecki.

As of mid-1992, the PSL was the third-largest single-party bloc in the Sejm. In 1992 the party's 180,000 dues-paying members made it the largest political party in the country. It showed considerable strength even in such heavily industrialized areas as Upper Silesia. Although not a member of the five-party coalition that installed Olszewski as prime minister in December 1991, the PSL provided critical support in securing Sejm approval for Olszewski's cabinet at a time when that coalition was already beginning to collapse. Despite its initial support for Olszewski, however, the party became disenchanted with the prime minister's agricultural program and voted for his removal in 1992.

Politics and the Media

Prior to the return of democracy in 1989, Poland's independent press defied state censorship and flourished to an extent unknown in other East European communist states. Active publication by opposition groups in the 1970s formed a tradition for the well-organized distribution of censored materials that flowered in the contentious decade that followed.

The Early Opposition Press

As early as 1970, underground groups had begun issuing opposition literature that included short-lived periodicals, strike announcements, and brochures. By 1976 opposition groups were better organized and began issuing influential carbon-copied and mimeographed serials. In the autumn of that year, KOR began producing its *Biuletyn Informacyjny* (Information Bulletin). During the period between 1976 and 1980, about 500 uncensored serial titles were recorded, some with circulations of more than 20,000 copies. At the same time, underground book publishing flourished as over thirty-five independent presses issued hundreds of uncensored monographs.

Following the Gdańsk Agreement of August 1980, Poland saw a new explosion of independent publishing. In addition to *Tygodnik Solidarność* (Solidarity Weekly), whose circulation was limited to 500,000 copies supplemented by ten regional weeklies, Solidarity and its rural affiliate published hundreds of new periodicals. Assisted by donations of printing equipment from the West, about 200 publishing houses had emerged by December 1981, when martial law abruptly curtailed independent publishing.

During Solidarity's first period of legal activity, reprints of opposition literature from abroad, particularly the influential émigré journals *Kultura* (Culture) and *Zeszyty Historyczne* (Historical Notebooks), were especially popular.

Liberalization in the 1980s

The imposition of martial law in December 1981 was a major setback for independent publishing. But, despite the confiscation of printing equipment and the arrest of opposition leaders, the clandestine press quickly resumed issuing bulletins. By the end of 1982, some forty publishing houses were producing a great variety of books, brochures, and serials. Not only did the Jaruzelski regime fail to infiltrate and shut down such publishing operations, it allowed considerable freedom of expression in the "legitimate" press. For example, the influential Catholic periodical, *Tygodnik Powszechny* (Universal Weekly), founded in 1945, provided an independent voice defending the rights of the Polish citizenry.

After the formal suspension of martial law in July 1983, the regime grew increasingly tolerant toward independent publishing. The underground press diversified to reflect the widening spectrum of opposition points of view. By 1986 only about half of the known independent serial titles were organs of Solidarity.

As the independent press grew more diverse, the state press increasingly cited articles published in underground periodicals and even began to publish "illegal" books. In 1986 the regime granted legal status to *Res Publica,* a scholarly underground journal representing a moderate social and political philosophy. Meanwhile, the Catholic press grew ever more prominent when dozens of church publications were resurrected after long being banned.

The Jaruzelski regime's increasingly liberal attitude toward the print media was motivated not only by a desire to achieve national reconciliation, but also by the realization that the state could not suppress three highly prolific publishing networks—the underground press, the church-sponsored press, and the émigré press in the West. After the mid-1980s, the nonstate publishing houses averaged 500 to 600 new titles annually.

The End of Press Censorship

A key element of the Round Table Agreement was the end of the communist monopoly of the news media. In April 1990, state censorship was abolished. The PZPR publishing and distribution monopoly, the Workers' Publication Cooperative Press-Book-Movement began to break up, and numerous communist-era periodicals were privatized. Some periodical titles, such as the daily *Rzeczpospolita* (Republic) and the weekly *Polityka* (Politics), were recast and gained respect for the quality of their journalism. Others, most notably the official party organ *Trybuna Ludu* (People's Tribune), changed their names but continued to represent a leftist political viewpoint (*Trybuna Ludu* became simply *Trybuna*). Many familiar communist ideological publications were discontinued, however. After mid-1989, hundreds of new periodicals appeared, failed, reappeared, and failed again. These failures were the result of the high cost of newsprint, ignorance of free-market business principles, and the unpredictable demand created by a newly liberated reading public.

As of mid-1992, nearly 1,000 Polish periodicals were being published. Among these were seventy-five daily and 164 weekly newspapers. The left-of-center *Gazeta Wyborcza* (Election Gazette), with a circulation of 550,000 weekday copies and more than 850,000 weekend copies, was the most widely read newspaper. *Gazeta Wyborcza,* issued in thirteen local editions, resembled Western papers in its layout and extensive commercial advertising. *Rzeczpospolita* claimed roughly 250,000 readers, followed closely by *Życie Warszawy* (Warsaw Life). Of the national political weeklies, *Polityka* and *Wprost*

(Straightforward) enjoyed the greatest success, with circulations of 350,000 and 250,000, respectively.

In the years following the Round Table Agreement, the Polish press presented a range of opinion that reflected the increasingly fractured political landscape. Following the schism between Mazowiecki and Wałęsa forces in 1990, *Tygodnik Solidarność* became the mouthpiece of the pro-Wałęsa Center Alliance, while Michnik's *Gazeta Wyborcza* and the Catholic church's *Tygodnik Powszechny* supported the Mazowiecki faction.

Book Publishing

After the Round Table Agreement, book publishing, distribution, and marketing entered a period of unprecedented upheaval. Together with the welcome lifting of censorship came the end of generous state subsidies for publishers. Thus, publishers of esoteric scholarly and literary works with limited market appeal suffered severe losses. At the same time, however, the newfound opportunity to gain profits by satisfying the reading tastes of the Polish public caused a dramatic proliferation of publishing houses. In mid-1992, between 1,200 and 2,000 publishing houses, most of them small enterprises, were in operation. Only about 100 of that number had all the trappings of full-scale publishing firms: catalogs, international standard book numbers, and observance of the copyright deposit law.

Radio and Television

To a significant extent, electronic news and information sources defied government control in the 1980s. Millions of Poles received uncensored radio broadcasts from Radio Free Europe, the Voice of America, the British Broadcasting Corporation, and other Western sources. Solidarity units also occasionally broadcast news programs from mobile radio stations. And hundreds of thousands of VCRs allowed the Polish population to view taboo films by prominent domestic and foreign directors.

Unlike periodicals, the electronic media adjusted slowly to the changed political environment following the Round Table Agreement. As of mid-1992, the Sejm had yet to enact legislation to regulate radio and television broadcasting. Decades of communist manipulation of the electronic media had taught politicians the power of those media in shaping public attitudes. In mid-1992, Wałęsa indicated his continuing distrust of broadcast journalism by stating that television should represent the government's views and that state television was not the place for contrary political opinions. The membership of the Committee for Radio and Television, a communist-era holdover agency regulating all broadcasting, was determined by the Council of Ministers, and appointment of the committee chairman became highly politicized.

In mid-1992 Poland continued to have only two national television channels, and by Western standards the program offerings were limited. Besides daily news broadcasts, the most popular program was a political satire, "Polish Zoo," a weekly puppet show that lampooned leading political figures and institutions, including the church. To supplement the meager offerings of domestic television, many Poles received foreign broadcasts. Small satellite antenna dishes were common throughout the country. Impatient with the government's inaction, private television stations in Warsaw, Lublin, Poznań, and Szczecin began to broadcast without licenses in the early 1990s.

The government interfered less with radio than with television broadcasting. In addition to the four national stations broadcasting to nearly 11 million Polish receivers, thirteen unlicensed radio stations had come into existence by mid-1992. Nearly 600 applications for broadcasting licenses awaited evaluation. Radio broadcasts were dominated by Western popular music, just as the publishing and film industries were overwhelmingly Western in orientation.

The continuing dominance of Western culture in the 1990s appeared to be assured, as unauthorized reproduction of films, literature, and music made inexpensive, high-quality copies easily accessible to the average citizen. In the postcommunist era, intellectual piracy in Poland emerged as one of the troublesome issues between Warsaw and the United States. In early 1992, it was estimated that the United States lost US$140 million dollars annually to Polish audio, video, and computer program piracy.

Foreign Relations

In mid-1992, Poland was enjoying the fruits of three years of skillful statesmanship by its foreign minister, Krzysztof Skubiszewski, who had directed foreign policy in five governments beginning with Mazowiecki in August 1989. Skubiszewski guided Poland through a tumultuous period during which Warsaw reclaimed full sovereignty in foreign affairs for the first time since World War II and moved resolutely to "rejoin Europe."

The Soviet-dominated Warsaw Treaty Organization (known as the Warsaw Pact—see Glossary) and its economic counterpart, the Council of Mutual Economic Cooperation (Comecon—see Glossary), which had set the parameters of Polish foreign policy for decades, no longer existed after mid-1991. By year's end, the Soviet

Anti-Soviet graffiti covering World War II monument in Warsaw
Courtesy Ronald D. Bachman

Union itself had disappeared, and by late 1992 Moscow was to complete the withdrawal of combat troops from Poland. Meanwhile, Warsaw pursued forward-looking bilateral relations with the many newly independent states of the former Soviet Union. Only in the case of Lithuania could relations with eastern neighbors be described as less than cordial.

To replace the old Soviet-dominated military and trade structures, Poland sought collective security with its southern neighbors, the Czech and Slovak Federative Republic (see Glossary), and Hungary, with which it formed the so-called Visegrád Triangle. This arrangement envisioned a bilateral free trade zone between Budapest and Warsaw, which both the Czechs and the Slovaks were invited to join. The Visegrád partners would also coordinate their strategies to join West European economic and military organizations.

·In mid-1992, Poland's relationship with its other traditional enemy, Germany, also was forward-looking. Acquiescing in German reunification, Warsaw won assurances that Bonn would recognize the Oder-Neisse Line as the official, permanent frontier between Germany and Poland, ratifying the postwar transfer of German lands to Poland. Germany offered economic assistance, investment, and support for Polish membership in the European Community (EC—see Glossary).

Relations with other Western nations in mid-1992 were generally excellent. Warsaw was frustrated, however, by its inability to gain full membership in the North Atlantic Treaty Organization (NATO), the Western European Union (WEU—see Glossary), and the EC and by the reluctance of the West to lower import tariffs on Polish goods (see Postcommunist Policy Adjustments, ch. 3). Traditionally warm ties with the United States returned to normal after the difficult 1980s, and Poland regained most-favored-nation trade status and benefited from a range of United States economic and technical assistance.

Soviet Union and Russia

The geopolitical realities of postwar Europe allowed Poland little room to maneuver in foreign policy. Until the late 1980s, the ever present threat of Soviet intervention kept Poland a compliant member of the Warsaw Pact. In fact, Jaruzelski maintained that the decision to impose martial law in December 1981 was taken to preempt a Soviet invasion. Such an invasion would have been consistent with the Brezhnev Doctrine, which justified military intervention in any Warsaw Pact member where socialism was threatened. In early 1992, Jaruzelski's claim received corroboration when a high official in the former Soviet Army revealed the Soviet Union's plan to invade Poland at the end of 1981 under precisely that pretext.

In the late 1980s, the Brezhnev Doctrine was suspended when Soviet leader Mikhail S. Gorbachev enunciated a new world view, which he called "new thinking." For the first time in the postwar era, the Soviet Union acknowledged the right of its East European neighbors to pursue their own paths of social and economic development. Thus, Moscow reluctantly accepted Poland's 1989 Round Table Agreement, the defeat of the communists in Poland's first open parliamentary elections, and the ensuing installation of a noncommunist government as beyond its legitimate concern.

As the first postcommunist leadership of Poland, the Mazowiecki government approached its relationship with the Soviet Union with cautious resolve, reassuring Moscow that Poland would fulfill its obligations as a member of the Warsaw Pact and Comecon. Nevertheless, Poland soon demonstrated its determination to transform these Soviet-dominated military and economic alliances into consultative bodies respecting the sovereignty of all member countries. Foreign Minister Skubiszewski guided foreign affairs skillfully through this delicate period, as the Warsaw Pact, Comecon, and the Soviet Union itself disintegrated.

Among the difficult issues the new government confronted in redefining its relationship with the Soviet Union were the presence of some 58,000 Soviet troops on Polish territory; the future role of the Warsaw Pact and Comecon; new terms of bilateral trade; the plight of more than 1 million ethnic Poles living on Soviet territory; clarification of the "blank spots" in the history of Soviet-Polish relations; and the Polish relationship to Soviet republics seeking independence.

Skubiszewski handled the issue of Soviet troop withdrawal delicately. In negotiating with Moscow, the government faced accusations of timidity from presidential candidate Wałęsa on the one hand and the risk of antagonizing Moscow and strengthening the position of Kremlin hardliners on the other. Wałęsa and some of the center-right parties believed the Mazowiecki government was moving too cautiously on the issue. But Mazowiecki viewed Warsaw Pact forces as a counterbalance to a reunited, possibly expansionist Germany. In September 1990, Mazowiecki yielded to domestic pressure by demanding negotiations on the withdrawal of Soviet forces and cleanup of the extensive environmental damage they had caused (see Environmental Conditions and Crises, ch. 2). By the end of 1990, the Polish side was pushing Moscow to remove all its forces within one year.

Postcommunist Poland's trade relationship with the Soviet Union also presented a complex problem. Moscow was Poland's most important trading partner, the source of nearly all its imported oil and gas, and the market for 70 percent of its industrial exports. Poland had benefited from the comfortable if inefficient Comecon trading arrangements of administered prices denominated in transferable rubles. Although the impending end of Comecon clearly signaled the need for drastic reorientation of trade policy, in 1990 no source could replace rapidly the fundamental supplies available from the old system. Thus, Moscow retained its economic influence on Polish foreign policy despite Gorbachev's pledges to respect Polish sovereignty.

Yet another obstacle to normalized relations was the legacy of Stalin's crimes against the Polish people in World War II and the plight of Polish nationals who remained in Soviet territory after the war. In April 1990, Gorbachev finally acknowledged Soviet culpability in the massacre of thousands of Polish officers in the Katyń Forest, which until that time the Soviets had attributed to the German army despite widespread knowledge of the true situation (see World War II, ch. 1). Indeed, early in 1989 the Jaruzelski government had declared that Stalin's secret police, not the German army, had committed the atrocities. Gorbachev's action in 1990 did not placate Poland. The Polish government continued to demand information on critical "blank spots" in the history of the World War II era, notably the fate of Poles whom Stalin exiled to Siberia and Central Asia.

In 1990 and 1991, the Bielecki government continued Mazowiecki's policy toward Moscow. The withdrawal of Soviet forces, the interruption of oil and gas deliveries, and the collapse of the Soviet market for Polish exports dominated bilateral relations during Bielecki's tenure. Moscow's decision to shift to hard-currency trade at world prices as of January 1, 1992 had painful consequences for Poland. In response to severe disruption of its export market, fuel delivery, and domestic employment, Warsaw established ad hoc barter arrangements with the Soviet Union and individual neighboring republics.

Meanwhile, on the security front, the Soviets pressured Poland and other members of the dying Warsaw Pact to sign new bilateral treaties giving Moscow the right to veto entry into alliances inimical to Soviet interests. Among the East European nations formerly in the Soviet sphere, however, only Romania yielded to Moscow's pressure. Poland refused to surrender its sovereign right to choose allies. After a failed attempt by hardliners to take over the Soviet government in August 1991, Moscow dropped its demand, and bilateral negotiations proceeded more smoothly.

The coup attempt in the Soviet Union placed Warsaw in a precarious situation and emphasized the real possibility that Soviet hegemony would return to Eastern Europe if reactionaries overthrew Gorbachev. For Warsaw such a scenario was quite plausible because substantial Soviet forces remained in Poland and the former German Democratic Republic (East Germany) at the time of the coup, and no bilateral treaty guaranteed withdrawal. Although Wałęsa's official statements during the crisis affirmed Poland's sovereignty and commitment to democracy, later rumors suggested that he had considered recognizing the Moscow junta.

Galvanized by the coup events, Poland pressed the Soviet Union for a withdrawal timetable. In October 1991, the countries initialed a treaty providing for the removal of all combat troops by November 15, 1992, leaving only 6,000 support personnel by the beginning of 1993. Signature of a final treaty, however, was delayed by disagreement on compensation details. Moscow claimed compensation for fixed assets left in Poland, while Warsaw demanded compensation for damage done to its environment and infrastructure by the basing and transport of Soviet troops and equipment. Wałęsa and Russian president Boris Yeltsin signed the final accords in May 1992.

The presidents also signed several other bilateral agreements on that occasion. The most important was a new cooperation treaty to replace the Polish-Soviet friendship treaty of 1965. The breakthrough on the new treaty had come soon after the failed August coup, which dramatically changed the relationship among the republics of the Soviet Union. Moscow conceded to Poland the right to pursue its own security relationships and to deal directly with individual republics. During his Moscow visit, Wałęsa announced the beginning of a new chapter in Polish-Russian relations; in return, Yeltsin expressed hope for mutual understanding and partnership in future relations.

Wałęsa's visit to Moscow also yielded a Polish-Russian consular convention; a declaration on cultural, scientific, and educational cooperation; a provisional settlement of the issue of double taxation; and an agreement on border crossing points. The presidents issued a joint statement condemning the crimes of Stalinism against both the Polish and Russian peoples and pledging to base bilateral relations on the principles of international law, democracy, and the observance of human rights.

Other Former Soviet Republics

From the outset, Foreign Minister Skubiszewski pursued a dual-track policy toward Poland's eastern neighbors, Russia, Belarus, Lithuania, and Ukraine. This approach enabled Warsaw to negotiate for Polish interests with the central political authority that remained in Moscow as the Soviet Union dissolved, while simultaneously developing bilateral ties with the individual republics that would emerge from that process as independent neighbors. The failure of the August coup signaled to Warsaw the end of the highly centralized Soviet state and the feasibility of officially recognizing independence-minded republics. Accordingly, immediately after the coup Poland became the first East European country to extend diplomatic recognition to the Baltic republics of Lithuania, Latvia, and Estonia. On the day following the formal dissolution of the Soviet Union, Poland announced that it was prepared to open normal diplomatic relations with all the members of the Commonwealth of Independent States (CIS—see Glossary).

Although it supported national self-determination, Warsaw feared that the breakup of the Soviet Union might bring regional instability, armed conflict fueled by rival territorial claims, and perhaps millions of displaced persons crossing into Poland. Still struggling with its own economic and political transition, Poland could not have borne the burden of resettling huge numbers of refugees. These concerns moved President Wałęsa to declare his support for Gorbachev's last-ditch effort in December 1991 to reconstitute the Soviet Union as a loose confederation. Then, after the formal demise of the Soviet Union, Wałęsa called for massive Western aid for the newly created CIS to avoid what he called a ''mass exodus of hungry refugees.''

Baltic States

On numerous occasions after mid-1989, the Polish government demonstrated sympathy for the increasingly vocal Lithuanian independence movement. After the Lithuanian declaration of independence in March 1990, a Polish senator was the first foreign government representative to address the Lithuanian parliament. Poland provided important moral support during the economic blockade imposed by the Kremlin, and after the Soviet military crackdown in Vilnius in January 1991, Poland joined Scandinavian nations, the Czech and Slovak Federative Republic, and Hungary in calling for a discussion of the action by the Conference on Security and Cooperation in Europe (CSCE—see Glossary).

Despite Warsaw's sympathetic actions, Vilnius grew impatient at the Poles' unwillingness to grant diplomatic recognition. At that time, however, such an action would have jeopardized negotiations on withdrawal of Soviet troops from Poland—especially because no major Western power had recognized Lithuania. Skubiszewski noted that although good relations with the Baltics were important to Poland, relations with the Soviet Union had immediate strategic significance.

The demise of the Soviet Union transformed Poland's relationship with Lithuania. As the threat of repression from Moscow diminished, Vilnius began to perceive Warsaw as a likely source of external pressure. The Lithuanian government grew suspicious that Warsaw coveted lost territories in Lithuania, where ethnic Poles still resided in heavy concentrations. From Poland's perspective, the respect of minority rights for roughly 260,000 ethnic Poles residing in Lithuania emerged as the most important issue in the bilateral relationship.

In 1988 and 1989, relations of the Polish minority in Lithuania with the Lithuanian government deteriorated with the enactment of language laws that discriminated against non-Lithuanian speakers. The laws provoked leaders of the Polish minority to declare an autonomous Polish national territorial district. In response, Vilnius dismissed numerous ethnic Polish local officials and placed districts with large Polish populations under direct parliamentary administration. Further contributing to the worsening relations between the two communities was a citizenship law requiring a loyalty oath that the Polish community viewed as oppressive. Relations reached their nadir in late 1991 when the Lithuanian defense minister called Poland his country's greatest threat. The following March, Skubiszewski charged Lithuania with delaying elections to local councils in districts with large concentrations of ethnic Poles.

Early 1992 also brought hopeful developments, however. The foreign ministers of the two nations signed a wide-ranging ten-point declaration of friendship and neighborly relations and a consular convention. In the declaration, each country renounced all territorial claims against the other and pledged to adhere to European standards in respecting the rights of its minorities, including native-language education rights.

Polish relations with the other two Baltic states were less complicated. In mid-1992, Skubiszewski visited Latvia to sign the first Polish bilateral treaty with any of the newly independent Baltic states. He also signed important accords on trade, travel, and minority rights. Skubiszewski praised Latvia's treatment of its sizable Polish population, which in mid-1992 was estimated at between 60,000 and 100,000. Skubiszewski then signed a similar treaty in Tallinn, where the Estonian foreign minister described relations with Warsaw as excellent. Both Estonia and Latvia viewed Poland as a benign neighbor whose experience in economic and political reform could facilitate their own transition and could promote their integration into Western Europe.

Belarus

For several reasons, Polish relations with Belarus were slow to develop. Belarus, which had never existed as an independent state, had been so firmly incorporated into the Soviet Union that it lacked the intense sense of nationhood found in the Baltic states and in Ukraine. Prior to the August coup attempt, Polish overtures were frustrated because the Belorussian Republic (as it was known before independence) hesitated to pursue foreign policy initiatives without the Kremlin's blessing. Most notably, in late 1990 the Belorussians refused to sign a declaration of friendship and cooperation, although Russia and Ukraine had already signed similar agreements. Minsk specifically objected to wording about its borders with Poland and to the treatment of the approximately 300,000 ethnic Belorussians in Poland (see Ethnic Groups, ch. 2).

After August 1991, relations evolved rapidly once Belarus had declared its independence. In a declaration of friendship and cooperation, signed in October 1991, each party renounced territorial claims against the other and promised to respect minority rights.

In December 1991, Poland extended diplomatic recognition to Belarus. Commercial ties between the two countries flourished in 1991 and 1992, and several important transportation and economic agreements took effect. A bilateral treaty of wide-ranging cooperation in security, environmental, economic, and other matters was prepared for signing in mid-1992.

Ukraine

Despite a centuries-old legacy of conflict, relations between Poland and Ukraine steadily improved after 1989, particularly after Ukraine gained its independence in late 1991. In the fall of 1990, the countries signed a declaration of friendship and cooperation, renouncing all territorial claims against one another and guaranteeing the rights of national minorities on their territories. Groundbreaking bilateral economic and cultural agreements followed in 1991, as Ukraine emerged from Moscow's domination and reoriented itself toward Central Europe and Western Europe.

Both countries had much to gain from improved ties. Kiev sought Polish intercession to gain acceptance in European economic and security organizations; Warsaw welcomed the prospect of a nonthreatening buffer state on its eastern border.

Hours after the results of a referendum on Ukrainian independence were announced in December 1991, Poland was the first country to grant diplomatic recognition to the new nation. A bilateral cooperation treaty ensuring minority rights on each side of the border was signed during the May 1992 visit to Warsaw of Ukraine's president, Leonid M. Kravchuk. The treaty called for annual consultations between the countries' foreign ministers and cooperation in economic, cultural, scientific, and environmental affairs. During Wałęsa's visit to Moscow (also in May 1992) to sign long-awaited troop withdrawal and bilateral cooperation treaties, Wałęsa noted the rapid progress in bilateral relations since 1989 and hailed the countries' new emphasis on future goals rather than past conflicts. Wałęsa also noted that the concept of a Warsaw-Moscow-Kiev alliance, raised in his talks with Yeltsin, would depend most heavily on peaceful relations between Russia and Ukraine. This observation reaffirmed Poland's neutrality in ongoing Russian-Ukrainian disagreements over the ownership of the Black Sea Fleet, Crimea, and other territories.

Southern Neighbors and the Visegrád Triangle

With the demise of the Warsaw Pact and Comecon, the so-called upper-tier nations of Eastern Europe (Poland, Hungary, and Czechoslovakia, which in 1990 became the Czech and Slovak Federative

Republic) found themselves in a security vacuum with both military and economic dimensions. But by late 1991, all three had gained associate status with NATO and the EC and were pursuing full membership in those organizations.

Poland, the Czech and Slovak Federative Republic, and Hungary all supported an enhanced peacekeeping role for the CSCE, and all joined emerging regional integration associations such as the Central European Initiative. Originally called the Pentagonale and including Italy, Yugoslavia, Austria, Hungary, and Czechoslovakia, this grouping aimed to strengthen economic, cultural, and ecological cooperation in the region. The organization became known as the Hexagonale when Poland joined in July 1991, only to be renamed the Central European Initiative a few months later when Yugoslavia's breakup brought the withdrawal of that nation.

Already in 1990, Poland, Hungary, and Czechoslovakia had begun to coordinate efforts toward shared goals, including the end of the Soviet-dominated Warsaw Pact and Comecon and entry into Western institutions. A milestone in trilateral cooperation was the February 1991 summit meeting of Hungary's Prime Minister József Antall, President Václav Havel of the Czech and Slovak Federative Republic, and Lech Wałęsa at Visegrád, Hungary. An earlier summit at Bratislava had initiated a series of meetings and exchanges among the leaders of the three potential partners, leading to the formation of a consultative committee to coordinate policy on regional problems. The following January, the foreign ministers met in Budapest and issued a joint communiqué criticizing the Kremlin's military crackdown in the Baltics. The foreign ministers also issued a statement of support for the United States-led coalition in the Kuwait crisis.

The outcome of the Visegrád summit was the Declaration on the Cooperation of the Hungarian Republic, the Czech and Slovak Federative Republic, and the Republic of Poland on the Road to European Integration. The document committed the signatories to eliminate the vestiges of totalitarianism, build democracy, ensure human rights, and totally integrate themselves into the "European political, economic, security, and legislative order." The triangle was not intended to become a military alliance, as Foreign Minister Skubiszewski carefully emphasized to allay fears in Moscow. Poland subsequently signed bilateral military accords with the other triangle partners, again insisting that the agreements were designed to promote communication and understanding and posed no threat to any specific country.

During the August coup attempt in Moscow, triangle political and military leaders were in frequent contact, agreeing to adopt a common position toward the crisis and the refugee and border security problems that might result from it. In October 1991, a second summit in Kraków formalized the Visegrád declaration, accelerated efforts to gain NATO and EC membership, and advocated an expanded role for the CSCE. The eight-point Kraków declaration also chastised Serbia as the aggressor in the Yugoslav conflict and called for national self-determination and the preservation of the previously existing republic boundaries in that country.

In the months following the Kraków summit, several key events strengthened ties among the triangle members and with the West. The triangle supported a proposal by the United States and Germany to establish a North Atlantic Cooperation Council that would promote stability and communication between NATO and the nations of Central Europe and the former Soviet Union. And in December, the triangle countries were accorded associate membership in the EC. This step established routine political contacts with the EC and set the course toward eventual full membership. Also in December, the triangle members agreed to coordinate their policy on recognition of the independence of Slovenia and Croatia, which they granted in January 1992. In April 1992, they jointly recognized the independence of Bosnia and Hercegovina.

By early autumn 1992, the future of the triangle was clouded by the impending division of the Czech and Slovak Federative Republic and by tensions between Hungary and Slovakia over a series of issues. After meeting Czech prime minister Václav Klaus in September, Polish prime minister Suchocka stated that Poland viewed the split as a settled matter and would treat the Czech Republic and Slovakia on equal terms. Klaus stressed that trilateral relations would become less important, and that closer bilateral ties among the members would be the way of the future. Polish foreign minister Skubiszewski, however, favored continuing the Visegrád Triangle, stating that there were problems that could be resolved better through regional cooperation than by unilateral or bilateral action.

Germany

Together with securing the removal of Soviet troops from Polish territory, the reemergence of a united, economically powerful Germany presented Warsaw's greatest foreign policy challenge after 1989. Fear of a resurgent Germany motivated Skubiszewski's initial desire to preserve the Warsaw Pact as a political alliance guaranteeing the Oder-Neisse Line as Poland's western border. Warsaw also welcomed the continued presence of United States forces in Europe as a check on potential German expansionism. At the same time, however, Germany represented the largest potential source of economic assistance and investment for Poland, accounting in 1990 for one-fifth of Warsaw's imports and one-quarter of its exports.

Throughout the postwar period, relations between Warsaw and the Federal Republic of Germany (West Germany) had ranged from cool to hostile. In 1981 Poland's international isolation following the imposition of martial law further set back bilateral relations. Despite the overall expansion of economic ties in the postwar period, intractable differences remained over such issues as treatment of the 300,000 ethnic Germans in Poland, German territorial claims on Poland, compensation for Polish victims of Nazi persecution, and the permanence of the Oder-Neisse border. Warsaw consistently and energetically opposed all movement toward German reunification and revanchism. On the other hand, bilateral relations between Poland and East Germany were never warm, in spite of their official alliance in the Warsaw Pact. Poles resented East Germany's general enthusiasm for communist orthodoxy and its support of Jaruzelski's martial law decree in 1981.

West German chancellor Helmut Kohl visited Warsaw in November 1989 to accelerate the recent improvement of relations between the traditional enemies. Kohl hoped to gain Polish guarantees for German minority rights and to quiet fears about German revanchism that had escalated with impending reunification. West Germany extended some US$2 billion in economic assistance to Warsaw and acknowledged Germany's guilt for attacking Poland in World War II. Kohl also reaffirmed a 1970 bilateral treaty promising to respect existing borders. After Kohl subsequently caused an international stir by hedging on that commitment, the border issue was buried when Germany officially renounced all claims on Polish territory and recognized the permanence of the existing border in May 1990.

December 1991 marked a milestone in Polish-German relations when the parliaments of both countries ratified a treaty of friendship and cooperation. On that occasion, Prime Minister Bielecki stated that the common strategic goal of a united Europe had inspired Poland and unified Germany to a level of mutual trust unprecedented in the long history of their coexistence. Bielecki and his successors viewed Germany as Poland's key to integration into the West. In turn, Germany considered Warsaw the gateway to vast economic opportunities in the East. A central element of the treaty was strict adherence to international standards in the treatment of ethnic minorities.

In 1992 bilateral relations continued to improve. On an official visit in the spring, Wałęsa praised Germany as a democratic, liberal, and modern state and urged greater investment in Poland. In July the new German foreign minister, Klaus Kinkel, visited Warsaw to sign routine customs and border agreements. Kinkel praised Poland's treatment of its German minority, which had gained seven representatives in the Sejm and one in the Senate in the October 1991 parliamentary elections.

Despite the many positive signs of a lasting rapprochement between Germany and Poland, however, in 1992 Poles remained suspicious of their powerful western neighbor. European economic instability during the late summer brought into question the feasibility of the EC goal of monetary and political union and rekindled fears of German economic domination. Widespread vandalism and violence by xenophobic extremists in Germany also contributed to Polish unease.

The United States

Over the years, a special relationship evolved between the peoples of Poland and the United States. Poles and persons of Polish ancestry made enormous contributions at every stage in the development of the United States. For Poles, family ties and genuine admiration for the United States negated decades of official anti-American propaganda. As official relations between Washington and Warsaw deteriorated after the December 1981 imposition of martial law, the United States maintained communication with the centers of Polish opposition, including leaders of labor, the intelligentsia, and the Roman Catholic Church. During the 1980s, United States policies of economic sanctions against the regime and support for the opposition contributed to the ultimate fall of the communist government.

Immediately after Jaruzelski imposed martial law in 1981, the United States invoked economic sanctions against Poland. In 1982 the United States suspended most-favored-nation trade status and vetoed Poland's application for membership in the International Monetary Fund (IMF—see Glossary). In the following years, Warsaw repeatedly blamed such United States policies for Poland's economic distress (see Reform Failure in the 1980s, ch. 3). For the period 1981 to 1985, the Polish government claimed that United States-inspired sanctions and Western refusal to reschedule debts and extend additional credit had cost the Polish economy US$15 billion in export income and other losses.

Despite the end of martial law and limited amnesty for political prisoners in 1983, relations with the United States did not improve.

President Lech Wałęsa meets with President George H.W.
Bush on an official visit to Washington, 1991.
Courtesy David Valdez, White House Photo Office

In the mid-1980s, Warsaw's determined efforts to prove its loyalty
to the Soviet Union made rapprochement with Washington impossible. Poland supported the Soviet version of events surrounding the shooting down of a Korean Airlines passenger plane in 1983,
an incident that greatly heightened Soviet Union-United States tensions. In 1984 Warsaw joined the Soviet boycott of the Los An-
geles Olympic Games in reprisal for the United States boycott of
the previous games in Moscow. Jaruzelski delivered a scathing attack against United States sanctions policy in a 1985 speech at the
United Nations. And in 1986 the Polish government condemned
a United States air strike against Libya.

Official relations between Washington and Warsaw began to improve after the Jaruzelski government's 1986 general amnesty
released all political prisoners. By early 1987, the administration
of Ronald W. Reagan lifted all economic sanctions and restored
Poland's most-favored-nation trading status. Vice President George
H.W. Bush visited Warsaw the following October and promised
United States support for debt rescheduling in return for the Polish government's pledge to respect human rights. In 1988, however,
the United States decided to withhold economic aid until Poland
reestablished political pluralism.

After the Round Table Agreement of mid-1989, the United States moved quickly to encourage democratic processes and assist economic reform in Poland. Toward this goal, President Bush initially promised some US$100 million in economic assistance, and a three-year package totaling US$1 billion was proposed later in the year. In November Wałęsa visited Washington and addressed a joint session of the United States Congress, which greeted his unprecedented speech with promises of additional economic assistance. The Congress enacted the Support for Eastern European Democracy Act (SEED) to streamline the delivery of humanitarian aid and assistance for the development of democracy and free-market institutions in postcommunist Eastern Europe. An interagency coordinating council led by the Department of State was established to direct assistance to Eastern Europe. The privately managed Polish-American Enterprise Fund (PAEF) was created in May 1990 to provide credit for Polish entrepreneurs to start businesses. Contingent on the level of congressional funding, the PAEF estimated that it would make US$130 million in loans in 1991. Another nongovernmental organization, the Overseas Private Investment Corporation, began providing loans, loan guarantees, insurance, and advice to facilitate United States private investment in Poland and other East European countries. In 1990 the United States led an international effort to create the US$200 million Polish Stabilization Fund, which was instrumental in making the zloty convertible with Western currencies (for value of the zloty—see Glossary).

As a major player in such international financial institutions as the World Bank (see Glossary), the IMF, the Organisation for Economic Co-operation and Development (OECD—see Glossary), the Paris Club (see Glossary), and the European Bank for Reconstruction and Development (EBRD—see Glossary), the United States led the effort to provide debt relief and other economic assistance to Poland. In early 1991, the United States pledged a further 20 percent reduction of Warsaw's debt to Washington. In a mid-1992 visit to Warsaw, President Bush praised Poland's political and economic reforms and proposed using the currency-stabilization fund to spur private-sector growth.

Other Western Countries

After December 1981, Polish relations with the West were generally unfriendly for several years. Few high-ranking Western delegations travelled to Warsaw, and the Polish government failed to end West European support of economic sanctions in response to martial law. In 1985 a brief meeting between Jaruzelski and French president François Mitterrand yielded no concrete results. Jaruzelski's first full-fledged official visit to the West was his 1987 trip to Italy, during which he signed an important agreement for automobile production with the Fiat Corporation.

British and French policy toward Poland throughout the 1980s was consistent with that of Washington. Both United States allies imposed sanctions against Warsaw after December 1981. Both cultivated contacts with nongovernment circles and assisted the development of pluralism. And both welcomed the round table talks of 1989 and supported economic assistance to the new government.

The visit of the British prime minister, Margaret Thatcher, to Warsaw in November 1988 sent a clear signal of Britain's support for pluralism and economic reform in Poland. Thatcher met with Solidarity leaders and made a symbolic visit to the grave of Father Jerzy Popiełuszko, a dissident killed by the Polish secret service in 1984. In June 1989, Mitterrand visited Poland. In March 1992, Prime Minister Olszewski traveled to Paris and received Mitterrand's assurances of support for Polish membership in the EC.

Relations with Israel improved dramatically after 1988, when Poland hosted an international conference to honor the victims of the Holocaust and to observe the forty-fifth anniversary of the Warsaw Ghetto uprising. Full diplomatic relations were reestablished in 1990.

International Organizations

Poland was a founding member of the United Nations (UN) and takes an active role in numerous UN agencies, including the United Nations Educational, Scientific, and Cultural Organization; the World Health Organization; the United Nations Children's Fund; the Food and Agriculture Organization; the United Nations Industrial Development Organization; and the United Nations Conference on Trade and Development. In the postcommunist era, Warsaw has consistently supported Western-led UN initiatives such as Operation Desert Storm and the condemnation of Serbian policies toward other republics of the former Yugoslavia. In 1992 Poland belonged to roughly 1,500 international governmental and private organizations.

After the change of government in mid-1989, Poland assigned the highest priority to obtaining full membership status in NATO and the EC as soon as possible. The West supported the concept of Poland's integration into Europe; however, only associate status in the EC and NATO had been achieved as of mid-1992. Meanwhile, in 1990 Warsaw had gained associate status in the Council of Europe, an organization including all West European nations and devoted to promoting democracy and the economic health of its members. The council granted Poland full membership after the free parliamentary elections in the autumn of 1991. In November 1991, the EC approved ten-year associate status for Poland, Hungary, and the Czech and Slovak Federative Republic (see Southern Neighbors and the Visegrád Triangle, this ch.). The agreement provided certain trade concessions and generally was viewed as a first step toward eventual full membership. Long and spirited debate preceded the Sejm's ratification of membership in mid-1992. Political factions voiced various objections to the terms of the agreement. One minister expressed reservations about the excessive length of the ten-year adjustment period for Poland to reach the general economic development level of EC members. Nationalist elements, including the KPN considered the agreement a threat to Polish sovereignty (see Political Parties, this ch.).

Poland also had serious disagreements with the IMF, which suspended credits in 1991 because Warsaw had failed to control its budget deficit. In March 1992, however, the IMF expressed general support for the Polish economic program. By terms of a subsequent agreement with the IMF, Poland came back into compliance with IMF deficit guidelines in exchange for access to US$1.5 billion in IMF loans.

Like its partners in the Visegrád Triangle, Poland remained frustrated in 1992 because the West was responding slowly to its attempts to obtain full membership in European international organizations. Nevertheless, Poland continued its full support of NATO and the European security role of the CSCE and left little doubt in mid-1992 of its long-term strategic goal, "to rejoin Europe."

*   *   *

Because of the ongoing transformation of Poland's system of governance, current political analyses and reports are an important source of information. The most useful of these are the *RFE/RL Research Report* and the Foreign Broadcast Information Service's *Daily Report: East Europe.* Arthur R. Rachwald's excellent summaries of Polish matters in the *Yearbook on International Communist Affairs* chronicle political events from the imposition of martial law in 1981 through the elections of 1991. *Informator Polska '91,* available only in Polish, is the best source on government structure at all levels after 1989. The communist government system of the 1980s is summarized in *Communist Regimes in Eastern Europe* by Richard Staar. Jane Leftwich Curry's *Poland's Journalists: Professionalism and Politics* is among useful sources on censorship and the print media.

Among many discussions of Poland's foreign policy, those meriting special attention are "Poland and the Soviet Union" by Roger E. Kanet and Brian V. Souders; *The Bloc That Failed: Soviet East European Relations in Transition* by Charles Gati; "From Visegrád to Kraków: Cooperation, Competition, and Coexistence in Central Europe" by Rudolf L. Tokes, and "Polish-Lithuanian Relations: Past, Present, and Future" by Stephen R. Burant. (For further information and complete citations, see Bibliography.)

Chapter 5. National Security

Syrena, mermaid of Warsaw, legendary protector of the city

IN THE EARLY 1990s, Poland addressed its national security issues as an independent state for the first time in more than fifty years. The loss and restoration of independence, and the fluctuations of national security that accompany such trauma, were not unusual in Polish history, however. When it was included in the Soviet Union's new empire after World War II, Poland lost control of its national security for the second time in two centuries. After functioning as two separate entities during the war, the Polish military was consolidated after the war as a subordinate component of a multinational military organization devoted primarily to defense of the Soviet Union. Following the Soviet model, the Polish communist government also established strong military-style internal security forces to protect the regime from internal and external threats.

In 1989 Poland's communist government fell unexpectedly after several decades of civil unrest that periodically had brought the threat of punitive intervention by the Soviet Union. The ensuing political chaos forced Poland to develop a new doctrine of national defense emphasizing cooperation with Western military and security organizations and friendly relations with previously hostile neighbor states. By 1991 the Warsaw Treaty Organization, better known as the Warsaw Pact, the multinational military structure created by the Soviet Union to dominate its East European empire, also had crumbled.

Poland's new doctrine developed slowly and fitfully in the first years of the 1990s. The country's economic need to trim its defense establishment clashed with perceptions of possible new threats and alliances in postcommunist Europe. After emerging from the Warsaw Pact, Poland found itself without military alliances at the same time as its military infrastructure was rapidly decaying. In this setting, harsh budget restrictions caused alarm that national security again might be compromised before restructuring and rearmament could take place.

Poland's location between two powerful neighbors, Germany and Russia, had influenced the country's national security for centuries. By the early 1990s, however, the changing political circumstances of the region had mitigated Polish concerns about German or Russian aggression for the foreseeable future. Beginning in 1990, Germany's attention was largely absorbed by the massive problems of reunification. The disintegration of the Soviet Union at the end of 1991 enabled the nations of Lithuania, Belarus, and Ukraine to emerge as newly independent states on Poland's eastern border. Thus, in less than three years the number of countries on Poland's borders increased from three to six. Under those circumstances, Poland was concerned about a security vacuum that might promote internal instability, border disputes, or even an armed regional conflict close to Polish territory. Poland's national security depended not only on the stability of neighboring states but also on domestic political and economic stability.

A healthy military was important for two reasons. Historically, the army had represented Polish self-esteem and the survival of the Polish state. National leaders were anxious to recapture that tradition to boost domestic morale. Also, a capable military establishment would help Poland present itself to the world as a viable, independent state. To achieve these goals, Polish leaders sought a complete restructuring of the defense establishment in the early 1990s. A new national military doctrine was formulated to reflect the end of the Warsaw Pact and the end of the political and military division of Europe into rival camps, as well as Poland's possible inclusion in existing Western security structures. The reform program was intended to streamline the Ministry of National Defense and military administration and to include civilians more closely in the process of defense decision making. The reform program sought to extricate the Polish Army from the constraints of Soviet-dominated Warsaw Pact military doctrine and training standards. Reform leaders also sought to reestablish the prestige of the armed forces as a national institution separate from and above politics. The quasimilitary forces that the Ministry of Internal Affairs had used to quell civil unrest during the communist era were abolished or redirected against genuine threats to the welfare of society.

Development of the Armed Forces

The Polish people possess remarkably strong military traditions. Throughout their history, they have demonstrated their will to resist foreign invasion and occupation. Military men who fought for national independence were viewed among the country's greatest patriots. In periods of national travail, the people sought leadership from their military heroes—Jan Sobieski, Tadeusz Kościuszko, Józef Poniatowski, the young officers who led the 1830 uprising, Józef Piłsudski, and Władysław Sikorski.

From Medieval Times to World War I

From the days of the earliest kings, the defense of Polish soil

Old fortress at Cieszyn, Silesian stronghold ceded by Piast
rulers to Bohemia in twelfth century
Courtesy Sam and Sarah Stulberg

demanded constant vigilance against Mongol, Tatar, and, later, German encroachment. In the 1400s, the first century of Poland's union with Lithuania, Polish soldiers often battled the Teutonic Knights (see Glossary), who threatened the union from their stronghold along the Baltic seacoast (see The Polish-Lithuanian Union, ch. 1). Poland was regarded as the outer bastion of Western Europe, and the Poles, led by an aristocratic military caste, accepted the mission to defend Western civilization against Eastern intrusions. Jan Sobieski's defeat of the Turks at Vienna in 1683, the last great military victory of the Polish-Lithuanian Commonwealth, was a turning point in the centuries-long struggle against westward expansion of the Ottoman Empire.

By 1725, however, Peter the Great had established a strong, unified Russian Empire that began to compete with the Ottoman Turks for dominance of the Slavic lands between them. At the same time, internal political decay weakened the Polish-Lithuanian Commonwealth, and Poland fell permanently behind Russia as a military power (see Decay of the Commonwealth, ch. 1). In the eighteenth century, Russia assumed the role of protector of Poland, first against Sweden and then against Prussia. In this period, the national army serving the Polish king degenerated from its previously honored

233

position. Manpower and royal prestige dwindled as local landlords raised their own private armies. Under these conditions, Poland lacked the military strength to resist the three partitions imposed by Austria, Prussia, and Russia between 1772 and 1795. The courageous but hopeless campaign of Tadeusz Kościuszko's insurgent army against the Russian Army in 1794 marked the final chapter in that era of Polish independence. By 1795, Poland had been erased from the map (see Partition of Poland, 1764–95, ch. 1).

Although the army could not prevent the final partition of the country, its veterans and graduates of the military college fought alongside the armies of Napoleon in his campaigns against Austria, Prussia, and Russia. Many Poles also served in the army of Congress Poland after 1815 (see The Napoleonic Period, ch. 1). Józef Poniatowski, nephew of the last Polish king, distinguished himself in Napoleon's 1809 campaign against Austria. The Polish Legion participated in Napoleon's invasion of Russia in 1812.

In the nineteenth century, Polish soldiers and officers served in the armies of Russia, Prussia (Germany), or Austria, depending on which power occupied their region. In this period, the practices of the partitioning powers exerted great influence on Polish military thought. Poles rose to high command positions, particularly in Austrian service. Poles fought on both sides during World War I, and all three occupying powers exerted great efforts to maintain the loyalty of the Poles in their jurisdictions. A Polish army was formed in France to help protect that country from the Central Powers, whereas Józef Piłsudski raised his Polish Legion to fight against Russia (and, more incidentally, for Austria) in the hope of eventually regaining Poland's independence from Russia. Much of the fighting on the eastern front in World War I took place on the territory of the former Polish Republic. Some 2 million Polish soldiers fought with the armies of the three occupying powers, and 450,000 Poles died in the war.

The Interwar Years

In 1918, after 123 years of partition, Poland regained its independence. The immediate military task was forming a new national army from soldiers and officers who had fought on both sides— although officers who had served on the side of the Central Powers dominated the new army. In the territorial uncertainty that followed the war, the Red Army pushed westward, aiming to use Poland as a bridge over which to spread socialism into postwar Germany. Piłsudski blocked this advance in 1919; then in 1920 he advanced eastward with the goal of including Ukrainian and Belorussian territory in a new Slavic state. Polish forces were thrown

*Tadeusz Kościuszko,
leader of the Polish
insurrection of 1794
Courtesy National Portrait
Gallery, Smithsonian
Institution, Washington*

back nearly to Warsaw, where Piłsudski defeated the Soviets and began an effective counterattack that preserved Poland's independence from Soviet domination in the interwar period.

Piłsudski's military and political prominence ensured that the armed forces became an important national institution in the new government. Many Poles saw the army as both the symbol and the guarantor of their country's independence and unity. In 1926, after Poland had experienced several years of political uncertainty and weak leadership, Piłsudski took over the state in a military coup, assuming the posts of minister of defense and general inspector of the army. In the interwar period, military officers held prominent positions in the national government, and their elevated status fostered intense political and personal rivalries as well as high-level corruption. After Piłsudski's death in 1935, Poland was ruled ineffectually by a group of his former subordinates, who remained in power until 1939.

After World War I, Polish national security rested on a military alliance with France, which guaranteed Poland's independence and territorial integrity. Poland was unsuccessful in joining the Little Entente, a French-sponsored alliance of Czechoslovakia, Romania, and Yugoslavia, because Czechoslovakia suspected Polish territorial ambitions along their mutual border. In protecting its sovereignty during this period, Poland had as its primary concerns maintaining a balance between its two powerful neighbors, Germany and the Soviet Union, and avoiding a situation where the two would take concerted action against Poland and divide it once again.

World War II

The Molotov-Ribbentrop pact between Nazi Germany and the Soviet Union realized Poland's worst fear. In September 1939, within one month of the signing of the treaty, Poland's two neighbors again attacked and divided the country. In the twenty years following World War I, Poland had been unable to modernize its armed forces or devise strategic and operational plans for defense against a Soviet or German attack. Hence in 1939 Poland was strategically isolated, unable to mobilize its troops, and technologically inferior. Although the Franco-Polish Alliance and Military Convention of 1921 required that a German attack on Poland trigger a French offensive against Germany in the West (terms that had been confirmed as recently as May 1939), the French did not come to Poland's aid when Adolf Hitler staged a border incident that brought Nazi forces storming onto Polish territory.

The large but underequipped Polish Army soon capitulated, and most of the force spent the war in prisoner-of-war camps. Underground resistance against German occupation began almost immediately, however, and resistance activity continued on Polish soil throughout the war. At its peak, the so-called Home Army (Armia Krajowa), directed by the London government-in-exile, included as many as 400,000 resistance fighters. Polish forces also fought under British and Soviet commands on the western and eastern fronts respectively. Poles fought with distinction with the Allies in Africa and Italy; the number of Polish soldiers on the Western Front reached 200,000 by the end of the war.

A separate Polish army, recruited by order of Joseph V. Stalin from among Polish prisoners of war on Soviet soil in 1943, initially lacked officers and expertise. As a result, by the war's end about 40 percent of the officers in that force had come directly from the Red Army. In July 1944, on the strength of occupation by this Soviet-Polish army, a Soviet-backed provisional government was established at Lublin in eastern Poland. At the same time, the Eastern Front force, augmented by Soviet conscription in liberated territory, reformed as the Polish First Army under command of General Zygmunt Berling, who had been a Polish officer before the war. The Polish First Army later joined the Lublin-based communist resistance command to form the Polish Armed Forces (Wojska Polskie). In late 1944, two additional armies were added to this umbrella command; all the Polish Eastern Front armies, which ultimately totaled about 400,000 troops, fought with distinction as the Soviet forces drove westward toward Germany in 1944–45 (see World War II, ch. 1).

The Polish armies on the eastern and western fronts remained under separate commands throughout the war, reflecting the political split that would substantively alter Poland's military doctrine after the war. The Soviet officer corps of the Eastern Front armies wielded a heavy political influence on their troops. Before the end of hostilities, an estimated 5,000 to 6,000 political officers were charged with indoctrinating military personnel in the philosophy of the new communist political order that the Soviets planned for postwar Poland. By mid-1945, the Polish Army had adopted Red Army equipment, organization, regulations, and strategy, as well as the Soviet-type political apparatus that would become standard for all the armies of postwar Eastern Europe.

The Communist Era

For forty-five years following World War II, the Polish military subordinated its organization and its doctrine to the larger geopolitical and military aims of the Soviet Union. Until 1981, however, Polish society largely retained the traditional notion that the first mission of its army was to represent and defend the Polish people, regardless of political conditions. The final eight years of communist rule marked an unnatural combination of military and political doctrines, triggering a reorganization process that continued into the noncommunist 1990s.

Postwar Consolidation

The noncommunist Home Army officially disbanded in January 1945, and the course of the war left the Eastern Front armies in control of all Polish territory. In the immediate postwar era, the army took second place to Poland's new internal security forces in purging political opponents and consolidating communist power. This purging process lasted until the formation of the Polish United Workers' Party (Polska Zjednoczona Partia Robotnicza— PZPR) in 1948 (see Consolidation of Communist Power, ch. 1).

Unlike other important institutions, the army did not suffer wholesale purges of its noncommunist elements in the immediate postwar period. Communists controlled the top ranks and leadership positions, however, and political commissars installed in military units taught communist party principles to regular soldiers and ensured their loyalty to the party. Many wartime political officers played a significant role in the indoctrination process and based glittering civilian careers on their contributions to the building of the communist state.

In the late 1940s, the main roles of the military were resettlement of Poland's newly acquired western territory, helping in economic reconstruction, and waging a three-year civil war against former Home Army supporters, Ukrainian nationalists, and various outlaw bands in the foothills of the Carpathian Mountains. Some 70,000 people were arrested by internal security and military authorities in the repression of civil uprisings between 1945 and 1948. In 1981 General Wojciech Jaruzelski, who later would head the last communist government, cited the threat that such uprisings would recur in his rationale for imposing martial law in Poland.

The sociological composition of Poland's army changed dramatically after World War II. The interwar officer corps had come mostly from the gentry and professional classes. By 1949, however, only 29 percent of Polish officers had begun service before the war, and peasants and workers were favored highly in postwar officer training programs. From 1948 through 1953, in keeping with Stalin's intrusive totalitarian influence throughout Eastern Europe, the PZPR and the Soviet Army exercised increasing influence in Polish military affairs. Soviet officers headed the Polish General Staff, all service branches, and all military districts during this period. A Soviet general, Konstantin Rokossovskii, served as minister of defense of Poland between 1949 and 1956. His first assignment was to purge the Polish armed forces of remaining prewar personnel who were considered ideologically unreliable. Accordingly, between 1950 and 1955, many faithful communist officers were imprisoned or executed. In 1949, as the Cold War set in, the Polish People's Army (as it was renamed after World War II) went on a war footing, conscription was reinstituted, and preparations were made to operate as part of the Soviet army in a future European land war.

The ravages of World War II somewhat eroded society's faith in the Polish military's ability to defend the country. Postwar politicization caused a further decline in the military's stature and a parallel decline in military morale and organization. Soviet army officers in close cooperation with the Committee for State Security (Komitet gosudarstvennoi bezopasnosti—KGB) occupied all key commands until 1956. This command structure bypassed Polish communist authorities often and openly in making military policy.

Defining the Military's Postwar Role

In June 1956, major failures of communist state economic policy brought a large-scale uprising of workers in Poznań demanding "bread and freedom." Polish troops refused to fire on the workers, heralding a political upheaval that ended the Stalinist era in Poland. The uprisings of 1956 greatly alarmed the Soviet Union and ultimately reduced Soviet control over the Polish military and internal security agencies. Poland's Security Service (Służba Bezpieczeństwa—SB), which had crushed the Poznań workers ruthlessly, was revamped in 1956. The widely unpopular Rokossovskii and thirty-two Soviet generals were recalled to the Soviet Union in spite of intense Soviet diplomatic pressure. At this critical point, Polish units went on alert in response to a massing of Soviet troops and tanks on the eastern border. Incoming party chief Władysław Gomułka skillfully negotiated Poland's position with the Soviets; backed by Poland's demonstrated willingness to defend itself, Gomułka was able to avert an invasion. Just two weeks later, in October 1956, Soviet tanks would roll into Hungary. The Moscow Declaration and the Treaty of December 17, 1956 then stipulated the sovereignty of the Polish communist elite over the Polish military and established limitations on the stationing and maneuver of Soviet forces in Poland.

Many of Gomułka's reforms proved short-lived, however, and no full offensive was mounted against Soviet control of the military. In his campaign against "revisionism," which began in 1957, Gomułka gradually returned pro-Moscow officers to key positions. Moscow continued to station troops in Poland, train Polish officers in the Soviet Union, supply Soviet-made weapons, and include Poland in regional defense plans. And in 1957, Gomułka formed the Military Counterintelligence Service to continue supplying the party information about political attitudes in the military. At the same time, he refined and professionalized the Internal Security Corps, which had been discredited in 1956. Political officers received training to give them a higher level of professional military competence and credibility with the troops and their professional counterparts. Nevertheless, experts consider the events of 1956 a watershed in Polish military history. Because Polish forces had helped the Polish communist government to a new autonomy, the military regained some of its prestige and influence in society.

Gomułka's government sought to consolidate PZPR control of military policy, which in the Stalinist years had been a tangled combination of informal Polish and Soviet lines of authority. Gomułka replaced departing Soviet commanders with Polish officers who had served with him in the wartime communist underground (as opposed to the Soviet-controlled Polish First Army) and with commanders who had prepared their troops to resist the threatened Soviet invasion in 1956. Nominal control of military affairs rested with the Council of Ministers and its National Defense Committee

(Komitet Obrony Kraju—KOK; see The Communist Tradition, this ch.). As in all other national policy matters, however, the Political Bureau (Politburo) of the PZPR had the final word in all important policy questions. Personalities and factions continued to dominate policy. Under Gomułka's trusted minister of national defense, General Marian Spychalski, the top grades of the officer corps were riven by political conflict. A conservative nationalist group known as the Partisans became a major force opposing military and political reform. Their leader, internal security chief Mieczysław Moczar, gained substantial power in the 1960s by playing factions against one another and purging reformist rivals. In 1967–68, using the June 1967 War between Israel and its Arab neighbors as a pretext, Moczar and his faction instigated the purge of the remaining 200 Jewish officers in the Polish People's Army and the ouster of Spychalski. Moczar's methodology did not yield him complete control, however, because most of the purged officers were replaced by young professionals uninterested in the ideological infighting of the military establishment.

One such figure was Wojciech Jaruzelski, the lieutenant general who capped a rapid rise through the ranks by replacing Spychalski as minister of national defense in 1968. Jaruzelski's appointment began the retreat of the Partisans' influence. In 1970 the military again was ordered to quell worker riots, this time in the Baltic ports of Gdańsk and Gdynia. Jaruzelski refused to transmit the order, and the army generally refrained from action. Although army units inflicted some civilian casualties, the Internal Security Corps again was the main force brought against Polish demonstrators. The army's reaction reinforced the message of 1956 that the Polish military could not be expected to defend a communist regime from the people by suppressing political unrest.

In the 1970s, the prestige of the military continued to grow while that of the PZPR plummeted because of the economic failures and corruption associated with the regime of Gomułka's successor, Edward Gierek. Through the 1970s and the 1980s, the military took a noncommittal attitude toward major episodes of civil unrest. In 1976 Minister of National Defense Jaruzelski informed Gierek that Polish soldiers could not be expected to fire on striking Polish workers. The army remained strictly loyal to the communist system, but it showed much less loyalty to particular regimes when they came under attack from the Polish population. In 1980, when the Solidarity (Solidarność) union set off a series of large-scale strikes in the Baltic ports, the government apparently did not consider using the military to quell unrest. A 1981 poll showed the military behind only the church and Solidarity in the level of respect afforded by Poles to their national institutions.

While the Polish military remained neutral in internal affairs, it fulfilled completely the foreign duties expected of a Warsaw Pact member. Two Polish divisions took part in the 1968 invasion of Czechoslovakia that was precipitated by Soviet alarm at that country's experimentation with economic and political reform. In keeping with the Soviet Union's decision to distribute defense responsibilities more widely among Warsaw Pact members, the Polish defense industry grew rapidly in the 1970s and early 1980s. Poland reached fifth place in world arms exports in 1987.

Martial Law

Although the military was taking a low public profile, Jaruzelski played a major behind-the-scenes role in unseating the discredited Gierek in 1980. The following year, Jaruzelski himself became prime minister as a compromise candidate acceptable to all factions of the PZPR's divided leadership. By 1981 military officers occupied fourteen seats in the PZPR Central Committee (three had been the norm during the Gierek regime). Until late 1981, Jaruzelski represented a moderate wing of the PZPR willing to negotiate with the ever-more powerful Solidarity movement. The restraint Jaruzelski had shown in using military force in 1970, 1976, and 1980 sustained his public prestige and that of the armed forces through 1980.

In 1981, however, the near-collapse of the PZPR caused civilian party leaders to tie the army, by way of Jaruzelski, closer to the role of defending the regime against popular dissent. Party leaders named Jaruzelski prime minister and then first secretary of the PZPR, making the general the most powerful political figure in Poland and completely closing the gap between military and political authority. In December 1981, the party's continued collapse, the country's economic decay, and Solidarity's increasingly radical demands and fear of a Soviet Army invasion triggered by those conditions caused Jaruzelski to declare martial law, in effect executing a military coup.

The military was mobilized but did not confront activists and demonstrators directly. The army staffed checkpoints and protected communications and transportation facilities while the specialized Motorized Units of the Citizens' Militia (Zmotoryzowane Oddziały Milicji Obywatelskiej—ZOMO) performed riot control functions on the streets (see Internal Security, this ch.). Nevertheless, martial law associated the military directly with the severe curtailment of civil liberties and the imprisonment of thousands of antigovernment activists. The use of the military to keep a Polish regime in power again tarnished the public perception of the armed forces. The prospect of facing fellow Poles in life-threatening confrontations fragmented and demoralized the army as well. Once the public regained its voice in government policy in 1989, the memory of martial law prompted strong insistence that control of the armed forces henceforth be distinctly lodged with responsible civilian officials and totally separate from any political party.

The state of emergency ended officially in mid-1983, but Jaruzelski and his military subordinates remained in control of top party and government offices for the next six years. Jaruzelski supporters replaced the discredited upper echelon of civilian PZPR officials, and during this period political officers remained in place at all levels of the military. Especially in the early and mid-1980s, the special police forces of the Ministry of Internal Affairs remained a potent arm of the government in suppressing dissident activity by surveillance and physical intimidation. The public's negative image of the military regime was reinforced in 1984 when Jaruzelski's government was implicated in the murder of dissident priest Jerzy Popiełuszko by internal security agents. After a unique public trial, the security service was reorganized, but dissidents still were harassed in the years that followed. During this period, military recruitment became increasingly difficult because the declaration of martial law had reduced the prestige of a military career.

By 1985 Mikhail S. Gorbachev's highly visible reforms in the Soviet Union removed the rationale that political reform in Poland might incite an invasion from the East, and Jaruzelski moved cautiously in the same direction as Gorbachev. Shortly thereafter, the Soviet Union also orchestrated changes in Poland's international military position by restructuring the Warsaw Pact and revising the military doctrine that justified the alliance. When the Soviet Union began streamlining military planning and increasing doctrinal reliance on reserve forces throughout the alliance in 1987, Poland was able to begin sorely-needed reductions in its military budget. In 1988 military personnel were reduced by 15,000 persons, and another 33,000 were cut in 1989 (see Military Manpower, this ch.). The military budget for 1989 was 4 percent less than that for 1988 (see Military Budget, this ch.).

Transition and Reform

In 1989 the peaceful transition from the Jaruzelski regime to the popularly elected Solidarity-led government had little immediate impact on the organization of the Polish military. General Florian Siwicki, who had been Jaruzelski's minister of national defense, served in the first cabinet of noncommunist Prime Minister Tadeusz Mazowiecki, even though Siwicki had been closely involved in the 1968 invasion of Czechoslovakia and the imposition of martial law. Under Mazowiecki, Siwicki directed a first phase of military reforms until he was replaced in mid-1990. General Czesław Kiszczak, Jaruzelski's minister of internal affairs throughout the martial law period, also was held over in Mazowiecki's first cabinet. Kiszczak began redirecting the charter of the infamous special police services away from their traditional communist role of support for the government in power and toward protection of society as a whole.

In 1989, for the first time since the interwar period, the military came under open scrutiny by the Polish media and parliament. Public resentment of the armed forces as a tool of communist repression was increased by exposures of brutality and corruption under Jaruzelski. The military responded with a campaign of openness and humanization that finally led to substantial reform and reduced hostility between the military and Solidarity. Reform measures taken by the end of 1990 included removal of all political organizations from the military, further budget and manpower reductions, conversion of thirty military installations to civilian use, shortened terms of service for draftees, and freedom of religious practice in the military (see The Military and Society, this ch.). Shortages of personnel already had forced passage of an alternative service law in 1988. Lech Wałęsa, the first popularly elected president, who came to power in December 1990, became commander in chief of the armed forces, and the Ministry of National Defense began a transition from a basically military body into a civilian agency of the government in which military authority would be distinctly subordinate (see Evolution and Restructuring, this ch.).

Externally, Poland's chief military goal in the first postcommunist years was ending the Warsaw Pact obligations that still placed Soviet troops on Polish soil in the early 1990s, then moving as quickly as possible to a new set of national security agreements. In 1990 Czechoslovakia, Hungary, and Poland began urging the dissolution of the Warsaw Pact, citing new geopolitical conditions that made such an arrangement superfluous for the security of both the Soviet Union and the East European member nations.

In late 1990, the Poles then entered long and difficult bilateral negotiations on the Soviet troop issue, including the timing for withdrawal from Poland and the method by which Soviet troops leaving Germany would cross Polish territory. Soviet negotiators resisted an early timetable (Wałęsa's initial bargaining position required complete withdrawal by the end of 1991) and demanded compensation for installations that Soviet forces had built. The Soviet position on Poland was determined by existing agreements for complete Soviet withdrawal from Czechoslovakia and Hungary, and by the recent reunification of Germany. After those events, Poland was perceived as the last pillar of the Soviet Union's European security structure. The issue was finally resolved in late 1991 with Soviet agreement to remove all combat troops from Poland by the end of 1992 and all support troops by the end of 1993. A separate agreement defined terms for transit of Soviet troops from Germany through Poland (see Threat Perception, this ch.).

National Security Policy

In mid-1991, the Warsaw Pact ceased to function as a military alliance, ending the dominating role of that organization in Polish national defense. Poland's approach to national security changed drastically, but the change really was a return to the geopolitical fundamentals that had formed the nation's long-term threat perception and military doctrine. Poland sought a new balance among its immediate neighbors (including Russia and Germany) and new security arrangements with other states, such as Hungary and the Czech and Slovak Federative Republic (CSFR—see Glossary), that were also emerging from Soviet domination. Like Poland, those nations now felt exposed on all sides. They were free to determine their own future, but they were also solely responsible for the results of their political and national security choices.

Threat Perception

Throughout the communist era, official threat perception by the Polish military was identical to that of the Soviet Union: the North Atlantic Treaty Organization (NATO—see Glossary) would confront the forces of the socialist nations on the plains of Northern Europe in a massive conventional war. Until 1990 Poland had the special threat perception of renewed invasion from Germany; although the Federal Republic of Germany (West Germany) was itself no longer a military power, it was the ostensible staging area for large numbers of NATO troops against the Warsaw Pact. On the other hand, the Soviet invasions of Czechoslovakia and Hungary exemplified the eastern threat perceived by both communist and noncommunist Poles with nationalist loyalties. That threat was also a convenient tool for the Jaruzelski government in justifying oppression of reform activity.

By 1987 the inefficient centralized industrial systems of the Warsaw Pact countries were increasingly unable to produce high-technology weaponry, and their national economies had become severely distorted by the priority given military production. Accordingly, Gorbachev's "new thinking" on Soviet security prompted a redesign of Warsaw Pact strategy based on sober reassessment of Warsaw Pact resources and on the belief that political means could replace military strategy in protecting the security of the alliance. The new strategy included reducing defense spending and emphasizing a pan-European security plan that might split NATO into American and European factions. Although the new structure continued to regard Poland as a central player in the coalition defense system, Poland was able to reduce and streamline key military units beginning in 1987. Thus, before the revolutions of 1989, the Warsaw Pact's combined threat perception had changed pragmatically, and member nations had the opportunity to relieve somewhat the onus of mandatory support of the alliance's military structure. For Poland, this change triggered the search for a more realistic and independent threat perception that continued into the early 1990s.

The postcommunist era complicated Poland's threat perception. The new outlook began with the recognition that Poland was not and could not be militarily comparable to its traditionally dangerous neighbors. To the east, the Soviet Union had fractured into numerous republics, abolishing any remaining threat of an attack launched from the east to keep Poland within ideological limits. The uneasy relations among the former Soviet republics, especially between Russia and Ukraine over issues such as jurisdiction over nuclear weapons and control of the Black Sea, caused alarm in Poland. So did the possibility that reform would fail in Russia, allowing an ultranationalist, hard-line regime to come to power, reassert Soviet or imperialist prerogatives, and renege on troop withdrawal schedules. Another threat was the rejection by the newly independent republics of arms control agreements signed by the Soviet Union. Such a move could lead to uncontrolled proliferation of nuclear weapons and the failure of limits on conventional forces in the region. In another scenario, central authority might fail entirely in former republics, causing conflicts among former Soviet forces to spill over onto adjacent Polish territory. In 1991 three events—the Soviet crackdown in Lithuania in January, the attempted reactionary coup in the Soviet Union in August, and the chaos of the Serbian-Croatian struggle in the last half of the year—lent urgency to the formation of Poland's new European security policy.

Polish concerns were magnified by the strength and disposition of forces in the former Soviet Union. Russian troops withdrawn from Germany and Poland went to Kaliningrad, the isolated Russian province on Poland's northern border, and often remained there because the surrounding republics, Belarus and Lithuania, would not permit Russian troops to pass through their territory. The continued concentration of Russian armored, artillery, and infantry forces in Kaliningrad was a source of alarm for Poland in 1992. (Poland did not seek a change in the political status of Kaliningrad, however.) To the east, the armed forces in Ukraine's Carpathian Military District adjoining Poland exceeded Poland's entire combat strength in 1992 (although bilateral relations with Ukraine were quite friendly). Many Polish storage depots were located close to the borders of both Kaliningrad and Ukraine, making them vulnerable in case of attack from either direction.

Past territorial and military conflicts with Belarus, Lithuania, and Ukraine were confined increasingly to the memories of the older generations on all sides. Nevertheless, Belarus, remembering that the Treaty of Riga had divided that republic between Poland and Soviet Russia in 1921, still claimed the Białystok region of eastern Poland, which was home to a substantial Belarusian population. And Ukrainian nationalists remembered the role of the Polish People's Army in helping the Soviet Union crush the anticommunist Ukrainian Resistance Army in 1947, as well as the interwar Polish hegemony in western Ukraine. The most divisive issue in Polish-Lithuanian relations was treatment of the Polish minority in Lithuania, estimated at 300,000 people in 1990. In 1991 and 1992, that well-organized minority pressed for autonomy, putting the Polish government in a difficult diplomatic position and blocking Poland's efforts to secure its eastern and northern borders from ethnic turmoil (see Other Former Soviet Republics, ch. 4).

Poland's evaluation of Germany's position was more reassuring. In the early 1990s, Polish policy makers saw the newly reunified Germany's strong commitments to NATO and the European Community (EC—see Glossary), the German national outlook, and continued deemphasis of the German military as indicators that Germany would remain a benign neighbor through the 1990s. Poles increasingly perceived the threat from Germany as one of economic rather than military domination. Accordingly, Poland's best defense appeared to lie in forming closer ties with the traditionally robust German economy and reinvigorating the Polish political system rather than in strategic military planning. Doubts about Germany's long-term territorial goals were revived briefly in 1990 when Germany hesitated in accepting the Oder-Neisse Line as a permanent border between the two countries, but tensions were eased by the signing of a border treaty in mid-1990 and a Polish-German friendship and cooperation treaty in late 1991 (see fig. 12;

Armor crew checking terrain on maneuvers
Courtesy Polish Information Agency, Warsaw

Germany, ch. 4). In pursuing closer German ties, however, Poland cautiously soothed Russian perceptions that a new alliance might be forming to its west.

Military Doctrine

Throughout the existence of the Warsaw Pact, Poland was a key element in the security system of the Soviet Union. The Polish armed forces were the largest non-Soviet national component of the alliance. Located in the "northern tier" between NATO countries and the Soviet Union, Poland was expected to play a major role in any major conventional conflict with West European forces. Polish force structure gave priority to armor in expectation of a blitzkrieg-style theater offensive across Europe. In joint offensive warfare training exercises in the early 1980s, Poland had the mission of attacking northern West Germany and Denmark. Poland was also the major corridor for supply and communications between the Soviet Union and the large Soviet force in place in the German Democratic Republic (East Germany). These factors were the rationale for the assignment of approximately 30,000 Soviet ground and air troops on Polish soil from the late 1940s until 1992.

After essentially following Soviet military doctrine for forty-five years, in 1990 Poland began formulating independent doctrine

247

taking into account a vastly different European strategic situation. The first public declaration of a new approach came in February 1990, when Poland was still a member of the Warsaw Pact. The guidelines issued by Jaruzelski's national security agency, the KOK (which at that point still included some communists), were clearly labeled as transitional, and the statement included a one-sentence reiteration of loyalty to Warsaw Pact obligations. Nevertheless, some independent positions were taken. Poland now categorically rejected initiation of military action against another state and participation in a war unless its allies were attacked. Maintenance of Polish troops beyond national borders was described as contradictory to national interests. In case of an attack on a Warsaw Pact member, only Polish authorities would determine the appropriate response of Poland, Polish commanders would retain full control of Polish troops, and Polish forces would remain discrete units rather than being integrated with Soviet troops. As an extension of the Warsaw Pact doctrinal revision that began in 1987, the guidelines assigned the highest priority to defending against attack by air, armored, and amphibious forces.

In 1990 the Commission on National Defense of the Sejm, the lower house of Parliament, strongly criticized the initial KOK reform program as insufficient for full military reform and as retaining too much of Poland's past subservience to the Warsaw Pact. The total collapse of the pact in the following year required more complete revision of military doctrine. A new program called Armed Forces '90 represented a second, truly postcommunist, phase of military reform. It was a long-term plan of steps to be completed by the year 2000. Already in mid-1990, the military began implementing plans to apportion defensive forces more evenly between Poland's eastern and western borders.

From mid-1990 to mid-1992, the topic of appropriate doctrine for Poland received extensive treatment in general and specialized forums, but doctrinal reform was stymied by internal political conflicts. All agreed that henceforth the basic mission of the Polish defense system should be protecting the sovereignty, independence, and territorial integrity of the Polish nation. The means to that end were more problematic, however. In mid-1991 a deputy to the chief of the General Staff proposed that the new Polish Army (the word *people's* having been dropped from the title in 1990) be built around assault-landing brigades, helicopter regiments, armored and motorized units, and special forces such as mountain infantry, to achieve optimal flexibility and mobility in the defensive posture. Poland would also begin manufacturing sophisticated modern weapons and purchase medium-class warships. The chief obstacle to this plan, however, was a military budget that in 1991 barely sustained routine maintenance.

A comprehensive doctrinal reform first proposed in mid-1991 was never approved because of disagreement between President Lech Wałęsa, on one side, and Prime Minister Jan Olszewski and Minister of National Defense Jan Parys, on the other, over the question of which office should control military policy. In mid-1992, after the Olszewski government fell, a new draft doctrine was prepared by the president's National Security Bureau (Biuro Bezpieczeństwa Narodowego—BBN) and officials of the ministries of foreign affairs and national defense.

The basic assumption of the new doctrine was that Poland was not threatened with any form of attack from outside, excepting possible spillover from ethnic or border conflicts in the former Soviet republics. Instead, the chief threats to Polish national security would be serious civil unrest or strikes, a massive influx of refugees from the east, or the failure of other countries to fulfill economic obligations. In early 1992, Russia provided a prime example of the third type of risk by unexpectedly demanding a revision of the terms of a crucial barter agreement to supply natural gas to Poland. Within Poland conversion from a centrally planned economy to free enterprise would cause social strains, leading to mass emigration, crime, and relaxation of social rules. The new doctrine therefore recommended completing social reconstruction as quickly as possible to minimize disruptions that might threaten national security. Given budgetary constraints, planners estimated that national security requirements could be met with a total force of about 200,000, or 60 percent of the force level in the 1980s, together with a National Guard force of unspecified size.

In the spirit of cooperation with all neighbors, the doctrine refused membership in any military alliance directed against any neighbor. It also rejected deployment of Polish forces abroad except in accordance with international agreements; a United Nations (UN) peacekeeping mission, for example, would be permitted. Specifically mentioned were close and friendly relations with Russia, Belarus, Ukraine, and Lithuania. Regional cooperation was described as the foundation of a general international security system that included North America. An important element of this general concept was membership in NATO and close cooperation with the Conference on Security and Cooperation in Europe (CSCE—see Glossary); (see Military Cooperation and Exchanges, this ch.).

Strategy and Tactics

Until 1990 Polish strategic missions were determined by the country's assigned role in the Warsaw Pact. The overall theme was prevention of war in peacetime and defense of the Soviet Union and its allies in wartime. Through the mid-1980s, the alliance emphasized strategic offense over strategic defense, with a single strategic plan integrating the two aspects. The plan heavily emphasized overlap and cooperation of strategic missions in a combined arms format. The Soviet Union initially used the Warsaw Pact primarily to retain military and political control of its East European allies beneath a facade of collective decision making. Soviet dominance began to diminish in the 1960s, however, and by the 1980s the alliance had become a forum for debate and bargaining over issues of national independence and autonomous decision making. Until 1989, Poland's military leaders remained cautious in expressing independent views on questions of strategy.

By mid-1990, international events fully revealed the obsolescence of Poland's Warsaw Pact membership. The anti-West German rationale behind the alliance seemed especially dated in view of Soviet approval of German reunification and Germany's approval of the Oder-Neisse Line as the permanent border with Poland. In the summer of 1990, Czechoslovak and Polish proposals for substantial reform in the alliance structure brought no constructive response from the Soviet Union. Shortly thereafter, the Polish Ministry of Foreign Affairs began making public reference to Poland's withdrawal from the Warsaw Pact and the pact's impending disintegration. Meanwhile, internal strife in the Soviet Union weakened the argument that deviation from Warsaw Pact strategic planning would provoke Soviet retaliation (an argument that in reality had been hollow at least since Gorbachev's reform programs began in the mid-1980s).

Beginning in 1990, Polish military strategists and tacticians shifted toward defensive techniques over offensive operations. Their theories promoted a mobile, nonlinear defense based on enhanced force maneuverability. The new strategic defense plan included creating conditions favorable to a war of maneuver, constructing tactical and permanent fortifications, protecting the military communications network in wartime, and preparing to destroy key objectives to prevent their use by the enemy. The context of this program was defensive battle against superior forces, using terrain features to channel the enemy into areas vulnerable to a Polish counterattack. If this goal were not possible, the mission would be to extend the engagement long enough to raise the political cost to

Trainees moving in camouflage on field exercise
Courtesy Polish Information Agency, Warsaw

the aggressor by making the conflict a threat to general European security. Partisan resistance after defeat of Poland's conventional forces was rejected because of projected human and material losses. New strategies featured defensive combat in the forested and flooded areas that predominate in the eastern border region—a strong indication of Poland's new threat perception. Air defense, although labeled a top priority by Polish planners, remained very poorly defined and equipped in mid-1992 (see Armed Services, this ch.).

Strategic writings in the early 1990s contemplated no action outside Poland. In keeping with Poland's shifting threat perceptions involving Kaliningrad and Ukraine, the military establishment agreed on a shift of force concentration to the eastern borders. Military districts were redesignated accordingly in 1991. Budget constraints and the lack of military basing infrastructure limited implementation of this policy by preventing large-scale force shifts, however. In 1992 about 65 percent of Polish forces remained west of the Vistula River (compared with 75 percent in the Warsaw Pact alignment), and Polish defensive lines remained static, deep, and echeloned, in keeping with standard Soviet practice.

Military Cooperation and Exchanges

Poland's pattern of military cooperation changed as drastically

251

as its political climate in 1989. Participation in Warsaw Pact joint exercises ended in 1988, and the Polish military establishment ended its close working relationship with its Soviet counterparts. The April 1990 appointment of Solidarity intellectual Janusz Onyszkiewicz as deputy minister of national defense for foreign military relations signaled a new orientation in the defense establishment. Once the disintegration of the Soviet Union altered the geopolitics of all Eastern Europe, however, Poland sought new, equal military partnerships with Russia and other former Soviet republics. A comprehensive cooperation treaty completed in late 1991 replaced the Polish-Soviet friendship treaty of 1965, which had legitimized Soviet domination of Polish military policy. The new pact, given urgency on the Soviet side by the failed coup attempt of August 1991, rejects all interference in Polish affairs by the current Soviet state or by any state that might succeed it.

With the goal of eventual close military relations that would guarantee military protection by the West, Poland took steps to prove itself a worthy military partner in the early 1990s. In the early 1990s, the Polish defense establishment was divided over the need for NATO membership because some officials believed that move would sacrifice Polish national integrity. Nevertheless, long-term military planning aimed at compatibility of Polish weaponry and doctrine with that of the West. In 1991 Minister of National Defense Piotr Kołodziejczyk visited NATO headquarters to promote Polish cooperation with the alliance and to establish information exchanges on doctrine and military exercises. Two months later, Chief of the General Staff General Zdzisław Stelmaszuk presented Poland's plans for reorganization of its armed forces to the NATO Supreme Allied Commander Europe, General John Galvin. Poland gained further concessions during Olszewski's visit to the United States in early 1992, and during NATO Secretary General Manfred Woerner's visit to Poland.

In the Persian Gulf War, Poland provided a hospital ship, a rescue ship, and a ground field hospital to U.N. forces. Polish troops were among U.N. peacekeeping forces in Croatia and Bosnia and Hercegovina in 1991–92. In 1992 the Polish navy was scheduled to participate with the Russian navy in a joint NATO exercise in the Baltic Sea. Beginning in 1990, Polish officers and civilian officials of the Ministry of National Defense attended Western military academies. The aim was to gain familiarity with Western military practice and to identify the defensive systems most appropriate for Poland's new international position.

Before the collapse of the Warsaw Pact in 1991, security specialists from the Visegrád Triangle member nations (the CSFR, Hungary, and Poland) discussed military cooperation to supplement the economic and political programs already underway (see Southern Neighbors and the Visegrád Triangle, ch. 4). National security cooperation within the grouping had already included decades of Warsaw Pact joint military exercises, use of standardized Soviet weapons, organization, and tactics, negotiation as a bloc for favorable arms purchase prices and joint licensing agreements for their arms industries, and collaboration in 1988–89 in demanding a restructured Warsaw Pact. Beginning in 1991, the Visegrád Triangle nations arranged group purchases of equipment from Western suppliers to reduce per-unit cost. The defense industries of Poland and the CSFR also began coproduction of specific armaments in 1991.

The common objective that emerged in the Visegrád talks was regional stability based on links with existing European security systems and complete abolition of neutral buffer zones and opposing security sectors. The Visegrád Triangle nations extended their economic rationale to strategic doctrine, seeking integration into West European groupings by presenting a united security position to organizations such as NATO and the CSCE. According to that position, security depended on the broadest possible European integration, eliminating formal bilateral and multilateral military alliances that excluded parts of the continent (see Foreign Relations, ch. 4).

Defense Organization

The overall reassessment of Poland's military position brought fundamental change in the structure of the military establishment, beginning with the separation of the military branches from the civilian administration. Ultimate command was firmly assigned to civilian officials. Such a change from the simplicity of the Jaruzelski government, where the military had occupied top government positions, caused considerable friction and confusion in the early 1990s.

The Communist Tradition

Under Poland's communist regimes, the Politburo of the PZPR was ultimately responsible for major military policy decisions, with nominal responsibility lodged with the Council of Ministers. The Administration Department of the PZPR's Central Committee closely supervised military affairs, monitoring such items as promotions and budgets. The minister of national defense, who was always a general officer and usually a full member of the Politburo, was supreme commander of the army and chief of operations. Beginning in 1982, however, Jaruzelski delegated this responsibility (which he nominally retained after becoming head of state) to General Siwicki. The Polish People's Army included all branches—ground forces, navy, air force, and air defense—but lines of command differed among the services. Commanders of the naval and air forces reported directly to the minister of national defense. The ground forces, on the other hand, reported to the minister of national defense through the General Staff. In practice, the minister of national defense often commanded all aspects of a military exercise, and the General Staff, which nominally commanded only the ground forces, made policy binding on all branches.

The armed forces were divided into the operational army and the National Territorial Defense Forces (Obrona Terytorium Kraju—OTK). The former was organized as an integral part of Warsaw Pact forces, whereas the latter was limited to service in Poland and had no role in Warsaw Pact activities. The operational army forces were administered in three military districts—Wrocław, Bydgoszcz, and Warsaw—each of which had a two-division corps and a rapid-reaction corps.

Evolution and Restructuring

The accommodation of the Polish Army's command structure to the domestic and foreign conditions of post-Warsaw Pact Europe was a fitful and controversial process. The transfer of military policy making to civilian authority, in itself a widely accepted goal, brought intragovernmental power struggles. Together with severe budgetary limitations, those struggles caused great uncertainty in the military community about future directions.

Civilian Command Structure

In mid-1991 an Interministerial Commission for the Reorganization of National Defense submitted its structural reform recommendations to the Council of Ministers, citing the need to amend the constitution and the law on military service. The Ministry of National Defense was to be converted into a civilian organ of state administration with a separate, subordinate armed forces section. Appointment of a civilian minister of national defense would improve the ministry's communications and joint activity with Parliament, state agencies, and the national economy, ensure depolitization of the military, and relieve the military of responsibility for budgets, administration, supply, social issues, and other matters judged more appropriate for a civilian agency. The military section would prepare concepts for national defense, forecast international situations that might bear on national security, plan long-term projects of the arms industry, and assist in export and import policy making.

Passage of the Little Constitution in the fall of 1992 was expected to define the previously hazy lines of national security authority. However, Wałęsa expressed open dissatisfaction with the control allotted the presidency, heralding possible future clashes with Parliament and the Council of Ministers over individual aspects of security policy. The Little Constitution specifies that peacetime command of the Polish Army be exercised by the president of the republic and by the prime minister and the Council of Ministers (see Constitutional Revisions after April 1989; Presidency; Council of Ministers, ch. 4). All levels of central and local government are charged with managing aspects of the national defense assigned them by the constitution and by legislation. The president oversees the activities of all such agencies. The president determines the composition of military advisory bodies in peacetime and the composition of a war staff in wartime. After consultation with the prime minister, the president appoints a minister of national defense, and after consultation with the minister of national defense, he appoints the chief of the General Staff. In turn, the minister is to consult with the president on appointment of commanders of military districts and the individual services.

The Sejm is responsible for assigning appropriate levels of annual funding and for passing laws regulating defense. The Sejm's Commission on National Defense was revamped and empowered to call a defense official to testify under oath on general questions of national defense policy. The wartime national defense system gives the president and the Council of Ministers supreme decision-making power; in wartime the Sejm is to appoint the chief commander of the Polish Army, who would have strategic command of all armed forces for the duration of wartime and who would be directly responsible to the president. If the Sejm were not in session when war began, the president would appoint the commander. The Council of Ministers has specific wartime responsibility for organizing supply and other support services from the civilian sector to the armed forces, and for protecting the civilian population from the effects of war. District governors have decision-making power for all administrative and economic units within their jurisdiction.

The minister of national defense is responsible for shaping and implementing national defense policy. The minister administers the development, education, and training of the armed forces; resolves issues of international cooperation; and oversees defense tasks assigned to outside agencies. The civilian component of the Ministry of National Defense includes vice ministers for social relations and education, defense policy, and armament. The Viceministry for Social Relations and Education includes veterans' affairs, public information, physical education, and departments of education and social policy. The Viceministry for Defense Policy includes strategic planning, foreign relations, legal affairs, mobilization policy, and the National Defense Academy (Akademia Obrony Narodowej—AON). And the Viceministry for Armament includes procurement, research and development, military technical inspection, and military and transportation infrastructure. The minister of national defense also is supported by offices or departments for intelligence (the so-called Department Two), control and supervision, personnel, and finances, as well as the office of the chief military prosecutor.

Military Command Structure

In peacetime the direct commander of the armed forces is the chief of the General Staff, who also carries the title general inspector of the armed forces. The General Staff is responsible for all phases of command, including training, strategic and organizational planning, mobilization, and logistics—activities previously divided among several departments in the Ministry of National Defense. The chief of the General Staff has three deputies: the chief of the training inspectorate, the chief of armed forces strategic planning and organization, and the chief inspector of logistics. Those officers in turn head the three main support commands of the military branch. The chief commands directly the four military districts, together with unified air and air defense, navy, and higher military education commands. Directorates for personnel, medicine, education, finances, and military police are commanded by the General Staff as a whole.

Throughout the 1980s, Poland's armed forces were administered through three military districts. In 1991, in keeping with the eastward shift of threat perception, plans were made to split the Warsaw Military District, which had covered all of eastern Poland, to form a fourth military district centered in Kraków. Although this step nominally gave Poland the strength of two districts facing eastward, the actual formation of the Kraków Military District was delayed in 1992 because funding was unavailable to make the necessary shifts of personnel and equipment.

The Military Prosecutor

Although the chief military prosecutor remains structurally subordinate to the Ministry of National Defense, since 1990 the scope of the military prosecutor's activities has been defined by the Ministry of Justice. This change adds another dimension of civilian control over the military. In the communist era, the military prosecutor's office acted as a specialized military command staffed by political officers, charged with maintaining party control in the armed forces, and given authority to interfere in civilian life to enforce "respect for the law."

The reform and integration of the military prosecutor's office into the general justice system was a high priority of the first Solidarity-led government in 1989. As part of the general overhaul of the justice system embodied in the 1990 Law on the Prosecution Office, the chief military prosecutor became a deputy of the minister of justice (who also served as prosecutor general), appointed by the prime minister in consultation with the ministers of justice and national defense. In his role as prosecutor general, the minister of justice makes all top military justice appointments in consultation with the minister of national defense; the minister of justice is also consulted on all special assignments given military prosecutors. The Office of the Chief Military Prosecutor also is assigned oversight of decisions by military bodies that might controvert civilian law.

Lines of Authority

Many proposals for restructuring the armed forces commands suffered the same fate as those for reforming military doctrine. In 1992 no clear apportionment of military and civilian policy-making powers existed in practice, and many civilian and military offices and directorates performed redundant functions. For example, the military Directorate of Logistics Planning and the civilian Department of Procurement performed similar tasks. The relative authority of officials at comparable levels of the two organizations (such as military chiefs of staff and viceministers of defense) also remained undefined.

The locus of ultimate military command remains a hot issue; Jan Parys, minister of national defense in the Olszewski government (and the first civilian to hold that position), was dismissed by President Wałęsa because Parys complained that his ministry was a powerless bureaucracy under Wałęsa's complete control. In mid-1992 Wałęsa ceded nominal approval of high military appointments to Janusz Onyszkiewicz, minister of national defense in the newly formed government of Hanna Suchocka. Although Wałęsa's move was presented as a concession to the stature of Onyszkiewicz, many observers believed that peacetime command of the Polish Army would remain an issue of contention between the presidency and the Council of Ministers.

Establishing civilian control over the Ministry of National Defense was a necessary move toward Western-style democratic rule. However, in the early 1990s high civilian officials often were named because of political influence rather than expertise, especially in the newly redesigned Department of Education (see Military Training and Education, this ch.). In fact, few civilians brought any military policy experience with them into Poland's postcommunist governments. This was mainly because Solidarity had avoided involvement with military and internal security policy in the contentious 1980s, fearing that opposition on those fronts might be a pretext for harsher government repression. Even after the fall of Jaruzelski, the first Solidarity government replaced communist officials in the defense and internal affairs establishments very cautiously to avoid antagonizing the PZPR in its last two government strongholds. Once the PZPR collapsed in 1990, however, the pace of reform increased.

National Security Agencies

In January 1991, Wałęsa began forming a National Security Council (Rada Bezpieczeństwa Narodowego—RBN) that would take the place of the KOK as the chief security policy advisory body to the executive branch. The KOK had been established by Gomułka for administration of wartime efforts (it also implemented communist party decisions during the martial law period). The RBN would have the broader task of determining appropriate defense measures against military, economic, and ecological threats to national security. It would be directed by the Bureau of National Security (BBN) and headed by a representative of Wałęsa. It would include experts in military, legal, foreign affairs, and domestic security matters. Because of this broad mission and RBN's direct subordination to the president, Wałęsa's plan immediately ran afoul of the Sejm, which refused to pass legislation making the RBN an official government body. The RBN then existed in 1991 and 1992 as an unofficial adjunct to the president's office, but the Sejm had no legal obligation to follow the RBN's policy recommendations.

By mid-1992 the RBN was taking an active and controversial role in defense planning, largely because the responsibility for national security planning had not been firmly assigned to any agency. Wałęsa's enemies attacked the RBN because the agency's bimonthly meetings allowed interested parties to attend unofficially and, under that stipulation, some of Wałęsa's cronies seemed to have access to classified information. Jan Parys, an advocate of higher force strength as a prerequisite for national security, engaged in polemics with RBN officials over budget cuts and restructuring during 1992 when he was minister of national defense.

In the meantime, the KOK had continued to exist as the official maker of national defense policy. Control of national security was a key issue of Olszewski's term as prime minister; after Olszewski's ouster, the atmosphere of defense policy making calmed, and the KOK recovered some of its stature. However, it was the BBN that issued a new defense doctrine, including potential threats and recommended responses, in July 1992. The doctrine, produced by a task force representing the General Staff and the ministries of national defense, foreign affairs, and internal affairs, became official when ratified by the KOK in the fall of 1992. The Little Constitution, ratified in October 1992, officially renamed the KOK as the RBN and prescribed changes in the structure and control of the existing agency.

Armed Services

In 1992 the Polish Army consisted of the ground forces, the navy, and the air force and air defense forces. The air force and air defense forces formally merged in 1991 when full command of the air force reverted to Poland from the Warsaw Pact and the strategic requirement for air combat outside Polish territory ended. The size of the Polish Army began to decrease dramatically in 1988, but changes in force structure were more gradual in the early 1990s. Between 1988 and 1992, the total number of armed forces personnel dropped from 897,000 (406,000 active, 491,000 reserves) to 731,500 (296,500 active, 435,000 reserves). Plans called for further reduction in the mid-1990s to a total active force of slightly over 200,000.

The armed forces model proposed in 1991 for the next ten years called for increased mobility of forces, principally provided by helicopters; improved equipment quality, especially in command, air defense, and radio-electronic systems; completion of force redeployment with operational and strategic supply support in place; increased staff professionalism; and a stronger position in the world market for selected military products such as helicopters, radio-electronic equipment, and tanks (see Arms Procurement, this ch.). The short-term model called for air traffic control and air defense system cooperation with partners in the Visegrád Triangle; reactivation of several mechanized divisions to balance reduction of the combat readiness of the two western military districts; and complete activation of the Kraków Military District, all within the next two to three years.

In 1989 some sixty-eight military units were disbanded, and another 147 units were reorganized. According to reports, this meant the retirement of 400 tanks, 700 artillery pieces, 600 armored personnel carriers, and eighty aircraft, as well as a cut of 30,000 active-duty personnel. The 1990 schedule called for elimination of fifty-seven more units and reorganization of seventy units, retiring 450 tanks, 200 artillery pieces, and 100 armored personnel carriers.

After completion of the restructuring program, planners envisioned ground forces of nine streamlined divisions, one airborne brigade, and one coastal defense brigade. The air and air defense forces would include one fighter division, two fighter-bomber divisions, an air reconnaissance regiment, two combat helicopter regiments, and one transport helicopter regiment. Five training regiments would serve the remaining active forces. The structure of the navy would remain essentially unchanged, featuring three flotillas and one coastal defense brigade.

Ground Forces

The ground forces underwent the most dramatic change in the Polish Army in the postcommunist era. They are administered in four military districts (the fourth of which, the Kraków Military District, was being established in 1992). The districts defend the northeast, southeast, northwest, and southwest quadrants of the country, respectively. Once forces were redeployed to balance defenses of the eastern and western borders, Poland would have a truly omnidirectional ground defense in which two districts would engage the aggressor and the other two would serve as reserves, depending on the direction of the attack. In 1992 the Pomeranian Military District (formerly the Bydgoszcz Military District) in the northwest included three mechanized divisions (formerly designated as motorized rifle divisions), one coastal defense unit, one artillery unit, one Scud missile installation, one engineer brigade, and one SA–6 missile installation. Between 1989 and 1992, a fourth mechanized division in the district had been converted into a supply base, and a tank division had been disbanded.

In the Silesian Military District (formerly the Wrocław Military District), two tank divisions were converted to mechanized divisions between 1990 and 1992, and one mechanized division was converted to a supply base in 1990. In 1992 those changes left the district with four mechanized divisions, two artillery units, one Scud missile installation, two engineer brigades, two SA–4 missile brigades, two antitank brigades, and one SA–6 missile regiment. Between 1990 and 1992, the Warsaw Military District, which covered all of eastern Poland pending organization of the Kraków Military District, went from one mechanized division to two

Chemical-biological-radiation warfare training
Courtesy Polish Information Agency, Warsaw

mechanized divisions, plus one engineer brigade, three ceremonial guard units, one artillery battery, and one SA–6 missile regiment. Once completed, the Kraków district was to have two mechanized divisions, one air assault unit, and one mountain infantry brigade. One mobile mechanized division was held in reserve in 1992.

In addition, Poland contributes small components to UN peacekeeping forces in several countries. In 1992 Polish forces abroad included 176 soldiers in Cambodia, one battalion (899 troops) in Croatia, seven soldiers in Kuwait, eighty-four soldiers in Lebanon, 159 logistical support personnel in Syria, and two observers in Western Sahara. Poland also contributed staff to the Neutral Nations Supervisory Commission for Korea (NNSC Korea).

Restructuring of the ground forces centers on eventual creation of a single type of multipurpose division emphasizing mobility and featuring limited offensive capability. Four active tank-heavy divisions, suitable for the Warsaw Pact era but not for Poland's new defensive doctrine, would be retired or redistributed (see Military Doctrine, this ch.). Equipment from two divisions would go into storage while equipment from the other two divisions would go for replacement in divisions remaining active. Two additional divisions were scheduled for reductions in personnel.

261

By 1992 the ground forces were reduced by nearly 40,000, to 194,200 troops, including 109,800 conscripts. Logistical units numbered 28,100; training personnel, 25,900; and centrally controlled staff, 2,900. The chief small arm of the Polish ground forces, the Kalashnikov rifle, is rated at the top of its class. The Radom Lucznik Works, a sewing-machine plant, is the domestic manufacturer. In 1992 main battle tanks totaled 2,850, of which 2,065 were T–55 and 785 were T–72. The Soviet–designed T–55 tanks, introduced in the 1950s, were considered extremely limited against much more sophisticated Western tanks. Although the Soviet-licensed and Polish-produced T–72 is comparable to top Western tanks in maneuverability and traction, its effective range is less than that of the best German and United States tanks, and night vision is inferior. Poland's last fifty-eight light amphibious PT–76 tanks were eliminated as obsolete in 1992.

Some 685 amphibious reconnaissance vehicles were in use in 1992. Two types, the Hungarian-designed FUG and the Soviet-designed BRDM–2, were included in that inventory; Poland began using the FUG in 1966 and the BRDM–2 around 1981. In 1991 Poland had 1,409 fully amphibious BMP–1 armored personnel carriers and sixty-two BMP–2 carriers. The BMPs were considered the only world-class armored vehicles in the Polish Army (although the BMP–1 had been in service since the early 1960s). Some 928 SKOT wheeled armored personnel carriers, a joint Polish and Czechoslovak design of 1959, remained in use in 1992. Many of these vehicles had been refitted as specialized command and communications vehicles, although the class was considered obsolete.

In 1992 the Polish ground forces had a total of 2,316 artillery pieces. Of that number, 883 were towed, including 715 M–1938 howitzers (122mm), 166 D–20 gun-howitzers (152mm), and two D–1 howitzers (152 mm). Another 617 artillery pieces were self-propelled, including 498 of the 2S1 model (122mm), 111 of the Dana (M–77, 152 mm), and eight of the 2S7 (203-mm) variety. The Soviet-built M–1938 howitzer had been upgraded and replaced several times in the Soviet arsenal since its introduction in 1938. The D–20 was designed shortly after World War II, and the D–1 was first used in 1943. The Dana (M–77) was the most modern self-propelled gun in use in 1992.

The artillery arsenal in 1992 also included 262 multiple rocket launchers, of which 232 were BM–21 and thirty RM–70 (both models 122mm). The BM–21 had been in Warsaw Pact arsenals since at least 1964; the RM–70 was added in the late 1980s to replace the older BM–14. Some 554 Soviet-designed 120mm mortars were also in service in 1992. In the surface-to-surface missile category,

Poland had forty FROG and twenty-five Scud B launchers. Four types of antitank guided weapons were in use in 1992. There were 271 AT-3s, 115 AT-4 Spigots, eighteen AT-5 Spandrels, and seven AT-6 Spirals. In the 85mm antitank gun class, Poland had 722 D-44 guns, which were of World War II vintage.

In 1992 Poland had 945 antiaircraft guns in the 23mm and 57mm classes. The former were ZU-23-2 and ZSU-23-4 SP, the latter S-60, which were introduced in 1950. Some 260 surface-to-air missile launchers were of the SA-6, SA-7, SA-8, SA-9, and SA-13 types.

Navy

During both the communist and postcommunist eras, the Polish navy received less emphasis and funding than other combat branches. Because the Polish navy had usually purchased the simplest and cheapest equipment offered by the Soviet Union, all other navies on the Baltic Sea were considered superior to Poland's. The assigned role of the Polish navy in the Warsaw Pact was to provide amphibious landing and mine warfare capability in the Baltic Sea; postcommunist restructuring deemphasized amphibious operations in favor of the navy's fast attack and patrol craft components. In 1992 the only short-term change envisioned for the navy, however, was retirement of antiquated equipment, much of which would not be replaced. To enhance coastal security, in 1989 military planners proposed Polish participation in a regional Baltic defense fleet.

Naval personnel in 1992 totaled 19,300 (including naval aviation forces), of which 10,600 were conscripts. Total naval personnel had dropped from 22,000 since 1981 (see table 21, Appendix). Another 1,800 individuals served in the coast guard, which operated forty small coastal craft; in wartime that component would be integrated into naval operations. Naval bases were located at Gdynia, Hel (just west of Gdynia), and Świnoujście, with a coast guard and border station at Kołobrzeg.

The origin and sophistication of Polish naval craft varies widely. Of the three Polish submarines existing in 1992, all built in the Soviet Union, the one Orzeł (corresponding to the Soviet Kilo model) vessel is the most advanced; two Wilk-class (Soviet Foxtrot) submarines are older and noisier. All three vessels feature 533mm torpedo tubes. Because they were designed for ocean combat, the three submarines maneuver clumsily in the Baltic Sea in comparison with the smaller submarines of the other Baltic nations. One Polish submarine was retired between 1989 and 1992.

In 1992 Poland had two principal surface combatants. The destroyer *Warszawa,* in the Soviet Kotlin class, was designed in the 1950s and transferred to Poland from the Soviet navy in 1970. The *Warszawa* displaces 2,850 tons (3,600 with a full load), is 127.5 meters long, has a top speed of thirty-six knots, and carries the following armaments: two twin SA–N–1 Goa surface-to-air missile launchers with twenty missiles each; four SS–N–2C Styx surface-to-surface missile launchers; two antisubmarine rocket launchers; five 533mm torpedo tubes, twin 130mm guns; four 45mm guns; and eight 30mm guns. The frigate *Kaszub* features two antisubmarine rocket launchers, four 533mm torpedo tubes, and a 76mm gun. The *Kaszub,* manufactured in cooperation with East Germany, was completed by the Poles after being left incomplete when German reunification occurred.

The twenty patrol and coastal combatants active in 1992 included missile corvettes, missile craft, and patrol boats. Four Górnik-type (Soviet Tarantul I) corvettes feature two twin SS–N–2C Styx surface-to-surface missile launchers. Designed in the Soviet Union in the late 1970s, the corvettes are among the most modern elements of the Polish navy. Displacement is 580 tons with a full load; length is fifty-six meters, maximum speed thirty-six knots. Eight Soviet Osa-1 fast patrol craft have four SS–N–2A surface-to-surface missile launchers. Full-load displacement is 210 tons; length is thirty-nine meters, maximum speed thirty-five knots. The Osa class, developed by the Soviet Union in the early 1960s, was considered outmoded by 1990. Poland's eight Obluze large inshore patrol craft were built domestically at the Oksywie Shipyard in Gdynia using a German design of the early 1960s.

The Polish navy has no specifically designed minelaying ships, but its Lublin-type landing ships, its submarines, and its Krogulec-type minesweepers can perform this function. Minesweeping ships total twenty-four, in three classes. The eight Krogulec coastal minesweepers were built in the 1960s at the Gdynia Shipyard; some vessels in this class had already been taken out of service by 1991. Noteć inshore minesweepers, a newer design featuring fiberglass hulls, were still being built in Poland in 1992; fourteen were operational that year. Two Leniwka inshore minesweepers complete Poland's mine countermeasure capability.

Six amphibious landing craft were in service in 1992. All had been built in Poland; the Północny was a Soviet design. Five Lublin-type craft have a capacity of 130 troops and eight tanks, and the single Północny craft could transport 180 troops and six tanks. The Lublins, introduced in 1989, were the last major upgrade of the Polish amphibious capability under the Warsaw Pact. The Północny

ZU-23-2 antiaircraft gun and crew on maneuvers
Courtesy Polish Information Agency, Warsaw

was used as a command ship in 1992. Three Deba-type utility landing craft are used, but not for amphibious operations. Ten craft serve in support of naval operations. These include two intelligence collection vessels, four support tankers, two survey ships, and two training ships.

The one naval aviation division has received special attention because its role in coastal reconnaissance, patrol, and search-and-rescue was considered an important element of the new national defense doctrine. In 1992 this division included 2,300 personnel, thirty-eight MiG-21 fighters, and four armed helicopters. Although the MiG-21 was considered inappropriate for action over the sea, in 1992 experts had little hope for modernization of the naval air fighter capability. The division's one search-and-rescue liaison squadron has three W-3 Sokol, three Mi-8, and nine Mi-2 helicopters, two AN-2 single-engine and two AN-28 two-engine transport planes, and four TS-11 jet trainers. In 1991 Poland ordered three W-3RM Anakonda helicopters, improved versions of the Soviet Sokol; one was delivered in 1992. All Poland's MiG-15 reconnaissance aircraft were withdrawn as obsolete in 1992; no replacement aircraft were available at that time. In 1992 the special naval air regiment included twelve Polish-built TS-11s and ten AN-2s; several of the former were revised TS-11Rs with upgraded radar and navigation systems. Another naval air regiment, designated for antisubmarine warfare and search-and-rescue, had eight Mi-2, one Mi-8, and fifteen Mi-14 helicopters. The coastal defense forces included 4,200 personnel manning six artillery batteries with M–1937 guns (152mm) and three surface-to-surface missile batteries with SS–C–2B launchers.

Air and Air Defense Forces

In 1992 a high military priority was establishing an air defense system based on existing assets of the air and air defense forces. Within that context, early warning and force integration were the most immediate problems. Resistance to enemy fire and maneuverability were rated as poor by Polish military experts. Restructuring plans called for one air defense corps in each of the four military districts, each corps having air intercept and rocket forces. Combined manpower was projected at 50,000.

In 1992 some 83,000 personnel, including 47,000 conscripts, served in the Polish air and air defense forces. Active combat aircraft numbered 423, with an additional eighty-six in storage awaiting sale, and thirty-one attack helicopters. The forces were divided into two air divisions. The four regiments of ground-attack fighters totaled twenty Su-20 and 104 Su-22 fighters supplied by the Soviet Union in the 1970s. For reconnaissance, the ground-attack regiments had twenty-four MiG-17 and eight Su-20 airplanes. Air combat forces were divided into eight regiments equipped with 221 MiG-21/U fighters, whose equivalents were long ago withdrawn from service in the West; thirty-seven more advanced variable wing-geometry MiG-23MF fighters; and nine MiG-29 fighters top-of-the-line Soviet aircraft whose delivery was curtailed in late 1990. Air combat forces utilized twenty-four MiG-21RU reconnaissance aircraft.

In 1992 the air force had two transport regiments equipped with ten AN–2 single–engine transports, one AN–12 four-turboprop general transport, eleven AN–26 two-turboprop short-haul transports, ten Yak-40 short-haul, three-turbofan jet transports, one Tu-154 long-range three-turbofan jet transport, three Il-14 piston-engine light transports, four Mi-8 helicopters, and one Bell 412 helicopter.

Polish helicopter attack forces were organized in three regiments in 1992. Altogether the regiments had thirty Mi-24, 130 Mi-2, and twenty-one Mi-8 assault helicopters. Of that component, the Mi-2 and Mi-8 were designed in the 1960s and the Mi-24 in the early 1970s. Eighteen Su-22 fighters were used for training. The Polish armed forces stored a large number of redundant or outmoded fighter airplanes and began selling them to Western collectors in the early 1990s. In storage in 1992 were forty MiG-21s and variants of that model, twenty-four MiG-17s, and twenty-two MiG-15 U7s.

Territorial Defense Forces

The National Territorial Defense Forces (OTK) were founded in 1965 to help defend Polish territory when the Polish People's Army was engaged under Warsaw Pact obligations outside the country. Although their primary mission was defending the homeland, the OTK also had the Warsaw Pact mission of transporting Soviet forces and supplies across Poland in wartime. Formed mainly from units shifted from the Ministry of Internal Affairs, the OTK went under a new Inspectorate for National Territorial Defense in the Ministry of National Defense. The OTK included the Internal Defense Forces (Wojska Obrony Wewnętrznej— WOW, the largest unit) and several smaller territorial defense units. Immediately after World War II, the WOW had suppressed the Home Army, which had been loyal to the London government-in-exile; the WOW had also played a large part in suppressing the Poznań workers in 1956 (see The Communist Era, this ch.).

The WOW, which totaled 65,000 troops in 1982, were equipped as mechanized infantry units, including tanks. The component units, which were organized at district level, had the missions of engaging hostile troops on Polish territory and eliminating local underground elements. The units were to receive the same individual training as regular ground forces, although they did not participate in large-scale coordinated exercises.

By 1990 the OTK was not a credible military force. The organization included many nonmilitary patriotic and social groups, such as the boy scouts, and many military retirees found soft assignments in OTK units. Although the force had a military commander, it was not under direct control of the Ministry of National Defense. By 1991 budget cuts were reducing personnel significantly, and plans called for transforming many OTK units into civil defense formations that would support production and service in the civilian economy. The OTK units remaining armed and attached to districts as regional defense forces would count as part of the ground forces' planned mid-1990s allotment of about 150,000 troops. They would function as cadre units reinforcing operational ground forces within their territorial boundaries.

Military Manpower

In 1992 several factors affected the supply and demand of

manpower for the Polish Army. Given reduced force levels, fewer individuals were needed; however, reduced terms of active duty created faster turnover. At the same time, reliance on sophisticated electronics, especially in the air force, made recruitment, training, and retention of highly qualified individuals more important. And the availability of qualified personnel was influenced by society's general attitude toward the military and by availability of employment in the civilian economy.

The Military and Society

The declaration of martial law in 1981 and the repression in the years that followed greatly harmed the image of the military in Polish society and within the military itself. Until that time, the Polish People's Army had consciously maintained an apolitical posture that was bolstered by its abstention from action against mass demonstrations in Polish cities in 1956 and 1970. At the same time, however, PZPR membership was strongly encouraged among military personnel and was practically a prerequisite for advancement to the senior officer grades. Party membership among military officers increased from about 50 percent in the mid-1950s to about 85 percent by 1980. Almost all senior officers were party members.

In the year 1981, however, the military became identified fully with the communist state for the first time when General Wojciech Jaruzelski became party leader and prime minister. Throughout the 1980s, the army was viewed with distrust and antagonism. With the fall of the Jaruzelski government in early 1989, the Polish military began an active campaign to separate itself from all political parties, to work with the former opposition leaders, and to "humanize" its image. In early 1990, Jaruzelski's announcement of his resignation from the PZPR precipitated the mass return of party cards by Polish officers, and at the last PZPR congress in 1990 the military delegation sat apart. Such symbolic acts were stimulated by the political reality that the military's symbiotic relationship with the PZPR had ended and that the military had no relationship whatever with Solidarity, the now-dominant political force that had enormous public support. And public support acquired a direct strategic value for planners in the post-Warsaw Pact world. In 1992 Professor Kazimierz Nóżko of the National Defense Academy stated that the new Polish defense system must be based on "the stable foundation of psychological and patriotic preparation of all society and the armed forces to repel aggression determinedly."

In 1990 officials of the ministries of national defense and internal affairs approached officials of the Roman Catholic Church with proposals to upgrade and increase chaplain positions in the military and security forces. In 1991 the Field Ordinariate was reestablished as the church's arm to minister to the armed services. A field bishop was appointed for the first time since World War II. Between 1989 and mid-1992, the number of military chaplains had risen from twenty-nine to sixty-two.

Participation of military personnel in religious services, long discouraged under the communist regimes, increased dramatically in 1990 and became an important element of the campaign by the Ministry of National Defense to refurbish the military's image. To reinforce the patriotic image of the armed forces, the military establishment revived historical traditions such as appointing officers by a sword stroke and playing the fife and drum at the changing of the guard at the Tomb of the Unknown Soldier.

All political organizations were banned from the military in 1989, and military personnel were forbidden from participating in political parties or trade unions during their term of active duty. Depolitization of the Polish military proceeded rapidly in the early 1990s, and outward manifestations of loyalty to the military in society increased accordingly. One survey showed that 80 percent of Poles had a positive view of the military as early as 1991, and a 1992 survey showed that the military had surpassed the Roman Catholic Church as the most trusted institution in Poland. Some experts believed that such results were premature and unrealistic, however, contending that the memory of the military's role in martial law would linger in Polish society, and that attitudes among career military personnel remaining from the Warsaw Pact era would lag behind organizational reform.

In 1990 the government called in army transport equipment and personnel during a rail workers' strike in Pomerania to prevent a collapse of the national transport system. Comparisons were made between that military intervention and the role of the military in suppressing the demonstrations of 1981. However, Deputy Minister of National Defense Onyszkiewicz, whose role in Solidarity gave him public credibility, cited this application of the military as an example of a justifiable, nonpolitical use of military assets to serve society in a national emergency, without the use of force toward strikers—in contrast to the repressive activities of the martial law period. In mid-1992 Wałęsa's power struggle with the Ministry of National Defense again aroused public fears that the military would be used to reach political goals. Again Onyszkiewicz, now acting minister of national defense, reassured Poles that competing political factions would use instruments of civilian government to resolve their differences.

A controversial issue after 1989 was the status of communist civilian officials and military officers who had been responsible for quashing civilian uprisings and labor strikes. Many individuals who had served during that era remained in command positions in 1992. According to a 1991 survey by the antiestablishment reformist Viritim officers' group, 40 percent of officers had "conservative" views, 45 percent were "indifferent" to reform, and only 5 percent were willing to speak openly for institutional reform. A second activist group, the illegal Association of Junior Officers for Promoting Change in the Army, sought purges of officers whose military policies did not conform to their philosophy. Their attempt to undermine the authority of the Ministry of National Defense became part of the ongoing public dispute between Wałęsa and the ministry over control of military policy making (see Evolution and Restructuring, this ch.).

The Polish public was not reluctant to express opinions on the military. Because of public pressure, Jaruzelski himself was called to testify about the killing of striking coal miners in 1981. Czesław Kiszczak, who had been minister of internal affairs in 1981, was scheduled for indictment in the fall of 1992 for issuing orders to shoot strikers. Some Poles demanded the large-scale trial of former communist authorities, but by mid-1992 none had gone to jail. Especially controversial was the case of Colonel Ryszard Kukliński, a Jaruzelski aide who defected in 1981 and revealed Warsaw Pact military secrets to the United States. Some Poles demanded that Kukliński be pardoned; others, including many military personnel, felt that because he had betrayed Poland as well as the Jaruzelski regime, Kukliński should remain in exile or return to serve the sentence given him in absentia.

Recruitment and Service Obligations

In 1949 Polish law stipulated universal, obligatory military service for males. The Military Service Law of 1967 and its amendments set the age of mandatory service at nineteen and the age for volunteering for service at seventeen. Failure to register and failure to report after being drafted were punishable by fine or imprisonment. The basic term of service was two years, except in highly technical positions, where the term was three years. The Council of Ministers could add one year to the term in case of national need. Soldiers entered the reserves after completing active duty. For enlisted personnel, reserve status continues until age fifty. For noncommissioned officers (NCOs) and officers, reserve status continues until age sixty. With permission of the recruitment command, a conscript could perform alternative service in a civilian social service organization, a civil defense unit, or the civilian police force. The term of service, housing, and discipline of such individuals are similar to those for active-duty personnel. The rank and grade structure of the Polish army is similar to that of other armed forces organizations. There are some variations, however, in the number and titles of authorized enlisted, warrant officer and officer grades (see fig 16; fig. 17; fig. 18).

In 1960 mandatory military training programs were instituted in civilian colleges; upon completion, a student was eligible to enter reserve status as an NCO or to secure a reserve commission in a short officer training program. In 1980 social resentment of this privilege and the inadequacy of such a training program led to a nominally mandatory one-year term of active duty upon completion of university studies. In practice, however, the training and assignments of graduating college students usually were not arduous, and many evaded the obligation entirely.

The first postcommunist regime immediately shortened the terms of active duty. Terms in the ground forces dropped from twenty-four months to eighteen months, and terms in the navy and air forces dropped from thirty-six months to twenty-four months. Planners projected an eventual twelve-month term for ground forces inductees. An alternative service option was continued from the policy established by the Jaruzelski regime in 1988.

In the early 1990s, an average of 250,000 individuals were examined yearly by recruiting commissions; fewer than half entered active duty. Inductions were scheduled for spring and fall of each year, but the fall 1991 and spring 1992 calls were either limited or eliminated entirely. Experts speculated that the change in schedule was caused by a combination of low budgeting and the lack of eligible individuals; at the 1992 induction rate, Poland's active-duty forces would fall below the limitations of the 1990 Conventional Forces in Europe (CFE) Treaty (see Glossary) that cut the forces of all NATO and Warsaw Pact nations (see table 22, Appendix). In mid-1992, some 220,000 billets were listed as filled, compared with the force level of 300,000 prescribed for that stage of force reduction. Of the 220,000 billets, about 100,000 were career military and more than half were in rear-echelon rather than combat units.

In the early 1990s, cities provided the majority of recruits, and students normally received deferments. In 1991 the armed forces showed about a 20 percent shortage of officers, warrant officers, and junior officers, although interest in attending military schools had increased after military reform began. In 1992 policy makers discussed offering qualified individuals five-year contracts as a

271

POLISH RANK	SZEREGOWIEC	STARSZY SZEREGOWIEC		KAPRAL	STARSZY KAPRAL	PLUTONOWY	SIERŻANT	STARSZY SIERŻANT		SIERŻANT SZTABOWY	STARSZY SIERŻANT SZTABOWY
ARMY											
U.S. RANK TITLE	BASIC PRIVATE	PRIVATE	PRIVATE 1ST CLASS	CORPORAL/ SPECIALIST	SERGEANT	STAFF SERGEANT	SERGEANT 1ST CLASS	MASTER SERGEANT	FIRST SERGEANT	SERGEANT MAJOR	COMMAND SERGEANT MAJOR
POLISH RANK	SZEREGOWIEC	STARSZY SZEREGOWIEC		KAPRAL	STARSZY KAPRAL	PLUTONOWY	SIERŻANT	STARSZY SIERŻANT		SIERŻANT SZTABOWY	STARSZY SIERŻANT SZTABOWY
AIR FORCE											
U.S. RANK TITLE	AIRMAN BASIC	AIRMAN	AIRMAN 1ST CLASS	SENIOR AIRMAN SERGEANT	STAFF SERGEANT	TECHNICAL SERGEANT	MASTER SERGEANT	SENIOR MASTER SERGEANT		CHIEF MASTER SERGEANT	
POLISH RANK	MARYNARZ	STARSZY MARYNARZ		MAT	STARSZY MAT	BOSANMAT	BOSMAN	STARSZY BOSMAN		BOSMAN SZTABOWY	STARSZY BOSMAN SZTABOWY
NAVY	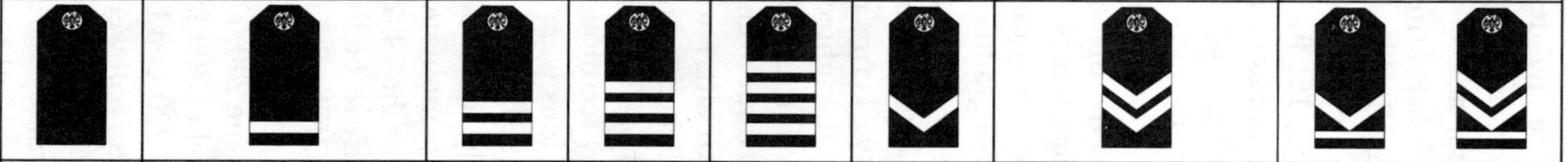										
U.S. RANK TITLE	SEAMAN RECRUIT	SEAMAN APPRENTICE	SEAMAN	PETTY OFFICER 3D CLASS	PETTY OFFICER 2D CLASS	PETTY OFFICER 1ST CLASS	CHIEF PETTY OFFICER	SENIOR CHIEF PETTY OFFICER		MASTER CHIEF PETTY OFFICER	

Figure 16. Enlisted Ranks and Insignia, 1992

POLISH RANK	PODPORUCZNIK	PORUCZNIK	KAPITAN	MAJOR	PODPUŁKOWNIK	PUŁKOWNIK	GENERAL BRYGADY	GENERAL DYWIZJI	GENERAL BRONI	GENERAL ARMII	MARSZAŁEK POLSKI
ARMY											
U.S. RANK TITLE	2D LIEUTENANT	1ST LIEUTENANT	CAPTAIN	MAJOR	LIEUTENANT COLONEL	COLONEL	BRIGADIER GENERAL	MAJOR GENERAL	LIEUTENANT GENERAL	GENERAL	
POLISH RANK	PODPORUCZNIK	PORUCZNIK	KAPITAN	MAJOR	PODPUŁKOWNIK	PUŁKOWNIK	GENERAL BRYGADY	GENERAL DYWIZJI	GENERAL BRONI		
AIR FORCE										NO RANK	
U.S. RANK TITLE	2D LIEUTENANT	1ST LIEUTENANT	CAPTAIN	MAJOR	LIEUTENANT COLONEL	COLONEL	BRIGADIER GENERAL	MAJOR GENERAL	LIEUTENANT GENERAL	GENERAL	
POLISH RANK	PODPORUCZNIK MARYNARSKI	PORUCZNIK MARYNARSKI	KAPITAN MARYNARSKI	KOMANDOR PODPORUCZNIK	KOMANDOR PORUCZNIK	KOMANDOR	KONTRADMIRAL	WICEADMIRAL	ADMIRAL		
NAVY										NO RANK	
U.S. RANK TITLE	ENSIGN	LIEUTENANT JUNIOR GRADE	LIEUTENANT	LIEUTENANT COMMANDER	COMMANDER	CAPTAIN	REAR ADMIRAL LOWER HALF	REAR ADMIRAL UPPER HALF	VICE ADMIRAL	ADMIRAL	

Figure 17. Officer Ranks and Insignia, 1992

means of augmenting skilled military specialties outside CFE limitations.

In 1990 the government enacted measures to improve military housing, living conditions of dependents, pay, and leave. By 1990 specialized personnel such as jet pilots had begun leaving the service in large numbers, partly because of personnel cutbacks but also because low pay, low prestige, and outdated equipment were not commensurate with the rigorous entrance and training requirements for their specialties. Because the military doctrine of the 1990s would rely heavily on sophisticated equipment and skilled personnel, improving service conditions for such individuals was an important planning goal in the early 1990s.

Military Training and Education

Under communist leadership, Poland's programs for military training and education received generous funding and formed a large network of institutions, all of which included political indoctrination as well as technical training. The doctrinal reorientation that began in 1987 and intensified in 1989 reduced the training load and made efficient use of training institutions an economic imperative. The new emphasis on public approval of the military brought civilian and military education programs closer together. And the political officers that had preserved party loyalty and taught communist doctrine in the Polish Army since 1944 were removed in favor of establishing a general education agency.

Conscript Training

Prior to 1990, individual and unit training followed the Soviet model because of Poland's regular participation in joint Warsaw Pact exercises with the Soviet Union and northern-tier allies Czechoslovakia and East Germany. Most conscripts served their entire term of active duty as privates or privates first class. Outstanding individuals were identified early for specialized schooling as NCO candidates. NCOs were required to commit to four years of additional service after completing their schooling. Thirteen warrant officer candidate schools operated in 1981, offering specialized technical programs of between one and three years that included more political indoctrination than did programs for NCOs.

The Main Political Administration (Główne Biuro Administracji, known in the West by its English-language acronym, MPA) was headed by a deputy in the Ministry of National Defense. But the MPA also exercised independent authority as a department of the PZPR Central Committee; ultimate responsibility was to the PZPR, and the head of the MPA was appointed by the PZPR Secretariat.

The MPA conducted political indoctrination in the armed forces and counseled the army in personnel policy making and appointments. Political officers in Polish People's Army units supervised party organizations and communist youth groups for conscripts. The most significant youth group was the Union of Military Youth, which sought to improve both the moral and ideological outlook of service personnel, at the same time reinforcing party control of society. In the 1980s, about half of Polish conscripts were members of the union.

In 1989 the first noncommunist government pressed hard to reform or replace the MPA. In late 1989, the organization was replaced by the Main Education Board (Główny Zarząd Wychowawczy—GZW), and party posts in the military were abolished. Party influence on military training continued, however, until late 1990, when the collapse of the PZPR and of the old state security system (together with strong pressure from Parliament), made clear to the military establishment that meaningful reform was necessary to garner crucial public support.

In the postcommunist years, conscript training has been limited by the budget. As of mid-1992, no division-scale exercises had been held since the Warsaw Pact era. Total exercise time for trainees was significantly reduced, and items such as projectile allotments were limited. Cruises by navy personnel and training flights for pilots, both very expensive phases of training, were curtailed; in 1992 Polish pilots averaged between forty and fifty flying hours annually, compared with an average of 200 hours for NATO pilots.

Officer Education

In the communist era, officer education began with the precepts of Marxism-Leninism and their importance in defending the socialist system. The MPA directed the officers' indoctrination in these precepts. By contrast, in training both officers and enlisted personnel the postcommunist military education system emphasized the individual's role in maintaining Poland's military heritage and traditions rather than in preserving a particular ideology. The Education Officers Corps was abolished, as was the post of deputy commanding officer in military units, which had been obligatory billets for political officers. In 1990, public skepticism toward the initial reshuffling of the military education program led to a second stage of reform. The GZW was then reconstituted as the Department of Education and given a broad educational mission. These moves were seen as a clean break with political indoctrination of the military and an opportunity to improve the professional level of military personnel.

POLISH RANK	MŁODSZY CHORAZY	CHORAZY	STARSZY CHORAZY	CHORAZY SZTABOWY	STARSZY CHORAZY SZTABOWY
ARMY					
U.S. RANK TITLE	WARRANT OFFICER (W-1)	CHIEF WARRANT OFFICER (W-2)	CHIEF WARRANT OFFICER (W-3)	CHIEF WARRANT OFFICER (W-4)	
POLISH RANK	MŁODSZY CHORAZY	CHORAZY	STARSZY CHORAZY	CHORAZY SZTABOWY	STARSZY CHORAZY SZTABOWY
AIR FORCE					
U.S. RANK TITLE	NO RANK	NO RANK	NO RANK	NO RANK	
POLISH RANK	MŁODSZY CHORAZY	CHORAZY	STARSZY CHORAZY	CHORAZY SZTABOWY	STARSZY CHORAZY SZTABOWY
NAVY					
U.S. RANK TITLE	NO RANK	CHIEF WARRANT OFFICER (W-2)	CHIEF WARRANT OFFICER (W-3)	CHIEF WARRANT OFFICER (W-4)	

Figure 18. Warrant Officer Ranks and Insignia, 1992

Higher officer candidate schools had been the major source of career officers in the Polish People's Army, although a few graduates of civilian schools switched to a military career after completing their active-duty obligation. Of the fourteen higher officer candidate schools in the 1980s, only the Technical Military Academy and the Medical Military Academy received sufficient qualified applicants. In the communist era, all schools offered programs for political officers as well. Graduation from a higher officer candidate school yielded a bachelors degree and a commission as a second lieutenant.

From 1949 to 1989, all instruction at Polish military schools was heavily politicized. At the higher officer schools and military graduate schools, mandatory courses included Marxist philosophy, political economy, and scientific socialism. The stated goal of such courses was "to instill the socialist outlook among soldiers."

Officer training reform in the early 1990s stressed defensive techniques and sought to blend military training with education to produce well-rounded officers who could be integrated more fully into Polish society. Low attendance and low budgets required closing some specialized schools, and several other specialized schools were merged. In some cases, joint programs were established with universities.

In another effort to depoliticize Polish military training, a single senior military school, the National Defense Academy (Akademia Obrony Narodowej—AON) was established in 1990. The AON merged the General Staff and military-political academies, which had been criticized as bastions of cronyism that provided nonfunctional instructor positions for senior officers. The AON's mission is to train commanders and senior staff officers as well as to prepare civilians for service in the upper echelons of the defense bureaucracy. Graduate programs have been established offering masters and doctoral degrees. The AON also develops policy recommendations for national defense, and its faculty often participates in intragovernmental working groups assembled to define future national security policy.

Reserves and Mobilization

In the communist era, reserve training programs were inadequate to maintain large numbers of personnel in service-ready condition. In fact, some reservists completed their twenty-year obligation without ever attending training. Regulations limited both total training time and total call-up time of reserve personnel to twenty-four months or less. In 1982 this system had produced

605,000 reservists whose training was labeled as adequate. In the early 1990s, reserve training remained quite spotty.

The new Polish defense system places special emphasis on the mobilization preparation of reserves because of drastic decreases in active-duty forces. In case of military threat or war, an estimated 5 to 6 percent of overall combat forces would come from reserve units. In this context, the training of reserve personnel, especially command, staff, and specialist positions, is much more important than it was under the communist system. According to 1992 policy, which did not vary greatly from communist-era doctrine on the subject, 400,000 to 500,000 reservists would be available for call-up. Reserve units are formed according to geographical location to achieve cohesiveness. In wartime their mission is to delay an enemy force in their area long enough for the regular army to engage. One difficulty with this system is the requirement that individual reservists maintain weapons at home specifically for emergency use, a practice at variance with Polish culture and criticized as introducing firearms into civilian society.

Defense and the National Economy

In the early 1990s, military planners recognized the crucial connection between the health of the national economy and the degree to which the Polish Army could be transformed into a lean and efficient defensive force. Given a stringent budget, key decisions were needed in arms procurement policy, particularly regarding foreign versus domestic manufacture and the degree of technological sophistication. The practicality and advisability of converting the Polish arms industry to civilian manufacture and budgetary allocations to defense were also major concerns.

Military Budget

The Polish military budget had begun to shrink somewhat by 1988, but major cuts occurred between 1989 and 1991. In 1991, for example, the Ministry of National Defense proposed to the Sejm a defense budget of 29 trillion zloty (for the value of the zloty—see Glossary); the Sejm approved a budget of 23 trillion zloty, but subsequent cuts lowered the total to 16 trillion zloty. Some 22.5 percent of the 1990 defense budget was allotted to purchase of arms and equipment, and 61.5 percent went to maintaining manpower levels. Military experts considered the former figure too low to even maintain Polish equipment in status quo condition, leaving no funds for modernization. At the same time, the manpower figure was inflated by the communist legacy of redundant bureaucracy filled with senior officers. The 1991 budget made a nominal allotment of 10 percent for procurement of new equipment. Although cuts in senior military staff were expected to remedy the chronic imbalance between personnel and equipment allocations, in the first part of 1992 some 80 percent of the military budget went to maintaining personnel.

The Sejm cut another 11 percent from the budget for 1992, causing planners again to reassess the structure and equipment of the armed forces. At that point, the Ministry of National Defense owed a debt of about US$70 million to Polish defense industries.

Arms Procurement

When communism fell, Poland's military equipment and arms supply changed as dramatically as its strategic position. In the Warsaw Pact era, the Soviet Union had been Poland's main supplier at prices far below world standards. Once the political advantage of offering such bargains disappeared, however, the Soviet/Russian arms industry ended preferential treatment. In the late 1980s, for example, the top-of-the-line MiG-29 fighter was offered to Soviet allies for US$2 million each; in 1991 the same aircraft was offered to the same customers at the approximate world market value of US$18 million. Given severe cuts in its military budget and the impending obsolescence of many of its existing armaments, Poland faces critical procurement choices that have generated heated debate in the military establishment in the early 1990s. Those choices are also conditioned by the technical requirements of Poland's new strategic defense doctrine of high mobility and flexibility—qualities lacking in many critical systems remaining from the Soviet supply line.

The debate centered on how much Poland should rely on supplies from its own arms industry (thrown into crisis by the cutbacks that began in the late 1980s), how much on purchases from Western suppliers, and how much on previous connections with Soviet/Russian suppliers. Production at home offered two significant advantages: technological continuity and lower cost. In 1990 some 64 percent of the equipment used by the Polish armed forces was domestically produced, and most Polish-produced armaments were compatible with existing Soviet-supplied products. (In 1991 the cost of an M–1–A1 Abrams tank from the United States was nearly ten times that of a Polish-made tank in the T–72 line.) Also a major planning factor were the arms reductions that would be required of former Warsaw Pact nations in nearly every category by the terms of the CFE Treaty.

According to statistics often cited in the arms-policy debates of the early 1990s, the ratio of equipment to personnel in the Polish

Army was significantly smaller than comparable ratios in former Warsaw Pact allies Bulgaria, the CSFR, East Germany, and Romania and much smaller than those of NATO countries. Planned personnel cuts in the Polish Army would improve the overall ratio, but significant technical modernization was needed to bring the percentage of state-of-the-art equipment to the desired 35 to 40 percent. In 1991 Chief of Staff General Zdzisław Stelmaszuk rated less than 25 percent of the Polish Army's equipment in this category, and over 40 percent of towed artillery and naval vessels were classified as obsolete. According to a General Staff analysis in 1991, about 500 trillion zloty of armaments purchases would be needed by the year 2000 to reach the desired level of modernity. This figure dwarfed the 1991 Ministry of National Defense budget allotment of 16 trillion zloty passed by Parliament.

In 1991 Stelmaszuk, who was also chairman of the Group for Restructuring the Polish Armed Forces, projected the following armament goals for the mid-1990s after restructuring and reductions to meet CFE requirements: 1,730 tanks; 2,150 armored vehicles, of which 1,700 would be infantry combat vehicles; 1,610 artillery systems over 100mm; 1,430 antitank systems; 3,175 antiaircraft systems (including 1,455 missile systems); 130 combat assault helicopters; and eighty naval vessels (including forty combat vessels).

In the early 1990s, the uncertainty of available annual funding complicated procurement. Although some specific long-range procurement goals had been determined by 1991, in 1992 civilian and military leaders had not yet reached a consensus about the best way to achieve those goals.

Arms Imports

Beginning in 1989, long-term defense contracts with the Soviet Union and East Germany were broken unexpectedly, resulting in shortages of crucial components and materials. From 1990 onwards, the Soviet Union simply refused to supply some spare parts and lubricants not available in Poland, while raising the price of others to world market levels. The withdrawal of Soviet forces removed nuclear warheads from Scud and other Warsaw Pact missile batteries, leaving the Poles to locate conventional warheads elsewhere to fit their disarmed missiles and launchers. Naval coproduction contracts with East Germany ended with German reunification in 1990, leaving Poland with empty hulls and ships lacking armaments.

Such situations caused planners to consider importing Western military equipment. This solution would move the Polish Army toward its long-range goal of compatibility with NATO doctrine and armaments. Three major obstacles confronted such a policy,

Sokol helicopter, manufactured at Swidnik Transport Factory
Courtesy Polish Information Agency, Warsaw

however. The introduction of Western technology would create a confused, hybrid system; sale of advanced technology by Western nations to a former Warsaw Pact member often was blocked by export restrictions of the Coordinating Committee for Multilateral Export Controls (CoCom—see Glossary); and the Polish defense budget simply lacked sufficient funds to buy advanced Western hardware.

Domestic Arms Production

Under the communist system, the Ministry of National Defense ran nineteen manufacturing and repair plants, but about eighty plants were designated as defense industry enterprises under branches of the Ministry of Industry. In the late 1980s, the largest military goods producers were the Stalowa Wola Steel Works, the Kasprzak Radio Works, the Krasnik Ball-Bearing Plant, the Wifama Textile Machinery Combine, the Stomil Tire Plant, the Polish Aviation Combine, the Pronit firm, the Northern and Wisła shipyards in Gdańsk, the Lucznik Works, the Starachowice Truck Factory, the Polish Optical Works, the Bumar-Łabędy Engineering Equipment Combine, and the Olkusz Enamel Plant. In most cases, over 85 percent of a plant's production went to nondefense customers; the shipyards, the Bumar-Łabędy combine, and the Stalowa Wola

Steel Works were among the few producers whose output went mostly to the military. In 1988 military goods producers employed about 260,000 people and accounted for about 3 percent of total output of enterprises under the Ministry of Industry. At the same time, over 6 percent of Poland's total exports were military products. Of military output, 49 percent went to the Polish military, 46 percent was exported, and 5 percent went to the ministries of justice and internal affairs. By 1992 military goods had dropped from 3 percent to 1 percent of total industrial output.

Polish military industries began planning for conversion to civilian production in 1987, when the Warsaw Pact was developing its new defensive posture. Some twenty of the eighty designated defense industry enterprises were considered for closure or conversion to civilian functions. Meanwhile, all defense industries made long-term plans for greatly reduced orders between 1991 and 1995. By 1990 military contracts had dropped by 30 to 80 percent, depending on the plant. Spending on weaponry had dropped by 84 percent. These reductions in demand led to unemployment and unused industrial capacity. Defense industries also lost the privileged position they had enjoyed in the communist economy. Gone in 1990 were supply priority, low-interest credit, state subsidies, and tax exemptions. Industry pessimism increased in 1990 and 1991 when military planners considered replacing Soviet- and Polish-made equipment with Western equipment.

Conversion of defense industry plants to civilian production faced serious obstacles. Deep cuts in the defense budget left little money for a centrally administered program or for the massive investment required to convert heavy industry. Because long-range military needs remained undefined in 1992, the degree of conversion would require guesswork. Finally, some plants simply could not be converted at any reasonable cost.

In 1992 the Ministry of Industry proposed a program to restructure the defense industry. The program would create three classes of linked holding companies, classified according to the degree of competition in which they engaged. One group, including producers of munitions and electronics, would be fully controlled by the State Treasury. The second group, including producers of aircraft, armored vehicles, and the Northern Shipyard at Gdańsk, would have the State Treasury as controlling shareholder. The third group, including private firms supplying specialized production, would operate as market-economy enterprises. This structure was designed to focus production on critical military items and efficiently convert remaining capacity to free-market production.

By 1992 budgetary uncertainty and the high cost of Western equipment caused planners to rely more on domestic production of high-technology equipment and on joint production projects between Polish and Western firms. Projects considered in 1992 included an improved T–72 tank, new armored combat vehicles, a new ground attack helicopter, and a light attack aircraft. Many new products were suggested to replace Soviet equipment. Among the new products developed by the Polish industry were the I–22 Iryda combat training jet, the first such airplane completely designed in Poland, and the PW light military vehicle. In its testing stage, the I–22 Iryda jet trainer was evaluated as a very well-made airplane lacking a first-class engine. In 1992 Polish manufacturers sought joint ventures with Western firms to supply appropriate Western components to upgrade the Iryda and the PW.

In the Warsaw Pact decades, Polish production of sophisticated guidance and communications equipment was generally discouraged. As a result, in 1990 Polish industry was unable to supply the armed forces with modern avionics, electronics, and guidance systems that would make up some of the ground lost by relying on Soviet technology. The greatest manufacturing capabilities were in airframe design, small weapons design, and ammunition manufacturing.

A top procurement priority was electronic friend-or-foe aircraft identification units to upgrade the primitive air defense system. In the late 1980s, the Soviet Union had refused to complete a contract to supply such equipment—a fortunate development in light of ensuing changes in Polish threat perception and the advantages design familiarity would have given Russian attack planes. In 1992 Polish planners were considering both domestic design of an identification system and coproduction with a Western firm.

The Bumar-Łabędy combine manufactured the T–72 tank by license with the Soviet Union, using Polish manufacturing technology. Until 1988 a seller of tanks to many countries of the world, Bumar-Łabędy suffered from reduced world and domestic demand, and by 1989 its plants were working at half capacity. Like many other defense-oriented heavy industries, Bumar-Łabędy found conversion to civilian production difficult. Meanwhile, the firm's financial condition deteriorated because of the high cost of maintaining a spare-parts inventory and serious payment lapses by the Ministry of National Defense.

Arms Exports

A possible solution to the critical condition of Poland's arms industry is increased exports. A 1992 study rated Poland twentieth in world arms exports in the period 1985–91, with an estimated total export value of more than US$1.6 billion. Between 60 and 70 percent of Poland's arms exports involved servicing and spare parts. At that point, three large companies—Bumar-Łabędy, Cenzin, and Cenrex—had government licenses for arms export, as did fifty small firms. In the transition period, regulations governing arms export were often murky, leading to a series of scandals when the extralegal activities of Polish exporters were disclosed. In 1991 high-ranking defense officials were arrested for selling US$96 million worth of arms to Iraq, and a number of smaller export deals were uncovered.

Law and Order

After 1989 the state's role in maintaining law and order changed, as did the definition of internal threats to national security. In accordance with Poland's commitment to representative democratic governance, the complex and sinister system of internal security organizations that had been established to eliminate opposition to communist regimes gave way to an apolitical and professional police force. Like most other reforms of the transition period, practical changes came slowly because of resistance from incumbent officials.

Internal Security

Until 1990 the internal security forces of the Ministry of Internal Affairs, which included the Security Service (Służba Bezpieczeństwa—SB), the regular police (Milicja Obywatelska—MO), the riot police, and a large Citizens' Militia Voluntary Reserve (Ochotnicza Rezerwa Milicji Obywatelskiej—ORMO), were charged with preserving public order and protecting the regime and the PZPR. These forces were especially active during the martial law period of the early 1980s because the Jaruzelski government sought to separate regular military forces from unpopular civilian control actions. All departments of the internal security forces came under intense public pressure for abolition or reform when the first noncommunist government was formed in 1989.

The first stage of reform in the Ministry of Internal Affairs was Kiszczak's reorganization program of 1989, which was designed to satisfy public demands for government rather than party control of the ministry. The reorganization sought to avoid the kind of frontal assault, advocated by radical reformers, that would bring confrontation with entrenched bureaucrats. Kiszczak was suspected of seeking to change his ministry's image without substantially reducing its power. Although the scope of the initial reform was quite broad and nominally separated the Ministry of Internal Affairs from PZPR control, the ministry also remained beyond the control of other branches of government. Kiszczak, who remained minister, refused to replace any of his deputies with Solidarity representatives. After the initial reform, internal affairs departments continued covert surveillance activity, although now with the nominal requirement of court approval.

Security Service

Kiszczak's reforms primarily affected the security service. The SB had been a plainclothes force of the Ministry of Internal Affairs, charged with seeking out subversive elements at home and abroad and investigating sabotage. Established in 1944 and controlled by the Soviet Union through the early 1950s, the SB faded during the Gomułka reform period, then revived as a totally secret force that stood over Polish society throughout the rest of the communist era.

The 1990 reform cut about 70 percent of SB personnel and most of the departments that had been most active in protecting the communist regimes from internal dangers. Department Three, which had monitored the activities of social, cultural, and political organizations and the press, was abolished. So was Department Four, which had monitored religious organizations and was assumed to be responsible for the murder of dissident leader Father Jerzy Popiełuszko in 1984. Three new, nominally apolitical departments were established in place of those abolished, and the name was changed from SB to the Office of State Protection (Urząd Ochrony Państwa—UOP). In mid-1990 an independent screening commission was established for former employees of abolished departments seeking jobs in remaining agencies of the ministry. All applicants over fifty-five years of age were rejected in an attempt to remove as many as possible of the communist-era SB administrators.

In 1992 the reputation of the new UOP was clouded by the discovery that many records from the communist era had been destroyed before the reform took place. An air of scandal surrounded the ministry as many top government figures, including Wałęsa, were implicated as collaborators in SB activities. Some Poles demanded that all SB records be opened to the public. However, the remaining files could not be relied upon to identify accurately the remaining government officials guilty of SB collaboration. In 1992 accusation of SB collaboration was a frequently used weapon in Poland's fractious political system.

Militia Forces

The ZOMO motorized riot troops, which played the most visible role in quelling demonstrations in 1980 and 1981, were reduced in size somewhat by the early 1990s and renamed Preventive Units of the Citizens' Militia (Oddziały Prewencji Milicji Obywatelskiej— OPMO). OPMO forces are restricted to roles such as crowd control at sporting events, ensuring safety in natural disasters, and assisting the regular police. In theory, higher government authority would be required for large OPMO contingents to be used.

From the 1960s through the 1980s, ORMO forces, which at one time numbered as many as 600,000 civilian volunteers, were used to augment regular police personnel at key trouble spots. In the early 1980s, ORMO harassed Solidarity members and prevented independent groups from organizing. Largely staffed by industrial workers who gained substantial privileges by monitoring their peers in the workplace, ORMO was the object of extreme resentment throughout the 1980s. Kiszczak attempted to promote ORMO as a valuable auxiliary police force, but the organization was abolished by the Sejm in 1990.

The Kiszczak reforms failed to reassure the public that the security agencies now were acting in the public interest. However, the collapse of the PZPR in 1990 made possible the ouster of Kiszczak and faster reduction of the autonomy of the security agencies. Kiszczak's successor, a journalist, put the Ministry of Internal Affairs under a civilian for the first time since martial law was declared.

Border Troops

Under the communist regimes, the Border Guard Troops (Wojska Ochrony Pogranicza—WOP) was an agency of the Ministry of Internal Affairs, which was responsible for tight border security as well as a variety of less specific missions. In 1991 the military-style WOP was disbanded and replaced by the Border Guard (Strażnik Graniczny—SG), whose commander was appointed by and reported directly to the prime minister. The force was reduced from 20,000 to 13,500 troops, with the top-heavy officer corps absorbing the largest cuts.

The newly configured force retrained the large numbers of lower- and mid-level cadre that remained in service and switched its operational strategy from tight border patrols to border reconnaissance. SG activity is now aimed at preventing illegal border crossings, smuggling, and the entry of environmentally harmful materials into Poland from adjoining countries. Between 1990 and 1991, border crossings into Poland increased from 2 million to 10 million. In

1991 and 1992, the major refugee movements from Eastern Europe and Southern Europe put great stress on Poland's reduced border force, which was responsible for customs and visa inspections at border crossings. A 1991 study showed alarming signs that Poland's borders were very porous. For example, 70 percent of goods declared as transiting Poland remained within the country once they entered (thus having avoided taxes and duties), and only 30 percent of automobiles going into the Soviet Union had proper transport documents.

Crime

In 1989 and 1990, the crime rate in Poland rose substantially. The increase was attributed to several factors: social stresses from the uncertainties of the transition period; the institutional inadequacy of the Ministry of Internal Affairs to deal with social unrest without wielding unlimited authority; and widespread skepticism that prevented public cooperation with police investigations. Public confidence had been destroyed by numerous incidents of arbitrary and unpunished police violence against civilians. In Warsaw, where robberies increased by 50 percent between 1988 and 1989, police solved only 16 percent of reported crimes in 1990. Police budgets were slashed, and recruitment became very difficult because police work now carried low prestige and offered few benefits. For personnel remaining from the communist era, the drop in institutional support was especially demoralizing.

By 1990 these conditions led to citizen complaints about being defenseless against crime and to complaints by the police that they could not do their work properly because of poor cooperation from citizens and insufficient budgetary support. Between 1990 and 1991, the police budget was cut by 13 percent and distance limitations were put on the use of patrol cars. Already in early 1990, however, legislation had been drafted to put the police under a separate chief appointed by and directly responsible to the prime minister. Such a shift meant that the Ministry of Internal Affairs could not issue direct orders on the conduct of police business. Local jurisdictions also could establish their own police forces as counterweights to the national police system; political qualifications could not be considered in hiring at any level. The new law also placed extensive limitations on police powers that interfered with citizen rights.

In 1991 the Citizens' Militia changed its name to simply the Police (Policja). Personnel were retrained, and a strong public relations campaign was established to gain public trust. Uniforms and operational methods were changed, and by 1992 police had begun to flush pockets of crime from the inner cities. In 1992 the aura of fear had dissipated, and a large part of the public came to believe the police were performing as well as possible under strict budget limitations. A major newspaper poll in early 1992 showed the police second to the military (and above the Roman Catholic Church) in respect afforded Polish institutions.

By 1991 large increases had occurred in white-collar crime and economic scandals connected with privatization, liberalization of foreign trade, and decentralization of economic policy making. The unsealing of Poland's borders also made the country vulnerable to foreign organized crime. Accordingly, the Ministry of Internal Affairs set up a special police unit to combat corruption and economic fraud. In 1991, with a total detail of 600, the special unit set up special departments at existing police stations in seventeen districts.

New international conditions fostered new types of crime in the early 1990s. By 1992 the large number of refugees entering Poland, many without legal status and without employment, had become a serious source of crime. And explosives and arms left behind by the Soviet armed forces combined with social unrest to contribute to a significant increase in terrorist bombings. In addition to actual bombings, police frequently had to cope with false reports. As many as 90 percent of false alarms involved Poles between eleven and sixteen years old.

By 1992 narcotics had also became a problem. Bands of Polish amphetamine producers and distributors had developed a complex underground organization that produced very pure amphetamine narcotics, laundered money, and smuggled large amounts of their products into Western Europe (see Health Issues, ch. 2). The "Polish pipeline" of agents abroad moved hashish, heroin, and cocaine into Western markets with increasing frequency. In the early 1990s, the entry of international traffickers into the indigenous Polish system threatened to raise the sophistication of local operations and make Poland a central distribution point for the world narcotics industry. Asian, Latin American, and African traffickers found Polish operatives useful because customs agents had not yet learned to identify East Europeans as potential smugglers. In 1991 some 20 percent of amphetamines captured in Western Europe originated in Poland.

Prevention of drug-related crime was hampered by policies remaining from the communist era and by budget limitations. Drug laws remained very lax in 1992; because drug trading was regarded as a minor offense, no Pole was convicted for amphetamine activities between 1985 and 1992. The nation's police force included only thirty full-time drug enforcement officers in 1992, with an annual operating budget of between US$100,000 and US$200,000.

Penal System

Under both communist and postcommunist governments, the Polish penal system operated under national authority. Beginning in 1956, the system was under jurisdiction of the Ministry of Justice through its Main Bureau of Penal Institutions. Institutions were categorized by the criminal records of the inmates and the severity of their crimes. Each institution had a prison commission that classified inmates and adjusted their treatment according to behavior.

Adopted in 1969, the Penal Code of the Polish People's Republic was one of the most punitive in Europe in actual practice—although the code's rhetoric was quite liberal. Nominally, members of the judiciary had free access to prisons to investigate prisoner grievances, examine documents, and assess prison conditions. In actuality, the Polish judiciary was completely controlled by the PZPR and therefore had no capacity for remedial action. Likewise, codified prisoner privileges such as medical treatment and access to libraries seldom existed in practice. In 1981 Western experts estimated that the penal system managed between 130,000 and 200,000 prisoners—a rate of imprisonment per 100,000 citizens of 350 to 580, compared with 212 in the United States and twenty-five in the Netherlands.

At its inception in 1980, Solidarity began distributing previously unseen information about Polish prison conditions. Patronat, an organization lobbying for liberalized prison policies, emerged in 1981 but was repressed in 1982. The political tensions of the early 1980s triggered a wave of prison strikes affecting two of every three penal institutions in Poland between 1980 and 1982. Press reports on the riots revealed chronic deficiencies in the system. Food standards did not meet human biological needs. Prisoners were routinely beaten, tortured, and denied medical treatment. Large prison populations caused overcrowding, and sanitation and recreational facilities were inadequate. Hard labor—the standard method of inmate rehabilitation—featured dangerous working conditions, and refusal to work led to solitary confinement and other harsh penalties. An uncodified set of prison regulations introduced in 1974 had given prison guards arbitrary power to inflict a wide range of punishments. Those punishments were a key motivation of inmate strikes in the early 1980s. Prisoners could complain only as individuals, never as a group, and until the riots the workings of the prison system were completely hidden from the Polish public.

Under Communism

In the communist era, the Polish penal system basically adapted the penal practices of the Soviet Union to suit local conditions. In both systems, cheap and disciplined prison labor played an important role in supporting the economy. Forced, uncompensated labor on private projects of prison officials was a source of particular resentment among inmates.

The civil upheavals of 1980 and 1981 expanded the political role of the penal system. Among the thousands of arrests made during that time, typical crimes were possession of underground leaflets, display of Solidarity symbols, organization of meetings and marches, and refusal to work in militarized enterprises. Solidarity activists generally were imprisoned in groups. The PZPR applied great pressure to civil and military judges trying such cases; under martial law, a military commissar monitored every court as well. Loyalty oaths were required of judges, and many who were deemed unreliable lost their positions.

When martial law ended in mid-1983, thousands of political prisoners who had been held without charges were conscripted into the army and sent to hard labor camps, where they were subject to military rather than civil law. In this period, military courts retained jurisdiction over all cases involving "public safety, order, or national security." The tougher sentences of the martial law period remained in force and the right to appeal remained void.

Postcommunist Reform

Beginning in 1989, former opposition groups (who during the 1980s had become quite familiar with the Polish prison system) achieved a government ban on violence in prisons and restoration of prisoner civil rights. In 1989 Parliament passed an amnesty law that released political prisoners but continued to confine recidivists. In late 1989, the disappointed hard-core prison population staged some 500 riots. In 1990 Paweł Moczydłowski, director of the Central Prison Administration, succeeded in ending the violence and corruption typical of the communist administration. About one-third of prison guards and three-quarters of prison governors were dismissed between 1990 and 1992. By mid-1992, nearly 50 percent of prison personnel had been in service less than three years.

Wherever possible, the physical structure of prisons was opened to give inmates greater contact; harassment and arbitrary punishment were eliminated, and visitation and appeal rights were extended. Patronat and Alcoholics Anonymous became active among prisoners, and clergymen had unlimited access. Increased public access eased tensions between inmates and guards. In 1992, however, a Helsinki Watch report noted poor material and sanitation conditions and overcrowding in many Polish prisons. Only fifteen prisons had their own hospitals, many of them with primitive facilities. The opportunity to work, an arduous but often welcome respite from prison tedium, was reduced significantly in the postcommunist economic decline; in mid-1992 only about 25 percent of prisoners held jobs, and only about 4 percent of prisoners worked for civilian companies.

In mid-1992 the Central Prison Administration had debts of US$8.3 million. The decline of prison enterprises meant that prisons no longer contributed to the budget of the Ministry of Justice. Prison budgets were consumed by the cost of housing prisoners (3 million zloty monthly per prisoner). Most Polish prisons were at least 100 years old, and several facilities had been condemned by 1992. In 1992 the prison population was 61,329. Although significantly lower than in the communist era, that figure climbed by 1,000 to 1,500 per month between 1989 (when the post-amnesty population was 40,000) and 1992 (when experts declared that the system had reached its capacity). Sentences still averaged two years, compared with six to eight months in the West. In most cases, courts still tended to impose maximum sentences even for trivial crimes. Lesser punishments, such as fines and restricted freedom, were rarely imposed as alternatives to imprisonment.

In the early 1990s, most aspects of internal security in Poland followed the same irregular pattern of reform as that which occurred in national security policy in the same years. By 1992 the mission of state security agencies had changed dramatically toward protection of all citizens rather than protection of the state, but the public retained from the communist era considerable suspicion of such agencies. The open society of the early 1990s fostered new types of crime, which were met with uncertain reform measures in police and border protection and in prison policy. Obtaining public support for internal security institutions was a difficult part of governance in the early postcommunist era, as all of Polish society adjusted to quite new internal and external conditions.

* * *

Background on Poland's military history is available in studies such as M.K. Dziewanowski's *Poland in the Twentieth Century* and Norman Davies's *God's Playground: A History of Poland.* A. Ross Johnson covers the development and organization of the Polish People's

Army in *East European Military Establishments: The Warsaw Pact Northern Tier;* he covers the role of the military in government in *Poland in Crisis.* Several valuable recent studies of Polish military doctrine and the international security position of Poland have been published by the Soviet Studies Research Center of the Royal Military Academy at Sandhurst and the Foreign Military Studies Office at Fort Leavenworth, Kansas. The RFE/RL Research Institute's *RFE/RL Research Report* series published between 1989 and 1992 contains comprehensive reports on the Polish prison system, reform of internal security agencies, and Poland's postcommunist military doctrine and strategy. The annual volumes of *The Military Balance,* published by the International Institute for Strategic Studies (London), provide detailed information on force and armament strength. The *Daily Report: East Europe,* a publication of the Foreign Broadcast Information Service, is an invaluable source of translations of up-to-date periodical articles on the Polish military and the political background of military policy. (For further information and complete citations, see Bibliography.)

Appendix

Table

1 Metric Conversion Coefficients and Factors
2 Level of Education of Females Aged Fifteen and Over, 1990
3 Marital and Family Position of Females Aged Eighteen to Fifty-Nine, 1987 and 1991
4 Housing Capacity, 1981–90
5 Religious Instruction in Primary and Secondary Schools, 1991
6 Schools, Students, and Teachers by Level of Education, 1981, 1986, and 1991
7 Foreign-Language Instruction in Primary and Secondary Schools, 1991
8 Incidence of Selected Diseases and Disability Days Caused, 1980, 1985, and 1989
9 Medical Personnel, 1980, 1985, and 1990
10 Medical Facilities, 1980, 1985, and 1990
11 Births, Marriages, and Deaths, 1984–90
12 Civilian Labor Force by Type of Occupation, 1987, 1988, and 1989
13 Selected Balance of Payments Data in Transferable Rubles, Selected Years, 1985–91
14 Selected Balance of Payments Data in Convertible Currencies, Selected Years, 1985–91
15 Industrial Output and Consumer Price Index, July 1990 to November 1991
16 Unemployment Rate by Age-Group and Sex, Summer 1992
17 Output of Selected Engineering Products, Selected Years, 1980–91
18 Principal Agricultural Products, 1988, 1989, and 1990
19 Principal Trading Partners, 1988, 1989, and 1990
20 Election Results for Sejm and Senate, 1991
21 Naval Craft and Personnel, Selected Years, 1970–95
22 Declared Holdings of the Polish Army and Arms Limitations According to the Conventional Forces in Europe Treaty, 1991

Table 1. Metric Conversion Coefficients and Factors

When you know	Multiply by	To find
Millimeters	0.04	inches
Centimeters	0.39	inches
Meters	3.3	feet
Kilometers	0.62	miles
Hectares (10,000 m²)	2.47	acres
Square kilometers	0.39	square miles
Cubic meters	35.3	cubic feet
Liters	0.26	gallons
Kilograms	2.2	pounds
Metric tons	0.98	long tons
	1.1	short tons
	2,204	pounds
Degrees Celsius (Centigrade)	1.8 and add 32	degrees Fahrenheit

Table 2. Level of Education of Females Aged Fifteen and Over, 1990

Highest Level Completed	Per 100 Males	Percentage of All Females	
		Urban	Rural
Higher education	89	8.3	1.8
Secondary education	150	36.0	15.8
Basic vocational education	56	16.1	16.8
Primary school	126	35.9	51.5
Did not complete primary school	181	3.7	14.1

Source: Based on information from Poland, Główny Urząd Statystyczny, *Sytuacja społeczno-zawodowa kobiet w 1990 r.,* Warsaw, 1990, 18.

*Table 3. Marital and Family Position of Females Aged Eighteen
to Fifty-Nine, 1987 and 1991*
(in percentages of age range)

Year	Children	Total	Single	Married	Divorced	Widowed	Separated
1987	None	37.4	93.6	25.8	29.2	64.7	27.7
1991	None	37.5	94.6	25.8	32.3	68.8	18.3
1987	One	23.4	6.1	25.7	40.2	18.0	40.4
1991	One	22.4	4.7	24.2	40.4	16.2	40.9
1987	Two	25.3	0.3	31.0	22.7	12.0	29.9
1991	Two	26.8	0.7	32.9	22.6	9.9	32.4
1987	Three or more	13.9	0.0	17.5	7.9	5.3	2.0
1991	Three or more	13.3	0.0	17.1	4.7	5.1	8.4
All females							
1987 * ..	n.a.	n.a.	13.6	75.2	4.5	5.1	1.0
1991 * ..	n.a.	n.a.	12.1	69.6	4.5	5.1	1.6

* Totals may not add to 100 because of rounding.
n.a.—not applicable.

Source: Based on information from Poland, Główny Urząd Statystyczny, *Sytuacja społeczno-
zawodowa kobiet w 1991 r.*, Warsaw, 1991, 7.

Table 4. Housing Capacity, 1981-90

Category	1981-85 *	1986-90 *	1990
Dwellings completed			
(in thousands)	190.9	170.0	134.2
Urban	144.8	124.5	98.8
Rural	46.1	45.5	35.4
Housing cooperatives	99.3	79.8	68.4
Privately built	54.2	56.9	47.4
Communal	2.8	5.2	3.0
Other	34.6	28.1	15.4
Rooms completed (in thousands)	740.4	698.6	567.3
Urban	535.5	486.6	396.3
Rural	204.9	212.0	171.0
Housing cooperatives	344.8	292.0	254.6
Privately built	266.1	291.6	248.0
Communal	9.1	17.1	10.0
Other	130.4	97.9	54.7
Average useful floor space per dwelling			
(in square meters)	67.1	74.1	77.2
Urban	60.4	66.8	69.6
Rural	88.0	93.9	98.4
Housing cooperatives	53.4	57.9	59.4
Privately owned	99.9	106.5	109.9
Communal	52.2	54.0	56.8

* Annual averages.

Source: Based on information from Poland, Główny Urząd Statystyczny, *Concise Statistical Yearbook of Poland, 1991,* Warsaw, 1991, 114-15.

Table 5. Religious Instruction in Primary and Secondary Schools, 1991

Level of Education	Percentage of Total Receiving Instruction	Non-Roman Catholic Students Receiving Instruction	Total
Primary			
Urban	97.9	26,600	5,161,200
Rural	99.3	15,800	1,868,300
All primary	95.8	42,400	7,029,500
Secondary			
College preparatory	92.2	1,900	409,300
Vocational	88.5	2,600	551,100
All secondary	90.1	4,500	960,400

Source: Based on information from Poland, Główny Urząd Statystyczny, *Concise Statistical Yearbook of Poland, 1991,* Warsaw, 1991, 128.

*Table 6. Schools, Students, and Teachers by Level
of Education, 1981, 1986, and 1991*

Level of Education	1981	1986	1991
Schools			
Primary [1]	13,524	17,013	18,501
College preparatory secondary [2]	1,230	1,131	1,334
Vocational secondary	5,977	4,801	5,190
Postsecondary	1,272	960	893
Students			
Primary [1]	4,259,800	4,897,600	5,276,400
College preparatory secondary [2]	415,000	382,900	493,600
Vocational secondary	909,000	634,800	795,000
Postsecondary	589,200	435,700	502,600
Graduates			
Primary	494,800	503,200	590,400
College preparatory secondary	105,300	85,800	99,900
Vocational secondary	207,100	127,500	150,600
Postsecondary	141,600	97,000	91,800
Teachers			
Primary	204,300	277,900	328,900
College preparatory secondary	22,900	22,300	25,100
Vocational, all levels	77,400	80,200	85,700
Postsecondary	54,700	57,300	62,100

[1] In 1991 eighty-six nonpublic primary schools enrolled 4,800 students.
[2] In 1991 ninety-three nonpublic college preparatory secondary schools enrolled 6,700 students.

Source: Based on information from Poland, Główny Urząd Statystyczny, *Concise Statistical Yearbook of Poland, 1991,* Warsaw, 1991, 128.

*Table 7. Foreign-Language Instruction in Primary
and Secondary Schools, 1991* [1]

| | | Secondary [2] | | |
| | | College | | |
Language	Primary [2]	Preparatory	Vocational	Total
Required				
English	5.0	52.6	17.5	627,600
French	0.8	16.2	5.0	147,400
German	3.7	44.1	31.7	628,200
Russian	40.6	85.6	73.0	3,648,300
Other	0.0	8.9	4.5	68,800
Elective				
English	5.8	0.5	5.7	339,500
French	0.7	0.1	1.3	44,600
German	3.8	0.3	10.0	263,900
Other	0.7	6.6	1.5	81,900

[1] Excludes special schools.
[2] In percentages

Source: Based on information from Poland, Główny Urząd Statystyczny, *Concise Statistical
Yearbook of Poland, 1991,* Warsaw, 1991, 128.

*Table 8. Incidence of Selected Diseases and Disability
Days Caused, 1980, 1985, and 1989*

Category	1980	1985	1989
Incidence of selected diseases			
Tuberculosis	25,807	21,650	16,185
Venereal diseases	42,370	14,973	10,399
Influenza	1,410,357	2,309,875	1,642,126
Cancer	64,959	76,938	82,494
Mental and nervous conditions	155,317	150,596	145,756
Disability days caused			
by disease (per 100 employees)			
Respiratory system	350.7	382.4	420.1
Circulatory system	207.2	196.1	215.2
Nervous system	163.4	186.5	230.4
Bone, muscle, or connective tissue	158.3	168.9	203.0

Source: Based on information from Poland, Główny Urząd Statystyczny, *Concise Statistical
Yearbook of Poland, 1991,* Warsaw, 1991, 121.

Table 9. Medical Personnel, 1980, 1985, and 1990

Category	1980	1985	1990
Physicians	63,550	73,172	81,674
Dentists	16,834	17,440	18,219
Hospital attendants	3,747	3,244	2,708
Nurses	156,975	179,727	207,654
Midwives	15,092	19,850	23,868

Source: Based on information from Poland, Główny Urząd Statystyczny, *Concise Statistical Yearbook of Poland, 1991,* Warsaw, 1991, 117.

Table 10. Medical Facilities, 1980, 1985, and 1990

Category	1980	1985	1990
Dispensaries			
Regional	n.a.	2,322	2,410
Industrial	2,481	2,469	2,450
Cooperative	418	377	316
Other	3,019	1,237	1,383
Total dispensaries	5,918	6,405	6,559
Health service centers	3,218	3,283	3,328
Beds			
General hospitals	200,752	210,611	217,717
Mental hospitals	36,535	34,381	33,135
Delivery rooms	1,968	1,487	811
Tuberculosis sanitoriums	8,850	8,850	5,977
Alcoholism treatment			
centers	755	946	750
Drug addiction treatment			
centers	n.a.	44	504
Total beds	248,860	256,319	258,894
First aid sections	397	404	412
Emergency stations	49	53	61
Ambulances	4,784	4,635	4,814
Hospital aircraft	75	78	69

n.a.—not available.

Source: Based on information from Poland, Główny Urząd Statystyczny, *Concise Statistical Yearbook of Poland, 1991,* Warsaw, 1991, 118–19.

Table 11. Births, Marriages, and Deaths, 1984-90

Year	Live Births Number	Per 1,000 Population	Marriages	Deaths Number	Per 1,000 Population
1984	699,041	18.9	285,258	364,862	9.9
1985	677,576	18.2	266,816	381,457	10.3
1986	634,748	17.0	257,887	376,316	10.1
1987	605,492	16.1	252,819	378,365	10.1
1988	587,741	15.5	246,791	370,821	9.8
1989	562,530	14.8	255,643	381,173	10.0
1990	545,800	14.3	255,369	388,440	10.2

Source: Based on information from *The Europa World Year Book, 1992,* 2, London, 1992, 2252.

Table 12. Civilian Labor Force by Type of Occupation, 1987, 1988, and 1989

Type of Occupation	1987	1988	1989
Agriculture, forestry, and fishing	5,059,000	4,923,900	4,729,500
Mining and quarrying	612,900	609,800	614,700
Manufacturing	4,710,800	4,684,900	4,630,600
Construction	1,457,600	1,471,400	1,418,300
Trade, restaurants, and hotels	1,816,300	1,808,600	1,787,000
Transportation, storage, and communications	1,378,500	1,367,600	1,303,200
Community, social, and personal services	2,860,900	2,917,200	3,066,600
Other	700,200	690,700	814,100
TOTAL	18,596,200	18,474,100	18,364,000

Source: Based on information from *The Europa World Year Book, 1992,* 2, London, 1992, 2252.

Poland: A Country Study

Table 13. Selected Balance of Payments Data in Transferable Rubles, Selected Years, 1985-91
(in millions)

	1985	1987	1989	1991 *
Merchandise exports	9,073	10,665	11,320	1,236
Merchandise imports	– 10,303	– 11,219	– 10,342	– 816
Balance of trade	– 1,230	– 554	978	420
Balance of services	319	373	427	n.a.
Interest payments	– 1,097	– 424	– 1,104	n.a.

n.a.—not available.
* Through November 1991.

Source: Based on information from Poland, Główny Urząd Statystyczny, *Rocznik statystyczny handlu zagranicznego,* Warsaw, 1989, 88; Poland, Główny Urząd Statystyczny, *Rocznik statystyczny handlu zagranicznego,* Warsaw, 1991, 92; and *Życie gospodarcze,* No. 14, 1992, 12.

Table 14. Selected Balance of Payments Data in Convertible Currencies, Selected Years, 1985-91
(in millions)

	1985	1987	1989	1991
Merchandise exports	5,768	6,920	8,113	12,760
Merchandise imports	– 4,594	– 5,878	– 7,987	– 12,709
Balance of trade	1,174	1,042	126	51
Balance of services	– 17	– 37	– 211	236
Cost of credits	– 2,444	– 2,804	– 3,069	– 2,863
Current account balance	– 523	– 392	– 1,922	– 1,359

Source: Based on information from Poland, Główny Urząd Statystyczny, *Rocznik statystyczny handlu zagranicznego,* Warsaw, 1989, 88; Poland, Główny Urząd Statystyczny, *Rocznik statystyczny handlu zagranicznego,* Warsaw, 1991, 92; and *Życie gospodarcze,* No. 14, 1992, 12.

Table 15. Industrial Output and Consumer Price Index, July 1990 to November 1991

Month	Output *	Consumer Price Index
July 1990	87.8	103.4
August 1990	107.6	103.6
September 1990	108.0	104.6
October 1990	100.4	105.7
November 1990	100.0	104.9
December 1990	103.2	105.9
January 1991	82.4	112.7
February 1991	100.8	106.7
March 1991	100.1	104.5
April 1991	91.7	102.7
May 1991	98.4	102.7
June 1991	102.2	104.9
July 1991	87.9	100.1
August 1991	105.9	100.6
September 1991	103.5	104.3
October 1991	101.5	103.2
November 1991	105.9	103.2

* The figure for each month is the percentage of the previous month.

Source: Based on information from Jan Winiecki, "The Polish Transition Programme: Underpinnings, Results, Interpretations," *Soviet Studies* [Glasgow], 44, No. 5, 1992, 814.

Table 16. Unemployment Rate by Age-Group and Sex, Summer 1992 (in percentages)

Age-Group	Males	Females	Total
18 and under	12.0	14.0	13.0
18–19	32.0	37.5	34.0
20–24	25.0	28.0	26.0
25–29	14.5	18.0	16.0
30–34	9.5	17.0	13.0
35–44	9.5	12.0	10.5
45 and over	7.0	7.0	7.0

Source: Based on information from Antoni Kowalik, "'Bluebirds' or Voluntarily Unemployed?" *Rzeczpospolita* [Warsaw], September 4, 1992, Joint Publications Research Service, *JPRS Report: East Europe* (JPRS-EER-92-146.), October 16, 1992, 29.

Table 17. Output of Selected Engineering Products, Selected Years, 1980–91

Product	1980	1985	1989	1991
Automobiles (in thousands of units)	351	283	285	167
Trucks (in thousands of units)	61	54	51	n.a.
Tractors (in thousands of units)	58	59	48	18
Train passenger cars (single units)	328	350	230	n.a.
Television sets (in thousands of units)	900	610	772	443
Radios (in thousands of units)	2,695	2,690	2,523	n.a.
Washing machines (in thousands of units)	809	739	811	335
Metallurgical machines (in thousands of tons) ...	60	28	30	n.a.
Agricultural machines (in thousands of tons)	343	460	381	n.a.

n.a.—not available.

Source: Based on information from Poland, Główny Urząd Statystyczny, *Rocznik statystyczny, 1990,* Warsaw, 1990, 267–69.

Table 18. Principal Agricultural Products, 1988, 1989, and 1990 (in thousands of tons)

Crop	1988	1989	1990
Potatoes	34,707	34,390	36,313
Sugar beet	14,069	14,374	16,721
Wheat	7,582	8,462	9,026
Rye	5,501	6,216	6,044
Barley	3,804	3,909	4,217
Mixed grains	3,387	3,466	3,554
Oats	2,222	2,185	2,119
Cabbages	1,574	1,617	1,749
Apples	1,393	1,312	812
Rapeseed	1,199	1,586	1,206

Source: Based on information from *The Europa World Year Book, 1992,* 2, London, 1992, 2253.

Table 19. Principal Trading Partners, 1988, 1989, and 1990
(in millions of zloty) [1]

Country	1988	1989	1990
Imports			
Soviet Union	1,228,447	2,608,802	15,369,501
West Germany	687,142	2,337,781	15,586,565 [2]
Czechoslovakia	335,978	846,166	2,761,817
East Germany	264,990	662,884	
Switzerland	239,866	782,392	4,988,089
Austria	230,123	886,892	4,403,499
Britain	221,728	663,918	4,382,049
Other	2,064,039	6,075,340	30,028,335
Total imports	5,272,313	14,864,175	77,519,855
Exports			
Soviet Union	1,474,580	4,048,255	19,767,703
West Germany	747,156	2,757,736	32,502,840 [2]
Czechoslovakia	359,139	1,075,301	5,282,084
Britain	301,766	1,262,563	9,227,183
East Germany	264,251	815,520	
Austria	183,865	690,865	4,988,514
Switzerland	153,738	504,375	6,078,434
Other	2,527,250	8,321,559	51,608,189
Total exports	6,011,745	19,476,174	129,454,947

[1] For value of the zloty—see Glossary.
[2] 1990 figures combine West Germany and East Germany.

Source: Based on information from *The Europa World Year Book, 1992,* 2, London, 1992, 2256.

Table 20. Election Results for Sejm and Senate, 1991

Party or Coalition	Percentage of Sejm Seats	Number of Senate Seats
Alliance of the Democratic Left	13.0	4
Center Alliance	9.6	9
Christian Democracy	1.1	1
Christian National Union	10.7	9
Confederation for an Independent Poland	10.9	4
Democratic Union	13.5	21
German Minority	1.5	1
Liberal-Democratic Congress	8.0	6
Party of Christian Democrats	0.9	3
Peasant Alliance	6.1	7
Polish Peasant Party	10.4	8
Solidarity	5.9	11
Parties with single seats in Senate	2.4	16
Parties with no seats in Senate	6.1	0
TOTAL	100.0 *	100

* Figures do not add to total because of rounding.

Source: Based on information from Louisa Vinton, "Poland's New Election Law: Fewer Parties, Same Impasse?" *RFE/RL Research Report* [Munich], 2, No. 28, July 9, 1993, 10.

Table 21. Naval Craft and Personnel, Selected Years, 1970–95

Category	1970	1980	1985	1990	1995 *
Destroyers and frigates	3	1	1	2	2
Submarines	6	4	3	3	3
Missile craft	12	29	20	11	0
Corvettes	0	0	2	4	5
Patrol boats	64	25	8	8	8
Mine countermeasures	51	44	49	32	26
Amphibious craft	16	23	23	26	5
Personnel	20,000	25,000	19,100	19,300	10,000

* Projected

Source: Based on information from John L. Green, ''The Baltic: A Sea in Transition,'' Monterey, California, 1991, 80.

Table 22. Declared Holdings of the Polish Army and Arms Limitations According to the Conventional Forces in Europe Treaty, 1991

Category	Holdings	Arms Limitations
Battle tanks	2,850	1,730
Armored combat vehicles	2,377	2,150
Artillery	2,300	1,610
Combat aircraft	551	460
Attack helicopters	29	130

Source: Based on information from *Jane's Defence Weekly* [Coulsdon, United Kingdom], 16, No. 1, July 6, 1991, 18–19.

Bibliography

Chapter 1

Abromsky, Chimen, et al. (eds.). *The Jews in Poland*. New York: Blackwell, 1986.

Ash, Timothy Garton. *The Magic Lantern: The Revolution of '89 Witnessed in Warsaw, Budapest, Berlin, and Prague*. New York: Random House, 1990.

_____. *The Polish Revolution: Solidarity*. New York: Vintage, 1985.

_____. *The Uses of Adversity: Essays on the Fate of Central Europe*. New York: Random House, 1989.

Barraclough, Geoffrey (ed.). *Eastern and Western Europe in the Middle Ages*. (History of European Civilization Library.) London: Harcourt Brace Jovanovich, 1970.

Bhutani, Surendra. "Poland under Gierek: 1970–1980," *IDSA Journal* [New Delhi], 16, July–September 1983, 40–55.

Davies, Norman. *God's Playground: A History of Poland*, 1 and 2. New York: Columbia University Press, 1982.

_____. *Heart of Europe: A Short History of Poland*. Oxford: Oxford University Press, 1986.

de Weydenthal, Jan B. "Poland Facing the Brink," *Current History*, 74, April 1978, 159–63.

Dziewanowski, M.K. *Poland in the Twentieth Century*. New York: Columbia University Press, 1977.

Gieysztor, Aleksander, et al. *History of Poland*. Warsaw: Polish Scientific Publishers, 1968.

Golan, Galia. "The Soviet Union and the Polish Crisis," *Slavic and Soviet Series*, 5, Nos. 1–2, 1980, 20–29.

Gross, Jan T. *Polish Society under German Occupation: The Generalgouvernement, 1939–1944*. Princeton: Princeton University Press, 1979.

_____. *Revolution from Abroad: The Soviet Conquest of Poland's Western Ukraine and Western Belorussia*. Princeton: Princeton University Press, 1988.

Halecki, Oskar. *The History of Poland*. Chicago: Regnery, 1966.

Jasienica, Pawel. *The Commonwealth of Both Nations: The Silver Age*. Miami: American Institute of Polish Culture, 1987.

_____. *Jagiellonian Poland*. Miami: American Institute of Polish Culture, 1978.

Karski, Jan. *The Great Powers and Poland, 1919–1945: From Versailles to Yalta*. Lanham, Maryland: University Press of America, 1985.

Korbonski, Andrzej. "Civil-Military Relations in Poland Between the Wars: 1918–1939,'' *Armed Forces and Society,* 14, Winter 1988, 169–89.

Kulski, W.W. "The Soviet Union, Germany, and Poland," *Polish Review,* 23, No. 1, 1978, 48–57.

Leslie, R.F. (ed.). *The History of Poland since 1863.* Cambridge: Cambridge University Press, 1980.

Lord, Robert Howard. *The Second Partition of Poland: A Study in Diplomatic History.* Cambridge: Harvard University Press, 1915.

Malia, Martin. "Poland's Eternal Return," *New York Review,* 30, September 29, 1983, 18–27.

Michnik, Adam. *Letters from Prison and Other Essays.* Berkeley: University of California Press, 1985.

Orzell, Laurence. "Poland and Russia, July 1941–April 1943: The 'Impossible' Alliance," *Polish Review,* 21, No. 4, 1976, 35–58.

"Poland: Self-Occupation and Resistance," *Survey,* 26, Summer–Autumn, 1982.

Polonsky, Antony. *Politics in Independent Poland, 1921–1939: The Crisis of Constitutional Government.* Oxford: Oxford University Press, 1972.

Rachwald, Arthur R. "Poland Between the Superpowers: Three Decades of Foreign Policy," *Orbis,* 20, Winter 1977, 1055–83.

Reddaway, W.F., et al. (eds.). *The Cambridge History of Poland,* 1 and 2. Cambridge: Cambridge University Press, 1941, 1950.

Roos, Hans. *A History of Modern Poland.* New York: Knopf, 1966.

Torońska, Teresa. *"Them": Stalin's Polish Puppets.* New York: Harper and Row, 1987.

Walesa, Lech. *A Way of Hope.* New York: Holt, 1987.

Wandycz, Piotr S. *The Lands of Partitioned Poland, 1795–1918.* (A History of East Central Europe series.) Seattle: University of Washington, 1974.

Watt, Richard M. *Bitter Glory: Poland and Its Fate, 1918–1939.* New York: Simon and Schuster, 1979.

World Bank. *Poland: Decentralization and Reform of the State.* (World Bank Country Studies.) Washington: 1992.

Zamoyski, Adam. *The Polish Way.* New York: Franklin Watts, 1988.

Zawodny, J.K. *Death in the Forest: The Story of the Katyn Forest Massacre.* New York: Hippocrene, 1988.

———. *Nothing but Honour: The Story of the Warsaw Uprising, 1944.* Stanford, California: Hoover Institution Press, 1979.

Zuzowski, Robert. "KOR after KOR: The Intelligentsia and Dissent in Poland, 1981–1987," *Polish Review,* 33, No. 2, 1988, 167–89.

Chapter 2

Adam, Jan (ed.). *Economic Reforms and Welfare Systems in the USSR, Poland, and Hungary.* New York: St. Martin's Press, 1991.

Applebaum, Anne. "Poles Face Life Without 'Them,' " *Orbis,* 34, No. 2, Spring 1990, 195–209.

Archer, Margaret Scotford, and Salvador Griner (eds.). *Contemporary Europe: Class, Status, and Power.* (Reading University Studies on Contemporary Europe.) London: Weidenfeld and Nicolson, 1971.

Blazyca, George, and Ryszard Rapacki (eds.). *Poland into the 1990s: Economy and Society in Transition.* New York: St. Martin's Press, 1991.

Clark, John, and Aaron Wildavsky. *The Moral Collapse of Communism: Poland as a Cautionary Tale.* San Francisco: Institute for Contemporary Studies, 1990.

Engelberg, Stephen. "Poland's Pity? The Fears of AIDS Burns Brighter," *New York Times,* July 7, 1992, A4.

The Europa World Year Book, 1992, 2. London: Europa, 1992.

Faber, Bernard Lewis (ed.). *The Social Structure of Eastern Europe.* New York: Praeger, 1976.

Fallenbuchl, Zbigniew M. "Economic Reform and Changes in the Welfare System in Poland." Pages 110–31 in Jan Adam (ed.), *Economic Reforms and Welfare Systems in the USSR, Poland, and Hungary.* New York: St. Martin's Press, 1991.

Fischoff, Baruch. "Report from Poland," *Environment,* 33, No. 2, March 1992, 12–17, 37.

Gella, Aleksander. *Development of Class Structure in Eastern Europe.* Albany: State University of New York Press, 1989.

Hann, C.M. *A Village Without Solidarity: Polish Peasants in Years of Crisis.* New Haven: Yale University Press, 1985.

Jasiński, Jerzy (ed.). *Problems of Social Maladjustment and Crime in Poland.* Warsaw: Polish Academy of Sciences, 1989.

Kabala, Stanley J. "Ecological Literature and Social Awareness in Poland: A Documentary Review, 1969–1988," *Environment Policy Review,* 3, No. 2, July 1989, 34–43.

Kennedy, Michael D., and Ireneusz Bialecki. "Power and the Logic of Distribution in Poland," *Eastern European Politics and Societies,* 3, No. 2, Spring 1989, 300–28.

Kolankiewicz, George, and Paul G. Lewis. *Poland: Politics, Economics, and Society.* (Marxist Regimes Series.) London: Pinter, 1988.

Lane, David, and George Kolankiewicz (eds.). *Social Groups in Polish Society*. London: Macmillan, 1973.

Łaszek, Jacek. "Housing." Pages 63–72 in George Blazyca and Ryszard Rapacki (eds.), *Poland into the 1990s: Economy and Society in Transition*. New York: St. Martin's Press, 1991.

Liroff, Richard A. "Environmental Legacy Mixed in Eastern Europe," *Forum for Applied Research ad Public Policy*, 6, Winter 1991, 31–38.

Mason, David S. "Solidarity as a New Social Movement," *Political Science Quarterly*, 104, No. 1, Spring 1989, 41–58.

"May Poles," *The Economist* [London], 323, No. 7755, May 16, 1992, 66.

Mazurski, Krzysztof R. "Communism and the Environment," *Forum for Applied Research and Public Policy*, 6, Winter 1991, 39–44.

Nagengast, Carole. *Reluctant Socialists, Rural Entrepreneurs*. (Studies in the Ethnographic Imagination.) Boulder, Colorado: Westview Press, 1991.

Osa, Maryjane. "Resistance, Persistence, and Change: The Transformation of the Catholic Church in Poland," *Eastern European Politics and Societies*, 3, No. 2, Spring 1989, 268–99.

Paltrow, Scot J. "Poland and the Pope: The Vatican's Relations with Poland, 1978 to the Present," *Millennium: Journal of Independent Studies* [London], 15, No. 1, Spring 1986, 1–26.

Piekarski, Adam. *Freedom of Conscience and Religion in Poland*. Warsaw: Interpress, 1979.

Pienkos, Donald E. "Changes in Peasant Political and Religious Attitudes and Behavior in Poland," *Polish Review*, 23, No. 1, 1978, 58–68.

Poland. Główny Urząd Statystyczny. *Concise Statistical Yearbook of Poland, 1991*. Warsaw: 1991.

_____. Główny Urząd Statystyczny. *Rocznik statystyczny, 1991*. Warsaw: 1991.

_____. Główny Urząd Statystyczny. *Sytuacja społeczno-zawodowa kobiet w 1990 r.* Warsaw: 1990.

_____. Główny Urząd Statystyczny. *Sytuacja społeczno-zawodowa kobiet w 1991 r.* Warsaw: 1991.

Ramet, Sabrina P. *Social Currents in Eastern Europe*. Durham, North Carolina: Duke University Press, 1991.

Rusiński, Michał. "Environment." Pages 32–43 in George Blazyca and Ryszard Rapacki (eds.), *Poland into the 1990s: Economy and Society in Transition*. New York: St. Martin's Press, 1991.

Sikorska, Grazyna. "The Polish Roman Catholic Church and the Fate of Former Lutheran Churches in the 'Recovered Lands,' " *Religion in Communist Lands*, 16, Autumn 1988, 196–209.

The Stateman's Year-Book, 1991–1992. (Ed., Brian Hunter.) New York: St. Martin's Press, 1991.

Steven, Stewart. *The Poles.* New York: Macmillan, 1982.

Szajkowski, Bogdan. "New Law for the Church in Poland," *Religion in Communist Lands,* 17, Autumn 1989, 196–208.

Tatur, Melanie. "Catholicism and Modernization in Poland," *Journal of Communist Studies* [London], 7, No. 3, September 1991, 335–49.

Turner, Bengt, Jozsef Hegedüs, and Ivan Tosics (eds.). *The Reform of Housing in Eastern Europe and the Soviet Union.* London: Routledge, 1992.

Turnock, David. *The Human Geography of Eastern Europe.* London: Routledge, 1989.

United States Information Agency. Office of Research. "Public Opinion on Environmental Issues in Poland," *United States Information Agency Research Memorandum,* April 22, 1992, 1–11.

Wedel, Janine. *The Private Poland.* New York: Facts on File, 1986.

Wnuk-Lipiński, Edmund. "Polish Society after the Communist Experiment." Pages 4–10 in George Blazyca and Ryszard Rapacki (eds.), *Poland into the 1990s: Economy and Society in Transition.* New York: St. Martin's Press, 1991.

Wöhlke, Wilhelm (ed.). *Länderbericht Polen.* (Studien zur Geschichte und Politik.) Bonn: Bundeszentrale für politische Bildung, 1991.

Wulff, Kenneth R. *Education in Poland: Past, Present, and Future.* Lanham, Maryland: University Press of America, 1992.

Zamoyski, Adam. *The Polish Way.* New York: Franklin Watts, 1988.

Zubek, Voytek. "The Rise and Fall of Rule by Poland's Best and Brightest," *Soviet Studies,* 44, No. 4, 1992, 579–608.

Zuzowski, Robert. "The State, the Church, and the Intelligentsia in Poland's Politics," *Australian Outlook* [Sydney], 42, August 1988, 106–13.

(Various issues of the following periodicals were also used in the preparation of this chapter: Foreign Broadcast Information Service, *Daily Report: East Europe;* Joint Publications Research Service, *JPRS Report: East Europe; Radio Free Europe Research Report* [Munich]; *RFE/RL Report on Eastern Europe* [Munich]; and *Washington Post.*)

Chapter 3

Adam, Jan. *Employment Policies in the Soviet Union and Eastern Europe.* London: Macmillan, 1987.

Baka, Władysław. *The Economic Program and Transformation of the Banking System in Poland.* Warsaw: Information and Publications Office, Narodowy Bank Polski, 1990.

Bienkowski, Wojciech. "Can Poland Deviate from IMF Requirements?" *RFE/RL Research Report* [Munich], 1, No. 30, July 31, 1992, 49–53.

Bienkowski, Wojciech, and Masumi Hakogi. "Poland's Economic Relations with the West in the 1980s: The Impact of Political and Economic Factors," *Coexistence,* 25, September 1988, 299–318.

Blazyca, George. *Poland's Next Five Years: The Dash for Capitalism.* New York: Economist Intelligence Unit, 1991.

Blommestein, Hans, and Michael Marrese (eds.). *Transformation of Planned Economies: Property Rights Reform and Macroeconomic Stability.* Paris: Organisation for Economic Co-operation and Development, 1991.

Bochniarz, Zbigniew, and Richard Bolan (eds.). *Designing Institutions for Sustainable Development: A New Challenge for Poland.* Minneapolis and Białystok: Białystok Technical University, 1991.

Bolan, Richard S. "Organizing for Sustainable Growth in Poland," *Journal of the American Planning Association,* 58, Summer 1992, 301–11.

Brada, Josef C., and Earl-Eugen Wadekin, (eds.). *Socialist Agriculture in Transition.* Boulder, Colorado: Westview Press, 1988.

Business International. *Doing Business with Eastern Europe: Poland.* London: 1989.

Clarke, Roger (ed.). *Poland: The Economy in the 1980s.* Harlow, United Kingdom: Longman and St. James Press, 1989.

Engelberg, Stephen. "Poland: Practical Politics Vs. Economic Necessity," *New York Times,* May 17, 1992, Sect. 4, 4.

The Europa World Year Book, 1991, 2. London: Europa, 1991.

The Europa World Year Book, 1992, 2. London: Europa, 1992.

Fallenbuchl, Adam, and Zbigniew M. Fallenbuchl. "Privatization and Marketization in Poland," *Studies in Comparative Communism,* 22, Nos. 3–4, 1990, 285–306.

Fallenbuchl, Zbigniew M. *East-West Technology Transfer: Study of Poland.* Paris: Organisation for Economic Co-operation and Development, 1983.

_____. "Poland: Foreign Trade Developments in 1990," *Radio Free Europe Report on Eastern Europe* [Munich], 1, No. 41, October 12, 1990, 25–28.

_____. "Poland's Economic Crisis," *Problems of Communism,* 31, No. 2, March–April 1982, 1–21.

_____. *The Polish Economy in the Year 2000: Need and Outlook for*

Systematic Reforms, Recovery, and Growth Strategy. Pittsburgh: University of Pittsburgh Center for Russian and East European Studies, 1988.

Gabrisch, Hubert, et al. *Depression and Inflation: Threats to Political and Social Stability.* Vienna: Vienna Institute for Comparative Economic Studies, 1992.

Gomulka, Stanislaw. "Polish Economic Reform, 1990–91: Principles, Policies, and Outcomes," *Cambridge Journal of Economics* [Cambridge, United Kingdom], 16, September 1992, 355–72.

Guinet, Jean. *Industry in Poland: Structural Adjustment Issues and Policy Options.* Paris: Organisation for Economic Co-operation and Development, 1992.

Joseph, Philip (ed.). *The Economies of Eastern Europe and Their Foreign Economic Relations.* Brussels: NATO, 1986.

Kaminski, Bartlomiej. "Systemic Underpinnings of the Transition in Poland: The Shadow of the Round-Table Agreement," *Studies in Comparative Communism,* 24, No. 2, Summer 1991, 173–90.

Karpinski, Andrzej. *Gospodarcza pozicja Polski w świecie.* Warsaw: Ksiązka i Wiedza, 1973.

Kolankiewicz, George, and Paul G. Lewis. *Poland: Politics, Economics, and Society.* (Marxist Regimes Series.) London: Pinter, 1988.

Kowalik, Antoni. "'Bluebirds' or Voluntarily Unemployed?" *Rzeczpospolita* [Warsaw], September 4, 1992. Joint Publications Research Service, *East Europe Report.* (JPRS-EPS-92-146.) October 16, 1992, 29.

Kowalik, Tadeusz. "The Costs of 'Shock Therapy,'" *Dissent,* 38, Fall 1991, 497–504.

Lane, Timothy D. "Transforming Poland's Economy: Early Experience after the 'Big Bang' of 1990," *Finance and Development,* 29, June 1992, 10–13.

Levitas, Anthony. "Rethinking Reform: Lessons From Polish Privatization," *World Policy Journal,* 9, Fall–Winter 1992, 779–94.

Marer, Paul, and Włodzimierz Siwiński (eds.). *Creditworthiness and Reform in Poland.* Bloomington: Indiana University Press, 1988.

Milanovic, Branko. "Poland's Quest for Economic Stabilisation, 1988–91: Interaction of Political Economy and Economics," *Soviet Studies* [Glasgow], 44, No. 3, 1992, 511–32.

_____. *Poverty in Poland, 1978–88.* Washington: World Bank, 1991.

Neuberger, Egon, and Laura Tyson (eds.). *The Impact of International Economic Disturbance on the Soviet Union and Eastern Europe.* New York: Pergamon, 1980.

Paszyński, Marian, (ed.). *The International and the Polish Economy in 1989 and 1990.* Warsaw: Foreign Trade Research Institute, 1990.

_____. *The International and the Polish Economy in 1990 and 1991.* Warsaw: Foreign Trade Research Institute, 1991.

Poland. Główny Urząd Statystyczny. *Rocznik statystyczny, 1989.* Warsaw: 1989.

_____. Główny Urząd Statystyczny. *Rocznik statystyczny, 1990.* Warsaw: 1990.

_____. Główny Urząd Statystyczny. *Rocznik statystyczny, 1991.* Warsaw: 1991.

_____. Główny Urząd Statystyczny. *Rocznik statystyczny handlu zagranicznego, 1989.* Warsaw: 1989.

_____. Główny Urząd Statystyczny. *Rocznik statystyczny handlu zagranicznego, 1990.* Warsaw: 1990.

_____. Główny Urząd Statystyczny. *Rocznik statystyczny handlu zagranicznego, 1991.* Warsaw: 1991.

_____. Główny Urząd Statystyczny. *Rocznik statystyczny przemysłu, 1989.* Warsaw: 1989.

_____. Główny Urząd Statystyczny. *Rocznik statystyczny przemysłu, 1990.* Warsaw: 1990.

_____. Główny Urząd Statystyczny. *Rocznik statystyczny przemysłu, 1991.* Warsaw: 1991.

_____. Główny Urząd Statystyczny. *Struktura gospodarki narodowej.* Warsaw: 1969.

Polanski, Zbigniew. "The Financial System in Post-Communist Countries: The Polish Lessons," *Intereconomics,* 27, November–December 1992, 261–68.

Poznanski, Kazimierz Z. "Privatisation of the Polish Economy: Problems of Transition," *Soviet Studies* [Glasgow], 44, No. 4, 1992, 641–64.

Rosati, Dariusz. *Poland: Economic Reform and Policy in the 1980s.* Warsaw: Foreign Trade Research Institute, 1990.

Sachs, Jeffrey. "Building a Market Economy in Poland," *Scientific American,* 266, March 1992, 34–40.

Slay, Ben. "Poland: The Rise and Fall of the Balcerowicz Plan," *RFE/RL Research Report* [Munich], 1, No. 5, January 31, 1992, 40–47.

The Statesman's Year-Book, 1990–1991. (Ed., John Paxton.) New York: St. Martin's Press, 1990.

United Nations. Industrial Development Organization. *Poland: Managing the Transition to a Market Economy.* Oxford: Blackwell, 1991.

United States. Central Intelligence Agency. *The World Factbook, 1989.* Washington: 1989.

_____. Congress. 95th, 1st Session. Joint Economic Committee. *East European Economies Post-Helsinki.* Washington: GPO, 1977.

_____. Congress. 96th, 2d Session. Joint Economic Committee. *East European Economic Assessment.* Washington: GPO, 1980.

_____. Congress. 99th, 2d Session. Joint Economic Committee. *East European Economics: Slow Growth in the 1980s.* Washington: GPO, 1986.

_____. Congress. 101st, 1st Session. Joint Economic Committee. *Pressures for Reform in the East European Countries.* Washington: GPO, 1989.

Vinton, Louisa. "The Polish Government in Search of a Program," *RFE/RL Research Report* [Munich], 1. No. 13, March 27, 1992, 5-12.

_____. "Polish Government Proposes Pact on State Firms," *RFE/RL Research Report* [Munich], 1, No. 42, October 23, 1992, 10-18.

Winiecki, Jan. "The Polish Transition Programme: Underpinnings, Results, Interpretations," *Soviet Studies* [Glasgow], 44, No. 5, 1992, 809-35.

World Radio TV Handbook, 1992. (Ed., Andrew G. Sennitt.) Hvidovre, Denmark: Billboard, 1992.

(Various editions of the following periodicals were also used in the preparation of this chapter: Foreign Broadcast Information Service, *Daily Report: East Europe* and Joint Publications Research Service, *JPRS Report: East Europe.*)

Chapter 4

Abet, Elie. *The Shattered Bloc: Behind the Upheaval in Eastern Europe.* Boston: Houghton Mifflin, 1990.

Ash, Timothy Garton. *The Magic Lantern: The Revolution of '89 Witnessed in Warsaw, Budapest, Berlin, and Prague.* New York: Random House, 1990.

_____. "Poland after Solidarity," *New York Review of Books,* 38, No. 12, June 13, 1991, 46-58.

_____. *The Uses of Adversity: Essays on the Fate of Central Europe.* New York: Random House, 1989.

Berglund, Sten, and Jan Ake Dellenbrandt (eds.). *The New Democracies in Eastern Europe: Party Systems and Political Cleavages.* Brookfield, Vermont: E. Elgar, 1991.

Blazyca, George, and Ryszard Rapacki (eds.). *Poland into the 1990s: Economy and Society in Transition.* New York: St. Martin's Press, 1991.

Brown, J.F. "Relief Without Relaxation: Eastern Europe Ponders the CIS," *RFE/RL Research Report* [Munich], 1, No. 8, February 21, 1992, 17-20.

Brzezinski, Mark F. "Constitutional Heritage and Renewal: The Case of Poland," *Virginia Law Review,* 77, No. 1, February 1991, 49-112.

Bugajski, Janusz, and Maxine Pollack. *East European Fault Lines: Dissent, Opposition, and Social Activism.* Boulder, Colorado: Westview Press, 1989.

Burant, Stephen R. "International Relations in a Regional Context: Poland and Its Eastern Neighbors—Lithuania, Belarus, Ukraine," *Europe-Asia Studies* [Glasgow], 45, No. 3, 1993, 395-418.

————. "Polish-Lithuanian Relations: Past, Present, and Future." *Problems of Communism,* 40, No. 3, May-June 1991, 67-84.

Clarke, Douglas L. "Arms Control and Security: After the Warsaw Pact," *RFE/RL Research Report* [Munich], 1, No. 1, January 3, 1992, 105-8.

————. "Central Europe: Military Cooperation in the Triangle," *RFE/RL Research Report* [Munich], 1, No. 2, January 10, 1992, 42-45.

Connor, Walter (ed.). *The Polish Road from Socialism: The Economics, Sociology, and Politics of Transition.* Armonk, New York: Sharpe, 1992.

"Constitution Watch," *East European Constitutional Review,* 1, No. 1, Spring 1992, 2-11.

Craig, Mary. *Lech Wałęsa and His Poland.* New York: Continuum, 1987.

Curry, Jane Leftwich. *Poland's Journalists: Professionalism and Politics.* Cambridge: Cambridge University Press, 1990.

Dahrendorf, Ralf. *Reflections on the Revolution in Europe: In a Letter Intended to Have Been Sent to a Gentleman in Warsaw.* New York: Times Books, 1990.

Dawisha, Karen. *Eastern Europe, Gorbachev, and Reform: The Great Challenge.* New York: Cambridge University Press, 1990.

de Weydenthal, Jan B. "The Cracow Summit," *Radio Free Europe Report on Eastern Europe* [Munich], 1, No. 43, October 25, 1991, 27-29.

————. "Czechoslovakia, Hungary, and Poland Gain Associate Membership in the EC," *RFE/RL Research Report* [Munich], 1, No. 6, February 7, 1992, 24-26.

————. "Finding a Place in Europe," *Radio Free Europe Report on Eastern Europe* [Munich], 1, No. 52, December 28, 1990, 21-24.

————. "The First Hundred Days of Walesa's Presidency," *Radio*

Free Europe Report on Eastern Europe [Munich], 2, No. 14, April 5, 1991, 9–11.

────── . "German Plan for Border Region Stirs Interest in Poland," *RFE/RL Research Report* [Munich], 1, No. 7, February 14, 1992, 39–42.

────── . "Poland and the Soviet Alliance System," *Radio Free Europe Report on Eastern Europe* [Munich], 1, No. 26, June 29, 1990, 30–32.

────── . *The Polish Drama, 1980–1982.* Lexington: Lexington Books, 1983.

────── . "Political Problems Affect Security Work in Poland," *RFE/RL Research Report* [Munich], 1, No. 16, April 17, 1992, 39–42.

────── . "The Presidential Contest Heats Up," *Radio Free Europe Report on Eastern Europe* [Munich], 1, No. 45, November 9, 1990, 15–17.

────── . "The Race for the Presidency," *Radio Free Europe Report on Eastern Europe* [Munich], 1, No. 42, October 19, 1990, 28–30.

────── . "Rapprochement with the West Continues," *Radio Free Europe Report on Eastern Europe* [Munich], 1, Nos. 51–52, December 20, 1991, 22–26.

────── . "Solidarity's Tenth Anniversary," *Radio Free Europe Report on Eastern Europe* [Munich], 1, No. 35, August 31, 1990, 22–24.

────── . "The Start of the Presidential Campaign?" *Radio Free Europe Report on Eastern Europe* [Munich], 1, No. 37, September 14, 1990, 26–28.

The Europa World Year Book, 1992, 2. London: Europa, 1992.

Fehér, Ferenc, and Andrew Arato. *Crisis and Reform in Eastern Europe.* New Brunswick, New Jersey: Transaction, 1991.

Frankland, Mark. *The Patriots' Revolution: How Eastern Europe Toppled Communism and Won Its Freedom.* Chicago: Dee, 1992.

Friszke, Andrzej. "The Polish Political Scene, 1989," *East European Politics and Societies,* 4, No. 2, Spring 1990, 305–41.

Gat, Charles. *The Bloc That Failed: Soviet-East European Relations in Transition.* Bloomington: Indiana University Press, 1990.

Grocholska, Janina, and Andrzej Wielgasiewicz (eds.). *Informator Polska '91.* Warsaw: Polska Agencja Prasowa, 1990.

Grzybowski, Marian. "The Transition of the Polish Party System." Pages 40–70 in Sten Berglund and Jan Ake Dellenbrant (eds.), *The New Democracies in Eastern Europe: Party Systems and Political Cleavages.* Brookfield, Vermont: Elgar, 1991.

Herman, Andrzej. "Germany and European Integration: A Polish View." Pages 171–79 in J.J. Lee and Walter Korter (eds.), *Europe in Transition: Political, Economic, and Security Prospects for the*

1990s. Austin: Lyndon B. Johnson School of Public Affairs, 1991.

Herman, Edward S., and Noam Chomsky. *Manufacturing Consent: The Political Economy of the Mass Media.* New York: Pantheon Books, 1988.

Heyns, Barbara, and Ireneusz Bialecki. "Solidarność: Reluctant Vanguard or Makeshift Coalition?" *American Political Science Review,* 85, No. 2, June 1991, 351-70.

Husarska, Anna. "'Mein Kampf' and the Plays of Szekspir: Adventures in the Polish Book Trade," *New York Times Book Review,* July 12, 1992, 14, 16-17.

Informator Polska '91. Warsaw: Polska Agencja Prasowa, 1991.

Institute for East-West Security Studies. *Eastern Europe and Democracy: The Case of Poland.* New York: 1990.

Kaminski, Bartlomiej. "Systemic Underpinnings of the Transition in Poland: The Shadow of the Round-Table Agreement," *Studies in Comparative Communism,* 24, No. 2, Summer 1991, 173-90.

Kanet, Roger E., and Brian V. Souders. "Poland and the Soviet Union." Pages 125-45 in Richard F. Staar (ed.), *East-Central Europe and the USSR.* New York: St. Martin's Press, 1991.

Kim, Julie, and Francis Miko. "Poland, Czechoslovakia, and Hungary: Recent Developments." (Library of Congress, Congressional Research Service, Issue Brief No. IB92051.) Washington: May 28, 1992.

Klis, Józef. "What Political System for the Third Republic of Poland?" *Poland Today* [Warsaw], 1, No. 1, January 1991, 4-5.

Kloc, Kazimierz. "Poland's Political System: Change and Future Scenarios." Pages 11-19 in George Blazyca and Ryszard Rapacki (eds.), *Poland into the 1990s.* New York: St. Martin's Press, 1991.

Kolankiewicz, George, and Paul G. Lewis. *Poland: Politics, Economics, and Society.* (Marxist Regimes Series.) London: Pinter, 1988.

Koralewicz, Jadwiga, and Ireneusz Bialecki (eds.). *Crisis and Transition: Polish Society in the 1980s.* New York: St. Martin's Press, 1987.

Laba, Roman. *The Roots of Solidarity: A Political Sociology of Poland's Working-Class Democratization.* Princeton: Princeton University Press, 1991.

Lee, J.J., and Walter Korter (eds.). *Europe in Transition: Political, Economic, and Security Prospects for the 1990s.* Austin: Lyndon B. Johnson School of Public Affairs, 1991.

Letowska, Ewa. "The Polish Ombudsman," *International and Comparative Law Quarterly* [London], 39, No. 2, June 1990, 206-17.

Lewis, Paul G. "The Long Goodbye: Party Rule and Political

Change in Poland since Martial Law," *Journal of Communist Studies* [London], 6, No. 1, March, 1990, 24-48.

Ludwikowski, Rett R., and Kenneth W. Thompson (eds.). *Constitutionalism and Human Rights: America, Poland, and France—A Bicentennial Colloquium at the Miller Center.* Lanham, Maryland: University Press of America, 1991.

Mason, David S. "Glasnost, Perestroika, and Eastern Europe," *International Affairs* [London], 64, No. 3, Summer 1998, 431-48.

_____. "Solidarity as a New Social Movement," *Political Science Quarterly*, 104, No. 2, Spring 1989, 40-58.

McQuaid, David. "The Parliamentary Elections: A Postmortem," *Radio Free Europe Report on Eastern Europe* [Munich], 2, No. 45, November 8, 1991, 15-21.

_____. "The War over the Election Law," *Radio Free Europe Report on Eastern Europe* [Munich], 2, No. 31, August 2, 1991, 11-28.

Michta, Andrew A. *East Central Europe after the Warsaw Pact: Security Dilemmas in the 1990s.* (Contributions in Political Science Series, No. 296.) New York: Greenwood Press, 1992.

Millard, Frances. "Emergent Pluralism in Poland: A Short Guide," *Journal of Communist Studies* [London], 6, No. 1, March 1990, 99-109.

Miller, Robert C. "The Polish Book Trade: Spring 1992," *Library Acquisitions, Practice and Theory*, 17, 1993, 439-47.

Mokrzycki, Edmund. "The Legacy of Real Socialism and Western Democracy," *Studies in Comparative Communism*, 24, No. 2, June 1991, 211-17.

Muravchik, Joshua. "Eastern Europe's 'Terrible Twos,'" *Journal of Democracy*, 3, No. 1, January 1992, 65-72.

Oleszek, Walter J. "Parliamentary Developments in Poland," *CRS Review*, 12, No. 8, August 1991, 31-33.

Rachwald, Arthur R. *In Search of Poland: The Superpowers' Response to Solidarity, 1980-1989.* Stanford, California: Hoover Institution Press, 1990.

_____. "Poland." Pages 302-24 in Richard F. Staar (ed.), *Yearbook on International Communist Affairs 1986: Parties and Revolutionary Movements.* Stanford, California: Hoover Institution Press, 1986.

_____. "Poland." Pages 310-30 in Richard F. Staar (ed.), *Yearbook on International Communist Affairs 1987: Parties and Revolutionary Movements.* Stanford, California: Hoover Institution Press, 1987.

_____. "Poland." Pages 285-304 in Richard F. Staar (ed.), *Yearbook on International Communist Affairs 1988: Parties and Revolutionary Movements.* Stanford, California: Hoover Institution Press, 1988.

_____. "Poland." Pages 335–47 in Richard F. Staar (ed.), *Yearbook on International Communist Affairs 1989: Parties and Revolutionary Movements*. Stanford, California: Hoover Institution Press, 1989.

_____. "Poland." Pages 358–84 in Richard F. Staar (ed.), *Yearbook on International Communist Affairs 1990: Parties and Revolutionary Movements*. Stanford, California: Hoover Institution Press, 1990.

_____. "Poland." Pages 316–32 in Richard F. Staar (ed.), *Yearbook on International Communist Affairs 1991: Parties and Revoluntary Movements*. Stanford, California: Hoover Institution Press, 1991.

Rapaczynski, Andrzej. "Constitutional Politics in Poland: A Report on the Constitutional Committee of the Polish Parliament," *University of Chicago Law Review*, 58, No. 2, Spring 1991, 595–631.

Roskin, Michael G. *The Rebirth of East Europe*. Englewood Cliffs, New Jersey: Prentice Hall, 1991.

Sabbat-Swidlicka, Anna. "Intellectual Piracy in Poland," *RFE/RL Research Report* [Munich], 1, No. 16, April 17, 1992, 57–60.

_____. "Local Self-Government: The Legal Framework," *Radio Free Europe Report on Eastern Europe* [Munich], 1, No. 18, May 4, 1990, 24–27.

_____. "The Media: Poland," *RFE/RL Research Report* [Munich], 1, No. 39, October 2, 1992, 47–52.

_____. "Poland: Weak Government, Fractious Sejm, Isolated President," *RFE/RL Research Report* [Munich], 1, No. 15, April 10, 1992, 1–7.

_____. "Poland Peasant Party Withdraws Support for Mazowiecki's Government," *Radio Free Europe Report on Eastern Europe* [Munich], 1, No. 41, October 12, 1990, 22–25.

_____. "The Polish Local Election Results," *Radio Free Europe Report on Eastern Europe* [Munich], 1, No. 26, June 29, 1990, 35–38.

_____. "Political Turmoil Overshadows Solidarity's Congress," *RFE/RL Research Report* [Munich], 1, No. 28, July 10, 1992, 16–19.

_____. "The Signing of the Polish-German Border Treaty," *Radio Free Europe Report on Eastern Europe* [Munich], 1, No. 49, December 7, 1990, 16–19.

_____. "Toward an Independent Judiciary," *Radio Free Europe Report on Eastern Europe* [Munich], 1, No. 37, September 14, 1990, 28–34.

_____. "Toward the Rule of Law: Poland," *RFE/RL Research Report* [Munich], 1, No. 27, July 3, 1992, 25–33.

Sadykiewicz, Michael, and Douglas L. Clarke. "The New Polish

Defense Doctrine: A Further Step Toward Sovereignty," *Radio Free Europe Report on Eastern Europe* [Munich], 1, No. 18, May 4, 1990, 20–23.

Sadykiewicz, Michael, and Louisa Vinton. "Politicization and the Polish Military," *Radio Free Europe Report on Eastern Europe* [Munich], 1, No. 13, March 30, 1990, 29–34.

Siekierski, Maciej, and Joseph D. Dwyer. "Polish Uncensored Publications since 1976: Holdings at the Hoover Institution." Stanford, California: Hoover Institution Press, March 11, 1988.

Slay, Ben (ed.). "Roundtable on Systemic Transformation," *RFE/RL Research Report* [Munich], 1, No. 31, July 31, 1992, 41–48.

Smolar, Aleksander. "The Polish Opposition." Pages 175–252 in Ferenc Fehér and Andrew Arato (eds.), *Crisis and Reform in Eastern Europe*. New Brunswick, New Jersey: Transaction, 1991.

Spero, Joshua B. "Central European Security," *Problems of Communism*, 11, No. 6, November–December, 1991, 141–51.

Staar, Richard F. *Communist Regimes in Eastern Europe*. (5th ed.) Stanford, California: Hoover Institution Press, 1988.

Staar, Richard F. (ed.). *East-Central Europe and the USSR*. New York: St. Martin's Press, 1991.

_____. *United States-East European Relations in the 1990s*. New York: Crane, Russak, 1989.

Staniszkis, Jadwiga. *The Dynamics of the Breakthrough in Eastern Europe: The Polish Experience*. Berkeley: University of California Press, 1991.

Thompson, Kenneth W. *Poland in a World in Change: Constitutions, Presidents, and Politics*. Lanham, Maryland: University Press of America, 1992.

Tökés, Rudolf L. "From Visegrád to Kraków: Cooperation, Competition, and Coexistence in Central Europe," *Problems of Communism*, 40, No. 6, November–December 1991, 100–14.

Valkenier, Elizabeth Kridl. "Glasnost' and Filling in the 'Blank Spots' in the History of Polish-Soviet Relations, 1987–1990," *The Polish Review*, 36, No. 3, 1991, 247–68.

Vinton, Louisa. "After the Elections: A 'Presidential Government'?" *Radio Free Europe Report on Eastern Europe* [Munich], 2, No. 45, November 8, 1991, 22–28.

_____. "Five-party Coalition Gains Strength, Walesa Proposes 'Little Constitution,' " *Radio Free Europe Report on Eastern Europe* [Munich], 2, No. 49, December 6, 1991, 5–12.

_____. "From the Margins to the Mainstream: The Confederation for an Independent Poland," *Radio Free Europe Report on Eastern Europe* [Munich], 2, No. 46, November 15, 1991, 20–24.

_____. "Government Wins Contest of Wills with Parliament," *Radio Free Europe Report on Eastern Europe* [Munich], 2, No. 37, September 13, 1991, 12–17.

_____. "Impasse Reached in Talks on New Government," *Radio Free Europe Report on Eastern Europe* [Munich], 2, No. 48, November 29, 1991, 19–25.

_____. "A New Team for Walesa," *Radio Free Europe Report on Eastern Europe* [Munich], 1, No. 41, October 12, 1990, 19–22.

_____. "Olszewski's Ouster Leaves Poland Polarized," *RFE/RL Research Report* [Munich], 1, No. 25, June 19, 1992, 1–10.

_____. "Poland: Government Crisis Ends, Budget Crisis Begins," *RFE/RL Research Report* [Munich], 1, No. 3, January 17, 1992, 14–21.

_____. "Poland: The Anguish of Transition," *RFE/RL Research Report* [Munich], 1, No. 1, January 3, 1992, 91–95.

_____. "Poland's Governing Coalition: Will the Truce Hold?" *RFE/RL Research Report* [Munich], 1, No. 31, July 31, 1992, 34–40.

_____. "Poland's 'Little Constitution' Clarifies Walesa's Powers," *RFE/RL Research Report* [Munich], 1, No. 35, September 4, 1992, 19–26.

_____. "Poland's New Election Law: Fewer Parties, Same Impasse?" *RFE/RL Research Report* [Munich], 2, No. 28, July 9, 1993, 7–17.

_____. "The Polish Government in Search of a Program," *RFE/RL Research Report* [Munich], 1, No. 13, March 27, 1992, 5–12.

_____. "Political Forces Grapple with the Tyminski Challenge," *Radio Free Europe Report on Eastern Europe* [Munich], 1, No. 51, December 21, 1990, 14–19.

_____. "Political Parties and Coalitions in the Local Government Elections," *Radio Free Europe Report on Eastern Europe* [Munich], 1, No. 26, June 29, 1990, 26–30.

_____. "The Presidential Elections: Walesa and Tyminski into the Second Round," *Radio Free Europe Report on Eastern Europe* [Munich], 1, No. 51, December 21, 1990, 10–13.

_____. "Sejm Approves New Law on Radio and Television," *RFE/RL Research Report* [Munich], 1, No. 43, October 30, 1992, 32–34.

_____. "Solidarity's Rival Offspring: Center Alliance and Democratic Action," *Radio Free Europe Report on Eastern Europe* [Munich], 1, No. 38, September 21, 1990, 15–25.

_____. "Walesa and the Elections," *Radio Free Europe Report on Eastern Europe* [Munich], 2, No. 44, November 1, 1991, 9–13.

————. "Walesa Elected President," *Radio Free Europe Report on Eastern Europe* [Munich], 1, No. 51, December 21, 1990, 19–21.

Walicki, Andrzej. "Notes on Jaruzelski's Poland." Pages 335–91 in Ferenc Fehér and Andrew Arato (eds.), *Crisis and Reform in Eastern Europe*. New Brunswick, New Jersey: Transaction, 1991.

Weschler, Lawrence. *Solidarity: Poland in the Season of Its Passion*. New York: Simon and Schuster, 1982.

White, Stephen (ed.). *Handbook of Reconstruction in Eastern Europe and the Soviet Union*. Harlow, United Kingdom: Longman, 1991.

White, Stephen, and John Gardner, George Schöpflin, and Tony Saich. *Communist and Postcommunist Political Systems: An Introduction*. New York: St. Martin's Press, 1990.

Wnuk-Lipiński, Edmund. "Polish Society after the Communist Experiment." Pages 4–10 in George Blazyca and Ryszard Rapacki (eds.), *Poland into the 1990s: Economy and Society in Transition*. New York: St. Martin's Press, 1991.

The World Bank. *Poland: Decentralization and Reform of the State*. (World Bank Country Studies.) Washington: 1992.

Yearbook on International Communist Affairs 1986: Parties and Revolutionary Movements. (Ed., Richard F. Staar.) Stanford, California: Hoover Institution Press, 1986.

Yearbook on International Communist Affairs 1987: Parties and Revolutionary Movements. (Ed., Richard F. Staar.) Stanford, California: Hoover Institution Press, 1987.

Yearbook on International Communist Affairs 1988: Parties and Revolutionary Movements. (Ed., Richard F. Staar.) Stanford, California: Hoover Institution Press, 1988.

Yearbook on International Communist Affairs 1989: Parties and Revolutionary Movements. (Ed., Richard F. Staar.) Stanford, California: Hoover Institution Press, 1989.

Yearbook on International Communist Affairs 1990: Parties and Revolutionary Movements. (Ed., Richard F. Staar.) Stanford, California: Hoover Institution Press, 1990.

Zmijewski, Norbert. "Vicissitudes of Political Realism in Poland: Tygodnik Powszechny and Znak," *Soviet Studies* [Abingdon, United Kingdom], 43, No. 1, 1991, 83–106.

Zubek, Vojtek. "Poland's Party Self-Destructs," *Orbis*, 34, No. 2, Spring 1990, 179–93.

————. "The Threshold of Poland's Transition: 1989 Electoral Campaign as the Last Act of a United Solidarity," *Studies in Comparative Communism*, 24, No. 12, December 1991, 355–76.

————. "Walesa's Leadership and Poland's Transition," *Problems of Communism*, 40, No. 1, January–April 1991, 69–83.

Zuzowski, Robert. "KOR after KOR: The Intelligentsia and

Dissent in Poland, 1981–1987," *Polish Review,* 33, No. 2, 1988, 167–89.

(Various editions of the following periodicals were also used in the preparation of this chapter: Foreign Broadcast Research Service, *Daily Report: East Europe* and Joint Publications Research Service, *JPRS Report: East Europe.*)

Chapter 5

Butowski, Piotr. "The Jane's Interview," *Jane's Defence Weekly* [Coulsdon, United Kingdom], 19, No. 5, January 30, 1993, 32.

Crane, Keith. *The Economic Implications of Reductions in Military Budgets and Force Levels in Eastern Europe.* (The Rand Publication Series—A Rand Note.) Santa Monica, California: Rand, 1991.

Davies, Norman. *God's Playground: A History of Poland,* 1 and 2. New York: Columbia University Press, 1982.

de Weydenthal, Jan B. "Building a National Security System," *Radio Free Europe Report on Eastern Europe* [Munich], 2, No. 24, June 14, 1991, 12–16.

_____. "Poland Prepares a New Military Doctrine," *RFE/RL Research Report* [Munich], 1, No. 33, August 21, 1992, 45–48.

Dziewanowski, M.K. *Poland in the Twentieth Century.* New York: Columbia University Press, 1977.

Fajfer, Luba. "The Polish Military and the Crisis of 1970," *Communist and Post-Communist Studies* [Oxford], 26, no. 2, June 1993, 205–25.

Green, John L. "The Baltic: A Sea in Transition." (Ph.D. dissertation.) Monterey, California: Naval Postgraduate School, 1991.

Hitchens, Theresa. "Ex-Warsaw Pact Nations Gear Up to Replace Arms," *Defense News,* 8, No. 18, May 10–16, 1993, 1, 21.

_____. "Poles, French Near Production Deal," *Defense News,* 8, No. 18, May 10–16, 1993, 1.

Institute for Foreign Policy Analysis. *Poland.* Cambridge, Massachusetts: 1993.

Johnson, A. Ross. *East European Military Establishments: The Warsaw Pact Northern Tier.* New York: Crane, Russak, 1982.

_____. *Poland in Crisis.* Santa Monica, California: Rand, 1982.

Koziej, Stanislaw. *Polish Defense Policy.* Ft. Leavenworth, Kansas: Foreign Military Studies Office, 1992.

_____. *Polish Ground Forces Operational Art: At the Threshold of the*

1990s. Ft. Leavenworth, Kansas: Foreign Military Studies Office; Sandhurst, United Kingdom: Soviet Studies Research Centre, 1992.

Lee, Rensselaer W., III, and Scott B. MacDonald. "Drugs in the East," *Foreign Policy*, 72, No. 90, Spring 1993, 89–107.

Los, Maria. "Law and Order in Contemporary Poland," *Canadian Slavonic Papers* [Edmonton], 25, September 1983, 392–410.

Madejski, Andrzej. *Assessment and Prognosis of Threats to the Polish Republic to 2010–2015*. Ft. Leavenworth, Kansas: Foreign Military Studies Office; Sandhurst, United Kingdom: Soviet Studies Research Centre, 1992.

Menkes, Jerzy. "The Changing Role of the Military in Democratic Societies: A Polish Perspective," *Arms Control* [London], 13, No. 2, September 1992, 222–33.

Michta, Andrew A. *East Central Europe after the Warsaw Pact: Security Dilemmas in the 1990s*. (Contributions in Political Science Series, No. 296.) New York: Greenwood Press, 1992.

———. *Red Eagle: The Army in Polish Politics, 1944–1988*. Stanford, California: Hoover Institution Press, 1990.

The Military Balance, 1981–1982. London: International Institute for Strategic Studies, 1981.

The Military Balance, 1988–1989. London: International Institute for Strategic Studies, 1988.

The Military Balance, 1991–1992. London: International Institute for Strategic Studies, 1991.

The Military Balance, 1992–1993. London: International Institute for Strategic Studies, 1992.

Nozko, Kazimierz. *Directions for Improving the Defense System of the Polish Republic*. Ft. Leavenworth, Kansas: Foreign Military Studies Office; Sandhurst, United Kingdom: Soviet Studies Research Centre, 1991.

Plugge, Matthias. "In Transition: The Polish Armed Forces," *International Defense Review*, 23, No. 2, February 1990, 133–35.

Podbielski, Peter J. *Whence Security? Polish Defence and Security after the Warsaw Pact*. Ft. Leavenworth, Kansas: Foreign Military Studies Office; Sandhurst, United Kingdom: Soviet Studies Research Centre, 1991.

Poland. Komitet Obrony Kraju. *Tenets of the Polish Security Policy and Security Policy and Defense Strategy of the Republic of Poland*. (Unpublished policy document.) 1992.

Rozenbaum, Wlodzimierz. "The Anti-Zionist Campaign in Poland, June–December 1967," *Canadian Slavonic Papers* [Edmonton], 20, June 1978, 218–36.

Sabbat-Swidlicka, Anna. "Changes in the Military Prosecution

Authorities," *Radio Free Europe Report on Eastern Europe* [Munich], 2, No. 2, January 11, 1991, 22-24.

_____. "Poland's Prison Chaplains," *RFE/RL Research Report* [Munich], 1, No. 46, November 20, 1992, 60-63.

_____. "Polish Prison Reform Focuses on Social Reintegration," *RFE/RL Research Report* [Munich], 1, No. 46, November 20, 1992, 53-59.

Sadykiewicz, Michael, and Douglas L. Clarke. "The New Polish Defense Doctrine: A Further Step Toward Sovereignty," *Radio Free Europe Report on Eastern Europe* [Munich], 1, No. 18, May 4, 1991, 20-23.

Sanford, George. *Military Rule in Poland: The Rebuilding of Communist Power, 1981-1983.* New York: St. Martin's Press, 1986.

Simon, Jeffrey (ed.). *European Security Policy after the Revolutions of 1989.* Washington: National Defense University Press, 1991.

Spero, Joshua B. "The Budapest-Prague-Warsaw Triangle: Central European Security after the Visegrad Summit," *European Security* [London], 1, No. 1, Spring 1992, 58-83.

Starr, Barbara. "Winners and Losers in the NATO CFE Share Out," *Jane's Defence Weekly* [Coulsdon, United Kingdom], 16, No. 1, July 6, 191, 18-19.

Szayna, Thomas S. *The Military in a Postcommunist Poland.* (The Rand Publication Series—A Rand Note.) Santa Monica, California: Rand, 1991.

United States. Department of Defense. *Soviet Military Power, 1990.* Washington: GPO, 1990.

Vermaat, J.A. Emerson. "The Polish Secret Police and the Popieluszko Case," *Journal of Church and State,* 28, Spring 1986, 249-67.

Vinton, Louisa. "Polish Internal Affairs Ministry Adapts to Changing Political System," *Radio Free Europe Report on Eastern Europe* [Munich], 1, No. 2, January 12, 1990, 24-29.

_____. "Sejm Opens Debate on Future of Police and Security Service," *Radio Free Europe Report on Eastern Europe* [Munich], 1, No. 8, February 23, 1990, 12-15.

Wisniewski, Grzegorz Kzysztof. *European Institutions and the Dilemmas of Polish Security.* Ft. Leavenworth, Kansas: Foreign Military Studies Office; Sandhurst, United Kingdom: Soviet Studies Research Centre, 1991.

_____. *Polish Security Doctrine.* Ft. Leavenworth, Kansas: Foreign Military Studies Office; Sandhurst, United Kingdom: Soviet Studies Research Centre, 1992.

Wohlfeld, Monika J. "Poland's Draft Defense Doctrine." (Research paper for NATO-OTAN Defense Support Division.) Brussels, November 1992.

(Various editions of the following periodicals were also used in the preparation of this chapter: Foreign Broadcast Information Service, *Daily Report: East Europe* and Joint Publications Research Service, *JPRS Report: East Europe.*)

Glossary

Bolsheviks—Members of the radical political faction that, under the leadership of Vladimir I. Lenin, staged the Bolshevik Revolution and in 1918 formed the Russian Communist Party (Bolshevik), precursor of the Communist Party of the Soviet Union (CPSU).

Byzantine—Medieval Christian civilization that combined European and Asian cultures on an ancient Greco-Roman foundation. Centered at Byzantium (known as Constantinople 330–1930, and later called Istanbul), the Byzantine Empire occupied western Turkey and the Balkans and, as the center of Orthodox Christianity, exerted strong influence on many of the Slavic peoples of Eastern Europe.

CoCom (Coordinating Committee for Multilateral Export Controls)—Loose arrangement of Western governments formed in 1949 to prevent the transfer of military-useful (dual-use) technology from the West to the Soviet Union and Eastern Europe; the group (whose membership was almost identical to that of the North Atlantic Treaty Organization, *q.v.*) operated on the basis of informal agreements covering items having military or nuclear applications.

Comecon (Council for Mutual Economic Assistance)—A multilateral economic alliance headquartered in Moscow; it existed from 1949–91. Members in 1990 included Bulgaria, Cuba, Czechoslovakia, the German Democratic Republic (East Germany), Hungary, Mongolia, Poland, Romania, the Soviet Union, and Vietnam. Also referred to as CMEA and CEMA.

Commonwealth of Independent States (CIS)—Official designation of the former republics that remained loosely federated in economic and security matters of common concern, after the Soviet Union disbanded as a unified state in 1991. Members in 1993 were Armenia, Azerbaijan, Belarus, Kazakhstan, Kyrgyzstan, Moldova, Russia, Tajikistan, Turkmenistan, Ukraine, and Uzbekistan.

Conference on Security and Cooperation in Europe (CSCE)—Originating at the meeting that produced the Helsinki Accords (*q.v.*) in 1975, a grouping of all European nations (the lone exception, Albania, joined in 1991) that subsequently sponsored joint sessions and consultations on political issues vital to European security.

Conventional Forces in Europe (CFE) Treaty—An agreement signed in 1990 by the members of the Warsaw Pact (*q.v.*) and the North Atlantic Treaty Organization (*q.v.*) to establish parity in conventional weapons between the two organizations from the Atlantic to the Urals. Included a strict system of inspections and information exchange.

Czech and Slovak Federative Republic (CSFR)—Official name of the former Czechoslovakia, adopted in December 1990 to recognize the two ethnic components of that country. (Czechoslovakia was still used as the short form designation after that date.) In January 1993, divided into two independent states, the Czech Republic and Slovakia, which retained some economic and security ties.

Enlightenment—Philosophical and spiritual movement in Europe in the seventeenth and eighteenth centuries, concerned with the relationship of God, nature, reason, and man, often challenging the tenets of conventional Christianity.

European Bank for Reconstruction and Development (EBRD)—A bank founded under sponsorship of the European Community (*q.v.*) in 1990, to provide loans to East European countries (Bulgaria, the Czech and Slovak Federative Republic, Hungary, Poland, Romania, the Soviet Union, and Yugoslavia) to establish independent, market-driven economies and democratic political institutions. Some fifty-eight countries were shareholders in 1993.

European Community (EC)—A group of primarily economic communities of Western European countries, including the European Atomic Energy Community (Euratom or EAEC) and the European Coal and Steel Community (ECSC). Executive power rests with the European Commission, which implements and defends the community treaties in the interests of the EC as a whole. Members in 1993 were Belgium, Britain, Denmark, France, Germany, Greece, Ireland, Italy, Luxembourg, the Netherlands, Portugal, and Spain. Name changed to European Union (EU), December 1993.

Gdańsk Agreement—The first of several major concessions made by the Polish communist government in late 1980 to the rising Solidarity movement. The agreement granted public expression to many groups in Polish society hitherto restricted, promised new economic concessions, removed discredited communist officials, and recognized workers' right to establish free trade unions.

glasnost'—Russian term, literally meaning "openness," applied in the Soviet Union beginning in the mid-1980s to official permission for public discussion of issues and public access to information. Identified with the tenure of Mikhail S. Gorbachev as leader of the Soviet Union.

gross domestic product (GDP)—The total value of goods and services produced exclusively within a nation's domestic economy, in contrast to gross national product (*q.v.*), usually computed over one year.

gross national product (GNP)—The total value of goods and services produced within a country's borders and the income received from abroad by residents, minus payments remitted abroad by nonresidents. Normally computed over one year.

Habsburg Empire—Also known as the House of Austria, one of the principal European dynasties between the fifteenth and twentieth centuries. Controlled a variety of separate monarchies, reaching its most powerful stage in the sixteenth century under Emperor Charles V of the Holy Roman Empire (*q.v.*). After 1867 what remained of the empire was commonly known as Austria-Hungary.

Helsinki Accords—Signed in 1975 by all countries of Europe except Albania (which signed in 1991), plus Canada and the United States, at the initial Conference on Security and Cooperation in Europe (*q.v.*). The pact outlined general principles of international behavior and security and addressed some economic, environmental, and humanitarian issues.

Holy Roman Empire—Enduring from A.D. 800 to 1806, official successor under papal authority to the Roman Empire. The title *king of the Romans,* first given to Charlemagne, was borne by a long succession of German kings. Centered in Germany, the empire at its peak (thirteenth century to sixteenth century) extended from the Low Countries to Czechoslovakia and southward into Italy. Weakened by struggles with the Roman Catholic Church and the Reformation, then scattered by the results of the Thirty Years' War (*q.v.*), 1648.

International Monetary Fund (IMF)—Established with the World Bank (*q.v.*) in 1945, a specialized agency affiliated with the United Nations and responsible for stabilizing international exchange rates and payments. Its main business is providing loans to its members when they experience balance of payments difficulties.

Jacobinism—Political philosophy of the leaders of the French revolutionary government. After reaching power in the revolutionary dictatorship of 1793, the Jacobins set about safeguarding the values of the revolution and public virtue by a Reign of Terror against opposing views.

London Club—A group of 500 major international commercial banks lending money under auspices of the International Monetary Fund (*q.v.*) to Poland for economic development, under conditions of continued economic reform.

net material product (NMP)—In countries having centrally planned economies, the official measure of the value of goods and services produced within the country. Roughly equivalent to the Western gross national product (*q.v.*), NMP is based on constant prices and does not account for depreciation.

North Atlantic Treaty Organization (NATO)—An alliance founded in 1949 by the United States, Canada, and their postwar European allies to oppose Soviet military presence in Europe. Until the dissolution of the Warsaw Pact (*q.v.*) in 1991, NATO was the primary collective defense agreement of the Western powers. Its military and administrative structure remained intact after the threat of Soviet expansionism had subsided.

Organisation for Economic Co-operation and Development (OECD)—Founded in 1961 to replace the all-European Organisation for European Economic Cooperation, assists member governments to form and coordinate economic and social aid policies in developing countries. In 1993, twenty-four nations had full membership, including Australia, Canada, New Zealand, and the United States.

Ottoman Empire—A Muslim empire that controlled southeastern Europe, the Middle East, and most of North Africa between the sixteenth and eighteenth centuries, and lesser territories from 1300 until 1913. Ottoman occupation was a major influence on all civilizations of southeastern Europe and caused ethnic animosities that remained after the disintegration of the empire.

Paris Club—A group of seventeen Western countries lending money under auspices of the International Monetary Fund (*q.v.*) to Poland for economic development, under conditions of continued economic reform.

perestroika—Russian word meaning "restructuring," applied in the late 1980s to an official Soviet program of revitalization of the communist party, economy, and society, by adjusting economic, social, and political mechanisms. Identified with the tenure of Mikhail S. Gorbachev as leader of the Soviet Union (1985–1991).

Prague Spring—Period of attempts to institute political and economic reforms in Czechoslovakia, led by communist party First Secretary Alexander Dubček, in 1968. The Soviet Union and four Warsaw Pact (*q.v.*) allies responded by invading Czecho-slovakia and forcing Dubček out of power.

Reformation—Sixteenth-century movement against dogma of the Roman Catholic Church, in favor of grace through faith, the authority of the Scriptures, and the direct relationship of believers with God. Met with resounding force by the established church, the Reformation influenced Christian practice to varying degrees in all European countries, resulting in a schism between the Roman Catholic church and Protestant reformers.

Teutonic Knights—In full, Knights of the Teutonic Order, an organization of German crusaders founded in Palestine in 1190. From their base in Prussia, consolidated the Eastern Baltic into a powerful feudal state in the fourteenth century, nominally as agents of the Roman Catholic Church. Expansion aroused hostility and revolts, which with Polish and Lithuanian support defeated the knights decisively at Grunwald in 1410. After rapid decline of military power and influence in the fifteenth century, disbanded in 1525.

Thirty Years' War—Conventional name for a fifty-year struggle (1610–60) of various factions including Protestant nobles and French kings against the Holy Roman Empire (*q.v.*) and its ruling Habsburg Dynasty for control of parts of Europe, including the Baltic coast. The fiercest period of the war was 1618–48, hence the misnomer *Thirty Years' War.*

Treaty of Versailles—Signed at the Paris Peace Conference, June 1919, dictating peace terms ending World War I. Harsh terms imposed by the Allies on Germany were cited as a major factor in the rise of Adolf Hitler and genesis of World War II.

Warsaw Pact—Informal name for Warsaw Treaty Organization, a mutual defense organization founded in 1955, including the Soviet Union, Albania (which withdrew in 1961), Bulgaria, Czechoslovakia, the German Democratic Republic (East Germany), Hungary, Poland, and Romania. The Warsaw Pact enabled the Soviet Union to station troops in the countries to its west to oppose the forces of the North Atlantic Treaty Organization (*q.v.*). The pact was the basis of the invasions of Hungary (1956) and Czechoslovakia (1968). Disbanded in July 1991.

Western European Union (WEU)—Signed in 1948 by Western European states as a regional defense, cultural, and economic pact, became inactive in 1954 but was revived in 1984 to improve European military preparedness and activity in the North Atlantic Treaty Organization (*q.v.*). Subsequently issued statements on European security and other international issues.

Members in 1993 were Belgium, Britain, France, Germany, Greece, Italy, Luxembourg, the Netherlands, Portugal, and Spain.

World Bank—Informal name for a group of four affiliated international institutions: the International Bank for Reconstruction and Development (IBRD), the International Development Association (IDA), the International Finance Corporation (IFC), and the Multilateral Investment Guarantee Agency (MIGA). The IBRD, established in 1945, has as its primary purpose making loans to developing countries for specific projects. The IDA, legally separate but administered by the IBRD, furnishes credits to the poorest developing countries on terms easier than those of the IBRD. The IFC supplements IBRD activity through loans to stimulate private enterprise in the less developed countries. The MIGA was founded in 1988 to insure private foreign investment in developing countries against noncommercial risks. The four institutions are owned by the governments of the countries that subscribed their capital. For a state to participate in the World Bank group, prior membership in the International Monetary Fund (IMF—*q.v.*) is required.

zloty—Polish national currency (Polish spelling, złoty) nominally divided into 100 groszy. Became convertible with Western currencies January 1, 1990. In March 1990, US$1 equaled 9,824 zloty; in March 1991, the exchange rate was US$1 = 9,520 zloty; in March 1993, it was US$1 = 16,330 zloty.

Index

abortion: church influence over, xxxi, xxxv, xliii, 96; controversy over, xxxiv, 182; demand for, 85, 86; outlawed, xxxi, xliii; restricted, 96

acquired immune deficiency syndrome (AIDS), 109-10; prevention efforts in, 109-10; victims of, 109

Adam Mickiewicz University (Poznań), 106

Agency for Industrial Development, 161

agricultural workers, 77, 78-81; living conditions of, 78; moving to industry, 81; as percentage of population, 78, 80

agriculture, 151-54; collectivization of, 42, 78, 152; decollectivization of, 126; export crops, 10; incomes in, 135; infrastructure for, 154; modernization of, 154; neglect of, 124; in Poland-Lithuania, 11; political problems in, 135; population working in, 68; privatization in, 43, 77; production of, 134, 151-52; resources for, 117, 120; state influence on, 117, 152; streamlining of, 154; subsidies for, xxxvii, xlviii; work force in, 120

AIDS. *See* acquired immune deficiency syndrome

air defense force, 266-67; lines of command in, 254; service terms in, 271

air force, 266-67; aircraft of, 266-67; divisions, 266; lines of command in, 254; number of personnel, 266; restructuring of, 266; service terms in, 271

airports, 159

Akademia Obrony Narodowej. *See* National Defense Academy

Alcoholics Anonymous, 290

alcoholism, 107, 109, 111

Aleksei (Alexis) (tsar), 16

Alexander II, 26

Alliance of the Democratic Left (Sojusz Lewicy Demokratycznej—SLD), xlvi, 205

All-Polish Alliance of Trade Unions (Ogólnopolskie Porozumienie Związ-ków Zawodowych—OPZZ), 175, 205-6

Andrusovo, Truce of (1667), 16

Antall, Jószef, 219

antisemitism, 28, 32, 71-72

AON. *See* National Defense Academy

Armament, Viceministry for, 256

armed forces, 259-67; service ages, 270; alternative service for, 270-71; attrition in, 274; chaplains in, 269; civilian command structure, 254-56; under communist rule, 237-44; conscripts in, 274; deployment of, 249, 261; education, 274-78; history of, 232-34; induction rate, 271; in interwar period, 234-36; lines of authority, 357-58; living conditions for, 274; military command structure, 255-56; military prosecutor, 256-57; missions of, 278; mobilization of, 277-78; modernization of, 280; political indoctrination in, 237, 274, 275; proposed model for, 259; public perceptions of, 240, 241, 242, 243, 268; purged, 238; recruitment for, 270-74; reform in, 243, 248, 257; reserves, 270, 277-78; restructuring of, 232, 254-58, 259-60; roles of, 238-39; service obligations of, 270-74; size of, 259, 277; and society, 268-70; term of service in, 270; training, 271, 274-78; in Warsaw Pact, 243

Armed Forces '90, 248

Armia Krajowa. *See* Home Army

Armia Ludowa. *See* People's Army

army. *See* ground forces

Association of Junior Officers for Promoting Change in the Army, 270

Association of Polish Catholics, 175

Augustus II of Saxony, 17

Augustus III, 17

Auschwitz: concentration camp, 36

Austria, 29; in Central European Initiative, xxxvii, 219; domination by, xxix, 19, 234

Austria-Hungary, 27

Autocephalous Orthodox Church, 89

balance of payments, 128, 130; deficit, 168

balance of trade, 164-66

Balcerowicz, Leszek, 131, 178, 179
Balcerowicz Plan (1990), 118, 131–33;
goals of, xxxvii–xxxviii; initial results,
132; long-term requirements, 132–33;
public reaction to, 139–40; social services under, 107
Baltic Council, xxxv
Baltic Sea: coastal plains, 60; oil fields in,
119; pollution in, 62
Bank Handlowy. *See* Commercial Bank
banking system, 159–60, 169; aid for,
160; inefficiencies in, 160; loans for-
given by, xl; modernization of, 131;
privatization of, 160; reform of, 160;
state, 159–60
Bank of Food Economy, 159
Bank of Poland, 159
banks: commercial, 132, 160; private, 160
Baptist Church, 100
Bar, Confederation of, 18
Batory, Stefan, 15
Battle of Grunwald (Tannenberg), 10
Battle of Mohács, 10
BBN. *See* National Security Bureau
Beck, Józef, 33
Belarus, 231; military conflicts with, 246;
relations with, xxxv, 215, 217–28, 249;
trade with, 137–38
Belarusians, 71, 74–75, 217; assimilation
of, 75; number of, 74–75
Belarusian Social and Cultural Society, 75
Belorussia (*see also* Belarus), 234; divid-
ed, 31; nationalist movement in, 14
Berling, Zygmunt, 236
BH. *See* Commercial Bank
Białystok: Belarusians in, 75; ghetto up-
rising in, 38
Bielecki, Jan, 183, 202, 221
Bielecki government, 139, 179–80, 214;
industry under, 148; mining under, 143
Bielsko-Biała automotive plant, 149
Bierut, Bolesław, 42–43, 93; death of, 198
Big Economic Organizations, 127
birth control, 96
Bismarck, Otto von, 27
Biuletyn Informacyjny (Information Bulle-
tin), 207
Biuro Bezpieczeństwa Narodowego. *See*
National Security Bureau
Black Madonna, 98
Bohemia: occupation by, 6
Bolesław I (the Brave), 4–5; conquests of,
4–5

Bonaparte, Napoleon, 22–23, 234
Border Guard (Strażik Graniczny—SG),
286–87
Border Guard Troops (Wojska Ochrony
Pogranicza—WOP), 286
border security, 286
Bosnia and Hercegovina, 220
Brest-Litovsk, Union of (1596), 99
Brezhnev Doctrine, 49, 212
Britain: investment from, 168; relations
with, 225
British Broadcasting Corporation, 209
British Eighth Army: Poles in, 37
budget, military, 242, 249
budget deficit, xxxviii, xlviii, 132, 226;
as percentage of gross domestic prod-
uct, 140
Bug River, 60
Bumar-Łabędy Engineering Equipment
Combine, 281, 283, 284
Bush, George H. W., 223, 224
Bydgoszcz: airport, 159; military district,
254, 260

capital: imported in the 1970s, 127; outflow, 130; shortages of, 122
capitalism: emergence of, 27
Carpathian Mountains, 57; oil fields in,
119
Carpathians Euroregion, xxxvi
Catherine the Great: partition of Poland
under, 18, 234
Catholic Action, 203
Catholic Church, Roman (*see also* church-
state relations): campaigns against, 27;
candidates for priesthood in, 97; under
communist rule, xxx, xxxi, 45, 92–93;
communists excommunicated from, 42;
conflict of, with other churches, 99;
criticism of, xliii; in democracy, xxxi-
xxxii; and education, xxxi, xxxv, xliii,
96, 102, 103, 106; losses by, in World
War II, 92–93; importance of, to national identity, 4, 7, 89; opposition of,
to communist rule, 45, 186; persecution by, of Protestants, 12; persecution
of, 42, 92, 93, 198; in politics, xlii–xliii,
xlvii, 95; publishing program of, 94,
207, 208; relationship of, with government, 43, 92–97; relationship of, with
other sects, 89; in rural areas, 97;

social activism by, 94, 96–97; support of, for Solidarity, xxxi, 46; support for, xxxi, 97–98

Catholics, Roman: as percentage of population, 89, 97; uprising by, 18

Catholic University of Lublin, 94, 99

CEI. *See* Central European Initiative

Cenrex, 284

censorship, 94; abolished, 208–9; loosening of, 43

Center Alliance (Porozumienie Centrum), 178, 181, 200–201; formed, 200; platform of, 201; support for, 200

Central Cooperatives Association, 88

Central European Initiative (CEI), xxxvii; members of, xxxvii, 219

Central Powers, 29

Central Prison Administration, 290, 291

Central Statistical Office, 135

Cenzin, 284

CFE Treaty. *See* Conventional Forces in Europe (CFE) Treaty

Charles X, 16

Chief Military Prosecutor, Office of the, 257

Chief Prosecutor, Office of the, 197

children, 84; daycare for, 86

Chopin, Frédéric, 24

Christianity (*see also under individual denominations*): celebration of millenium of, 93; conversion to, 3, 4

Christian National Union (Zjednoczenie Chrześcijańsko-Narodowe—ZChN), xxxiv, 182, 184, 203–4

Christian Social Union, 175

Churchill, Winston, 40

church-state relations, 92–97; controversy over, xxxii, xxxv, xliii, 95; law on, 95

CIS. *See* Commonwealth of Independent States

Citizens' Committee, 200

Citizens' Militia Voluntary Reserve (Ochotnicza Reserwa Milicji Obywatelskiej—ORMO), 284

Citizens' Movement for Democratic Action, 178

Citizens' Parliamentary Club, 200

civil liberties: restricted, 48

civil war, 238

classes: mobility among, 56, 76; structure, 68

clergy, 291

climate, 60–61, 120; precipitation, 60, 61, 120; seasons, 61; temperature, 61, 120

Clinton, William J., xlix

coal, 127, 142–43; demand for, 142; dependence on, 141; deposits, 57, 118–19, 143; mining, 124, 141, 142; supplies of, xlii, 117

CoCom. *See* Coordinating Committee for Multilateral Export Controls

Comecon. *See* Council for Mutual Economic Assistance

Commercial Bank (Bank Handlowy—BH), 159

Commissioner for Citizens' Rights, Office of the, 187, 188, 197–98; public response to, 198; role of, 197–98

Commonwealth of Independent States (CIS), 215–16

communications, 159; modernization of, 131; work force in, 120

communist rule: armed forces under, 237–44, 253; consolidation of, 39–41; economy under, 121–29; effects of, 55; elite under, 68, 71; end of, 49, 130; ethnic groups under, 71; features of, 42; judiciary under, 194; labor allocation in, 121; opposition to, 45; social engineering under, 41–42, 55

community councils, 194

concentration camps (Nazi), 29; Poles doing forced labor in, 36; Poles exterminated in, xxxi, 34, 36

Confederation for an Independent Poland (Konfederacja Polski Niepodległej—KPN), 181, 184, 204–5; founded, 204

Conference on Security and Cooperation in Europe (CSCE), 216, 249

Congress Kingdom of Poland, 25, 26

Constitutional Commission, 187–88; draft by, 187–88

Constitutional Tribunal, 186, 188, 196

constitution of May 3 (1791), 19, 184, 195; abrogated, 21

constitution of 1921, 31

constitution of 1952, xxxii, 184–87; amendments to, 185, 186, 187; execution of, 185; ideals of, 184

constitution of 1992 ("Little Constitution"), xxxii–xxxiii, 188; approved, xxxiii; Council of Ministers under, 193; issues resolved by, xxxiii; military under, 255, 259; National Assembly under, 189; president under, 189, 193;

prime minister under, 189; religion under, 95; Sejm under, 192; special powers under, xxxiii

construction: export of, 166; private-sector, 139; work force in, 120

consumer goods, 118, 127; neglect of, 124; shortage of, 128

consumers: protection of, 133

consumption, 134

Conventional Forces in Europe (CFE) Treaty (1990), 271, 279

cooperation, military, 251-53

Coordinating Committee for Multilateral Export Controls (CoCom), 281

Copernicus, Nicolaus, 13

copper, 119; mining, 124

Cossacks: uprising by, 16

Council for Mutual Economic Assistance (Comecon): collapse of, 136, 137, 138, 166, 210; membership in, xxix, 45; obligations to, 117, 123, 129, 130

Council of Elders (Konwent Seniorów), 191

Council of Europe, xxxvi; membership in, 225-26

Council of Ministers, 193; military affairs under, 239, 253, 254

Council of State, 186; replaced, 189

coups d'état: of 1926, 31, 235; of 1981, 47, 241

courts, 194-98; administrative, 196; lower, 196; supreme, 195-96; tribunal, 196-97

credits: caps on, 132

crime, 287-89; drug-related, 110-11, 288-89; increase in, 287; organized, 288; rate, 287; white-collar, 288

Croatia, 220

CSCE. *See* Conference on Security and Cooperation in Europe

Cultural Struggle (Kulturkampf), 27

currency: deficits, 130; devaluation of, xxxviii, 167; exchange, 166-68; foreign, reserves of, 162; for trade, 137

current accounts deficit, 130

Czarniecki, Stefan, 16

Czartoryski, Adam, 25

Czech and Slovak Federated Republic: in European Community, 226; exports to, xxxix-xl; relations with, 211, 218; security arrangements with, 244; in Visegrád Triangle, xxxvii, 211

Czechoslovakia (*see also* Czech Republic;

Slovak Republic): border disputes with, 31; in Central European Initiative, xxxvii, 219; in Little Entente, 235; Nazi occupation of, 33-34; relations with, 218; Warsaw Pact invasion of, 44, 199, 241, 243; withdrawal of Soviet troops from, 244

Czech Republic (*see also* Czechoslovakia): in Visegrád Group, xxxvii

Częstochowa, 119

Danzig: as free city, 31

daycare, 86

debt: under communist rule, 44, 128; forgiveness of, 118; foreign, 162; to London Club, xlix; to Paris Club, xli

Declaration on the Cooperation of the Hungarian Republic, the Czech and Slovak Federative Republic, and the Republic of Poland on the Road to European Integration, 219

defense industry: domestic, 279, 281-83; aircraft produced by, 283; conversion to civilian production, 282; reductions in, 282; restructuring of, 282

Defense of Workers, Committee for (Komitet Obrony Robotników—KOR), 45, 199

defense organization, 253-67; under communist rule, 253-54

Defense Policy, Viceministry for, 256

defense spending, 278-79; budget cuts, 278-79

Democratic Bloc, 41

Democratic Party, 175, 176, 186, 198, 206

Democratic Union (Unia Demokratyczna—UD), xlvi, 181, 182, 201-2; relations of, with Wałęsa, 201

demonstrations. *See* political demonstrations

Department of Education, 258

Department of Procurement, 257

de-Stalinization, 42, 198-99

development, economic, 123-24

Development of Education Systems, Law on (1961), 103

diet, 107

Directorate of Logistics Planning, 257

Dmowski, Roman, 28

doctrine, military, 237, 242-49

dojście (connections), 82–83
drainage, 60
drug addiction, 109, 110–11; treatments for, 110, 111
drug trafficking, 110–11, 288–89; measures to combat, 110–11
Druzhba Pipeline, 143

Eastern Orthodox Church, 13, 100; dissension in, 18
East Germany. *See* German Democratic Republic
EBRD. *See* European Bank for Reconstruction and Development
EC. *See* European Community
Ecofund, xliv
economic growth, xxx; indicators, 133–37; stabilization, 130–33
Economic Reform, Commission for, 129
economy, centrally planned, 42, 117, 121–29; agriculture under, 152; causes of decline in, 135–37; development of, 124–29; formula for, 124–26; inefficiencies in, 122, 126; plans for, 126; statistical distortions of, 134–35; structure of, 121–23
education (*see also* schools), 100–107; commission on (1989), 104; language in, 73; levels of, 56; new laws on, 104; reform of, 19, 102, 103–4; religious, xxxi, xxxv, xliii, 96, 102; repression of, 101–3; restructuring of, 101; role of, 100–101; structure of, 104–7; tradition, 101; underground, 102; vocational, 102; of workers, 81, 120
Education Officers Corps, 275
EFTA. *See* European Free Trade Agreement
election law, 180
elections: called by Wałęsa, 179–80; of 1989, 50, 130, 200, 204, 205; of 1990, 139, 178–89, 200, 204; of 1991, 139, 173, 180, 204; of 1993, xlv–xlvi, xlvii; presidential, 177–79; under Round Table Agreement, 175
electric power: generation, 119, 141, 144–47; conservation of, 144; hydro, 147; industry, 144; modernization of, 144; nuclear, 147; reorganization of, 147
emigration, 66; causes of, 67; to Germany, 75; to North America, 28

Employment Fund, 161
energy: resources, 141–47; subsidies, 141
Enigma code machine, 37
Enlightenment, 19
Enterprise Consulting Foundation, 161
environment: conditions in, 62–63; crises in, 62–63; groups concerned with, 63–64; protection systems for, 133
environmental policy, 64–65
environmental pollution, xxx, xliv, 61–65; caused by coal, xlii, 119, 127, 142; economic losses from, 63; health effects of, 107; public attitudes toward, 64
Environmental Protection and Natural Resources, Ministry of: ecodevelopment policy of, 65; established, 64
Estonia: recognition of, 215; relations with, 217
ethnic characteristics: xxxi, 55–56, 68, 71–75
ethnic tensions, xlvii–xlviii
Europe: orientation toward, 7
European Bank for Reconstruction and Development (EBRD), 162, 224
European Community (EC): financial aid from, 164; membership in, 174, 211, 219, 225, 226; trade with, xxxix–xl, 129, 164
European Free Trade Agreement (EFTA), xlviii
European Union, xlix
Euroregions (*see also* Nysa Euroregion; Pomerania Euroregion), xxxvi
Evangelical Church of the Augsburg Confession, 99–100
exchanges, military, 251–53
Export Development Bank, 160
Export Finance Insurance Corporation, 161
exports (*see also under individual products*): under communist rule, 44, 128; for hard currency, xxxix–xl, 166; of military products, 282, 283–84; of minerals, 119; share of world, 163; to Soviet Union, 123, 138, 164
Eysymontt, Jerzy, 181, 183

families: social role of, 82–83
farmers: demonstrations by, 135
Farm Ownership Agency, 154

farms: number of, 152; private, 152–53; restructuring of, 153–54; size of, 80, 152; state, 152–53; women on, 85–86; yields, 153

Fiat Corporation, 149

Field Ordinariate, 269

finance, 160–62; securities reform, 160–61

fishing, 154–55; exports, 155; work force in, 120

food, 117; prices, 45, 94; processing, 167; shortages, 83; subsidies for, xxxvii

foreign investment, 168–69; in Polish enterprises, 168

foreign policy, 173; under Piłsudski, 33

foreign trade organizations (FTOs), 163

forestry, 155–56; production, 156; work force in, 120

forests: location of, 155; primeval, 60, 155; size of, 155

France: alliance with, 23, 235; investment from, 168; problems with, 33; relations with, 225

Franco-Polish Alliance and Military Convention (1921), 236

Frederick the Great, 18

FTOs. *See* foreign trade organizations

fuel (*see also* coal; gas; oil), 141–47; consumption, 141–42; supplies, xlii

Galvin, John, 252

gas, natural, 119, 144; consumption of, 119; import of, 144, 213, 214; pipelines, 156; production, 119, 144; refining, 141; reserves, 60; supplies, xlii, 124

Gazeta Wyborcza (Election Gazette), 208

Gdańsk, 10; airport, 159; port of, 156; riots in, 240

Gdańsk Agreement (1980), 46, 186, 199

GDP. *See* gross domestic product

Gdynia: naval base, 263; port of, 156; riots in, 240

Gdynia Shipyard, 150–51, 264

General Savings Office, 160

General Staff, 256

Geremek, Bronisław, 188, 200, 201

German Democratic Republic (East Germany), 247

German Empire (Holy Roman Empire), 4

Germans, 71, 72–73, 221, 222; discrimination against, 72–73; geographic distribution of, 72, 73; language of, 72; number of, 72; percentage of, in population, xxxi; religion of, 99

Germany: compensation by, 221; domination by, xxix, 29, 233; emigration to, 75; fear of, 220, 222, 231, 236, 244; policy toward, xxxvii; as potential source of assistance, 221, 246; recognition by, of Oder-Neisse Line, 174, 211, 221, 246; refugees to, xxxvi; relations with, xxxvii, xlvii, 211, 220–22; trade with, 144, 167; treaty with, 221, 246

Germany, Nazi: invasion of Poland by, 34, 68; Molotov-Ribbentrop pact, 34, 236; occupation of Czechoslovakia by, 33–34; occupation by, 36, 68, 93, 102, 221, 236; resistance to, 37–38, 236; territorial demands by, 34

Gierek, Edward, 44

Gierek government, 93–95; education under, 103

glasnost', 49

Glemp, Józef, 94

Gliwice, port of, 156

Główne Biuro Administracji. *See* Main Political Administration

Główny Zarząd Wychowawczy. *See* Main Education Board

Gomułka, Władysław, 43–44, 239, 258; as first secretary, 43

Gomułka government, 43–44, 126; education under, 102; end of, 199

Gorbachev, Mikhail S., 49; new thinking of, 212

government: changes of, xxix; environmental policies of, 64; influence over agriculture, 117; special powers of, xxxiii; structure of, 188–98

government, local, 194

government, regional, 194

government-in-exile, 37

Greek Catholic Church, 74, 99; conflict of, with other churches, 99

Greek Orthodox Church, 74; conflict of, with other churches, 99; members of, 89

Green Solidarity, 63

gross domestic product (GDP): budget deficit as percentage of, 140; decline in, 134, 135, 139; growth of, xlviii

ground forces, 260-63; lines of command in, 254; matériel of, 262-63; purges in, 237, 240; reductions in, 626; restructuring of, 248; roles of, 269; service terms in, 271; vehicles of, 262
Group for Restructuring the Polish Armed Forces, 280
Gulf of Gdansk, 60
Gypsies, 75
GZW. *See* Main Education Board

Hangman of Wilno. *See* Muravev, Mikhail
Havel, Václav, 219
health, 107-11; conditions, 107; issues, 109-11
Health and Social Welfare, Ministry of, 111-12
health care: access to, 108, 121; under Balcerowicz Plan, 140; problems in, 107; system, 107-9
health care professionals, 108
health facilities, 108
health problems, xliv, 109; caused by coal, xlii
Hel: naval base, 263
Helsinki Accords (1975), 45
Helsinki Watch, 291
Hexagonale. *See* Central European Initiative
history, early, 3-7; starting date of, 4
history, medieval, 5-7
Hitler, Adolf: expansionist policies of, 33
Home Army (Armia Krajowa), 37, 236; disbanded, 237; rebellion by, 39, 238
housing, 86-89; benefits program, 88; construction, 87; cooperative, 87; modernization of, 131; neglect of, 124; ownership of, 89; persons per dwelling, 88; policy, under communist rule, 86-87; private, 88, 89; quality of, 87-88; reform, 88-89; rents for, 87, 88; shortage, 86-87
Hungary: in Central European Initiative, xxxvii, 219; in European Community, 226; exports to, xxxix-xl; relations with, 211, 218; security arrangements with, 244; Soviet invasion of, 239; in Visegrád Group, xxxvii; in Visegrád Triangle, xxxvii, 211; withdrawal of Soviet troops from, 244

IMF. *See* International Monetary Fund
imports, 167; of capital, 127; decline in, xl; of matériel, 280-81; reform of policy on, 132; share of world, 163; from Soviet Union, 119; from Sweden, 119; of technology, 128
income policy, 132
indicators, economic, 133-37
industrial associations, 123
industrialization, 126
industrial output, 134, 135, 139, 147; decline in, 148
Industrial Revolution, 19
industrial workers, 77, 78, 81-82; from agriculture, 81; education of, 81; moonlighting by, 82; prestige of, 81
industry, 136-37; automotive, 149-50; chemical, 147, 148, 166, 167; construction machinery, 150; debt in, xlii; development of, 42; engineering, 147, 148, 166, 167; government influence over, 117; growth in, 124; licensing agreements in, 150; light, 148-49; privatization of, 77, 149; restructuring of, xxxviii, 127, 150; shipbuilding, 150-51; steel, 148
inflation, xxxix, 129, 134, 136, 167
infrastructure, 127; improvement of, 131; neglect of, 124
Innovation and Independent Schools, Office of, 104
Inspectorate for National Territorial Defense, 267
Insurance and Reinsurance Company: abolished, 160
insurance services, 160-61; reform of, 160-61
intelligentsia, 56, 68, 75-77; Catholic, 94, 96; intimidation of, 198; members of, 75, 76; opposition of, to communist rule, 45, 77, 96, 186; role of, 75-76; values of, 76, 77
interest rates, 132
Interfactory Strike Committee (*see also* Solidarity), 199
Interministerial Commission for the Reorganization of National Defense, 254
Internal Affairs, Ministry of, xlviii, 95; quasi-military force of, 232, 242; reform in, 284-85
Internal Defense Forces (Wojska Obrony Wewnętrznej—WOW), 267

internal security, 1, 284–87
Internal Security Corps, 239, 240
International Monetary Fund (IMF), 131, 224; aid from, 140, 226; application for membership in, 222; credit arrangements with, 181
investment, 127; decrease in, 134; drive, 127–28; effects of, 128; from Germany, 221; outlays, 122; rate of, 122
iron, 119; supplies, 124
Israel, 225
Italy, 225; in Central European Initiative, xxxvii, 219; as source of artistic inspiration, 13

Jadwiga, 8
Jagiello, Władysław (*see also* Władysław II), 8
Jagiellon dynasty, 7–15
Jagiellon Era, 7–15; golden age of, 10–15
Jan II Kaziemierz, 16
January Insurrection (1863), 26
Japan: investment from, 168
Jaruzelski, Wojciech, 212, 240; as party leader, 47, 48; as president, 176, 189, 268; as prime minister, 241, 268; resignation of, from party, 268; retirement of, 178; talks by, with Solidarity, 49
Jaruzelski government, 47–50, 129, 174, 205; Catholic Church under, 94; end of, 130; freedom of expression under, 207–8; military under, 284; resistance to, 48
Jasna Góra Monastery, 98
Jews, 71–72; emigration of, xxxi; killed in concentration camps, xxxi, 34, 36, 56, 65, 71; population of, 71, 89; percentage of, in population, xxxi; purged, 44, 240; sentiment against, 28, 32
Jogaila. *See* Jagiello
John Paul II, 45; support of, for Solidarity, 46; visits to Poland by, 94, 95
Joint Episcopal and Government Commission, 94
Joint Investment Fund, 162
judges: appointment of, 195
judiciary, 194–98; under communism, 194; under Round Table Agreement, 175, 194–98
Justice, Ministry of, xlviii, 257

Kaczyński, Jarosław, xxxiv, 200
Kaliningrad, xxxvi, 246
Kania, Stanisław, 47
Kania government, 129
Karkonosze Mountains, 57
Karlowicz, Treaty of (1699), 16
Kasprzak Radio Works, 281
Kaszub, 264
Katowice: airport, 159
Katowice District, 68
Katowice Steel Mill, 138
Katyń Massacre, 36, 213–14
Kazimierz III (the Great), 6–7, 101; conquests of, 6
KGB. *See* Committee for State Security
Khrushchev, Nikita S., 42
Kinkel, Klaus, 222
Kiszczak, Czesław, 176, 243, 270, 284, 286
Klaus, Václav, 220
KLD. *See* Liberal-Democratic Congress
Kochanowski, Jan, 13
Kohl, Helmut, 221
Kołobrzeg naval base, 263
Kołodziejczyk, Piotr, 252
Komitet Obrony Robotników. *See* Committee for Defense of Workers
Konfederacja Polski Niepodległej. *See* Confederation for an Independent Poland
Kongres Liberalno-Demokratyczny. *See* Liberal-Democratic Congress
Konwent Seniorów. *See* Council of Elders
Kopernik, Mikołaj. *See* Copernicus, Nicolaus
KOR. *See* Committee for Defense of Workers
Kościuszko, Tadeusz, 22, 234
Koszalin airport, 159
KPN. *See* Confederation for an Independent Poland
Kraków: airport, 159; military district in, 256, 259, 260–61
Kraków, Congress of (1364), 6
Kraków University, 101
Krasnik Ball-Bearing Plant, 281
Kravchuk, Leonid, 218
Krewo, Union of (1385), 8
Kukliński, Ryszard, 270
Kultura (Culture), 207
Kuroń, Jacek, 183, 199, 201
Kwasniewski, Aleksander, xlvi

labor: allocation, 121; shortages of, 122; transfers, 122
Labor and Social Policy, Ministry of, 112
Labor Party: outlawed, 198
labor unions, 47, 121; participation in, by soldiers, 269
Łączkowski, Paweł, 204
Lake District, 56; forests in, 60
lakes: pollution in, 63
land: area, 56-57; distribution, 78; privatization of, 43
Latvia: recognition of, 215; relations with, 217
lead, 119
Lenin, Vladimir I., 31
Lenin Iron and Steel Plant, 148
Lenin Shipyard: strikes in, 44, 46
Łętowska, Ewa, 84
Lewandowski, Janusz, 202
Liberal-Democratic Congress (Kongres Liberalno-Demokratyczny—KLD), 179, 181, 182, 202
literacy rate, 56, 102
literature, 13, 24
Lithuania (*see also* Poland-Lithuania), 7, 232; ethnic Poles in, 216, 246; military conflicts with, 246; nationalist movement in, 14; recognition of, 215; relations with, xlix, 211, 215, 216-17, 249; and Teutonic Knights, 8-10
Little Coalition, 184, 201-2
Little Entente: attempt to join, 33, 235
livestock, 152
living standards, 124
Locarno Pact (1926), 33
Łódź, 138; population density in, 68
Łokietek, Władysław (the Short), 6
London Club, xlix
LOT. *See* Polish Airlines, 156
Lublin: coal deposits in, 118
Lublin, Union of (1569), 15
Lucznik Works, 281
Lutheran Church, 100

Main Bureau of Penal Institutions, 289
Main Education Board (Główny Zarząd Wychowawczy—GZW), 275
Main Political Administration (Główne Biuro Administracji—MPA), 274-75
Majdanek concentration camp, 36
manufacturing: work force in, 120

Mariavite Catholic Church of Poland, 100
Marie Curie-Skłodowska University (Lublin), 106
marketization, 130-33
martial law, 191, 205, 241-42; declared, 47, 129, 186, 199, 212, 238, 243; lifted, 48, 242; publishing under, 207
Masuria, 60
matériel, 248; domestic, 279, 281-83; exports of, 282, 283-84; goals, 280; imports, 280; modernization of, 280; procurement of, 279-84; reductions in, 279; retirement of, 260; from the Soviet Union, 279
Mazowiecki, Tadeusz, 178, 201; as prime minister, 50, 63, 130, 243
Mazowiecki government, 176, 178, 212; criticism of, 177, 178
media: censorship of, 208; and politics, 206-10
Medical Military Academy, 277
merchant marine, 156
Methodist Church, 100
Michnik, Adam, 199, 201
Mickiewicz, Adam, 24
Mieszko (prince), 4
Milicja Obywatelska. *See* police, regular
Military Counterintelligence Service, 239
military districts, 254, 256, 260
military officers: candidate schools, 277; education of, 275-77; nobles as, 238; as party members, 268; political, 237, 274, 275, 275; shortage of, 271-74
military personnel, 267-78; needs, 268; political involvement of, 268, 269; reductions in, 242, 260, 261; service requirements for, 243
Military Service Law (1967), 270
military strategy, 250-51, 253; air defense, 251; force concentration, 251; nonlinear defense, 250-51
military training, 274-78; of conscripts, 274-75; limits on, 275; reform of, 277
mines: closed, 142; inefficiencies in, 142; subsidies for, 142
mining: restructuring of, xlii, 142; work force in, 120
Mitterrand, François, 224, 225
MO. *See* police, regular
Moczar, Mieczysław, 240
Moczulski, Leszek, 204
Moczydłowski, Paweł, 290

Molotov-Ribbentrop pact, 236
MONAR. *See* Young People's Movement
to Combat Drug Addiction
monarch: election of, 11, 15; foreign, 15;
loss of power by, 17
money supply, 162
Mongol invasions, 6, 233
monopolies, 137
Moscow Declaration, 239
Motorized Units of the Citizens' Militia
(Zmotoryzowane Oddziały Milicji Oby-
watelskiej—ZOMO), 241, 286
mountains, 57-60
Mount Rysy, 57
MPA. *See* Main Political Administration
Muravev, Mikhail, 26

Najwyższa Izba Kontroli. *See* Supreme
Control Chamber
Narodowy Bank Polski. *See* National Bank
of Poland
National Assembly, xxxii
National Bank of Poland (Narodowy
Bank Polski—NBP), 84, 136, 159, 160
national cleansing (*sanacja*), 32
National Coalition of Labor Unions, 121
National Defense, Commission on, 248,
255
National Defense, Ministry of, xlviii, 256,
267, 270; civilian control over, 258; re-
form of, 232, 243, 254
National Defense Academy (Akademia
Obrony Narodowej—AON), 256, 277
National Defense Committee, xlvii, 248;
military affairs under, 239
National Democracy, 28; outlawed, 198
National Drug Bureau, 110
National Economic Plan, 126
National Education, Commission on, 101
National Education, Ministry of, 103, 104
national income. *See* net material product
nationalism, 23-25
National Judicial Council, 195
national origins, 3-5
national security, 244-53; agencies,
258-59; influences on, 231; threat perception in, 244-47; threats to, 232
National Security Bureau (Biuro Bezpieczeństwa Narodowego—BBN), 249,
258; defense doctrine, 259
National Security Council, xlvii; formed,
258; tasks of, 258

National Territorial Defense Forces
(Obrona Terytorium Kraju—OTK),
254, 267
NATO. *See* North Atlantic Treaty Organization
natural resources, 117, 118-21; fuels,
118-20; minerals, 118-20
naval aviation, 265-66; equipment of,
265-66; personnel, 265
navy, 263-66; bases, 263; fleet of,
263-65; lines of command in, 254;
number of personnel in, 263; service
terms in, 271
NBP. *See* National Bank of Poland
Netherlands: investment from, 168
net material product (NMP): growth rate
of, 121, 129
Neutral Nations Supervisory Commission
for Korea (NNSC Korea), 261
NIK. *See* Supreme Control Chamber
1967 Arab-Israeli War, 240
NMP. *See* net material product
NNSC Korea. *See* Neutral Nations Supervisory Commission for Korea
nobility, 11, 14; end of, 55; expansion of,
15; revolts against, 26; rights of, 11; in
rural areas, 10; solidarity of, 11
North Atlantic Cooperation Council, 220
North Atlantic Treaty Organization
(NATO): membership in, xlix, 174,
201, 212, 219, 225, 249, 252; role of,
244
Northern Shipyards, 281, 282
Norway: trade with, 143
Noteć River, 60
November Revolt, 25
Nóżko, Kazimierz, 268
Nysa Euroregion, xxxvi

Obrona Terytorium Kraju. *See* National
Territorial Defense Forces
Ochotnicza Reserwa Milicji Obywatel-
skiej. *See* Citizens' Militia Voluntary
Reserve
Oddziały Prewencji Milicji Obywatel-
skiej. *See* Preventive Units of the Citi-
zens' Militia
Oder-Neisse Line, 41; German recogni-
tion of, 174, 211, 221, 246, 250
Oder (Odra) River, 57, 60
OECD. *See* Organisation for Economic
Co-operation and Development

Ogólnopolskie Porozumienie Związków Zawodowych. *See* All-Polish Alliance of Trade Unions

oil, 143–44; fields, 119; imports, 143–44, 213, 214; pipelines, 143, 156; production, 143; refining, 141, 143; reserves, 119; supplies of, xliii, 124, 143

Okęcie International airport, 156

Old Lutheran Church, 99–100

Olkusz Enamel Plant, 281

Olszewski, Jan, 179, 201, 204; economic plan of, xxxviii–xxxix; as prime minister, xxxii, 249, 259; voted out, 182

Olszewski government, 181–83; coalition in, 181, 182; economic reform under, 140; scandals in, 182

Olsztyn District, 73

Onyszkiewicz, Janusz, 183, 252, 257, 269

OPEC. *See* Organization of Petroleum Exporting Countries

Operation Desert Storm, 225

OPMO. *See* Preventive Units of the Citizens' Militia

OPZZ. *See* All-Polish Alliance of Trade Unions

Organic Work, 26–27

Organisation for Economic Co-operation and Development (OECD), 224

Organization of Petroleum Exporting Countries (OPEC): imports from, 144

ORMO. *See* Citizens' Militia Voluntary Reserve

Oświęcim Basin, 60

OTK. *See* National Territorial Defense Forces

Otto I, 4

Ottoman Empire, 16; conquest by, 10; peace concluded with, (1533), 10; wars with, 16, 233

Overseas Private Investment Corporation, 224

Ownership Transformation, Ministry of, xli

Paris Club, xli, 167, 224

parliament. *See* Sejm

Partia Chrześcijańskich Demokratów. *See* Party of Christian Democrats

partitions, 17–22, 234; first, 17–19; second, 21; third, 22

Partnership for Peace, xlix

Partisans, 240

Party of Christian Democrats (Partia Chrześcijańskich Demokratów—PChD), 204

Parys, Jan, 182, 249, 257, 258

Passenger Car Plant, 149

Patriotic Movement for National Rebirth (Patriotyczny Ruch Odrodzenia Narodowego—PRON), 197

Patriotyczny Ruch Odrodzenia Narodowego. *See* Patriotic Movement for National Rebirth

Patronat, 290

Pawlak, Waldemar, 205; as prime minister, xlvi, 183, 201, 203

PC. *See* Center Alliance

PChD. *See* Party of the Christian Democrats

Peasant Alliance (Porozumienie Ludowe—PL), 202–3

peasants: conditions for, 11, 14; education of, 76; emancipated, 19; resistance by, to collectivization, 42, 78; revolts by, 26; social welfare for, 80–81

Penal Code of the Polish People's Republic (1969), 289

penal system, 289–91; under communism, 290; political role of, 290; reform of, 290–91

Pentagonale. *See* Central European Initiative

People's Army (Armia Ludowa), 39

perestroika, 49

Permanent Council, 19

Persian Gulf War, 252

Piast Dynasty, 4; end of, 6

Piłsudski, Józef, 28, 29, 235; jailed, 30; as military leader, 31, 234; as head of state, 30, 31–33, 235

Pius XII (pope), 99

PL. *See* Peasant Alliance

planning, economic, xxix, xxxvii, 123–24, 127, 131

Planning Commission, 112

Płock oil refinery, 143

Poland-Lithuania, xxix, 7–15, 233; decline of, 16–17; as a European Power, 10; government of, 11; during the Reformation, 12–13

Polanie (Poliane), 4

police, 287; budget for, 287; changes in, 287–88; public view of, 288

police, regular (Milicja Obywatelska—MO), 1
police, riot, 284
police, secret: collaboration with, 285; under Gomułka, 43
Policja, 287
Polish Academy of Learning, 102
Polish Airlines (Polskie Linie Lotnicze—LOT), 156
Polish-American Enterprise Fund (PAEF), 224
Polish Armed Forces (Wojska Polskie). *See* armed forces
Polish Autocephalous Orthodox Church, 74
Polish Aviation Combine, 281
Polish Beer-Lovers' Party (Polska Partia Przyjaciół Piwa—PPPP), 202
Polish Catholic Bishops' Conference, 100
Polish Committee of National Liberation (*see also* Lublin Committee), 39
Polish Democratic Society: revolt by, 25–26
Polish Development Bank, 161, 162
Polish Economic Program, 202
Polish Economic Society, 129
Polish Ecumenical Council, 98, 100
Polish Episcopate, 95
Polish First Army, 236
Polish General Staff, 238
Polish language, 65–66; dialects of, 66; and national identity, 65; restrictions on, 27, 92
Polish Legion, 234
Polish National Catholic Church, 100
Polish National Committee: formed, 29
Polish October, 43
Polish Optical Works, 281
Polish Peasant Party (Polskie Stronnictwo Ludowe—PSL), xlvi, 41, 181, 203, 206; outlawed, 198
Polish Peasant Party "Renewal," 206
Polish People's Army. *See* army
Polish Radio and Television Network, 159
Polish Republic, Second, 30–31
Polish Savings Office, 159
Polish Socialist Party, 28
Polish Stabilization Fund, 224
Polish State Railroads, 156
Polish Teachers' Association, 102
Polish United Workers' Party (Polska Zjednoczona Partia Robotnicza—

PZPR), xxxii, 41, 126, 205–6; congresses of, 50; under constitution of 1952, 185; as elite class, 68, 71, 76; formed, 198, 237; loss of power by, 174, 200, 205, 268; members, 47, 205, 241, 268; military policy under, 253; split in, 42
Polish Workers' Party (Polska Partia Robotnicza), 39
political parties (*see also under individual parties*), 198–206; participation in, by soldiers, 269
political reform, 242; following revolution of 1989, xxx; under Jaruzelski, 49
political unrest (*see also* revolutions of 1989), 22, 25, 43, 55, 95, 124; and changes of government, xxix–xx, 93; over education, 103; by farmers, 135; over food prices, 94; over housing, 87; over inflation, 129; repression of, 238; by workers, 44, 45, 126, 127, 128, 238, 240
Polityka (Politics), 208
Polska Partia Przyjaciół Piwa. *See* Polish Beer-Lovers' Party
Polska Partia Robotnicza. *See* Polish Workers' Party
Polska Zjednoczona Partia Robotnicza. *See* Polish United Workers' Party
Polskie Linie Lotnicze. *See* Polish Airlines
Polskie Stronnictwo Ludowe. *See* Polish Peasant Party
Pomerania, 60
Pomerania Euroregion, xxxvi
Pomeranian Bay, 60
Pomeranian Military District, 260
Poniatowski, Józef, 23, 234
Poniatowski, Stanisław August, 17–19
Popiełuszko, Jerzy, 48, 94, 225, 242, 285
population: age distribution in, 56, 66, 67, 120; of Belarusians, 74–75; density, 62, 68; distribution of, 68; of Germans, 72; of Gypsies, 75; of Jews, 71; in 1939, 65; in 1946, 65; in 1991, 66; in 2000, 66; percentage of, involved in agriculture, 78; percentage of Catholics in, 89; urban, 67, 120; of Ukrainians, 74
population statistics: birth rate, 56, 67; death rate, 67; growth rate, xliv, 66–67; infant mortality rate, 62, 109; life expectancy, 62, 66; mortality rate, 107, 109; sex ratio, 66; structure of, 66–67

Porozumienie Centrum. *See* Center Alliance

Porozumienie Ludowe. *See* Peasant Alliance

ports, 156

potop (deluge), 15-16

Potsdam Conference (1945), 40

poverty, 113

Poznań: airport, 159; riots in, 43, 126, 238

Poznań University, 101

PPPP. *See* Polish Beer-Lovers' Party

Prague Spring, 44

president (*see also* executive branch): under communist rule, xxxii; duties of, 190; election of, 187, 189; eligibility requirements, 189; legislative prerogatives of, 190-91; military under, 255; powers of, 179, 189; role of, xxxiii-xxxiv; under Round Table Agreement, 175, 189; term of, 189; vacating office, 189-90

Presidium of the Sejm, 191

press: freedom of expression in, 207-8; opposition, 207; role of, 173

Preventive Units of the Citizens' Militia (Oddziały Prewencji Milicji Obywatelskiej—OPMO), 286

prices: of coal, 143; deregulation of, xxxviii; for food, 45; increases in, 45, 134; regulation of, 122-23, 128

prime minister: military under, 255; naming of, 190

prime minister, deputy, 183

prisoners: number of, 289; political, 290; rate of imprisonment of, 289

prisons: conditions in, 289, 291; population of, 291

private sector: employment in, xxxix; farms, 152; growth of, xlviii; percentage of work force in, xlviii; productivity, xxxix

privatization, xxx, xxxviii, xliv, 118, 138-39, 149, 169; of agriculture, 43; of banking, 160; capital vouchers in, 139; of housing, 89; method of, xli-xlii; preparations for, 138; rate of, xli; of state enterprises, xli

productivity, xxxix, 134

professional classes, 82

PRON. *See* Patriotic Movement for National Rebirth

Pronit firm, 281

Prosecution Office, Law on the (1990), 257

prosecutor general, 197

Protestantism, 13; followers in population, 89; persecution of, 12

Prussia, 19, 234

PSL. *See* Polish Peasant Party

Public Education, Committee for, 102

publishing: books, 209; of Catholic Church, 94, 207, 208; under martial law, 207; underground, 207

purges: of Jews, 44

PZPR. *See* Polish United Workers' Party

radio, 159, 209-10; church influence over, xxxv, xliii; freedom in, 173; stations, private, 159; stations, state, 159

Radio and Television, Committee for, 208-9

Radio Free Europe, 209

railroads, 156

Rakowski, Miczysław, 175

recovery, economic, xliv-xlv

Red Army, 234-35

reform economic, xxxvii; accomplishments of, 169; attempts at, 44, 117, 126; under Mazowiecki government, 130-31; under Olszewski government, 140, 181-82

Reformation, 12-13

Reformed (Calvinist) Church, 100

refugees, 29, 288; crimes by, 288; to Germany, xxxvi; from former Soviet Union, xxxvi; from Yugoslavia, xxxvi

religion (*see also under individual sects*), 89-100; distribution of, in population, 89; diversity of, 13; freedom of, 12-13; intolerance of, 16; military participation in, 269; tolerance of, 12

Rej, Mikołaj, 13

Renaissance, 13

rents, 121

Res Publica, 208

revenue: sources of, xlviii

revolutions of 1989: role of Poland in, xxx

Riga, Treaty of (1921), 31, 246

rivers: pollution in, 62-63

roads, 156

Rokossovskii, Konstantin, 238, 239

Roman Catholic Church. *See* Catholic Church, Roman

Romania, 214; in Little Entente, 235
romanticism: impact of, 23-25
Roosevelt, Franklin Delano, 40
Round Table Agreement (1989), xxxii, 103-4, 173, 175-76, 208; constitutional amendments under, 187; freedoms under, 175; government under, 198
Round Table talks (1989), 173
rural areas: agricultural workers in, 80; infrastructure of, 80; migration to, 81; nobility in, 10; population in, 67, 68; religion in, 97; women in, 66
Rural Solidarity, 46, 202, 206
Rurik, 14
Russia (*see also* Soviet Union), 29, 245; domination by, xxix, 17, 19, 25, 30, 231, 233-34; fear of, 244; invasion by, 20; military conflict with, 15; policy toward, xxxv-xxxvi, xxxvii; relations with, xxxvii, 212-15, 249; revolt against, 25; trade with, 137-38, 144; treaty with, 252; withdrawal of troops by, 173-74, 213, 214
Russian Revolution, 30
Rzeczpospolita (Republic), 208

salt mining, 119-20
Samsonowicz, Henryk, 104
Sandomierz Basin, 57
SB. *See* Security Service
scandals, 182, 285
schools: college preparatory, 105-6; enrollment in, 104, 105; kindergarten, 105; primary, 105; private, 104; religious, 103, 106; secondary, 105; vocational, 102, 105-6
SdRP. *See* Social Democracy of the Republic of Poland
Security Service (Służba Bezpieczeństwa—SB), 239, 284
Sejm, 175, 191-92; accomplishments of, xxxiv; budget under, 192; coalition in, 180; committees of, 191-92; elections for, 180; marshal of, 191; members of, xxxiv, 191, 198; military under, 255; operation of, 11; terms in, 191
Senate, xxxii; elections for, 192; functions of, 192; members of, 192; revived, 175
serfs: liberated, 26
service sector: neglect of, 124; workers in, 78

SG. *See* Border Guard
shipbuilding, xlii, 150-51; exports by, 150; license agreements in, 150; restructuring of, 151
Sienkewicz, Henryk, 16
Sigismund II Augustus, 14; death of, 15
Sigismund III Vasa, 15
Sikorski, Władysław, 37
Silesia: coal deposits in, 118; division of, 31; ethnic tensions in, xlvii-xlviii; Germans in, 72
Silesia-Kraków Upthrust, 57
Silesian Lowlands, 57
Silesian Military District, 260
Silesian University (Katowice), 106
Siwicki, Florian, 242-43, 254
Six-Year Plan, First (1950-55), 42, 126
Skubiszewski, Krzysztof, xxxv, 179, 184, 210, 212, 213, 215, 216, 219, 220
slavery: under Nazis, 36
Slavic tribes; migration of, 4
SLD. *See* Alliance of the Democratic Left
Slovakia: in Visegrád Group, xxxvii
Slovak people, 4
Slovenia, 220
Słupsk airport, 159
Służba Bezpieczeństwa. *See* Security Service
Sobieski, Jan, 16, 233
Social Cultural Association, 73
Social Democracy of the Republic of Poland (Socjaldemokracja Rzeczypospolitej Polski—SdRP), 178, 180, 181, 184; platform of, 205
social policy: role of church in, xlii-xliii
Social Relations and Education, Vice-ministry for, 256
social relationships, 82-83
social services, xxx; under Balcerowicz Plan, 107, 140; for peasants, 80-81
Sofia Agreement (1949), 122
Socjaldemokracja Rzeczypospolitej Polski. *See* Social Democracy of the Republic of Poland
Sojusz Lewicy Demokratycznej. *See* Alliance of the Democratic Left
Solidarity (Solidarność) (*see also* Interfactory Strike Committee), 49, 121, 198-99, 240; banned, 48, 174, 199-200; church support for, xxxi; communist resistance to, 46-47; in elections, 130, 176; formed, 129; in government, 176; legalized, 174, 175; loss of power,

xxxiv, 47; members of, 46; negotiations of, with communists, 95, 174; origins of, 39, 45-47; political dissension by, xxx; social impact of, 83; support for, 46, 77, 240-41; underground operation of, 48, 199-200
Solidarność. *See* Solidarity
Soviet Bloc: role in, xxix
Soviet Union (*see also* Russia): attack by, 31, 34; attempted coup d'état in, 214, 219-20, 252; end of, 137, 245; influence of, 45, 185-86, 198, 236, 237; invasion of Hungary by, 239; liberation by, from Nazis, 38-39, 234; matériel acquired from, 279; military assistance from, 238, 239; Molotov-Ribbentrop pact, 34, 236; occupation by, 36, 68, 231, 247; policy toward, xxxv; relations with, 212-15; trade balance with, 164-66; trade with, 119, 123, 124, 137, 138, 143, 164, 167, 213; treaty with, 214, 215; withdrawal of troops by, 173-74, 213, 214, 243-44, 246, 280
Spychalski, Marian, 240
stabilization, economic, 130-33
Stalin, Joseph V., 34, 37, 117; Khrushchev's attack on, 42
Stalowa Wola Steel Works, 281, 282
Stanisław (saint), 5
Stanisław August (king), 19, 101
Starachowice Truck Factory, 281
state enterprises, 118; accounting system in, 136; financial structure of, xl; privatization of, xli, 138-39; reorganization of, 127, 132, 137, 138; work force in, 120
State Environmental Protection Inspectorate, 64
State Insurance Company, 160
state of emergency, 191
State Protection, Office of (Urząd Ochrony Państwa—UOP), 285
State Security, Committee for (Komitet gosudarstvennoi bezopasnosti—KGB), 238
State Treasury, xli
State Tribunal, 186, 188, 196-97
Stelmaszuk, Zdzisław, 252, 280
Stomil Tire Plant, 281
Strażnik Graniczny. *See* Border Guard
strikes, xl, 44, 46, 49, 82, 95, 199; armed forces used in, 269, 270
student demonstrations, 103

Student Solidarity, Committee for, 45
subsidies, xlviii, 123; end of, xxxvii, 132; for mines, 142; for transportation, 156; for utility bills, 121, 141
Suchocka, Hanna, 84, 202, 205, 220; support for, xxxv, xlv, xlvi
Suchocka government, xxx-xxxi, xxxiv-xxxv, 183-84, 257; expansion of special powers of, xxxiii
Sudeten Mountains, 57
sulfur, 119; mining, 124
Support for Eastern European Democracy Act, 224
Supreme Administrative Court, 196
Supreme Control Chamber (Najwyższa Izba Kontroli—NIK), 186, 192-93
Supreme Court, 195-96; duties of, 195; justices of, 195, 196
Suvorov, Aleksandr, 22
Sweden: investment from, 168; military conflict with, 15; trade with, 119
Świnoujście: naval base, 263; port of, 156
Switzerland: investment from, 168
Szczecin, port of, 156
szlachta. *See* nobility

tactics, military, 250-51
Targowica, Confederation of, 20
Tatars, 233
Tatra Range, 57
taxes, xlviii
Technical Military Academy, 277
technology: imported, 127, 148
telephones, 159
television, 159, 209-10; church influence over, xxxv, xliii; freedom in, 173; stations, private, 159, 210; stations, state, 159
Teutonic Knights, 6, 7; campaigns against, 8-10, 233; defeat of, 10
Thatcher, Margaret, 225
threat perception, 244-47
topography, 57-60; elevation, 57; zones, 57-60
trade (*see also* exports; imports; balance of trade), 162-70; with Comecon, 117, 123, 129, 130, 163; deficit, xlix; with European Community, xxxix-xl, 129; mechanisms, 163-64; policy, xlviii, 117; by private sector, xxxix; reform of, 164; with Soviet Union, 119, 123, 124,

213; state monopoly on, 163; with West, 137

transportation, 156–59; airports, 156–59; modernization of, 131; private-sector, 139; railroads, 156; roads, 156; work force in, 120

Treblinka concentration camp, 36

Trybuna Ludu (People's Tribune), 208

Turkey: military conflict with, 15, 233

Tusk, Donald, 202

Tygodnik Powszechny (Universal Weekly), 207, 209

Tygodnik Solidarność (Solidarity Weekly), 207, 209

Tymiński, Stanisław, 178

UD. *See* Democratic Union

Ukraine, 231, 234, 245; divided, 31; military conflicts with, 246; nationalist movement in, 14; relations with, xxxv, xlix, 215, 218, 249; trade with, 137–38

Ukrainian Resistance Army, 246

Ukrainians, 71, 73–74, 238; number of, 74; percentage of, in population, xxi, 74

Ukrainian Social and Cultural Society, 74

unemployment, xxxviii, xxxix, 77, 282; under Balcerowicz Plan, 118, 121, 136, 138; benefits, 112–13; rate of, 134; of women, 85

Unia Demokratyczna. *See* Democratic Union

Uniate Church. *See* Greek Catholic Church

Union of Military Youth, 275

Union of Polish Patriots, 37

Union of Ukrainians in Poland, 74

United Nations: advice from, 148–49; membership in, 225; peacekeeping forces, 261

United Nations Children's Emergency Fund, 225

United Nations Conference on Trade and Development, 225

United Nations Educational, Scientific, and Cultural Organization, 225

United Nations Food and Agriculture Organization, 225

United Nations Industrial Development Organization, 225

United Peasant Party (Zjednoczone Stronnictwo Ludowe—ZSL), 175, 176, 186, 198, 206

United States: advice from, 148–49; aid from, 140, 224; economic sanctions by, 222; investment from, 168, 224; relations with, 212, 222–24; trade with, 212

universities: brain drain from, 107; closed, 48; degrees from, 106; enrollment in, 106; entrance exams for, 106; military training in, 271

University of Kraków, 6, 13, 27

University of L'vov, 27

UOP. *See* Office of State Protection

urban areas: population in, 67, 120; professional class in, 28; working class in, 120

urbanization, 10, 27, 68

urban migration, 28, 81

Urząd Ochrony Państwa. *See* Office of State Protection

Utrecht, Union of, 100

Versailles, Treaty of (1919), 31

Vienna, Congress of (1815), 23

Vilnius: ghetto uprising in, 38

Viritim officers' group, 270

Visegrád Group, xlix; members of, xxxvii

Visegrád Triangle, 252–53; defense cooperation in, 259; exports to, xxxix–xl; members of, xxxvii, 211; relations with, 218–20; summit, 219

Vistula Basin, 60

Vistula (Wisła) River, 57, 60; pollution in, 62

Voice of America, 209

Volvo, 149–50

wages, xxxviii, 121, 124, 132, 134; declines in, 134, 135; increases in, 127, 128

Wałęsa, Lech, 72, 178, 219; awarded Nobel Peace Prize, 48; decline in support for, xxxv, xlv, xlvi; jailed, 48; as president, xxxii, xxxiii–xxxiv, 176, 177, 179, 189, 218, 243, 249, 257, 269, 270; relations of, with Democratic Union, 201; secret police scandal, 285; as strike leader, 46, 199; visit to Moscow, 214, 215; visit to Washington, 224

Warsaw (Warszawa): airport, 159; ghetto uprising in, 38; military district, 254, 260–61; population density in, 68;

port of, 156
Warsaw, Duchy of, 23
Warsaw Pact, 241, 250; end of, 210, 231, 244, 252; invasion of Czechoslovakia by, 44, 241, 243; obligations in, 243, 244–45, 247, 250, 252, 263; restructuring of, 242, 245
Warsaw Stock Exchange, xli, 161, 169
Warsaw Technical School, 106
Warsaw University, 84, 101, 106
Warszawa, 264
Warta River, 60
waterways, 156
welfare, 107, 111–13; assistance, demand for, 113; benefits, 112–13; cuts in, 111; pensions, 112, 140; restructuring of, 111; structure of, 112
Western European Union (WEU), 212
WEU. *See* Western European Union
Wifama Textile Machinery Combine, 281
Wilno (Vilnius) University, 101
Wilson, Woodrow, 30
Wisła Shipyards, 281
Władysław II (*see also* Jagiello, Władysław), 8
Woerner, Manfred, 252
Wojska Obrony Wewnętrznej. *See* Internal Defense Forces
Wojska Ochrony Pogranicza. *See* Border Guard Troops
Wojska Polskie. *See* armed forces
women: discrimination against, 86; education of, 84; as farmers, 85–86; as mothers, 84; opportunities for, 84; as percentage of population, 66; in positions of power, 84; professions of, 84; rights of, 86; roles of, 83–86; rural, 66; traditional roles of, 84, 86; unemployment of, 85; work day of, 85; in work force, 83, 122
women's liberation movement, 84–85
WOP. *See* Border Guard Troops
workers, xxxiv; education of, 76, 120; layoffs of, 138; opposition of, to communist rule, 45; protests by, 44, 45, 46, 126, 127, 128, 238, 240
Workers' Publication Cooperative Press-Book-Movement, 208
work force, 120–21; percentage of, in private sector, xlviii; percentage of, unemployed, 134; size of, 120; women as

percentage of, 83
working class, 77–82; composition of, 77; origins of, 41; role of family in, 82; urban, 120
World Bank: advice from, 143, 147, 154; aid from, 140, 160, 168
World Health Organization (WHO), 109, 225
World War I, 28–30, 234; casualties in, 29, 234
World War II, 34–39, 236–37; casualties in, 34; effects of, 55; origins of, 34
WOW. *See* Internal Defense Forces 267
Wojtyła, Karol (*see also* John Paul II (pope)), 45, 94
Wprost (Straightforward), 208–9
Wrocław: military district, 254, 260; port of, 156
Wyszyński, Stefan (cardinal), 45, 99; death of, 94; jailed, 42, 93; opposition to, 96

Yalta Conference (1945), 40
Yeltsin, Boris, 214
Young People's Movement to Combat Drug Addiction (MONAR), 111
Yugoslavia: in Central European Initiative, xxxvii, 219; in Little Entente, 235

ZChN. *See* Christian National Union
Zeszyty Historyczne (Historical Notebooks), 207
Zielona Góra: airport, 159; coal deposits in, 118
zinc, 119
Zjednoczenie Chrześcijańsko-Narodowe. *See* Christian National Union
Zjednoczone Stronnictwo Ludowe. *See* United Peasant Party
Zmotoryzowane Oddziały Milicji Obywatelskiej. *See* Motorized Units of the Citizens' Militia
Znak, 198, 199
ZOMO. *See* Motorized Units of the Citizens' Militia
ZSL. *See* United Peasant Party

Contributors

Ronald D. Bachman is Area Specialist for Poland and Eastern Europe, European Division, Library of Congress, Washington, D.C.

Glenn E. Curtis is Senior Research Analyst in East European Affairs, Federal Research Division, Library of Congress, Washington, D.C.

Zbigniew M. Fallenbuchl is Professor Emeritus of Economics, University of Windsor, Windsor, Ontario, Canada.

Neal Pease is Associate Professor of History, University of Wisconsin-Green Bay.

Published Country Studies

(Area Handbook Series)

550-65	Afghanistan		550-87	Greece
550-98	Albania		550-78	Guatemala
550-44	Algeria		550-174	Guinea
550-59	Angola		550-82	Guyana and Belize
550-73	Argentina		550-151	Honduras
550-169	Australia		550-165	Hungary
550-176	Austria		550-21	India
550-175	Bangladesh		550-154	Indian Ocean
550-170	Belgium		550-39	Indonesia
550-66	Bolivia		550-68	Iran
550-20	Brazil		550-31	Iraq
550-168	Bulgaria		550-25	Israel
550-61	Burma		550-182	Italy
550-50	Cambodia		550-30	Japan
550-166	Cameroon		550-34	Jordan
550-159	Chad		550-56	Kenya
550-77	Chile		550-81	Korea, North
550-60	China		550-41	Korea, South
550-26	Colombia		550-58	Laos
550-33	Commonwealth Caribbean, Islands of the		550-24	Lebanon
550-91	Congo		550-38	Liberia
550-90	Costa Rica		550-85	Libya
550-69	Côte d'Ivoire (Ivory Coast)		550-172	Malawi
550-152	Cuba		550-45	Malaysia
550-22	Cyprus		550-161	Mauritania
550-158	Czechoslovakia		550-79	Mexico
550-36	Dominican Republic and Haiti		550-76	Mongolia
550-52	Ecuador		550-49	Morocco
550-43	Egypt		550-64	Mozambique
550-150	El Salvador		550-35	Nepal and Bhutan
550-28	Ethiopia		550-88	Nicaragua
550-167	Finland		550-157	Nigeria
550-155	Germany, East		550-94	Oceania
550-173	Germany, Fed. Rep. of		550-48	Pakistan
550-153	Ghana		550-46	Panama

550-156	Paraguay		550-53	Thailand
550-185	Persian Gulf States		550-89	Tunisia
550-42	Peru		550-80	Turkey
550-72	Philippines		550-74	Uganda
550-162	Poland		550-97	Uruguay
550-181	Portugal		550-71	Venezuela
550-160	Romania		550-32	Vietnam
550-37	Rwanda and Burundi		550-183	Yemens, The
550-51	Saudi Arabia		550-99	Yugoslavia
550-70	Senegal		550-67	Zaire
550-180	Sierra Leone		550-75	Zambia
550-184	Singapore		550-171	Zimbabwe
550-86	Somalia			
550-93	South Africa			
550-95	Soviet Union			
550-179	Spain			
550-96	Sri Lanka			
550-27	Sudan			
550-47	Syria			
550-62	Tanzania			